HUMANITARIAN INTERVENTION
Ethical, Legal, and Political Dilemmas

WITHDRAWN

"The genocide in Rwanda showed us how terrible the consequences of inaction can be in the face of mass murder. But the conflict in Kosovo raised equally important questions about the consequences of action without international consensus and clear legal authority. On the one hand, is it legitimate for a regional organization to use force without a UN mandate? On the other, is it permissible to let gross and systematic violations of human rights, with grave humanitarian consequences, continue unchecked?" (United Nations Secretary-General Kofi Annan, September 1999). This book is a comprehensive, integrated discussion of "the dilemma" of humanitarian intervention. Written by leading analysts of international politics, ethics, and law, it seeks, among other things, to identify strategies that may, if not resolve, at least reduce the current tension between human rights and state sovereignty. This volume is an invaluable contribution to the debate on this vital global issue.

J. L. HOLZGREFE is a Visiting Research Scholar in the Department of Political Science, Duke University. He is a former Lecturer in International Relations at the University of St. Andrews, Scotland and visiting scholar at the Center of International Studies, Princeton University.

ROBERT O. KEOHANE is James B. Duke Professor of Political Science, Duke University. His publications include the award-winning *After Hegemony: Cooperation and Discord in the World Political Economy* (1984), and *Power and Governance in a Partially Globalized World* (2002).

HUMANITARIAN INTERVENTION

Ethical, Legal, and Political Dilemmas

Edited by

J. L. HOLZGREFE

AND ROBERT O. KEOHANE

CAMBRIDGE
UNIVERSITY PRESS

CAMBRIDGE UNIVERSITY PRESS
Cambridge, New York, Melbourne, Madrid, Cape Town, Singapore,
São Paulo, Delhi, Dubai, Tokyo, Mexico City

Cambridge University Press
The Edinburgh Building, Cambridge CB2 8RU, UK

Published in the United States of America by Cambridge University Press, New York

www.cambridge.org
Information on this title: www.cambridge.org/9780521529280

First published 2003
Third printing 2004

A catalogue record for this publication is available from the British Library

ISBN 978-0-521-82198-8 Hardback
ISBN 978-0-521-52928-0 Paperback

CONTENTS

CONTRIBUTORS

Allen Buchanan is Professor of Public Policy and of Philosophy at Duke University. He has authored numerous books and articles in the fields of ethics and bioethics as well as the following works on political philosophy: *Marx and Justice* (Rowman & Littlefield, 1982); *Ethics, Efficiency, and the Market* (Rowman & Allenheld, 1985); *Secession: The Morality of Political Divorce* (Westview Press, 1991); and *Justice, Legitimacy, and Self-determination: Moral Foundations for International Law* (forthcoming, 2003).

Michael Byers is Associate Professor of Law at Duke University. He was recently the Peter North Visiting Fellow at Keble College and the Centre for Socio-Legal Studies, Oxford University. He is the author of *Custom, Power and the Power of Rules* (Cambridge University Press, 1999), editor of *The Role of Law in International Politics* (Oxford University Press, 2000) and translator of Wilhelm Grewe, *The Epochs of International Law* (Walter de Gruyter, 2000). He is a regular contributor to the *London Review of Books*.

Simon Chesterman is a Research Associate at the International Peace Academy, where he directs the project on Transitional Administrations. He is the author of *Just War or Just Peace? Humanitarian Intervention and International Law* (Oxford University Press, 2001) and the editor of *Civilians in War* (Lynne Rienner, 2001). Before joining the International Peace Academy, he worked for the Office for the Coordination of Humanitarian Affairs in Belgrade, Yugoslavia, and at the International Criminal Tribunal for Rwanda.

Tom Farer, a former president of the University of New Mexico and the Inter-American Human Rights Commission, is currently Dean of the Graduate School of International Studies at the University of Denver and

Director of its Center for China–United States Cooperation. He is an honorary professor at Peking University and a member of the editorial boards of the *American Journal of International Law* and the *Human Rights Quarterly*. A former fellow of the Carnegie Endowment for International Peace, the Council on Foreign Relations, and the Smithsonian's Wilson Center, he has served as special assistant to the General Counsel of the Department of Defense and to the Assistant Secretary of State for Inter-American Affairs. His most recent book is *Transnational Crime in the Americas* (Routledge, 1999).

Thomas M. Franck is Murry and Ida Becker Professor of Law and Director of the Center for International Studies at New York University Law School. He is the author of numerous books and articles on international and comparative law, and teaches in both fields. His most recent work, *Recourse to Force: State Action Against Threats and Armed Attacks*, will be published by Cambridge University Press in 2003. He has also acted as legal adviser or counsel to many governments, including Kenya, El Salvador, Guatemala, Greece, and Cyprus. As an advocate before the International Court of Justice, he has successfully represented Chad and recently represented Bosnia in a suit brought against Yugoslavia under the Genocide Convention. Professor Franck currently serves as a judge ad hoc at the International Court of Justice.

J. L. Holzgrefe is a Visiting Research Scholar in the Department of Political Science, Duke University. He is a former Lecturer in International Relations at the University of St. Andrews, Scotland and visiting scholar at the Center of International Studies, Princeton University, the Center for International Affairs, Harvard University, and elsewhere. He was educated at Monash University, Melbourne, Australia and Balliol College, Oxford University, England. He has published on the history of international relations thought.

Michael Ignatieff is Carr Professor of the Practice of Human Rights at the Kennedy School of Government, Harvard University. He served as a member of the Independent International Commission on Kosovo and the International Commission on Sovereignty and Intervention and is the author of a trilogy of books on ethnic war and intervention, as well as a biography of Isaiah Berlin. His most recent book is *Human Rights as Politics and Idolatry* (Princeton University Press, 2001).

Robert O. Keohane is James B. Duke Professor of Political Science, Duke University. He is the author of *After Hegemony: Cooperation and Discord in the World Political Economy* (Princeton University Press, 1984), for which he was awarded the second annual Grawemeyer Award in 1989 for Ideas Improving World Order. He is also co-author (with Joseph S. Nye, Jr.) of *Power and Interdependence* (Addison-Wesley, third edition 2001), and co-author (with Gary King and Sidney Verba) of *Designing Social Inquiry: Scientific Inference in Qualitative Research* (Princeton University Press, 1994). He was president of the International Studies Association, 1988–89, and the American Political Science Association, 1999–2000. He is a fellow of the American Academy of Arts and Sciences and has been the recipient of a Guggenheim fellowship.

Jane E. Stromseth is Professor of Law at Georgetown University Law Center. She teaches in the fields of international law and constitutional law. She is the author of *The Origins of Flexible Response: NATO's Debate Over Strategy in the 1960s* (Macmillan, 1988), and she has written widely on constitutional war powers and on various topics in international law. She has served in government as Director for Multilateral and Humanitarian Affairs at the National Security Council, and as an Attorney-Adviser in the Office of the Legal Adviser in the Department of State. She is editing a book on accountability for atrocities (forthcoming, Transnational Publishers, 2003).

Fernando R. Tesón is the Tobias Simon Eminent Scholar Professor of Law at Florida State University, and Permanent Visiting Professor, Universidad Torcuato Di Tella School of Law, Buenos Aires, Argentina. He is the author of *Humanitarian Intervention: An Inquiry into Law and Morality* (Transnational Publishers, second edition 1997) and *A Philosophy of International Law* (Westview Press, 1998), as well as numerous articles including, most recently, "Self-Defeating Symbolism in Politics" (with Guido Pincione) which appears in the *Journal of Philosophy*, December 2001. Before entering academia, he was a diplomat for the Argentine Foreign Ministry in Buenos Aires for four years, and Second Secretary at the Argentine Embassy in Brussels for two years.

ACKNOWLEDGMENTS

This volume would not have been possible without the involvement of many institutions and individuals whose names do not appear in the list of contributors. First, we thank the institutions that provided financial support for our conferences: the Kenan Institute for Ethics at Duke University, the Carr Center for Human Rights Policy at Harvard University, and the Minda de Gunzberg Center for European Studies at Harvard University. We are particularly grateful to the leaders of these institutions: Elizabeth Kiss of the Kenan Institute, Michael Ignatieff of the Carr Center, and Peter A. Hall of the Center for European Studies. We are equally grateful to their supporting staff members, who organized our meetings. Lisa Eschenbach, Laurie Calhoun, and Abigail Collins of the Center for European Studies deserve particular thanks for organizing the large conference that was held at Harvard University in January 2001. We also particularly thank Camille Catenza of the Carr Center staff, who organized the conference at the Carr Center in September 2001, and Jill Clarke and Sarah B. Sewell of the Carr Center staff.

Equally important were those scholars who wrote memos or papers for our conferences, or who served formally or informally as commentators, but who did not write chapters for this volume. Their ideas and insights had an impact on many of the chapters, and on the organization of the volume as a whole; indeed, we may not even be aware of the extent to which our thinking has been influenced by them. These scholars include Charles R. Beitz, Antonia Handler Chayes, Lori Fisler Damrosch, Jack Donnelly, Peter A. Hall, J. Bryan Hehir, Bruce Jentleson, Elizabeth Kiss, Stephen D. Krasner, Dino Kritsiotis, Julie Mertus, Sean D. Murphy, Terry Nardin, Joseph S. Nye Jr., Louise Richardson, John Gerard Ruggie, Jerome Slater, Anne-Marie Slaughter, Thomas G. Weiss, and Nicholas J. Wheeler. This is truly a "who's who" of international law and institutions, and we are grateful to these individuals for generously offering their time and thought to this project. We also appreciate the presence and participation at the January conference of Karen Alter, Ina Breuer, Ioannis Evrigenis, Helen Fein, Samuel Houshower, Nancy Kokaz, Jens Meierhenrich, Andrew Moravcsik, Samantha Power, Zachary Shore, and Michael Werz.

We appreciate the efforts of Finola O'Sullivan, our wonderfully efficient and supportive commissioning editor at Cambridge University Press. We also wish to thank Treena Hall, Ms O'Sullivan's assistant, and Diane Ilott, our copy-editor.

In his capacity as co-editor Robert Keohane thanks Jeff Holzgrefe for providing the basic design for the cover.

One of the pleasures of working together on a project is developing a friendship. The two of us have intervened in each others' lives over the past two years – interventions that we have found enriching. We have played equal but complementary roles in defining the scope of the enterprise; selecting and coaxing authors, editing draft chapters, sometimes quite intrusively; and making final judgments on the quality of potential contributions. Our contributors, and some of the other participants in our conferences, may sometimes have regarded us as the Corinthians portrayed the Athenians: "they were born into the world to take no rest themselves and give none to others."[1] We, however, have learned from the process and have taken pleasure in it, and we hope that our readers will benefit as well.

J. L. Holzgrefe and Robert O. Keohane
Durham, North Carolina
5 March 2002

[1] Thucydides, *The Peloponnesian War*, Book I, ch. III (Modern Library, New York, 1951), p. 40.

Introduction

ROBERT O. KEOHANE

Saying "humanitarian intervention" in a room full of philosophers, legal scholars, and political scientists is a little bit like crying "fire" in a crowded theatre: it can create a clear and present danger to everyone within earshot. Arguments burn fiercely – although fortunately not literally – on the subject. Some people regard humanitarian intervention as an obscene oxymoron. How can military intervention ever be humanitarian? Others are so suspicious of the intentions of powerful governments that they reach, in practice, the same conclusion: humanitarian intervention should be outlawed.

Humanitarian intervention is defined by J. L. Holzgrefe in the first chapter in this volume. The term refers to the threat or use of force across state borders by a state (or group of states) aimed at preventing or ending widespread and grave violations of the fundamental human rights of individuals other than its own citizens, without the permission of the state within whose territory force is applied. *Unauthorized* humanitarian intervention refers to humanitarian intervention that has not been authorized by the United Nations Security Council under Chapter VII of the Charter. NATO's military actions in Kosovo are a prominent example of unauthorized humanitarian intervention.

The central question that we pose pertains to the conditions under which unauthorized humanitarian intervention is ethically, legally, or politically justified. None of the contributors regards humanitarian intervention as anathema under all conditions, but all of them are well aware of the potential for abuse inherent in its practice. Unlike many volumes on similar subjects, we do not focus specifically on Kosovo or other interventions, although Kosovo does receive particular attention in several essays. Our

The author expresses his appreciation to his co-editor, Jeff Holzgrefe, and to Allen Buchanan and Jane Stromseth for their comments on an earlier draft of this introduction.

concerns are more general and fundamental. This book analyzes humanitarian intervention in the context of state failure in many parts of the world, and explores fundamental issues of moral theory, processes of change in international law, and how conceptions of sovereignty are shifting as a result of changes in norms of human rights.

Since ethical, legal, and political conditions are all relevant to the evaluation of humanitarian intervention, it is appropriate that the contributors come from a variety of backgrounds, including law, philosophy, and political science. The legal scholars are notably sophisticated about politics as well as about moral philosophy, and by no means limit themselves to explicating the law.

We have sought to make this book not merely multidisciplinary but genuinely interdisciplinary: an integrated volume rather than merely a set of essays. The authors of eight of the chapters attended a conference sponsored by the Center for European Studies at Harvard University and the Kenan Institute for Ethics at Duke University, which took place in Cambridge, Massachusetts, during January 2001. At this conference, about twenty scholars presented memos, and a vigorous debate ensued. These authors also attended a follow-up conference at the Carr Center for Human Rights at Harvard University, in late September 2001, at which draft papers were discussed. This meeting was co-sponsored by the Carr Center, directed by Michael Ignatieff, and the Kenan Institute, directed by Elizabeth Kiss. We have also circulated drafts of relevant papers to authors, during the process of revision, in order to facilitate cross-references and discussions of disputed points.

The volume is divided into parts under the headings of ethics, law, and politics; but these labels are somewhat artificial. All of the chapters take both law and politics into account, and all are motivated in considerable measure by normative concerns. Other ways of organizing the volume would have been equally feasible.

Chapter 1, by J. L. Holzgrefe, offers a systematic review of the multifaceted debate on humanitarian intervention. Holzgrefe critically explores the ethics of humanitarian intervention, distinguishing various theories according to the source, objects, weight, and breadth of moral concern. His discussion focuses on the following ethical theories: utilitarianism, natural law, social contractarianism, communitarianism, and legal positivism. Holzgrefe goes on to relate these ethical arguments to current debates about the legality of humanitarian intervention. He concludes by identifying the key disagreements, and suggests several ways in which they may be resolved. His chapter provides a clear baseline of past controversy against which the contributions of the other chapters can be evaluated.

Tom J. Farer also discusses past debates on intervention, focusing principally on legal theorists. He neatly juxtaposes legal realists with those commentators that he refers to as classicists or textualists. Farer's emphasis on the legal debate complements Holzgrefe's examination of ethical issues, and deepens the discussion, begun by Holzgrefe, of legal issues. One of Farer's contributions is explicitly to consider the potential for abuse of a doctrine of humanitarian intervention that enables states to intervene without the consent of the United Nations Security Council. This theme is explicated later by the legal analyses of the three chapters in Part III.

The attacks of 11 September 2001 ("9/11") on the Pentagon and the World Trade Center occurred as we were preparing for our conference later that month. They raise the question of whether humanitarian intervention has become an obsolete topic in light of the struggle against terrorism being led by the United States. This issue is also addressed by Farer. He acknowledges that the war against terrorism could eclipse humanitarian intervention entirely in American foreign policy. However, the war against terrorism could lead instead to more intervention justified at least in part on humanitarian grounds. Indeed, insofar as the United States and its allies decide that fighting terrorism requires efforts to restructure failed states, they could engage in interventions that are designed both to prevent terrorism and to help save the people of those states from misery and chaos.

Humanitarian intervention will surely be different after 9/11 than it was before. Some of the arguments formerly heard that only "disinterested" intervention is permissible will ring hollow as long as terrorism is a serious threat. But whether 9/11 will lead to more or less humanitarian intervention as defined in this volume remains to be seen.

Part II contains two chapters that assess the ethics of humanitarian intervention. In chapter 3, Fernando Tesón, an international legal scholar who is also the author of *A Philosophy of International Law*,[1] puts forward a liberal argument for humanitarian intervention when human rights are being seriously abused. Human rights are intrinsic values and must prevail, where a choice has to be made, over the merely instrumental value of state sovereignty. Indeed, states may have not only the right to intervene but also

---

[1] Westview Press, Boulder, 1998.

the moral obligation to do so. Tesón's argument is self-consciously Kantian. He criticizes contentions that national borders, an obligation to obey existing international law, or concern about global stability have moral standing sufficient to override the duty to intervene when states are engaging in, or permitting, severe abuses of human rights. Tesón acknowledges that innocent people are often killed or hurt in military interventions. To evaluate such actions, he employs the doctrine of double effect from just war theory: it is permissible for intervenors to cause the deaths of innocent people if by so doing they prevent much greater harm, and if the damage they do is unintended. In marshalling his arguments for humanitarian intervention, Tesón seeks to trump the principle of non-intervention with the principle of protecting human rights.

In the terms used by Allen Buchanan, a philosopher and the author of chapter 4, Tesón's argument is based not merely on "simple moral necessity" but on an argument about lawfulness. What Buchanan calls "the Lawfulness Justification" expresses "a commitment to values embodied in the legal system – not just those of morality – in this case the protection of human rights." The distinctive contribution of Buchanan's chapter is to evaluate a third justification for humanitarian intervention, which he calls the "Illegal Legal Reform Justification." Such a justification could be used to defend intervention that is illegal on strict textual grounds, such as NATO's actions in Kosovo in 1999, as a means of reforming the international legal system. Defenders of reform through illegal action point out that it is hard to achieve reform through either treaties or efforts to change customary law: lacking a coherent legislative process, the system has a strong status quo bias. Major advances, such as those in the Nuremberg trials, have been made through actions that were arguably illegal under then-existing international law.

Like Tesón, Buchanan dismisses arguments that presume the sanctity of existing international law. What he calls "the state consent supernorm" does not always trump. On the contrary, doctrines of moral authority can be developed that do not rest on mere subjective preferences, but that justify actions taken without necessarily obtaining state consent. Buchanan then puts forward some guidelines for attempts at illegal reform of international law. However, when he applies these guidelines to the Kosovo intervention, he finds that NATO did not put forward a preferable alternative rule to the existing rules requiring Security Council endorsement of military intervention, and that its actions do not, therefore, constitute a justifiable example of illegal legal reform. Buchanan's analysis, although it begins with a narrow issue, deeply probes issues as fundamental as the nature of state consent and the status of customary international law.

Between them, Tesón and Buchanan show the power of philosophical analysis as applied to issues of intervention. They both make cogent arguments against the view that existing international law, made by and for states, necessarily carries moral weight. For Tesón, the international legal system should be reformed to fulfill values of human rights. If states override conventional international law but effectively protect human rights, more power to them. Buchanan does not undertake such a radical critique of the sources of international law. He argues that states seeking to promote human rights through intervention must meet a number of demanding criteria, and, in particular, must be able to show that the rule they endorse is likely to be superior to the rule they are breaking. These different philosophical positions clearly have consequences for policy evaluation. Tesón implies that NATO's intervention in Kosovo was justified, while Buchanan views it as unjustified, at least in terms of the illegal legal reform criteria that he evaluates.

Michael Byers and Simon Chesterman provide a striking contrast to Tesón's dismissal of the principle of non-intervention and Buchanan's critique of customary international law. In chapter 5, Byers and Chesterman declare that if any justification is to be provided for NATO's Kosovo intervention, it should be one of "exceptional illegality." In Buchanan's terms, Byers and Chesterman put forward a version of the "Simple Moral Necessity Justification," which declares that "basic moral values can trump the obligation to obey the law."[2] They strongly defend the principle of non-intervention as firmly established, as a general rule, in international law. To denigrate this principle would be to assume a radical and unsound change in the international legal system. The United Nations Charter, customary international law, and the repeated declarations of bodies such as the UN General Assembly, all have reinforced the non-intervention norm over the last six decades; the only credible conflicting precedent is the no-fly zone over Iraq, dating from 1991. In their view, the United States, aided by a small group of Anglo-American lawyers, is seeking to loosen the constraints of the non-intervention norm, but opinion from Africa and elsewhere in the world remains strongly opposed. Byers and Chesterman argue that customary

---

[2] See Allen Buchanan, "Reforming the International Law of Humanitarian Intervention," ch. 4 in this volume, p. 132.

international law cannot be changed simply by the most powerful states in the system, or by prominent international legal specialists from those states. Relaxing the non-intervention norm would alter the principle of sovereign equality – a principle manifestly as valuable to weak states as it is inconvenient to powerful ones. If intervention is morally required, it should be defended as such, and not used as part of "an unwarranted attempt to revise by stealth the fundamental principles of international law."[3]

Thomas Franck views international law as part of an evolving discourse, subject to reinterpretation in a way that is reminiscent of how the common law changes over time. Indeed, each organ of the United Nations is authorized to interpret the Charter's mandate for itself, and must do so to prevent the emergence of a large gap between law and a "common sense of values." Such a gap would threaten the legitimacy of international law and international organizations.

One way to narrow this gap is to consider "necessity" and "mitigation" as justifications for what otherwise would be clear violations of law. Franck examines the institutional practice, in the United Nations, of humanitarian intervention, arguing that specific facts have often trumped abstract legal principles in the name of necessity and mitigation. UN responses to India's invasion of East Pakistan in 1971, Vietnam's invasion of Cambodia in 1978, and Tanzania's invasion of Uganda in 1978, all reveal that the United Nations has been willing to acquiesce in unilateral intervention under certain circumstances. The UN also acquiesced in military intervention by West African regional forces in Liberia in 1990 and in Sierra Leone in 1997. In this light, NATO's Kosovo intervention is not obviously illegal. Although the Security Council failed to endorse the action in advance, it did reject a resolution condemning it, and engaged in "a form of retroactive endorsement" through resolutions at the end of the conflict. Franck asks whether the intervention was unlawful and answers: "Yes and no."[4] It violated Article 2(4) of the Charter; but the consequences were not bad since the action led to a result consistent with the intention of the law. In Buchanan's terms, Franck resorts to the Lawfulness Justification of NATO's intervention. In his view, UN organs perform a "jurying" function: like juries, they weigh the evidence and decide whether, in view of all of it, a nominal

---

[3] See Michael Byers and Simon Chesterman, "Changing the Rules about Rules? Unilateral Humanitarian Intervention and the Future of International Law," ch. 5 in this volume, p. 197.

[4] Thomas M. Franck, "Interpretation and Change in the Law of Humanitarian Intervention," ch. 6 in this volume, p. 226.

violation of law should be punished. The result, in practice, is an evolving international law that takes account of changing ethical understandings.

The chapters by Byers and Chesterman, on the one hand, and by Franck, on the other, are studies in contrast. Byers and Chesterman seek to preserve what Franck calls the "freeze-frame" of Article 2(4), prohibiting intervention not authorized by the Security Council. They fear that powerful states such as the United States, aided by clever legal scholars such as Franck, will poke loopholes in Article 2(4) large enough to fly bombers and missiles through, virtually at will. Franck, on the other hand, is concerned to maintain the legitimacy of international law. For him, legitimacy depends on law not being so strongly at odds with the ethical views of influential people that powerful states find it easy to discard. Both Byers and Chesterman and Franck seek to uphold the role of international law, but their strategies for doing so are diametrically opposed.

In chapter 7, Jane Stromseth takes up a related issue: should principles governing humanitarian intervention be codified? Recall Farer's discussion of legal realists vs. textualists in international law. Textualists such as Byers and Chesterman seek clear, bright-line law to restrain the depravations of powerful states. Byers and Chesterman, as we have seen, oppose loosening restraints on intervention; but those textualists who favor Tesón's liberalism might therefore want to codify their new principles, as a means of encouraging states to fulfill their supposed obligations to intervene in appropriate circumstances, while guarding against abuse. Stromseth, however, argues not only that codification would be a mistake, but that the uncertain legal status of humanitarian intervention is a good thing, since it provides "fertile ground for the gradual emergence of normative consensus, over time, based on practice and case-by-case decision-making."[5] Stromseth is therefore firmly in Franck's camp, as opposed to that of Byers and Chesterman: she is an incrementalist rather than a textualist.

Stromseth provides the most sustained discussion in this volume of the various legal positions taken with respect to the Kosovo intervention. She discusses not only Security Council actions but also the legal justifications – which were quite different – of various NATO states. She then analyzes four distinct approaches to humanitarian intervention: (1) the status quo approach, denying the legitimacy of unauthorized intervention; (2) the

---

[5] Jane Stromseth, "Rethinking Humanitarian Intervention: The Case for Incremental Change," ch. 7 in this volume, p. 233.

"excusable breach" approach, as exemplified by the Byers/Chesterman chapter; (3) a "customary law evolution of a legal justification" approach, which is close to what Franck advocates; and (4) an approach advocating a clear right of humanitarian intervention, such as that of Tesón. Stromseth views international law now as somewhere between positions (2) and (3), and she favors further movement towards the customary evolution view. Codification, under current conditions, is a false hope because codification would be difficult to enact; if enacted, the rules agreed would be vague; and the very process of codification would harden attitudes just when flexibility is needed. Discourse about incremental change, with a special emphasis not just on legality but on effectiveness, would be much superior as a way of generating salutary change in international law concerning humanitarian intervention.

The legal and philosophical arguments represented in this volume cover a broad range of views, omitting only those of doctrinaire opponents of all unauthorized humanitarian intervention. The categories employed by Holzgrefe, Farer, and Buchanan come alive in the passionate advocacy, on different sides of the issues, of Tesón, and of Byers and Chesterman. Natural law thinkers confront issues raised by utilitarians; textualists contend with incrementalists if not with strict legal realists; justifications from Simple Moral Necessity contrast with those from Lawfulness. Franck and Stromseth illustrate the subtlety and nuance of international legal scholars accustomed to work back and forth between doctrine and practice, while Tesón and Byers/Chesterman (who, despite their differences, share a more principled or doctrinaire approach) demonstrate the power of principles in providing criteria for action. As our discussion of Tesón and Byers and Chesterman has indicated, two sets of authors may be separated along one line of cleavage, but united with respect to another. Points of difference as well as agreement are interesting and subtle; the reader should be ready to put components of positions together for herself, rather than simply to choose between contrasting worldviews.

The final section of this volume turns to explicitly political issues, moving away from law. My own chapter develops a point made by Stromseth: that more attention should be paid to the effectiveness of intervention. In my view, traditional conceptions of sovereignty are a serious barrier to effectiveness, and I therefore advocate the "unbundling" of sovereignty. Domestic sovereignty should, where possible, be sustained, but the classical ideal of external sovereignty – involving the exclusion of external authority structures from decision-making – should be abandoned for many of the troubled societies in which intervention is contemplated. External sovereignty creates "winner-take-all" situations that aggravate conflict, and makes it very difficult for participants to make credible promises. In my view, societies with low capacity for self-governance will have to accept very limited sovereignty, which can be gradually enhanced as they develop effective institutions of their own for conflict management. For many societies, political authority will need to be institutionalized on a multilateral basis for a very long period of time.

I do not hold that limitations on sovereignty are desirable only for troubled societies. On the contrary, German sovereignty was limited throughout the Cold War, and the European Union has accepted a view of pooled sovereignty in which individual states are subject to the supremacy of European law. Indeed, the European Union illustrates an important point: that creating effective governance institutions is much easier in "good neighborhoods," with peaceful and democratic neighbors, than in bad ones. The divided societies of south-eastern Europe therefore have better prospects than those of Africa. The impact of the neighborhood makes it all the more important to engage in efforts to support countries in troubled areas where there is relatively good governance, to create a basis for its gradual expansion. The policy lesson of my analysis is that sustained involvement after intervention will be necessary for intervention to be effective – a lesson that is reinforced by our growing understanding of the sources of terrorism after 9/11.

In the final essay, Michael Ignatieff focuses on state failure, building on some of the themes introduced in my chapter. Ignatieff agrees that to fix failed states we need to rethink sovereignty,[6] but he also argues that we have to rethink the concept and practice of neutrality. State failure, in Africa, the former Soviet Union, and elsewhere, has its roots in weak state capacity, but is often aggravated by democracy. Inserted into ethnically divided societies without strong institutions for conflict resolution, the competition for office institutionalized in democracy can foster polarization, leading to civil war. Resource riches are also part of the problem rather than the solution, as competing factions fight for diamonds, gold, or oil. When two quite equally matched factions vie for power, external sovereignty merely perpetuates the problem, and some form of international protectorate becomes essential

---

[6] Michael Ignatieff, "State Failure and Nation-building," ch. 9 in this volume, p. 307.

for restoring order. Pooling and limitation of sovereignty are as essential for these societies as they are desirable for the wealthy democracies of the European Union and the North American Free Trade Area.

Interventions are often hindered, according to Ignatieff, by the desire of intervenors to remain neutral between competing factions. But UN involvement in Bosnia demonstrated the disastrous results of seeking to remain neutral between oppressor and victim. Furthermore, politically naive insertion of aid into conflict-ridden societies may accentuate conflict by giving armed participants more to fight about, and by helping civilian populations to endure continual civil war. Aid in Afghanistan, for instance, could merely strengthen the various warlords, enabling them to fight longer. Aid cannot, therefore, be regarded as neutral, but has political implications, which can be adverse as well as benign. Neutral intervention can also reward aggression, through mediation that takes facts on the ground as given. Hence Ignatieff argues for more vigorous and sustained intervention: "the idea of a responsibility to protect also implies a responsibility to prevent and a responsibility to follow through."[7]

One strand of thinking in this volume could be described as that of forceful liberalism. It emphasizes the defense of human rights through humanitarian intervention, whether authorized by the Security Council or not. Sovereignty for these thinkers is only an instrumental value: useful under some conditions, but not a shibboleth. Sins of omission, exemplified by the absence of intervention to stop the genocide in Rwanda in 1994, are more serious threats than sins of commission. Strong, sustained action is needed to help troubled societies and rebuild failed states. This line of argument runs from Tesón in chapter 3 to Keohane and Ignatieff in chapters 8 and 9.

To this theme, however, there are several counterpoints. Byers and Chesterman warn that powerful states typically seek to devalue sovereignty norms, since sovereignty limits their freedom of action. If the weak are to be protected, they say, beware of hegemonic states and their supporters bearing the gifts of humanitarian intervention and nation-building. Franck and Stromseth also implicitly counsel against letting action be determined too strictly by principles, which can wreak havoc in situations that may call for incremental change and the humility born from discourse and practice. Buchanan shows that criteria derived from principles, with respect to

---

[7] Ibid., p. 320.

questions such as those raised by illegal legal reform, may not justify the forceful action that advocates of humanitarian intervention prefer.

Perhaps Farer's stage-setting chapter provides the most encompassing conclusion to this debate. Farer is well attuned to the dangers of inaction, of policy hamstrung by legalism. But he is also aware of the dangers of abuse. And he puts the whole debate in the context of the struggle against terrorism in which many states are now engaged. Debates about humanitarianism, such as those in this volume, are important; but their character and significance will change after 9/11. Justifications of arguably illegal acts on the basis of necessity are likely to become more plausible; appeals "in mitigation" are also likely to be more persuasive. We may see more instances of impure humanitarian intervention, in which other motives (such as combating terrorism) play the predominant role in initial decisions, but in which actions to improve peoples' conditions of life are used to reinforce justifications of military force. Humanitarian intervention is likely to become more firmly connected to the high politics of strategy than it was in the 1990s. The issues, therefore, will become even more complex, and volumes such as this one even more essential, as the struggle against terrorism takes on new dimensions, and new forms.

PART I

The context for humanitarian intervention

1

The humanitarian intervention debate

J. L. HOLZGREFE

On 6 April 1994, President Habyarimana of Rwanda and several top government officials were killed when their plane was shot down by a surface-to-air missile on its approach to Kigali airport. Within hours, members of the Hutu-dominated government, presidential guard, police, and military started rounding up and executing opposition politicians. The army set up roadblocks at 50 to 100 meter intervals throughout Kigali. The airport was surrounded and sealed. Telephone lines were cut. Military intelligence distributed lists of the government's political opponents to death squads: "every journalist, every lawyer, every professor, every teacher, every civil servant, every priest, every doctor, every clerk, every student, every civil rights activist were hunted down in a house-to-house operation. The first targets were members of the never-to-be-constituted broad-based transitional government."[1]

Once the Tutsi leadership and intelligentsia were killed, the army, presidential guard, and the Interahamwe militia, the youth wing of the ruling Hutu party, began executing anyone whose identity cards identified them as Tutsis. When checking identity cards became too time-consuming, they executed anyone with stereotypical Tutsi features. On 9 April, the Interahamwe militia directed by presidential guards hacked to death 500 men, women, and children who had taken shelter in the Catholic mission in Kigali. In another incident, the Interahamwe shot 120 men and boys who had taken

I would like to thank Elizabeth Kiss, Bob Keohane, and Allen Buchanan for their extraordinarily valuable comments on earlier drafts of this chapter.

[1] Linda Melvern, *A People Betrayed: The Role of the West in Rwanda's Genocide* (Zed Books, London, 2000), p. 127.

refuge in St. Famille Church in Kigali. Soldiers killed any wounded Tutsis who made it to hospital. One killer went so far as to thank hospital staff for providing a "Tutsi collection point."[2] The Hutu radio station Radio Télévision Libre Milles Collines coordinated the killing. "You have missed some of the enemies [in such and such a place]," it told its listeners, "Some are still alive. You must go back there and finish them off... The graves are not yet quite full. Who is going to do the good work and help us fill them completely?"[3] In Taba, the Interahamwe killed all male Tutsis, forced the women to dig graves to bury the men, and then threw the children in the graves. "I will never forget the sight of my son pleading with me not to bury him alive," one survivor recalled. "[H]e kept trying to come out and was beaten back. And we had to keep covering the pit with earth until there was no movement left."[4]

Massacres such as these became commonplace throughout Rwanda. An estimated 43,000 Tutsis were killed in Karama Gikongoro, a further 100,000 massacred in Butare. Over 16,000 people were killed around Cyangugu; 4,000 in Kibeho; 5,500 in Cyahinda; 2,500 in Kibungo.[5] Other examples are not hard to find.[6] By early May, one journalist observed that one bloated and mutilated body plunged over the Rusomo Falls on the Kagera River every minute. "Hundreds and hundreds must have passed down the river in the past week and they are still coming... A terrible genocidal madness has taken over Rwanda. It is now completely out of control."[7] So many bodies littered the streets of Kigali that prisoners were detailed to load them into dump trucks. As one eyewitness recounted: "Some one flagged [the dump truck] down and dragged [a] body from under the tree and threw it into the ... truck which was almost full and people were moaning and crying, you

---

[2] Ibid., p. 142.

[3] Quoted in G. Prunier, *The Rwanda Crisis: History of a Genocide* (Hurst & Co., London, 1995), p. 224.

[4] UN Commission on Human Rights, *Report of the Special Rapporteur on Violence against Women, its Causes and Consequences*, Ms Radhika Coomaraswamy (E/CN.4/1998/54/Add. 1), 4 February 1998, p. 10. Quoted in Melvern, *A People Betrayed*, p. 158.

[5] Alison L. Des Forges, *"Leave None to Tell the Story": Genocide in Rwanda* (Human Rights Watch, New York, c. 1999), pp. 303–594; quoted in Melvern, *A People Betrayed*, p. 200.

[6] Ibid.

[7] Richard Dowden, "Sweet Sour Stench of Death Fills Rwanda," *Independent*, 7 May 1994. Quoted in Melvern, *A People Betrayed*, p. 189.

could see that some were not dead."[8] The sub-prefect of Kigali prefecture later admitted that 67,000 bodies were disposed of in this way. In three short months, as many as 1 million Tutsis were shot, burned, starved, tortured, stabbed, or hacked to death.[9]

The international community did nothing to stop the Rwandan genocide.[10] A complete holocaust was only prevented by the military victory of the Rwandan Patriotic Front – a Tutsi guerrilla army based in the north of the country. *But what, if anything, should the international community have done to stop the carnage? Did it have a moral duty to intervene? Did it have a legal right to do so? What should it have done if the United Nations Security Council had refused to authorize a military intervention? If it had a duty to intervene, how could it have overcome the political barriers to intervention? And, most importantly, what measures should be taken to prevent similar catastrophes in the future?*

It is the aim of this chapter to examine some of the answers commonly given to these and other questions. The first section very briefly defines humanitarian intervention. The second section discusses the ethics of humanitarian intervention, distinguishing various theories according to the source, objects, weight, and breadth of moral concern. The discussion focuses on the following ethical theories: utilitarianism; natural law; social contractarianism; communitarianism; and legal positivism. The third section surveys classicist and legal realist readings of the sources of international law with a view to determining the present legality of humanitarian intervention. The literature on the ethics and legality of humanitarian intervention is riven with disagreement. This chapter seeks to identify and critically assess the (often unexamined) moral and empirical assumptions behind these disagreements.

---

[8] Interview with Colonel Quist, transcript, tape 28. *Twenty-Twenty Television,* July 1994. Quoted in Melvern, *A People Betrayed,* p. 133.

[9] Boutros Boutros-Ghali, "Introduction," *The United Nations and Rwanda 1993–1996* (Department of Public Information, United Nations, New York, 1996), p. 4.

[10] "We must all recognise that … we have failed in our response to the agony of Rwanda, and thus have acquiesced in the continued loss of human life. Our readiness and capacity for action has been demonstrated to be inadequate at best, and deplorable at worst, owing to the absence of the collective political will." "Report of the Secretary-General on the Situation in Rwanda [S/1994/640, 31 May 1994]," *UN and Rwanda 1993–1996,* p. 291. See also Nicholas J. Wheeler, *Saving Strangers: Humanitarian Intervention in International Society* (Oxford University Press, Oxford, 2000), pp. 219–30; Melvern, *A People Betrayed,* pp. 186–206.

Definition of humanitarian intervention

What is humanitarian intervention? For the purposes of this volume, it is

the threat or use of force across state borders by a state (or group of states) aimed at preventing or ending widespread and grave violations of the fundamental human rights of individuals other than its own citizens, without the permission of the state within whose territory force is applied.[11]

In defining humanitarian intervention in this way, I deliberately exclude two types of behavior occasionally associated with the term. They are: non-forcible interventions such as the threat or use of economic, diplomatic, or other sanctions;[12] and forcible interventions aimed at protecting or rescuing the intervening state's own nationals.[13] I do this, not because the legality or morality of these types of interventions is uninteresting or unimportant, but because the question of whether states may use *force* to protect the human rights of individuals other than their own citizens is more urgent and controversial.

The ethics of humanitarian intervention

Does the international community have a moral duty to intervene to end massive human rights violations like the Rwandan genocide? The arguments for or against the justice of humanitarian intervention are classified in a wide variety of ways. Michael J. Smith distinguishes political realist and liberal

---

[11] I am indebted to Allen Buchanan for his help in formulating this definition of humanitarian intervention.

[12] "Humanitarian intervention should be understood to encompass ... non-forcible methods, namely intervention undertaken without military force to alleviate mass human suffering within sovereign borders." David J. Scheffer, "Towards a Modern Doctrine of Humanitarian Intervention," 23 *University of Toledo Law Review* (1992), 266; Fernando R. Tesón, *Humanitarian Intervention: An Inquiry into Law and Morality* (2nd edn, Transnational Publishers, Irvington-on-Hudson, 1997), p. 135; Fernando R. Tesón, "Collective Humanitarian Intervention," 17 *University of Michigan Law School Journal* (1996), 325–27.

[13] "I assume that humanitarian intervention ... is a short-term use of armed force by a government ... for the protection from death or grave injury of nationals of the acting State ... by their removal from the territory of the foreign State." R. Baxter in Richard B. Lillich ed., *Humanitarian Intervention and the United Nations* (University Press of Virginia, Charlottesville, 1973), p. 53; Ulrich Beyerlin, "Humanitarian Intervention," in Rudolf Bernhardt ed., 3 *Encyclopedia of Public International Law* (North-Holland Publishing Co., Amsterdam, 1982), pp. 213–14; Natolino Ronzitti, *Rescuing Nationals Abroad Through Military Coercion and Intervention on Grounds of Humanity* (Martinus Nijhoff, Dordrecht, 1985), pp. 89–113.

views.[14] J. Bryan Hehir differentiates moral and legal arguments, whereas Mark R. Wicclair contrasts rule-oriented and consequence-oriented ones.[15] Other scholars categorize the subject in still different ways.[16] All these taxonomies have much to recommend them. Nevertheless, no single dichotomy adequately captures all the important differences between the principal views on the justice of humanitarian intervention. It is for this reason that I shall classify these views according to which side of not one, but four ethical divides they fall.

The first ethical divide concerns the proper *source* of moral concern. *Naturalist* theories of international justice contend that morally binding international norms are an inherent feature of the world; a feature that is discovered through reason or experience. These theories maintain that particular facts about the world possess an intrinsic moral significance which human beings are powerless to alter. In contrast, *consensualist* theories of international justice claim that the moral authority of any given international norm derives from the explicit or tacit consent of the agents subject to that norm. On this view, just norms are made, not discovered. They are the product of consent and so only binding on the parties to the agreement.

The second ethical divide concerns the appropriate *objects* of moral concern. *Individualist* theories of international justice are concerned ultimately only with the welfare of individual human beings. In contrast, *collectivist* theories of international justice maintain that groups – typically ethnic groups, races, nations, or states – are proper objects of moral concern. It is crucial to note, however, that collectivists view groups entirely "in non-aggregative terms, that is, without reference to the rights, interests or

[14] Michael J. Smith, "Humanitarian Intervention: An Overview of the Ethical Issues," 12 *Ethics and International Affairs* (1998), 63–79.

[15] J. Bryan Hehir, "The Ethics of Non-intervention: Two Traditions," in Peter G. Brown and Douglas Maclean eds., *Human Rights and US Foreign Policy: Principles and Applications* (Lexington Books, Lexington, 1979), pp. 121–39; J. Bryan Hehir, "Intervention: From Theories to Cases," 9 *Ethics and International Affairs* (1995), 1–13; Mark R. Wicclair, "Human Rights and Intervention," in Brown and Maclean, *Human Rights and US Foreign Policy*, pp. 141–57. See also David R. Mapel and Terry Nardin, "Convergence and Divergence in International Ethics," in Terry Nardin and David R. Mapel eds., *Traditions of International Ethics* (Cambridge University Press, Cambridge, 1992), pp. 299–318.

[16] See Jeff McMahan, "The Ethics of International Intervention," in Anthony Ellis ed., *Ethics and International Affairs* (Manchester University Press, Manchester, 1986), pp. 24–51; Howard Adelman, "The Ethics of Humanitarian Intervention: The Case of the Kurdish Refugees," 6 *Public Affairs Quarterly* (1992), 62–87; Pierre Laberge, "Humanitarian Intervention: Three Ethical Positions," 9 *Ethics and International Affairs* (1995), 15–35.

preferences of the individuals" that compose them.[17] In other words, collectivists hold that groups can have interests independent of, and potentially in conflict with, those of their members.

The third ethical divide concerns the appropriate *weight* of moral concern. *Egalitarian* theories of international justice claim that the objects of moral concern must be treated equally. By this they mean that no object of moral concern should count for more than any other object of moral concern. *Inegalitarian* theories, in contrast, require or permit them to be treated unequally.

The final ethical divide concerns the proper *breadth* of moral concern. *Universalist* theories assert that *all* relevant agents – wherever they exist – are the proper objects of moral concern. *Particularist* theories, in contrast, hold that only *certain* agents – some human beings, but not others; some races, nations, states, but not others – are the proper objects of moral concern.

Readers should bear these distinctions in mind as I survey the principal theories of the justice of humanitarian intervention: utilitarianism; natural law; social contractarianism; communitarianism; and legal positivism.

Utilitarianism

Utilitarianism is the naturalist doctrine that an action is just if its consequences are more favorable than unfavorable to all concerned. For utilitarians, an action's consequences are everything. Conduct is never good or bad in itself. Only its effects on human well-being make it good or bad. Utilitarianism is naturalist because it holds that human well-being is an intrinsic good. It is individualist, egalitarian, and universalist because, in Jeremy Bentham's famous phrase, "each is to count for one and no one for more than one."[18]

Most versions of utilitarianism are more precisely formulated than the general principle stated above. First, the nature of well-being must be specified. Most nineteenth-century utilitarians held that acts are good to the extent they satisfy individuals' preferences. However, some utilitarians, noting people's propensity to want only what is realistically attainable rather than their actual desires, argue that it is individuals' objective "interests" or

---

[17] Fernando R. Tesón, *A Philosophy of International Law* (Westview Press, Boulder, 1998), p. 41. See also Tesón, *Humanitarian Intervention*, pp. 55–61.

[18] Quoted in R. M. Hare, "Rules of War and Moral Reasoning," 1 *Philosophy and Public Affairs* (1972), 170.

"welfare" rather than their subjective preferences that should be maximized. Second, the object of moral evaluation must be specified. "Act-utilitarians" contend that *each human action* is the proper object of moral evaluation. By this, they mean that a specific act is just if its immediate and direct consequences are more favorable than unfavorable to all concerned. In contrast, "rule-utilitarians" hold that a *specific class of actions* (rules, norms, and maxims) is the proper object of moral evaluation. By this, they mean that an act is just if it conforms to a set of rules whose general adoption increases aggregate well-being more than the general adoption of any other set of rules.

A simple example will illustrate the difference between act- and rule-utilitarianism. Take the question: "Should individuals keep their promises?" Act-utilitarians contend that the morality of keeping a promise depends solely upon whether keeping it would maximize human well-being. Rule-utilitarians, in contrast, argue that individuals should keep their promises if general adherence to the rule "individuals should keep their promises" best promotes human well-being.

As with promise-keeping, act-utilitarians argue that the justice of any humanitarian intervention depends entirely on its consequences. If its effect is to increase aggregate well-being, then it is just; if its immediate and direct effect is to decrease aggregate well-being, then it is unjust. Crudely put, act-utilitarians argue that a humanitarian intervention is just if it saves more lives than it costs, and unjust if it costs more lives than it saves. An act-utilitarian could argue that Tanzania's intervention in Uganda was just because, by overthrowing the Amin dictatorship, it saved more lives than it cost. For the same reason, an act-utilitarian could argue that India's intervention in Bangladesh was unjust because "more people died in Bangladesh during the two or three weeks when the Indian army was liberating the country than had been killed previously."[19]

Act-utilitarianism is commonly criticized for asking both too much and too little of people. It asks too much because it obliges us to aid anyone who would gain more from our assistance than we would lose by giving it. Put slightly differently, it obliges us to help others to the point at which our own well-being is reduced to the same level as those whose well-being we are attempting to improve.[20] Jeremy Bentham thus writes that it is unjust if a

---

[19] Thomas M. Franck in Lillich, *Humanitarian Intervention and the UN*, p. 65.
[20] Peter Singer, "Famine, Affluence and Morality," 1 *Philosophy and Public Affairs* (1972), 231.

nation should refuse to render positive services to a foreign nation, when the rendering of them would produce more good to the last-mentioned nation, than would produce evil to itself. For example if the given nation, without having reason to fear for its own preservation ... should obstinately prohibit commerce with them and a foreign nation: – or if when a foreign nation should be visited with misfortune, and require assistance, it should neglect to furnish it.[21]

Act-utilitarianism's extreme altruism is the logical consequence of its individualist, egalitarian, and universalist premises. Such demanding moral obligations, however, are widely considered far beyond the moral capacities of ordinary men and women.

Act-utilitarianism also asks too little because it does not prohibit some actions that seem intuitively quite wrong. Supporters claim that any sort of military action is permissible if it saves more lives than it loses.[22] Thus, for example, NATO's killing of ten civilian employees of Radio Television Serbia (RTS) in Belgrade during Operation Allied Force could be justified on act-utilitarian grounds if destroying "a source of propaganda that's prolonging this war and causing untold new suffering to the people of Kosovo" saved more lives than it cost.[23] Act-utilitarianism is thus sharply at odds with the natural law view that some harms (e.g. the torture or execution of prisoners of war, terror bombing, attacks on neutrals, and the like) are forbidden without exception or qualification.

Unlike act-utilitarianism, rule-utilitarianism claims that rules are the proper objects of moral evaluation because, as Robert E. Goodin points out, a significant portion of human well-being comes from coordinating the actions of a great many individual agents.

Often the only way to maximize the utility that arises from my act is by knowing (or guessing) what others are likely to do. But knowing with any certainty is ... impossible (or impossibly costly) in a world populated by act-utilitarian agents. The best way to coordinate our actions with those of others,

[21] Jeremy Bentham, "Principles of International Law," in John Bowring ed., *The Works of Jeremy Bentham* (Russell & Russell, New York, 1962), vol. II, pp. 538–89.

[22] "[A] military action (e.g. a bombing raid) is permissible only if the utility ... of victory to all concerned, multiplied by the increase in its probability if the action is executed, on the evidence (when the evidence is reasonably solid, considering the stakes), is greater than the possible disutility of the action to both sides multiplied by its probability." R. B. Brandt, "Utilitarianism and War," 1 *Philosophy and Public Affairs* (1972), 157.

[23] Clare Short, United Kingdom International Development Secretary. Quoted in Derek Brown, "Killing the Messengers," *Guardian*, London, 23 April 1999.

and thereby to maximize the utility from each of our actions as individuals as well as from each of our actions collectively, is to promulgate rules (themselves chosen with an eye to maximizing utility, of course) and to adhere to them.[24]

If people do not observe the same moral rules, trust will erode and aggregate well-being decrease. Thus, for instance, if the rule "individuals must keep their promises" is not generally observed, economic activity will decline and with it aggregate well-being. At its deepest level, then, act-utilitarianism is inimical to the rule of law. As Michael J. Glennon points out:

> While the law may sometimes incorporate cost-benefit analysis in various "balancing tests", cost-benefit analysis is, at a fundamental level, not law. Indeed, one can question whether a legal system does not admit failure when it adopts case-bound balancing tests, which in their subjectivity and non-universality rob law of its predictability. The case-by-case approach is, *juridically*, a cop-out, and an acknowledgement that no reasonable rule can be fashioned to govern all circumstances that can foreseeably arise.[25]

Act-utilitarians reply that if the consequences of a specific act (including damage to social trust and therefore future human well-being) are still more favorable than unfavorable to all concerned, then it should be performed. Anything else is "rule fetishism" – the unutilitarian adherence to rules for their own sake. Act-utilitarians thus feel perfectly justified in lying to Hutu death squads about the Tutsis hiding in their basements – even though observing the rule "tell the truth" maximizes utility in all other circumstances.[26]

For rule-utilitarians, the justice of a humanitarian intervention depends, not on its consequences, but on whether it is permitted or required by a rule that, if followed by everyone, produces the best consequences for all concerned. Unfortunately, though not unsurprisingly, there is considerable disagreement between rule-utilitarians as to which rule satisfies this

---

[24] Robert E. Goodin, *Utilitarianism as a Public Philosophy* (Cambridge University Press, Cambridge, 1995), p. 18.

[25] Michael J. Glennon, *Limits of Law, Prerogatives and Power: Interventionism after Kosovo* (Palgrave, New York, 2001), pp. 6–7.

[26] Rule-utilitarians can respond to this criticism by limiting the application of rules. For example, they may qualify the rule "Always tell the truth" with the phrase "except where doing so will cause the death of innocents." Act-utilitarians, however, counter that, if such a rule applies to only one act, rule-utilitarianism collapses into act-utilitarianism and, if it applies to a class of actions, it remains susceptible to the criticism outlined above. J. J. C. Smart, "An Outline of a System of Utilitarian Ethics," in J. J. C. Smart and Bernard Williams eds., *Utilitarianism: For and Against* (Cambridge University Press, Cambridge, 1973), pp. 1–73.

criterion. Some rule-utilitarians – or, more accurately, some writers who use rule-utilitarian arguments – claim that humanitarian interventions fail, on balance, to secure the best consequences for all concerned. H. Scott Fairley, for instance, asserts that "the use of force for humanitarian ends more often than not has become self-defeating, increasing the human misery and loss of life it was intended originally to relieve."[27] Ian Brownlie and Caroline Thomas likewise doubt that the positive consequences of the United States intervention in the Dominican Republic and the Tanzanian intervention in Uganda exceeded their negative ones.[28] Other authors make the case that humanitarian interventions reduce well-being by increasing the likelihood of international society "collapsing into a state of war."[29] "Violations of human rights are indeed all too common," writes Louis Henkin, "and if it were permissible to remedy them by external use of force, there would be no law to forbid the use of force by almost any state against almost any other."[30] If humanitarian intervention were legal, powerful states would receive "an almost unlimited right to overthrow governments alleged to be unresponsive to the popular will or the goal of self-determination."[31]

[27] H. Scott Fairley, "State Actors, Humanitarian Intervention and International Law: Reopening Pandora's Box," 10 *Georgia Journal of International and Comparative Law* (1980), 63. See also R. George Wright, "A Contemporary Theory of Humanitarian Intervention," 4 *Florida International Law Journal* (1989), 440.

[28] Ian Brownlie, "Humanitarian Intervention," in John Norton Moore ed., *Law and Civil War in the Modern World* (Johns Hopkins University Press, Baltimore, 1974), p. 224; Caroline Thomas, "The Pragmatic Case against Intervention," in Ian Forbes and Mark Hoffman eds., *Political Theory, International Relations and the Ethics of Intervention* (St. Martin's Press, New York, 1993), pp. 93–94.

[29] Michael Walzer, *Just and Unjust Wars: A Moral Argument with Historical Illustrations* (3rd edn, Basic Books, New York, 2000), p. 59.

[30] Louis Henkin, *How Nations Behave: Law and Foreign Policy* (2nd edn, Columbia University Press, New York, 1979), p. 145.

[31] Oscar Schachter, "The Legality of Pro-democratic Invasion," 78 *American Journal of International Law* (1984), 649. See also Ian Brownlie, *International Law and the Use of Force by States* (Clarendon Press, Oxford, 1991), pp. 340–41; Ian Brownlie, "Thoughts on Kind-hearted Gunmen," in Lillich, *Humanitarian Intervention and the UN*, pp. 139–48; Farooq Hassan, "*Realpolitik* in International Law: After Tanzanian–Ugandan Conflict 'Humanitarian Intervention' Reexamined," 17 *Willamette Law Review* (1981), 862; Jack Donnelly, "Human Rights, Humanitarian Intervention, and American Foreign Policy: Law, Morality, and Politics," 37 *Journal of International Affairs* (1984), 321–22; Oscar Schachter, "The Lawful Resort to Unilateral Force," 10 *Yale Journal of International Law* (1985), 294; Ved P. Nanda, "Tragedies in Northern Iraq, Liberia, Yugoslavia, and Haiti – Revisiting the Validity of Humanitarian Intervention under International Law – Part I," 20 *Denver Journal of International Law and Policy* (1992), 309; Peter Malanczuk, *Humanitarian Intervention and the Legitimacy of the Use of Force* (Het Spinhuis, Amsterdam, 1993), pp. 30–31.

Other rule-utilitarians disagree. Andrew Mason and Nicholas J. Wheeler, to cite only one example, conclude that non-interventionists "are unable to show that a properly regulated and suitably constrained practice of humanitarian intervention would be morally impermissible, or create a worse world than the one we currently live in . . . [A]llowing humanitarian intervention in some cases . . . would promote overall well-being. So far from forbidding humanitarian intervention, consequentialist reasoning will support it . . ."[32]

An exasperating feature of the debate within and between act- and rule-utilitarianism is that neither side supports their claims with anything more than anecdotal evidence. A systematic analysis of the welfare consequences of humanitarian interventions and non-interventions is sadly lacking. Until such a study is completed, our ability to judge the merits of the competing utilitarian claims is gravely handicapped.

Natural law

Natural law is the naturalist doctrine that human beings have certain moral duties by virtue of their common humanity. Its basic precepts are discovered through reason and therefore available to anyone capable of rational thought. Like human nature, they are also universal and immutable.[33]

For natural law theorists, our common human nature generates common moral duties – including, in some versions, a right of humanitarian intervention.[34] Our moral obligations to others, writes Joseph Boyle,

are not limited to people with whom we are bound in community by contract, political ties, or common locale. We are obliged to help whoever [sic] we

---

[32] Andrew Mason and Nick Wheeler, "Realist Objections to Humanitarian Intervention," in Barry Holden ed., *The Ethical Dimensions of Global Change* (Macmillan Press, Basingstoke, 1996), p. 106.

[33] Natural law is "right reason in harmony with nature; it is of universal application, unchanging and everlasting; it summons to duty by its commands, and averts from wrongdoing by its prohibitions . . . we cannot be freed from its obligations by senate or people, and we need not look outside ourselves for an expounder or interpreter of it." Marcus Tullius Cicero, "De Re Publica," III, xxii, 3: in Marcus Tullius Cicero, *De Re Publica and De Legibus* (Harvard University Press, Cambridge, Mass., 1928), p. 211.

[34] Terry Nardin, "The Moral Basis of Humanitarian Intervention," 16 *Ethics and International Affairs* (2002), 57–70. See also Alan Donagan, *The Theory of Morality* (University of Chicago Press, Chicago, 1977); John Finnis, *Natural Law and Natural Rights* (Oxford University Press, Oxford, 1980); Robert P. George, "Natural Law and International Order," in David R. Mapel and Terry Nardin eds., *International Society: Diverse Ethical Perspectives* (Princeton University Press, Princeton, 1998), pp. 54–69.

can...and to be ready to form and promote decent relations with them...
This general duty to help others is the most basic ground within this common
morality for interference in the internal affairs of one nation by outsiders,
including other nations and international bodies. The specific implications
of the general duty to provide help depend on a number of highly contingent
factors, including respect for a nation's sovereignty and awareness of the
limits of outside aid. But the normative ground is there, and...in extreme
circumstances it can justify the use of force.[35]

The Dutch jurist Hugo Grotius is a famous proponent of this view. In *De
Jure Belli ac Pacis*, he argues that, where a tyrant "should inflict upon his
subjects such treatment as no one is warranted in inflicting," other states
may exercise a right of humanitarian intervention.[36] Grotius bases this right
on the natural law notion of *societas humana* – the universal community of
humankind.[37] "The fact must also be recognized," he writes, "that kings, and
those who possess rights equal to those kings, have the right of demanding
punishments not only on account of injuries committed against themselves
or their subjects, but also on account of injuries which do not directly affect
them but excessively violate the law of nature or of nations in regard of any
person whatsoever."[38]

Note that Grotius talks of the right – not the duty – of humanitarian
intervention. States have a discretionary right to intervene on behalf of the
oppressed. But they do not have to exercise the right if their own citizens are
unduly burdened in doing so.[39] Natural law theorists who defend a duty of
humanitarian intervention conceive it as an imperfect duty, like the duties
of charity and beneficence.[40] States may discharge it at their own discretion

---

[35] Joseph Boyle, "Natural Law and International Ethics," in Nardin and Mapel, *Traditions of International Ethics*, p. 123.

[36] Hugo Grotius, *De Jure Belli ac Pacis* (Oxford University Press, Oxford, 1925), Book II, ch. 25, sec. 8, vol. II, p. 584.

[37] Ibid., Book II, ch. 20, sec. 8, vol. II, pp. 472–73.

[38] Ibid., Book II, ch. 20, sec. 40, vol. II, p. 503.

[39] Ibid., Book II, ch. 25, sec. 7, vol. II, pp. 582–83.

[40] Moral duties are often classified as perfect or imperfect. A perfect duty is one for which there is a corresponding right. For example, if I have a duty not to execute prisoners of war, you, as a prisoner of war, have a right not to be executed. An imperfect duty is one for which there is no corresponding right. "Duties of charity, for example, require us to contribute to one or another of a large number of eligible recipients, no one of whom can claim our contribution from us as his due. Charitable contributions are more like gratuitous services, favours, and gifts than like repayments of debts or reparations; and yet we do have duties to be charitable." Joel Feinberg, *Rights, Justice and the Bounds of Liberty: Essays in Social Philosophy* (Princeton University Press, Princeton, 1980), p. 144. See also David Lyons, "The Correlativity of Rights and Duties,"

and in the manner of their own choosing. The victims of genocide, mass murder, and slavery possess no "right of humanitarian rescue" – no moral claim to the help of any specific state.

Although an imperfect duty of humanitarian intervention comports easily with the belief that states should privilege the well-being of their own citizens over the well-being of foreigners, it can have terrible consequences. "The general problem," writes Michael Walzer,

> is that intervention, even when it is justified, even when it is necessary to prevent terrible crimes – even when it poses no threat to regional or global stability, is an imperfect duty – a duty that doesn't belong to any particular agent. Somebody ought to intervene, but no specific state or society is morally bound to do so. And in many of these cases, no one does. People are indeed capable of watching and listening and doing nothing. The massacres go on, and every country that is able to stop them decides that it has more urgent tasks and conflicting priorities; the likely costs of intervention are too high.[41]

If one is concerned about preventing or stopping genocide, mass murder, and slavery, an imperfect duty of humanitarian intervention will not do. If "persons as such have certain rights," writes Allen Buchanan, "then surely one ought not only to respect persons' rights by not violating them. *One ought also to contribute to creating arrangements that will ensure that persons' rights are not violated.* To put the same point somewhat differently, respect for persons requires doing something to ensure that they are treated respectfully."[42] It is not enough for a state to refrain from violating human rights itself. It also must create and participate in international institutions that prevent or stop gross human rights violations wherever they occur. A perfect duty of humanitarian intervention is, in principle, wholly compatible with the precepts of natural law. But in practice no natural law theorists advocate it.

By contrast, many natural law theorists maintain that, far from possessing an imperfect duty of humanitarian intervention, states have a perfect duty of non-intervention. Christian Wolff, Emer de Vattel, and Immanuel Kant, for example, contend that states have a duty to refrain from interfering in each other's affairs for the same reason that individuals have a duty to respect each

4 *Noûs* (1970), 45–55; John Rawls, *A Theory of Justice* (Belknap Press, Cambridge, Mass., 1971), pp. 108–17.

41 Walzer, *Just and Unjust Wars*, p. xiii.

42 Allen Buchanan, "The Internal Legitimacy of Humanitarian Intervention," 7 *Journal of Political Philosophy* (1999), 84. Emphasis added.

other's autonomy.[43] "To interfere in the government of another..." writes Christian Wolff, "is opposed to the natural liberty of nations, by virtue of which one nation is altogether independent of the will of other nations in its actions...If any such things are done, they are done altogether without right."[44] This argument rests on an analogy between persons and states. "Just as persons are autonomous agents, and are entitled to determine their own action free from interference as long as the exercise of their autonomy does not involve the transgression of certain moral constraints, so, it is claimed, states are also autonomous agents, whose autonomy is similarly deserving of respect."[45] The collectivist analogy, however, is a poor one. As Charles R. Beitz, Fernando R. Tesón, and many others argue, states are simply not unified agents with unified wills.[46] Indeed, at no time is this clearer than when a government commits gross human rights abuses against its own citizens.

Social contractarianism

Social contractarianism is the naturalist doctrine that moral norms derive their binding force from the mutual consent of the people subject to them. This mutual consent, however, is not between real people in real choice situations. Rather, it is between ideal agents in ideal choice situations. For social contractarians, norms are morally obligatory only *if* free, equal, and rational agents would consent to them. By defining justice in this way, they avoid the criticism that actual norms are rarely, if ever, chosen freely. It is by idealizing the choice situation that social contractarians ensure that mutual consent is genuine; that it is not the product of force or fraud.

---

[43] Christian Wolff, *Jus Gentium Methodo Scientifica Pertractatum* (Carnegie Classics of International Law, New York, 1934), ch. I, secs. 256–57, p. 131; Emer de Vattel, *The Law of Nations or the Principles of Natural Law* (Carnegie Institution, Washington, DC, 1916), Book I, ch. III, sec. 37; Book II, ch. IV, sec. 54, pp. 19, 131; Immanuel Kant, "Perpetual Peace: A Philosophical Sketch," in Hans Reiss ed., *Kant: Political Writings* (2nd enlarged edn, Cambridge University Press, Cambridge, 1991), p. 96; Immanuel Kant, *The Metaphysical Elements of Justice: Part I of the Metaphysics of Morals* (Macmillan, New York, 1965), part II, sec. 2, subsection 60, p. 123. See also Alan H. Goldman, "The Moral Significance of National Boundaries," 7 *Midwest Studies in Philosophy* (1982), 438–41; Gerald Elfstrom, "On Dilemmas of Intervention," 93 *Ethics* (1983), 713.

[44] Wolff, *Jus Gentium Methodo Scientifica Pertractatum*, ch. I, secs. 256–57, p. 131.

[45] McMahan, "Ethics of International Intervention," pp. 28–29.

[46] Charles R. Beitz, *Political Theory and International Relations* (Princeton University Press, Princeton, 1979), pp. 71–83; Tesón, *Humanitarian Intervention*, pp. 55–100; Tesón, *Philosophy of International Law*, pp. 39–47.

Although social contractarian arguments possess a similar structure, they are far from identical. One area of disagreement concerns the identity of the contracting parties. Some social contractarians contend that norms are just if the *citizens of a state* would consent to them.[47] Others claim that they are just if the *states* themselves would consent to them.[48] Still others argue that they are just if all *human beings* would consent to them.[49] The identity of the contracting parties is important because it affects which norms would be chosen – and hence which are morally binding. For example, if the citizens of a state were the contracting parties, then a duty to maximize the "national interest" would be selected. As Allen Buchanan explains:

> The state is understood as the creation of a hypothetical contract among those who are to be its citizens, and the terms of the contract they agree on are justified by showing how observance of those terms serves their interests. No one else's interests are represented, so legitimate political authority is naturally defined as authority exercised for the good of the parties to the contract, the citizens of this state... The justifying function of the state – what justifies the interference with liberty that it entails – is the well-being and freedom of its members. There is no suggestion that the state must do anything to serve the cause of justice in the world at large. What makes the government legitimate is that it acts as the faithful agent of its own citizens. And to that extent, government acts legitimately only when it occupies itself exclusively with the interests of the citizens of the state of which it is the government.[50]

[47] Richard Cox, *Locke on War and Peace* (Clarendon Press, Oxford, 1960); David Gauthier, "Hobbes on International Relations," in David Gauthier ed., *The Logic of Leviathan* (Oxford University Press, Oxford, 1969), pp. 206–12; Murray Forsyth, "Thomas Hobbes and the External Relations of States," 5 *British Journal of International Studies* (1979), 196–209; Hedley Bull, "Hobbes and the International Anarchy," 48 *Social Research* (1981), 717–38; H. Williams, *International Relations and the Limits of Political Theory* (Macmillan, Basingstoke, 1996), pp. 90–109. See also Thomas L. Pangle, "The Moral Basis of National Security: Four Historical Perspectives," in Klaus Knorr ed., *Historical Dimensions of National Security Studies* (University Press of Kansas, Lawrence, 1976), pp. 307–72.

[48] Rawls, *Theory of Justice*, p. 378; John Charvet, "International Society from a Contractarian Perspective," in Mapel and Nardin, *International Society*, pp. 114–31; John Rawls, *The Law of Peoples* (Harvard University Press, Cambridge, Mass., 1999).

[49] Beitz, *Political Theory*; Charles R. Beitz, "Justice and International Relations," in H. Gene Blocker and Elizabeth H. Smith eds., *John Rawls' Theory of Social Justice* (Ohio University Press, Athens, 1980), pp. 211–38; Charles R. Beitz, "Nonintervention and Communal Integrity," 9 *Philosophy and Public Affairs* (1980), 385–91; Thomas W. Pogge, *Realizing Rawls* (Cornell University Press, Ithaca, 1989); Thomas W. Pogge, "Cosmopolitanism and Sovereignty," 103 *Ethics* (1992), 48–75; Charles R. Beitz, "Cosmopolitan, Liberalism and the States System," in Chris Brown ed., *Political Restructuring in Europe: Ethical Perspectives* (Routledge, London, 1994), pp. 123–36.

[50] Buchanan, "Internal Legitimacy," pp. 74–75.

The justice of any given intervention thus hinges on whether it benefits or harms the "national interest." For writers who define this term narrowly (i.e. as the sum of security and material interests), interventions aimed at ending gross human rights abuses in foreign countries are almost always unjust.[51] Samuel P. Huntington's assertion that "it is morally unjustifiable and politically indefensible that members of the [United States] Armed Forces should be killed to prevent Somalis from killing one another" is a recent example of this view.[52] For authors who define "national interest" more expansively (i.e. as the sum of security, material, and what Joseph S. Nye, Jr. calls "humanitarian interests"), interventions aimed at ending genocide, mass murder, or slavery can be morally obligatory in certain circumstances.[53] In either case, the interests of the intervening state count for *everything* in assessing an intervention's legitimacy; the interests of the target state count for *nothing*.

The particularist conclusions of this argument are also inconsistent with its universalist premises. As Allen Buchanan makes clear, this variety of social contractarianism

> justifies the state as a coercive apparatus by appeal to the need to protect *universal* interests, while at the same time limiting the right of the state to use its coercive power to the protection of a *particular* group of persons, identified by the purely contingent characteristic of happening to be members of the same political society... If the interests whose protection justifies the state are human interests, common to all persons, then surely a way of thinking about the nature of states and the role of government that provides no basis for obligations to help ensure that the interests of all persons are protected is fundamentally flawed.[54]

The widespread appeal of the "national interest" argument rests in large measure on the inegalitarian, particularist view that states should privilege the well-being of their own citizens over the well-being of nameless persons in distant lands. This claim, however, needs to be justified.[55]

---

[51] Hans J. Morgenthau, *In Defense of the National Interest: A Critical Examination of American Foreign Policy* (Knopf, New York, 1951).

[52] Samuel P. Huntington, "New Contingencies, Old Roles," 2 *Joint Forces Quarterly* (1992), 338. See also Robert H. Jackson, "The Political Theory of International Society," in K. Booth and S. Smith eds., *International Relations Theory Today* (Polity Press, Cambridge, 1995), p. 123.

[53] Joseph S. Nye Jr., "Redefining the National Interest," 78 *Foreign Affairs* (1999), 22–35.

[54] Buchanan, "Internal Legitimacy," p. 79. Emphasis added.

[55] See below, p. 51.

Other social contractarians claim that international norms are morally binding if *states* would consent to them. The early John Rawls (the Rawls of *A Theory of Justice*), for example, contends that international norms are morally binding if the rational representatives of states deciding behind a "veil of ignorance" – deciding without "knowing anything about the particular circumstances of their own society, its power and strength in comparison to other nations" – would consent to them.[56] In this "original position,"

> the contracting parties, in this case representatives of states, are allowed only enough knowledge to make a rational choice to protect their interests but not so much that the more fortunate among them can take advantage of their special situation. This original position is fair between nations; it nullifies the contingencies and biases of historical fate. Justice between states is determined by the principles that would be chosen in the original position so interpreted.[57]

Rawls concludes that "the right of a people to settle their own affairs without the intervention of foreign powers" is an international norm that state representatives would consent to if deprived of this information.[58]

Other social contractarians disagree.[59] They reject the collectivist assumptions of Rawls's argument in *A Theory of Justice*, claiming instead that international norms are just only to the extent that they would be assented to by *human beings* deciding behind a "veil of ignorance." These scholars argue that a duty of humanitarian intervention is just because human beings deciding behind a "veil of ignorance" (i.e. deciding in ignorance of the type of state in which they lived) would consent to it. As Fernando R. Tesón explains:

> If the parties [deciding behind the veil of ignorance] believed that some societies were likely to be grossly unjust then it is plausible to conclude that . . . they would prefer a principle of limited intervention on behalf of human rights. And this is so because the first aim of the parties in the original position is to see that the fundamental rights of *individuals* within every

---

[56] Rawls, *Theory of Justice*, p. 378.   [57] Ibid., p. 378.   [58] Ibid., p. 378.

[59] Beitz, *Political Theory*; Wicclair, "Human Rights and Intervention," pp. 141–57; Mark R. Wicclair, "Rawls and the Principle of Non-intervention," in Blocker and Smith, *John Rawls' Theory of Social Justice*, pp. 289–308; Beitz, "Justice and International Relations," pp. 211–38; Beitz, "Nonintervention and Communal Integrity," pp. 385–91; Tesón, *Humanitarian Intervention*, pp. 61–74.

state are recognized and observed. The purpose of the state organization is to protect the rights of individuals. Because the parties in the original position [would] agree to terms of cooperation that are mutually acceptable and fair, the aim of the international community thus created . . . should also be the protection of the rights of individuals, and not the prerogatives of princes. Therefore it is doubtful that the parties in the original position would agree to the unqualified rule of non-intervention that would jeopardize the very rights the original position is primarily supposed to secure.[60]

In recent years, John Rawls has added a lot of communitarian water to his social contractarian wine. He now argues that international norms are just to the extent that the rational representatives of "decent" peoples deciding behind a "veil of ignorance" would assent to them. In *The Law of Peoples*, he maintains that states owe a duty of humanitarian rescue to the citizens of "outlaw" states; that is, to peoples whose governments fail to protect such basic human rights "as freedom from slavery and serfdom, liberty (but not equal liberty) of conscience, and security of ethnic groups from mass murder and genocide."[61] But, significantly, he also contends that states do not owe a duty of humanitarian intervention to the citizens of so-called "decent" states; that is, to peoples whose governments guarantee basic human rights, but fail to protect so-called "rights of liberal democratic citizenship," i.e. rights of civic equality, democratic governance, free speech, free association, free movement, and the like. Violations of these liberal–democratic rights are not a *casus belli*, he reasons, because a duty of humanitarian intervention on these grounds would not be assented to by the rational representatives of "decent" peoples (i.e. peoples who respect human, though not necessarily liberal–democratic, rights) deciding behind a "veil of ignorance."[62] This raises the crucial question why "decent" peoples rather than rational individuals should be parties to the original contract. As Rawls simply stipulates that they should, his argument is at best incomplete – at worst arbitrary.[63]

---

[60] Tesón, *Humanitarian Intervention*, pp. 65–66.   [61] Rawls, *Law of Peoples*, p. 79.

[62] Ibid., pp. 32–33. See also Fernando R. Tesón, "The Rawlsian Theory of International Law," 9 *Ethics and International Affairs* (1995), 83–99.

[63] "This account of decency . . . is developed by setting out various criteria and explaining their meaning. The reader has to judge whether a decent people . . . is to be tolerated and accepted as a member in good standing of the Society of Peoples. It is my conjecture that most reasonable citizens of a liberal society will find peoples who meet these two criteria acceptable as peoples in good standing. Not all reasonable persons will, certainly, yet most will." Rawls, *Law of Peoples*, p. 67.

Communitarianism

Communitarianism is the consensualist, particularist doctrine that norms are morally binding insofar as they "fit" the cultural beliefs and practices of specific communities.[64] "Justice is relative to social meanings," writes a leading communitarian, Michael Walzer.[65] "There are an infinite number of possible lives, shaped by an infinite number of possible cultures, religions, political arrangements, geographical conditions, and so on. A given society is just if its substantive life is lived in a certain way – that is, in a way faithful to the shared understandings of its members."[66] In the hands of communitarians, moral philosophy thus becomes moral anthropology – the discovery and description of the "inherited cultures" that rule peoples' lives.[67] These "inherited cultures" are morally binding because they are the product of long processes of "association and mutuality," "shared experience," "cooperative activity" – in short, they are binding because they are the product of consent.[68]

A duty of humanitarian intervention is just, according to Walzer, because it "fits" the "inherited cultures" of political communities everywhere.[69] It is justified, he writes,

> when it is a response ... to acts "that shock the moral conscience of mankind." The old-fashioned language seems to me exactly right. It is not the conscience

---

[64] Melvyn Frost, *Towards a Normative Theory of International Relations* (Cambridge University Press, Cambridge, 1986); David Miller, "The Ethical Significance of Nationality," 98 *Ethics* (1988), 647–62; N. J. Rengger, "A City which Sustains All Things? Communitarianism and International Society," 21 *Millennium: Journal of International Studies* (1992), 353–69; Anthony Black, "Nation and Community in the International Order," 19 *Review of International Studies* (1993), 81–89; Robert H. Jackson, "Armed Humanitarianism," 48 *International Journal* (1993), 579–606; David Miller, *On Nationality* (Oxford University Press, Oxford, 1995); David Morrice, "The Liberal–Communitarian Debate in Contemporary Political Philosophy and its Significance for International Relations," 26 *Review of International Studies* (2000), 233–51; Robert H. Jackson, *The Global Covenant: Human Conduct in a World of States* (Oxford University Press, Oxford, 2000), pp. 249–93.

[65] Michael Walzer, *Spheres of Justice: A Defense of Pluralism and Equality* (Basil Blackwell, Oxford, 1983), p. 312.

[66] Ibid., p. 313.

[67] Michael Walzer, "The Moral Standing of States: A Response to Four Critics," 9 *Philosophy and Public Affairs* (1980), 211. See also Walzer, *Spheres of Justice*, pp. 28–29; Walzer, *Just and Unjust Wars*, p. 45.

[68] Walzer, *Spheres of Justice*, p. 313; Walzer, *Just and Unjust Wars*, p. 54.

[69] Walzer, "Moral Standing of States," pp. 211–12; Michael Walzer, *Thick and Thin: Moral Argument at Home and Abroad* (University of Notre Dame Press, Notre Dame, 1994), pp. 15–19; Michael Walzer, "The Politics of Rescue," 62 *Social Research* (1995), 53–66.

of political leaders that one refers to in such cases. They have other things to worry about and may well be required to repress their feelings of indignation and outrage. The reference is to the moral convictions of ordinary men and women, acquired in the course of everyday activities.[70]

This global culture of human solidarity demands that states intervene whenever one of their number massacres, enslaves, or forcibly expels large numbers of its citizens or collapses into a frenzied, murderous anarchy.[71] Other communitarians, however, are not so sure. Hedley Bull, for instance, observes that "there is no present tendency for states to claim, or for the international community to recognize, any such right."[72]

The principal flaws of communitarianism – its moral relativism and conservatism – are well known and need not be rehearsed here.[73] A less well-known, though equally important, failing is that "consent," as communitarians conceive it, cannot generate morally binding norms. The communitarian conception of consent, writes Gerald Doppelt,

> is supposed to refer to a social process in which the activity of individuals "makes" or "shapes" a common life and independent community. But this picture is inherently vague and blurs important distinctions between the radically different terms on which individuals and groups are able to participate in, or influence, the life of a particular society . . . [Wherever societies are divided] into racial, economic, or religious groups with radically unequal political freedoms, civil rights, economic opportunities, living conditions, literacy or health . . . the oppressed group has little, if any, real choice or control concerning the harsh terms of its social participation. At the very least, all reflective people (and nations) distinguish between the social participation of a group or individual based on force, coercion, bare material survival,

---

[70] Walzer, *Just and Unjust Wars*, p. 107.   [71] Walzer, "Moral Standing of States," pp. 217–18.

[72] Hedley Bull, "Conclusion," in Hedley Bull ed., *Intervention in World Politics* (Clarendon Press, Oxford, 1984), p. 193.

[73] Richard A. Wasserstrom, "Review of *Just and Unjust Wars*," 92 *Harvard Law Review* (1978), 536–45; David Luban, "Just War and Human Rights," 9 *Philosophy and Public Affairs* (1980), 160–81; David Luban, "The Romance of the Nation-State," 9 *Philosophy and Public Affairs* (1980), 392–97; Beitz, "Nonintervention and Communal Integrity," pp. 385–91; Gerald Doppelt, "Statism without Foundations," 9 *Philosophy and Public Affairs* (1980), 398–403; Jerome Slater and Terry Nardin, "Nonintervention and Human Rights," 48 *Journal of Politics* (1986), 86–96; Tesón, *Humanitarian Intervention*, pp. 92–99; Richard Bellamy, "Justice in the Community: Walzer on Pluralism, Equality and Democracy," in David Boucher and Paul Kelly eds., *Social Justice: From Hume to Walzer* (Routledge, London, 1998), pp. 157–80; Tom J. Farer, "Does Walzer Still Work?" 41 *Public Affairs* (2000), 12–13.

ignorance, or blind habit and another kind which is "free" and approximates a meaningful sense of consent.[74]

Simply put, naturalists claim that communitarianism ignores the warping effects that asymmetries of wealth, power, and status have on expressions of consent. If individuals were truly free to construct their communities as they saw fit, they would choose norms quite different from those thrust on them by the dead hand of tradition.

Legal positivism

Legal positivism, as a normative doctrine, is the consensualist, collectivist view that norms are just if they are lawful; that is, if they are enacted according to accepted procedures.[75] The content of the norm is irrelevant to its binding force. One has a moral obligation to obey the law *qua* law. As Kenneth Einar Himma explains:

> To claim that there is a moral obligation to obey law qua law is to claim that a legal standard is morally obligatory ... *because* that standard is a law; in other words, it is to claim that a proposition of law is morally obligatory *in virtue of* being legally valid. Thus, someone who violates the law commits a moral wrong *in virtue of* performing an act that is inconsistent with the law.[76]

This view is known within legal positivism as the "separability thesis" – the claim that binding laws have absolutely no need to "reproduce or satisfy certain demands of morality, though in fact they have often done so."[77]

The separability thesis is vigorously contested by naturalists of all stripes. Joel Feinberg, to give only one example, asks: "Why should I have any

---

[74] Gerald Doppelt, "Walzer's Theory of Morality in International Relations," 8 *Philosophy and Public Affairs* (1978), 20–21. See also Beitz, *Political Theory*, pp. 67–105; Charles R. Beitz, "Bounded Morality: Justice and the State in World Politics," 33 *International Organization* (1979), 412–14.

[75] Legal positivism is also an analytic doctrine that seeks to distinguish legal norms from non-legal ones.

[76] Kenneth Einar Himma, "Positivism, Naturalism, and the Obligation to Obey Law," 36 *Southern Journal of Philosophy* (1998), 151.

[77] H. L. A. Hart, "Positivism and the Separation of Law and Morals," 71 *Harvard Law Review* (1958), 593–629; H. L. A. Hart, *The Concept of Law* (2nd edn, Oxford University Press, Oxford, 1994), pp. 181–82. See also Joseph Raz, *The Authority of Law: Essays on Law and Morality* (Clarendon Press, Oxford, 1979); Joseph Raz, *The Concept of a Legal System: An Introduction to the Theory of Legal Systems* (2nd edn, Clarendon Press, Oxford, 1980).

respect or duty of fidelity toward a statute with a wicked or stupid content just because it was passed into law by a bunch of men (possibly very wicked men like the Nazi legislators) according to the accepted recipes for making law?"[78] A small number of legal positivists concede Feinberg's point – arguing instead that one has a moral obligation to obey the law *qua* law only if it is enacted according to just legislative procedures.[79] But what is a just legislative procedure? In international law, "state consent" – expressed in the form of treaties and international custom – is the accepted procedure for enacting legal norms. But is "state consent" a just legislative procedure? Legal positivists could argue that "state consent" is the legally valid (and hence morally binding) legislative procedure because it is the legislative procedure that states recognize as legally valid (and hence morally binding). Such a claim, however, would be self-referential at best – tautological at worst. One could argue with equal consistency that "Nazi Party consent" was the legally valid (and hence morally binding) legislative procedure in Nazi Germany because it was the legislative procedure that the Nazi Party recognized as legally valid (and hence morally binding). To have a plausible normative theory, legal positivists need to justify (i) their collectivist assumption that states are the *proper agents* to enact binding norms, and (ii) their consensualist assumption that actual consent – whose problems we have briefly noted above – is the *proper means* for enacting such norms. To do this, however, they must employ the sorts of naturalist arguments that the separability thesis expressly forbids.[80]

The legality of humanitarian intervention

Legal positivists argue that there is a moral duty to obey the law. But what is the law? According to Article 38(I) of the Statute of the International Court of Justice, international norms are legally binding if they are incorporated

---

[78] Joel Feinberg, "Civil Disobedience in the Modern World," 2 *Humanities in Society* (1979), 43–44. See also Lon L. Fuller, "Positivism and Fidelity to Law: A Reply to Professor Hart," 71 *Harvard Law Review* (1958), 630; Jules Coleman, "On the Relationship between Law and Morality," 2 *Ratio Juris* (1989), 66–78; Tesón, *Philosophy of International Law*, pp. 92–97.

[79] Himma, "Positivism, Naturalism," pp. 145–61.

[80] John Rawls, "Legal Obligation and the Duty of Fair Play," in Sidney Hook ed., *Law and Philosophy* (New York University Press, New York, 1964), pp. 3–18; M. B. E. Smith, "Do We Have a Prima Facie Obligation to Obey the Law?" 82 *Yale Law Journal* (1973), 950–76; Klaus Füsser, "Farewell to 'Legal Positivism': The Separation Thesis Unravelling," in Robert George ed., *The Autonomy of Law: Essays on Legal Positivism* (Clarendon Press, Oxford, 1996), pp. 119–62.

in "a. international conventions, whether general or particular, establishing rules expressly recognized by the contesting states; b. international custom, as evidence of a general practice accepted as law ... " Although this Statute is technically only binding on the International Court of Justice, it is widely accepted as the authoritative statement of the sources of international law.

International conventions

The Charter of the United Nations

The paramount international convention governing the exercise of armed force in the international community is the Charter of the United Nations. Opponents of humanitarian intervention point to Article 2(4)'s injunction that "[a]ll states ... refrain in their international relations from the threat or use of force against the territorial integrity and political independence of any state, or in any other manner inconsistent with the purpose of the United Nations." They also note Article 2(7)'s declaration that "[n]othing in the present Charter shall authorize the United Nations to intervene in matters which are essentially within the domestic jurisdiction of any state."

For most international lawyers, this is the end of the matter. The meaning of the UN Charter is clear. A small, but growing, number of international legal scholars, however, beg to disagree. They advance three arguments aimed at reconciling humanitarian intervention with the UN's *jus ad bellum* regime.

First, they argue that "Article 2(4) does not forbid the threat or use of force *simpliciter*; it forbids it only when directed against the territorial integrity or political independence of any State."[81] Thus, if a "genuine humanitarian intervention does not result in territorial conquest or political subjugation ... it is a distortion to argue that [it] is prohibited by article 2(4)."[82]

---

[81] Julius Stone, *Aggression and World Order: A Critique of United Nations' Theories of Aggression* (Stevens, London, 1958), p. 95.

[82] Tesón, *Humanitarian Intervention*, p. 151. "Since a humanitarian intervention seeks neither a territorial change nor a challenge to the political independence of the State involved and is not only not inconsistent with the purposes of the United Nations but is rather in conformity with the most fundamental peremptory norms of the Charter, it is a distortion to argue that it is precluded by Article 2(4)." W. Michael Reisman with the collaboration of Myres S. McDougal, "Humanitarian Intervention to Protect the Ibos," in Lillich, *Humanitarian Intervention and the UN*, p. 177.

Most international lawyers dispute this argument on the ground that the drafters of the Charter clearly intended the phrase "territorial integrity or political independence of any State" to reinforce, rather than restrict, the ban on the use of force in international relations. "If it is asserted," writes Ian Brownlie, "that the phrase may have a qualifying effect then the writers making this assertion face the difficulty that it involves an admission that there is an ambiguity, and in such a case recourse may be had to the *travaux préparatoires*, which reveal a meaning contrary to that asserted."[83] Oscar Schachter is blunter: "The idea that wars waged in a good cause such as democracy and human rights would not involve a violation of territorial integrity or political independence demands an Orwellian construction of those terms."[84]

This debate, like so many in international law, turns on how to interpret the relevant international conventions. There are, broadly speaking, two approaches to the question. The advocates of what Tom J. Farer calls the "classicist view" presume that the parties to a treaty "had an original intention which can be discovered primarily through textual analysis and which, in the absence of some unforeseen change in circumstances, must be respected until the agreement has expired or has been replaced by mutual consent."[85] In contrast, champions of the rival approach, "legal realism," see

> explicit and implicit agreements, formal texts, and state behavior as being in a condition of effervescent interaction, unceasingly creating, modifying, and replacing norms. Texts themselves are but one among a large number of means for ascertaining original intention. Moreover, realists postulate an accelerating contraction in the capacity and the authority of original intention to govern state behavior. Indeed, original intention does not govern at any point in time. For original intention has no intrinsic authority. The past is relevant only to the extent that it helps us to identify currently prevailing attitudes about the propriety of a government's acts and omissions.[86]

---

[83] Brownlie, *International Law and the Use of Force*, p. 267. See also Michael Akehurst, "Humanitarian Intervention," in Bull, *Intervention in World Politics*, p. 105; Rosalyn Higgins, *The Development of International Law through the Political Organs of the United Nations* (Oxford University Press, Oxford, 1963), p. 183.

[84] Schachter, "Legality of Pro-democratic Invasion," p. 649.

[85] Tom J. Farer, "An Inquiry into the Legitimacy of Humanitarian Intervention," in Lori Fisler Damrosch and David J. Scheffer eds., *Law and Force in the New International Order* (Westview Press, Boulder, 1991), p. 186.

[86] *Ibid.*, p. 186.

If one accepts the classicist view, the illegality of unauthorized humanitarian intervention is patent. If one adopts the legal realist view, however, its legal status depends in large measure on the attitude of the contemporary international community towards it.

The second way many legal realists have sought to reconcile humanitarian intervention with the UN's *jus ad bellum* regime is to claim the phrase "or in any other manner inconsistent with the purposes of the United Nations" permits unauthorized humanitarian intervention where the Security Council fails to realize one of its chief purposes – the protection of human rights.[87] According to W. Michael Reisman, if the Security Council had functioned as originally designed,

> it would have obviated the need for the [unauthorized] use of force. States with a grievance could have repaired to the Security Council, which could then apply the appropriate quantum and form of authoritative coercion and thereby vindicate the rights it found had been violated... But the security system of the United Nations was premised on a consensus between the permanent members of the Security Council.[88] Lamentably, that consensus dissolved early in the history of the organisation. Thereafter... [p]art of the systematic justification for the theory of Article 2(4) disappeared.[89]

[87] "The purposes of the United Nations are... [t]o achieve international co-operation in... encouraging respect for human rights and for fundamental freedoms for all without distinction as to race, sex, language or religion" (Article 1(3)). "[T]he United Nations shall promote... universal respect for, and observance of, human rights and fundamental freedoms for all" (Article 55). "All members shall pledge themselves to take joint and separate action in co-operation with the Organisation for the achievement of the purposes set forth in Article 55" (Article 56).

[88] Reisman's assumption that the UN security system presupposed a continuation of the wartime alliance between the United States, the United Kingdom, the Soviet Union, France, and China is not without its critics. "During the formation of the United Nations," writes Judy A. Gallant, "numerous states initially hoped to eliminate the veto but quickly understood that it was a precondition to ensuring the very existence of the United Nations. The veto power was the cost that the less influential nations paid for the inclusion of the five major powers in the new collective security system." Judy A. Gallant, "Humanitarian Intervention and Security Council Resolution 688: A Reappraisal in Light of a Changing World Order," 7 *American University Journal of International Law and Policy* (1992), 898–99.

[89] W. Michael Reisman, "Criteria for the Lawful Use of Force in International Law," 10 *Yale Journal of International Law* (1985), 279–80. See also Stone, *Aggression and World Order*, pp. 43, 95–96; W. Friedmann, *The Changing Structure of International Law* (Columbia University Press, New York, 1964), p. 259; Richard B. Lillich, "Humanitarian Intervention: A Reply to Ian Brownlie and a Plea for Constructive Alternatives," in Moore, *Law and Civil War*, p. 230; W. Michael Reisman, "Coercion and Self-determination: Construing Charter Article 2(4)," 78 *American Journal of International Law* (1984), 642–45; Daniel Wolf, "Humanitarian Intervention," 9 *Michigan Year Book of International Legal Studies* (1988), 368.

On this view, if the Security Council fails to end massive human rights violations, states may do so without authorization.[90]

Classicists respond by noting that the negotiating history of the Charter supports the contention that the conjunction "or" in the phrase "or in any other manner inconsistent with the purposes of the United Nations" was meant to supplement, rather than qualify, the prohibition on the unauthorized use of armed force. In other words, the drafters of Article 2(4) intended to ban states from using force *against both the territorial integrity and political independence* of other states *and* in any other manner inconsistent with the promotion of human rights.[91] They also note that the contrary interpretation has twice been rejected by the International Court of Justice.[92]

Once again, if one accepts the classicist view, the illegality of unauthorized humanitarian intervention is clear. If one adopts the legal realist view, however, its legal status depends in large measure on the international community's current attitude towards such interventions. This is examined below.[93]

The third way legal realists seek to legitimate humanitarian intervention is through an expansive interpretation of Article 39 of the UN Charter. This article states that the Security Council may authorize the use of force in response to "any threat to the peace, breach of the peace or act of aggression." Legal realists argue that this article, by giving the Security Council jurisdiction over any "threat to *the* peace," rather than over any threat to

---

[90] "The deterioration of the Charter security regime has stimulated a partial revival of a type of [unauthorized] *jus ad bellum*... Nine basic categories appear to have emerged in which one finds varying support for [unauthorized] uses of force. They [include] ... humanitarian intervention." Reisman, "Criteria for the Lawful Use of Force," p. 281. See also Tesón, *Humanitarian Intervention*, pp. 157–62; David M. Kresock, "'Ethnic Cleansing' in the Balkans: The Legal Foundations of Foreign Intervention," 27 *Cornell International Law Journal* (1994), 234–37.

[91] "The delegate of Brazil adverted to the possibility of a restricted interpretation of the phrase. The United States delegate 'made it clear that the intention of the authors of the original text was to state in the broadest terms an absolute all-inclusive prohibition; the phrase "or in any other manner" was designed to insure that there should be no loop-holes.'" Brownlie, *International Law and the Use of Force*, p. 268, n. 6; Sean Murphy, *Humanitarian Intervention: The United Nations in an Evolving World Order* (University of Pennsylvania Press, Philadelphia, 1996), p. 73. Even as notable a proponent of humanitarian intervention as Anthony A. D'Amato concedes the drafters of the Charter intended to ban forcible self-help in defense of human rights. Anthony A. D'Amato, *International Law: Process and Prospect* (Transnational Publishers, Dobbs Ferry, 1987), p. 54.

[92] *Corfu Channel Case (Merits), ICJ Reports, 1949*, p. 35; *Nicaragua v. US (Merits), ICJ Reports, 1986*, p. 97.

[93] See below, pp. 46–49.

international peace, permits it to intervene to end human rights violations that lack transboundary effects.[94]

Once again, classicists beg to differ. Massive and pervasive human rights violations, writes Lori Fisler Damrosch,

> do not necessarily entail threats to peace and security ... Economic sanctions and other nonforcible measures are quite acceptable methods for enforcement of the full range of international human rights law, whether or not the human rights violations in question endanger international security. States may adopt such nonforcible measures of their own or through collective mechanisms, including those sponsored by the United Nations as well as by regional organizations. But there is no clear authority to be found in the UN Charter for transboundary *uses of force* against violations that do not themselves pose a transboundary threat to peace and security.[95]

This view, as Damrosch herself acknowledges, is difficult to defend on purely legal grounds.[96] First, the records of both the Dumbarton Oaks and San Francisco Conferences plainly show the drafters of the UN Charter wanted the Security Council to have wide discretion in determining the existence of any threat to the peace.[97] Second, and more importantly, the Security Council itself rejects it. The UN's interventions in Somalia (1992), Rwanda (1994), and Haiti (1994) all support the contention that the Security Council presently believes it is empowered under Chapter VII of the UN Charter to authorize the use of military force to end massive human rights abuses.[98]

[94] "[T]he decision of the Security Council on what constitutes a threat to international peace and security is a political one and subject to its political discretion." Malanczuk, *Humanitarian Intervention*, p. 26; Jost Delbrück, "A Fresh Look at Humanitarian Intervention under the Authority of the United Nations," 67 *Indiana Law Journal* (1992), 898–99.

[95] Lori Fisler Damrosch, "Commentary on Collective Military Intervention to Enforce Human Rights," in Damrosch and Scheffer, *Law and Force*, p. 219.

[96] "My concern about using the Security Council or the General Assembly in the kinds of situations under discussion relates not so much to the constitutional law of the UN Charter as to the wisdom of starting down this road." Ibid., p. 220.

[97] "[A]n overwhelming majority of the participating governments were of the opinion that the circumstances in which threats to the peace or aggression might occur are so varied that [Article 39] should be left as broad and as flexible as possible." US Department of State, *Charter of the United Nations: Report to the President on the Result of the San Francisco Conference (1945)* (Greenwood Press, New York, 1969), p. 91. See also Jochen A. Frowein, "Article 39," in Simma et al., *Charter of the UN*, pp. 607–08.

[98] Humanitarian interventions in Liberia (1990), northern Iraq (1991), southern Iraq (1992), and Sierra Leone (1998) neither support nor undermine the proposition that the UN has a right to use military force to end massive human rights abuses. In all four cases, the Security Council acquiesced in, rather than formally authorized, the use of armed force to protect human

In Somalia, for example, the Security Council determined that the civil war was "a threat to international peace and security."[99] To be sure, the collapse of the Somali state produced refugee flows that affected neighboring countries. But, as Sean D. Murphy notes,

> the Security Council's resolution made no mention of refugees, and the subsequent intervention was not designed simply to repatriate those refugees. The primary focus of the intervention under UNITAF was, rather, to open food relief lines into Somalia so as to prevent widespread starvation and disease among Somalis *in Somalia*... [O]ne benefit of these actions was the creation of conditions for the repatriation of Somali refugees, but to cast the intervention as designed wholly or predominantly to address that issue would be incorrect.[100]

In Rwanda, the Security Council likewise determined that the massacre of up to a million Tutsis constituted "a threat to peace."[101] And while it parenthetically noted the "massive exodus of refugees to neighbouring countries," the Security Council's preoccupation was with ending the "acts of genocide... *in Rwanda*"; "the ongoing violence *in Rwanda*"; "the continuation of systematic and widespread killings of the civilian population *in Rwanda*"; and the "*internal* displacement of some 1.5 million Rwandans."[102] Again, no impartial observer could conclude that the Security Council thought that it was only the transboundary effects of the Rwandan genocide, rather than the genocide itself, that permitted it to intervene.

Finally, in Haiti, the Security Council determined that the "deterioration of the humanitarian situation in Haiti, in particular the continuing escalation... of systematic violations of *civil* liberties"[103] constituted a "threat to peace" in the region.[104] In addition, although it expressed grave concern

---

rights. Security Council Resolution 688, UNSCOR, 2982nd mtg., 5 April 1991; Security Council Resolution 788, UNSCOR, 3138th mtg., 19 November 1992; Security Council Resolution 813, UNSCOR, 3187th mtg., 26 March 1993; Security Council Resolution 1156, UNSCOR, 3861st mtg., 16 March 1998; Security Council Resolution 1162, UNSCOR, 3872nd mtg., 17 April 1998; Security Council Resolution 1181, UNSCOR, 3902nd mtg., 13 July 1998.

[99] Security Council Resolution 688, UNSCOR, 2982nd mtg., 3 December 1992.

[100] Murphy, *Humanitarian Intervention*, pp. 286–87.

[101] Security Council Resolution 929, UNSCOR, 3392nd mtg., 22 June 1994.

[102] Security Council Resolution 925, UNSCOR, 3388th mtg., 8 June 1994; Security Council Resolution 929, UNSCOR, 3392nd mtg., 22 June 1994, para. 3. Emphases added.

[103] Security Council Resolution 940, UNSCOR, 3413th mtg., 31 July 1994. Emphasis added.

[104] Fernando R. Tesón contends that "the Security Council did *not* determine that the situation in Haiti constituted a threat to international peace and security while asserting that it was acting under Chapter VII." Tesón, "Collective Humanitarian Intervention," p. 358. This claim is mistaken, as the relevant sections of Security Council Resolutions 841 and 940 plainly show:

for the "desperate plight of Haitian refugees,"[105] there is little evidence that it thought that these transboundary effects alone, and not the "climate of fear" created by the "illegal de facto regime," gave it the right to intervene.[106]

The Charter's drafting history and recent Security Council practice thus strongly support the legal realist contention that UN-sanctioned humanitarian interventions are lawful exceptions to the Charter's general prohibition of forcible self-help in international relations.[107]

Human rights conventions

The UN Charter's apparent ban on unauthorized humanitarian intervention does not mean that states are free to treat their own citizens as they wish. To the contrary, most states are signatories to conventions that legally oblige them to respect the human rights of their citizens.[108] Nevertheless, the mere existence of these obligations, as Jack Donnelly observes,

---

"*The Security Council . . . [d]etermining* that . . . the continuation of this situation threatens international peace and security in the region . . . [and *a*]*cting*, therefore, under Chapter VII of the Charter of the United Nations . . . [*d*]*ecides* . . ." "*The Security Council . . . [d]etermining* that the situation in Haiti continues to constitute a threat to peace and security in the region . . . [and *a*]*cting* under Chapter VII of the Charter of the United Nations authorises Member States to form a multinational force under unified command and control and, in this framework, to use all necessary means to facilitate the departure from Haiti of the military leadership . . . [and] the prompt return of the legitimately elected President . . ." Security Council Resolution 841, UNSCOR, 3238th mtg., 16 June 1993; Security Council Resolution 940, UNSCOR, 3413th mtg., 31 July 1994.

[105] Security Council Resolution 940, UNSCOR, 3413th mtg., 31 July 1994.

[106] Security Council Resolution 841, UNSCOR, 3238th mtg., 16 June 1993.

[107] While it is widely accepted that the UN Security Council can authorize humanitarian interventions, there is considerable disagreement about whether a state or group of states claiming to be acting pursuant to *implied* or *ambiguous* Security Council authorizations is acting lawfully. See Thomas M. Franck, "Interpretation and Change in the Law of Humanitarian Intervention," ch. 6 in this volume; Jules Lobel and Michael Ratner, "Bypassing the Security Council: Ambiguous Authorizations to Use Force, Cease-fires and the Iraqi Inspection Regime," 93 *American Journal of International Law* (1999), 124–54.

[108] These include: Covenant to Suppress the Slave Trade and Slavery (1926); Convention on the Prevention and Punishment of the Crime of Genocide (1948); European Convention for the Protection of Human Rights and Fundamental Freedoms (1950); International Covenant on Economic, Social and Cultural Rights (1966); International Convention on the Elimination of All Forms of Racial Discrimination (1965); International Covenant on Civil and Political Rights (1966); Optional Protocol to the International Covenant on Civil and Political Rights (1966); American Convention on Human Rights (1969); Convention on the Elimination of All Forms of Discrimination against Women (1979); African Charter on Human and Peoples' Rights (1981); United Nations Convention against Torture and Other Cruel, Inhuman or Degrading Treatment (1984); United Nations Convention on the Rights of the Child (1989). For texts see Ian Brownlie, *Basic Documents on Human Rights* (3rd edn, Oxford University Press, New York, 1992).

does not imply that any international actor is authorized to implement or enforce those obligations. Just as in domestic politics, governments are free to adopt legislation with extremely weak, or even non-existent, implementation measures, states are free to create and accept international legal obligations that are to be implemented entirely through national action. And this is in fact what states have done with international human rights. None of the obligations to be found in multilateral human rights treaties may be coercively enforced by any external actor.[109]

It has been suggested that the Genocide Convention (1948), by enjoining its signatories to "prevent and punish" the "crime of genocide," may be the exception that proves this rule.[110] But, as the text of that convention makes clear, the only way in which the contracting parties may legally prevent acts of genocide is by calling upon "the competent organs of the United Nations to take such action as they consider appropriate."[111] Such an "enforcement" mechanism clearly does not establish a right of unauthorized humanitarian intervention.

In sum, the most important source of international law, international conventions, seems to permit the UN Security Council to authorize humanitarian interventions by its members. More controversial, however, is the claim that it also allows unauthorized humanitarian interventions.

Customary international law

Some scholars argue for the continued existence of a customary right of unauthorized humanitarian intervention.[112] According to them, state

---

[109] Jack Donnelly, "Human Rights, Humanitarian Crisis, and Humanitarian Intervention," 48 *International Journal* (1993), 623. See also Jack Donnelly, *International Human Rights* (Westview Press, Boulder, 1993), pp. 57–97.

[110] Scheffer, "Towards a Modern Doctrine," p. 289; United Nations Convention on the Prevention and Punishment of the Crime of Genocide (1948), Article I. Julie Mertus goes further: "If the target state is party to any of the relevant human rights conventions, or if the human right can be said to be customary international law applicable to all states, humanitarian intervention can be grounded or categorized as a means of enforcing these obligations on behalf of victims." Julie Mertus, "The Legality of Humanitarian Intervention: Lessons from Kosovo," 41 *William and Mary Law Review* (2000), 1773.

[111] United Nations Convention on the Prevention and Punishment of the Crime of Genocide (1948), Article VIII.

[112] Richard B. Lillich, "Forcible Self-help by States to Protect Human Rights," 53 *Iowa Law Review* (1967), 334; Jean-Pierre L. Fonteyne, "The Customary International Law Doctrine of Humanitarian Intervention: Its Current Validity under the UN Charter," 4 *California Western International Law Journal* (1974), 203–70; Lillich, "Reply to Ian Brownlie," pp. 229–51; Michael

practice in the nineteenth and early twentieth centuries established such a right; a right that was "neither terminated nor weakened" by the creation of the United Nations.[113] This right remains so secure, they argue, that "only its limits and not its existence is subject to debate."[114]

Classicists contest this view on two grounds. First, they contend that the handful of pre-Charter humanitarian interventions (Britain, France, and Russia in Greece [1827–30]; France in Syria [1860–61]; Russia in Bosnia-Herzegovina and Bulgaria [1877–78]; United States in Cuba [1898]; and Greece, Bulgaria, and Serbia in Macedonia [1903–08, 1912–13]) were insufficient to establish a customary right of humanitarian intervention.[115] Indeed, such a right was not even invoked, let alone exercised, in the face of the greatest humanitarian catastrophes of the pre-Charter era, including the massacre of 1 million Armenians by the Turks (1914–19), the forced starvation of 4 million Ukrainians by the Soviets (1930s); the massacre of hundreds of thousands of Chinese by the Japanese (1931–45); and the extermination of 6 million Jews by the Nazis (1939–45). It may also be noted that there is little or no evidence that the international community considered such a right legally binding (*opinio juris sive necessitatis*), a *sine qua non* of customary international law.[116]

J. Bazyler, "Re-examining the Doctrine of Humanitarian Intervention in Light of the Atrocities in Kampuchea and Ethiopia," 23 *Stanford Journal of International Law* (1987), 547–619.

[113] Reisman, "Humanitarian Intervention to Protect the Ibos," p. 171.

[114] International Law Association, *The International Protection of Human Rights by General International Law* (Interim Report of the Sub-Committee, International Committee on Human Rights, The Hague, 1970), p. 11, quoted in Fonteyne, "Customary International Law Doctrine," pp. 235–36. See also M. Ganji, *International Protection of Human Rights* (Librairie E. Droz, Geneva, 1962); Nanda, "Tragedies in Northern Iraq, Liberia, Yugoslavia and Haiti," p. 310; Bazyler, "Re-examining the Doctrine," p. 573; M. Trachtenberg, "Intervention in Historical Perspective," in Laura W. Reed and Carl Kaysen eds., *Emerging Norms of Justified Intervention* (Committee on International Security Studies, American Academy of Arts and Sciences, Cambridge, Mass., 1993), pp. 15–36; Barry M. Benjamin, "Unilateral Humanitarian Intervention: Legalizing the Use of Force to Prevent Human Rights Atrocities," 16 *Fordham International Law Journal* (1992–93), 126.

[115] Brownlie, *International Law and the Use of Force*, pp. 339–41; Thomas M. Franck and Nigel S. Rodley, "After Bangladesh: The Law of Humanitarian Intervention by Military Force," 67 *American Journal of International Law* (1973), 279–85; Brownlie, "Humanitarian Intervention," pp. 220–21; Beyerlin, "Humanitarian Intervention," p. 212; Ronzitti, *Rescuing Nationals Abroad*, pp. 89–93; Malanczuk, *Humanitarian Intervention*, pp. 7–11.

[116] J. Charney, "The Persistent Objector Rule and the Development of Customary International Law," 56 *British Yearbook of International Law* (1985), 1–24; R. Bernhardt, "Customary International Law," in Bernhardt, 1 *Encyclopedia of Public International Law*, pp. 898–905; G. Danilenko, *Law-making in the International Community* (Martinus Nijhoff, Dordrecht, 1993), pp. 81–109; Ian Brownlie, *Principles of Public International Law* (5th edn, Clarendon

Second, classicists contend that, even if one concedes that a customary right of humanitarian intervention existed in the pre-Charter era, it did not legally survive the creation of the UN's *jus ad bellum* regime. If one accepts the strictures of classicism, the only way such a right could have endured was if it were a peremptory international norm (*jus cogens*), i.e. a norm that was "accepted and recognised by the international community . . . as a norm from which no derogation is permitted."[117] Yet, as noted above, there is considerable doubt as to whether such a right even existed, let alone possessed the status of a peremptory international norm. Indeed, the very establishment of the United Nations, with its ostensible ban on unauthorized humanitarian intervention, is strong prima facie evidence to the contrary.

Of course, the burden of proving the continued existence of a customary right of unauthorized humanitarian intervention is lightened considerably if one accepts a legal realist interpretation of the UN Charter. In addition to avoiding the need to show that the doctrine of humanitarian intervention was a peremptory international norm in the pre-Charter period, one may point to a number of post-Charter interventions – the United States in the Dominican Republic (1965); India in East Pakistan (1971); Vietnam in Kampuchea (1978–93); Tanzania in Uganda (1979); ECOWAS in Liberia (1990–95); Britain, France, and the United States in Iraq (since 1991); ECOWAS in Sierra Leone (since 1998); and NATO in Kosovo (since 1999) – as evidence of its continued existence.

Yet having to meet a lighter burden of proof is not identical to actually doing so. Classicists still note that this alleged right lacks the two recognized attributes of a binding international norm: general observance and widespread acceptance that it is lawful (*opinio juris sive necessitatis*).[118] In support of this contention, they point to the highly selective exercise of the right of unauthorized humanitarian intervention in recent history. No

---

Press, Oxford, 1998), pp. 4–11; Michael Byers, *Custom, Power and the Power of Rules: International Relations and Customary International Law* (Cambridge University Press, Cambridge, 1999), pp. 129–203.

[117] Vienna Convention on the Law of Treaties (1969), Article 53. See also Jochen A. Frowein, "*Jus Cogens*," in Bernhardt, 7 *Encyclopedia of Public International Law*, pp. 327–30; L. Hannikainen, *Peremptory Norms (Jus Cogens) in International Law: Historical Development, Criteria, Present Status* (Lakimiesliiton Kustannus, Helsinki, 1988); G. Danilenko, "International *Jus Cogens*: Issues of Law-making," 2 *European Journal of International Law* (1991), 42–65.

[118] Franck and Rodley, "After Bangladesh," p. 296; Ian Brownlie, "Non-use of Force in Contemporary International Law," in William E. Butler ed., *Non-use of Force in International Law* (Martinus Nijhoff, Dordrecht, 1989), pp. 25–26; Farer, "An Inquiry into the Legitimacy," pp. 192–95.

state or regional organization, for example, intervened to prevent or end the massacre of several hundred thousand ethnic Chinese in Indonesia (mid-1960s); the killing and forced starvation of almost half a million Ibos in Nigeria (1966–70); the slaughter and forced starvation of well over a million black Christians by the Sudanese government (since the late 1960s); the killing of tens of thousands of Tutsis in Rwanda (early 1970s); the murder of tens of thousands of Hutus in Burundi (1972); the slaying of 100,000 East Timorese by the Indonesian government (1975–99); the forced starvation of up to 1 million Ethiopians by their government (mid-1980s); the murder of 100,000 Kurds in Iraq (1988–89); and the killing of tens of thousands of Hutus in Burundi (since 1993). But while the classicists are correct to highlight the selective exercise of this putative right, their argument, as Dino Kritsiotis notes,

> misconceives the theoretical and traditional understanding of humanitarian intervention in international law, which has been framed as a *right* of states and not as an *obligation* requiring action. Inherent in the very conception of a right is an element of selectivity in the exercise of that right. This is in keeping with the right-holder's sovereign discretion to decide whether or not to exercise the right in question and commit its armed forces to foreign territories and explains why it is the right *of* – rather than the right *to* – humanitarian intervention that has taken hold in practice as well as legal scholarship.[119]

Because the doctrine of unauthorized humanitarian intervention is a permissive rather than a mandatory norm, the selectivity of its exercise is no barrier to its being a customary international law.

The task of showing that a right of unauthorized humanitarian intervention possesses the second attribute of a customary international norm (widespread acceptance that it is lawful [*opinio juris sive necessitatis*]) is more difficult. The long list of UN General Assembly resolutions rejecting such a right argues strongly against this claim.[120] In 1999, for example,

---

[119] Dino Kritsiotis, "Reappraising Policy Objections to Humanitarian Intervention," 19 *Michigan Journal of International Law* (1998), 1027.

[120] "No state has the right to intervene, directly or indirectly, for any reason whatever, in the internal or external affairs of any other State." Declaration on the Inadmissibility of Intervention in the Domestic Affairs of States (1965), GA Res. 2131, UNGAOR, 20th sess., UN Doc. A/6220 (1965).

"Armed intervention and all other forms of interference or attempted threats against the personality of the State or against its political, economic and cultural elements, are in violation of international law." Declaration on Principles of International Law concerning Friendly

that august body passed, by a vote of 107 to 7 (with 48 abstentions), the following denunciation of NATO's intervention in Kosovo:

> *The General Assembly ... Reaffirming ...* that no State may use or encourage the use of economic, political or any other type of measures to coerce another State in order to obtain from it the subordination of the exercise of its sovereign rights ... [and] *Deeply concerned* that, despite the recommendations adopted on this question by the General Assembly ... [unauthorized] coercive measures continue to be promulgated and implemented with all their extraterritorial effects ... *Rejects* [unauthorized] coercive measures with all their extraterritorial effects as tools for political or economic pressure against any country.[121]

More significantly, even states that have intervened to end heinous human rights abuses have been loath to invoke a customary right of unauthorized humanitarian intervention to defend their actions. India's ostensible justification of its invasion of East Pakistan was self-defense.[122] Vietnam claimed that it was responding to a "large-scale aggressive war" being waged by Cambodia.[123] Tanzania defended its overthrow of the Amin regime as an appropriate response to Uganda's invasion, occupation, and annexation of the Kagera salient the preceding year.[124] ECOWAS's justification of its invasions of Liberia and Sierra Leone was that it was invited to intervene by the legitimate governments of those states.[125] NATO defended Operation Allied Force on the grounds that it was "consistent with" Security Council

Relations and Cooperation among States (1970), GA Res. 2625, UNGAOR, 25th sess., UN Doc. A/8028 (1970).

"The sovereignty, territorial integrity and national unity of States must be fully respected in accordance with the Charter of the United Nations. In this context, humanitarian assistance *should be provided with the consent of the affected country* and in principle on the basis of an appeal by the affected country." Declaration on Strengthening of the Coordination of Humanitarian Emergency Assistance of the United Nations (1991), GA Res. 46/182, UNGAOR, 46th sess., UN Doc. A/RES/46/182 (1991).

[121] GA Res. 54/172, UNGAOR, 54th sess., UN Doc. A/RES/54/172 (1999).

[122] Akehurst, "Humanitarian Intervention," p. 96; Franck and Rodley, "After Bangladesh," pp. 276–77; Ronzitti, *Rescuing Nationals Abroad*, pp. 96, 108–09; Wil D. Verwey, "Humanitarian Intervention under International Law," 32 *Netherlands International Law Review* (1985), 401–02.

[123] Foreign Ministry Statement (6 January 1979), quoted in Murphy, *Humanitarian Intervention*, p. 104. See also Gary Klintworth, *Vietnam's Intervention in Cambodia in International Law* (Australian Government Publishing Service, Canberra, 1989), pp. 15–33.

[124] Ronzitti, *Rescuing Nationals Abroad*, pp. 102–06; Hassan, "Realpolitik," pp. 859–912.

[125] Murphy, *Humanitarian Intervention*, pp. 146–58; Karsten Nowrot and Emily W. Schabacker, "The Use of Force to Restore Democracy: International Legal Implications of the ECOWAS Intervention in Sierra Leone," 14 *American University International Law Review* (1998), 321–412;

Resolutions 1160, 1199, and 1203.[126] It is irrelevant that these justifications are specious if not false. What is noteworthy is the fact that the states concerned felt they could not appeal to a right of unauthorized humanitarian intervention to legitimate their actions. If there is presently a right of unauthorized humanitarian intervention, it is a right that dares not speak its name.[127]

In sum, even if one accepts legal realism's relaxed attitude to the sources of international law, it still takes a highly selective reading of those sources to conclude that a right of unauthorized humanitarian intervention is presently legal. One must bear in mind, however, that demonstrating that unauthorized humanitarian intervention is illegal is not, unless you are a legal positivist, the same as proving that it is immoral.

Conclusion

Having surveyed the principal arguments about the morality and legality of humanitarian intervention, let me conclude by offering the following three observations.

First, any attempt to separate legal questions from moral ones is doomed to failure. Take, for example, the debate between classicists and legal realists. This debate is ostensibly about how best to identify state intent. Classicists aver that it is best found in the plain meaning of international conventions. Legal realists claim that it is best distilled from the widest range of relevant

---

J. Levitt, "Humanitarian Intervention by Regional Actors in Internal Conflicts: The Cases of ECOWAS in Liberia and Sierra Leone," 12 *Temple International and Comparative Law Journal* (1998), 333–75.

[126] Wheeler, *Saving Strangers*, pp. 275–81.

[127] Belgium was the lone NATO member to claim that Operation Allied Force was a legitimate exercise of a customary right of humanitarian intervention. "NATO, and the Kingdom of Belgium in particular, felt obliged to intervene to forestall an ongoing humanitarian catastrophe, acknowledged in Security Council resolutions. To safeguard what? To safeguard, Mr. President, essential values which also rank as *jus cogens*. Are the right to life, physical integrity, the prohibition of torture, are these not norms with the status of *jus cogens*? They undeniably have this status, so much so that international instruments on human rights (the European Human Rights Convention, the agreements mentioned above) protect them in a waiver clause (the power of suspension in case of war of all human rights except right to life and integrity of the individual): thus they are absolute rights, from which we may conclude that they belong to the *jus cogens*. Thus, NATO intervened to protect fundamental values enshrined in the *jus cogens* and to prevent an impending catastrophe recognized as such by the Security Council." "Public sitting held on Monday 10 May 1999, at the Peace Palace, Vice-President Weeramantry, Acting President, presiding in the case concerning *Legality of Use of Force* (*Yugoslavia* v. *Belgium*)." Available at http://www.icj-cij.org/icjwww/idocket/iybe/iybeframe.htm (5 March 2002).

sources. Still one cannot help feeling that the debate is, at a deeper level, about quite different issues. Classicists claim that international law is the lone, best, hope of stopping powerful states from running amok, and view legal realist attempts to weaken its already all-too-feeble restraining effects with barely concealed horror. Legal realists, for their part, fear that international law, in the hands of classicists, risks becoming an irrelevance at best, and a hindrance at worst. They worry that, in a rapidly changing world with precious few resources for legal reform, past expressions of state intent will become obstacles to new expressions of state intent. The relative merits of these two views, however, cannot be decided *a priori*. They depend instead on the character of the system's powerful states and the types of international reform those states are trying to pursue. Legal realism is unquestionably more appealing when the international system is dominated by liberal democracies pursuing a human rights agenda. By the same token, classicism is more appealing when the international system is dominated by totalitarian and authoritarian states pursuing imperialist policies. My point here is that, even in the selection of interpretive methods, legal positivists cannot avoid making moral judgments.

Second, much theorizing about the justice of humanitarian intervention takes place in a state of vincible ignorance. All too often, the empirical claims upon which different ethical theories rest are little more than guesswork. To be sure, the task of testing a claim that this or that humanitarian intervention will (or would) affect human well-being in this or that way is fraught with methodological and practical difficulties. To begin with, there is the problem of identifying a humanitarian intervention's direct and immediate consequences – let alone its peripheral and remote ones. Next, there is the problem of determining how these consequences affect human well-being. While these problems are formidable, they are not insurmountable. One can crudely measure how a humanitarian intervention will affect human well-being by comparing the number of people who actually died in a similar intervention in the past with the number of people *who would have died had that intervention not occurred*.[128] One way of testing this counterfactual proposition is to (i) find out how mortality rates changed in the course of the humanitarian catastrophe; (ii) discover where

[128] James D. Fearon, "Counterfactuals and Hypothesis Testing in Political Science," 43 *World Politics* (1991), 169–95; Philip E. Tetlock and Aaron Barkin eds., *Counterfactual Thought Experiments in World Politics: Logical, Methodological and Psychological Perspectives* (Princeton University Press, Princeton, 1997).

in the catastrophe's "natural" course the intervention occurred; and (iii) compare the actual post-intervention mortality rates with the projected ones. If the latter exceed the former, then one can reasonably conclude that the humanitarian intervention (and any others like it) is, on utilitarian terms, just; if the former exceed the latter, then one can assume that the reverse is true. Given the importance of various factual claims to both defenders and critics of humanitarian intervention, empirical studies of this kind are absolutely essential if these disagreements are ever to be resolved.

Finally, most disagreements about the justice of humanitarian intervention are caused less by differing conceptions of the *source* of moral concern than by differing conceptions of the proper *breadth* and *weight* of that concern. As we have just seen, some naturalists support a duty of humanitarian intervention – others do not. Some consensualists support a duty of humanitarian intervention – others do not. Identical meta-ethical premises simply do not generate identical, or even broadly similar, ethical conclusions. But, as we have also just seen, similar views about the proper weight and breadth of moral concern *do* produce similar ethical conclusions. Most egalitarians and universalists, for instance, strongly favor a duty of humanitarian intervention, while most inegalitarians and particularists strongly oppose it. The justice of humanitarian intervention thus seems to turn on how one answers the following questions:

What should the breadth and weight of one's moral concern be?
Should it extend beyond one's family, friends, and fellow citizens?
Should it extend to those nameless strangers in distant lands facing genocide, massacre, or enslavement?
Should the needs of these strangers weigh as much as the needs of family, friends, and fellow citizens?

Inegalitarian-particularists reply that we owe a greater duty of care to our family, friends, and fellow citizens than we owe to nameless strangers in distant lands. This view is intuitively appealing – within limits. Egalitarian-universalists respond that all human beings have a right to life and liberty. Duties to family, friends, and fellow citizens are owed once this moral minimum is secured. This is intuitively appealing – again within limits. Is there any way to reconcile these conflicting moral feelings?

One possible solution is offered by Robert E. Goodin who argues that the inegalitarian-particularist – or "special" – duties we owe our families, friends, and fellow citizens are simply the ways in which the egalitarian-universalist – or "general" – duties we owe humanity are assigned to particular people.[129]

> A great many general duties point to tasks that, for one reason or another, are pursued more effectively if they are subdivided and particular people are assigned special responsibility for particular portions of the task. Sometimes the reason this is so has to do with the advantages of specialization and division of labor. Other times it has to do with [irregularity in the distribution of] the information required to do a good job, and the limits on people's capacity for processing requisite quantities of information about a great many cases at once ... Whatever the reason, however, it is simply the case that our general duties toward people are sometimes more effectively discharged by assigning special responsibility for that matter to some particular agents ... The duties that states (or, more precisely, their officials) have vis-à-vis their own citizens [therefore] are not in any deep sense special. At root, they are merely the general duties that everyone has toward everyone else worldwide. National boundaries simply visit upon those particular state agents special responsibility for discharging those general obligations vis-à-vis those individuals who happen to be their own citizens.[130]

But Goodin also recognizes that if states are unwilling or unable to protect the lives and liberties of their citizens – if they degenerate into anarchy or tyranny – then the duty to safeguard these rights reverts to the international community.[131] In other words, if the duties we owe to families, friends, and fellow citizens derive their moral force from the duties we owe to human beings in general, "then they are susceptible to being overridden (at least at the margins, or in exceptional circumstances) by those more general considerations."[132] A very strong case can be made that humanitarian catastrophes such as the Rwandan genocide are just these sorts of "exceptional circumstances."

---

[129] Goodin, *Utilitarianism*, p. 280.   [130] Ibid., pp. 282, 283.
[131] Ibid., pp. 284–87.   [132] Ibid., p. 280.

2

Humanitarian intervention before and after 9/11: legality and legitimacy

TOM J. FARER

Introduction: why the fuss?

On the eve of the 11 September (hereafter "9/11") terrorist attacks on New York and Washington, articles, monographs, anthologies, conferences, and symposia on "Humanitarian Intervention" were proliferating even faster than weapons of mass destruction.[1] This metastasis of policy-focused cerebration coincided curiously with the paucity of the thing itself. Not, to be sure, of the exquisite suffering that was its notional target. Central Africa remained, as it remains today, in search of a contemporary Hieronymus Bosch to record its quotidian triumphs of death.[2] The elites of northern Sudan had not ceased their efforts, marked by a fine lack of discrimination, to subordinate, mutilate, or murder the Christians and Animists of the south. In Afghanistan, an entire gender was held in close captivity, and deviance by either sex from eighth-century views of the proper limits of human agency summoned eighth-century sanctions.[3]

The author notes with gratitude the advice of Bob Keohane on the themes and organization of this chapter and the multifaceted support of his research assistant, Sharon Healey.

[1] For example, a LEXIS search revealed thirty-five articles discussing humanitarian intervention written in the ten months after 9/11.

[2] For the ten years that the Human Development Report has been produced, African countries have dominated the lower quartile of the UNDP's Index. Since 1970, more than thirty wars have been fought in Africa, the vast majority of them intra-state in origin. In 1996 alone, fourteen of the fifty-three countries of Africa were afflicted by armed conflicts, accounting for more than half of all war-related deaths worldwide and resulting in more than 8 million refugees, returnees, and displaced persons. J. Oloka-Onyango, "Human Rights and Sustainable Development in Contemporary Africa: A New Dawn, or Retreating Horizons?" 6 *Buffalo Human Rights Law Review* (2000), 39, 43.

[3] Those places were instances of potentially telegenic torment: people being maimed and killed by acts of commission more or less grotesque. Omission can be equally efficient. The Nobel laureate Amartya Sen once calculated that the number of poor Indians who died over two

Suddenly experiencing the pre-9/11 frenzy of debate about the legality, legitimacy, and appropriate occasions and instruments for humanitarian intervention, a stranger to our planet might fairly have concluded that every Western government with the means to project force beyond its frontiers, above all the United States Government, was straining against the leash woven out of *normative* uncertainties, awaiting only their resolution to hurl itself into the humanitarian fray. But if he had taken brief leave of the conference circuit to note the multiple hesitations and evasions of the Clinton Administration,[4] or to parse the self-constraining declarations of President George W. Bush and his colleagues[5] and the doctrinal pronouncements of the American military establishment,[6] or to survey the extent of

decades from the avoidable results of immiseration – from malnutrition, disease, and all of the other pathologies that decimate the very poor – was roughly equal to the famine victims of Mao's Great Leap Forward. Guatemala City in this blessed time of peace has more helicopters, mostly private, per person than any other city in the world and a stunted indigenous population, the country's majority, that quietly suffers the regular attrition of poverty. "Small, Vulnerable – and Disunited, Mexico City and San Salvador," *The Economist*, US edn, The Americas, 11 August 2001.

[4] See David Halberstam, *War in a Time of Peace* (Scribner, New York, 2001), discussing the foreign policy of the Clinton Administration.

[5] Before the 9/11 attacks, Bush had stated that he opposed the use of the American military for peacekeeping and nation-building, and believed that, with extremely rare exceptions, the US should not be engaged in humanitarian interventions. He had stated that if another Rwanda occurred on his watch, he would not send American troops, though he would speak with the United Nations and "encourage them to move." Many of his advisers also shared the view that humanitarian interventions should be undertaken in extremely limited circumstances. For example, Dov Zakheim, Bush's Undersecretary for Defense, had written that violating another nation's sovereignty through humanitarian intervention threatens "to unravel the entire fabric of international relations." Zakheim concluded that we should intervene "only when our own interests are clearly at stake, or when genocide is so manifest that refusal to act would destroy our moral leadership of the free world." James Traub, "The Bush Years: W.'s World," *New York Times Magazine*, 14 January 2001.

[6] American military leaders have traditionally taken a narrow view of humanitarian intervention. In claiming that US humanitarian interventions over the last decade have been neither "just nor practical," former army officer and Secretary of State Alexander Haig argued that the US should be on guard that "the promise of America's values does not become the excuse for an American crusade," and that humanitarian interventions "should never be undertaken in the absence of careful calculations that include costs and benefits." Alexander M. Haig, Jr., "The Question of Humanitarian Intervention," 9(2) *Foreign Policy Research Institute WIRE, A Catalyst for Ideas* (12 February 2001).

The so-called "Weinberger–Powell Doctrine" of humanitarian intervention that gained hegemony within the American defense establishment in recent years holds that vital national interests (as opposed to values) must be at stake. For a critical examination of the Weinberger–Powell Doctrine, see Jeffrey Record, "Weinberger–Powell Doctrine Doesn't Cut It," *US Naval Institute Proceedings*, October 2000. Available at http://www.mtholyoke.edu/acad/intrel/bush/record.htm (5 March 2002).

essential preparation, whether in the United States or the United Nations, he would doubtless have arrived at a quite different view of the matter. The prospect, he would have decided, was not for an excess of poorly guided, confused, or fraudulent interventions. Rather it was for continuation of that repulsive marriage of noble rhetoric and heroic constraint in the face of evil that appeared before 9/11 to be the principal feature of contemporary statecraft for the United States and its European allies.

Humanitarian intervention is defined in this volume as the use of force *across state borders* by a state (or group of states) aimed at preventing or ending widespread and grave violations of the fundamental human rights of individuals other than its own citizens, *without the permission of the government of the state within whose territory force is applied.*[7] Why was humanitarian intervention, thus defined, so prominent in the discourse of practitioners hardly less than of scholars concerned with transnational relations? It was not as if the academic and governmental elites of powerful states had few other preoccupying subjects, few other outlets for their ameliorative vocations. What was there about the pre-9/11 political, moral, or intellectual context that drove debate about something far more talked about than done?

Part of the answer, I believe, is the challenge that claims on behalf of humanitarian intervention posed to the inherited structure and the associated ideas, values, and norms of the global order. In other words, one could fairly see humanitarian intervention as very much more than a minor exception or adjustment to the received organization of the human race. Instead, it arguably exemplified and acted as the doctrinal advance guard of the whole constellation of forces confronting the sovereign state's once indisputable claim to be the principal locus of power and loyalty. Defenses of humanitarian intervention also undermined the parallel claim of governments to an unfettered discretion with respect to producing and distributing public goods and determining the rights and obligations of persons living within the state's recognized frontiers.

To be sure, even at its doctrinal apogee, sovereignty never amounted to an unquestionable right of governments to do anything they pleased within their recognized space.[8] Like private property owners in Anglo-American common law, they enjoyed bundles of rights in relation to their space and

---

[7] See J. L. Holzgrefe, "The Humanitarian Intervention Debate," ch. 1 in this volume, p. 18.
[8] See e.g. Daniel Philpott, "Usurping the Sovereignty of Sovereignty?" 53(2) *World Politics* (2001), 297–324.

obligations to other sovereigns. Over time, both the rights and the obligations have varied. But in general sovereignty meant immunity from external challenge to forms and a very broad discretion respecting methods of governance.

While humanitarian intervention had been advocated primarily as a response to outrageous methods, the precedents invoked by advocates and scholars included cases like Haiti where the main stated purpose of intervention was the defense of democracy. There is a powerful logic to challenging forms as well as methods of governance. Concern for democracy, a form of governance, and concern over methods crippling to individual rights spring from the same liberal root. They spring, that is, from the view that human beings are equal moral agents entitled to an extensive freedom limited only by the equal freedom of others, and that freedom includes – as a substantive as well as an instrumental value – participation in processes by which people govern themselves. Consistent with this logic, it was in the name of liberalism that right-wing ideologues in the Presidential Administration of Ronald Reagan declared democracy to be the most important human right and the operational core of the Administration's human rights policy.[9] As soon as the Cold War ended, many of the same ideologues or their progeny, seeing the US as Prometheus unbound by the Soviet Union's collapse, advocated a pro-democracy crusade.[10]

The logic of liberalism, one of humanitarian intervention's ethical sources, can be invoked not only to challenge the forms and methods of governance within sovereign states, but the state's very existence in cases where one of several constituent nationalities, feeling oppressed, struggles to secede. Some liberal theoreticians have even placed the group right to national self-determination above the individual right to democratic government and denied any ethical basis for foreign intervention when only the latter is at stake.[11]

---

[9] For a discussion of human rights policy under the Reagan Administration, see Tamar Jacoby, "The Reagan Turnaround on Human Rights," 64 *Foreign Affairs* (1986), 1066; J. Kirkpatrick, "The Reagan Phenomenon and the Liberal Tradition," in *The Reagan Phenomenon and Other Speeches on Foreign Policy* (American Enterprise Institute for Public Policy Research, Washington, DC, 1983); Tom Farer, "Reagan's Latin America," *New York Review of Books*, 19 March 1981, pp. 10–16.

[10] See e.g. Charles Krauthammer, "Beyond the Cold War," *New Republic*, 19 December 1988.

[11] Michael Walzer, *Just and Unjust Wars: A Moral Argument with Historical Illustrations* (Basic Books, New York, 1977), ch. 6.

Few if any states currently recognize a right to intervene primarily in order to help peoples struggling to secede.[12] NATO's intervention in the case of Kosovo was ethically and legally premised on massive violations of human rights, not a Kosovar right to self-determination. To be sure, its position, before the intervention, was ambiguous. The Rambouillet draft agreement, unsuccessfully pressed on Serbia by the United States and its principal NATO allies before the bombing began, did include a referendum by means of which the inhabitants of Kosovo could vote for independence following a period of de facto occupation by an international force.[13] But any such provision was conspicuously missing from the NATO settlement proposal finally accepted by the Serbians which served as a basis for the administrative regime established by the Security Council in the wake of the conflict. Indeed, the settlement emphasized the territorial integrity of Serbia–Montenegro and purported to limit the aspirations of the Kosovars to autonomy within ex-Yugoslavia.[14] Nevertheless, the prospects for ultimate de facto reintegration of Kosovo in the Serb-dominated rump of former Yugoslavia seem slight and, indeed, seemed slight once the intervention began.

The Australian-led and Security-Council authorized occupation of East Timor[15] in the wake of the devastation wrought by paramilitary groups,

---

[12] See "Competing Claims: Self Determination and Security in the United Nations," an Occasional Paper of the International Peace Academy, Report of a Conference held in Vail, Colorado, 29 November–1 December 2000.

[13] "Rambouillet Accords: Interim Agreement for Peace and Self-Government in Kosovo," S/1999/648, 7 June 1999.

[14] "Military Technical Agreement between the International Security Force ('KFOR') and the Governments of the Federal Republic of Yugoslavia and the Republic of Serbia." Available at http://www.nato. int/kosovo/docu/a990609a.html (5 March 2002).

[15] On 5 May 1999, a set of agreements between Indonesia, Portugal, and the United Nations memorialized a proposal suggested by Indonesia's president recognizing the autonomy of East Timor and conceding that the special autonomy proposal would be submitted to the people of East Timor through a "popular consultation." (See Agreement Between Indonesia and Portugal on the Question of East Timor [5 May 1999]. Available at http://www.un.org/peace/etimor99/agreement/agreeEng01.htm [5 March 2002].) Subsequently, the Security Council adopted Resolution 1246, which established the United Nations Mission in East Timor (UNAMET) to organize and conduct a popular consultation consistent with the 5 May Agreements. (See SC Res. 1246, UNSCOR, 54th sess., 4013th mtg., UN Doc. S/INF/55 [1999].) In the wake of the vote, pro-integration militias, supported at times by the Indonesian military, waged a campaign of violence and destruction throughout East Timor. In response, the Security Council adopted Resolution 1264, which authorized the establishment of a multinational force – the International Force for East Timor (INTERFET) – to restore peace and security, protect and support UNAMET, and facilitate humanitarian assistance operations. (See SC Res. 1264, UNSCOR, 54th sess., 4045th mtg., UN Doc. S/INF/55 [1999].)

following a referendum favoring independence, laid the groundwork for its separation from Indonesia. While not formally a case of humanitarian intervention in that Indonesia consented to the occupation, the intense economic pressure from the US and other Western countries manifestly employed to induce that consent made the operation appear to be a very close cousin of humanitarian intervention.

The perceptual association of humanitarian intervention and secessionist struggles as a result of Kosovo and East Timor is not entirely adventitious. Secessionist campaigns usually are responses to, and invariably aggravate violations of, human rights by the existing state. So, in practice, the possibility of humanitarian intervention will probably be implicated with some regularity in the process by means of which an aggrieved ethnic group segues from demands for protection of its minority rights to a struggle for self-determination. The tendency of secessionist conflicts to create the triggering conditions for humanitarian intervention heightens the latter's implications for the traditional privileges of sovereignty, as well as its potential impact on the stability of the state-based international order.

A second reason, related but analytically distinct, for the pre-9/11 prominence of humanitarian intervention discourse was the way in which it served to focus debate on the legitimate use of force and, coincidentally, on the authority and hierarchy of intergovernmental institutions. For many observers in 1945, the United Nations Charter appeared to declare a new era in international relations marked by unprecedented legal restraints on the use of force.[16] The Cold War strained them severely to the point, some argued, where were no longer binding.[17] That war's end opened the prospect of effectively reasserting a three-fold division of the universe of force into aggression, self-defense, and enforcement action authorized by the Security Council.[18] Doing so is obviously incompatible with affirming a unilateral right to march across borders in pursuit of liberal or, for that matter, any other ends arguably including the preemption of suspected terrorists. So a debate about humanitarian intervention is inseparable from the larger debate about the conditions of legitimate violence.

---

[16] I will elaborate below on their content.

[17] See e.g. Myres S. McDougal and Florentino P. Feliciano, "Resort to Coercion, Aggression and Self Defense in Policy Perspective," in *Law and Minimum World Public Order* (Yale University Press, New Haven and London, 1961).

[18] See Tom J. Farer, "Law and War," in Cyril E. Black and Richard A. Falk eds., *The Future of the International Legal Order* (Princeton University Press, Princeton, 1969).

A third reason for the prominence of humanitarian intervention in contemporary inquiry about foreign policy was its entanglement in challenges to traditional conceptions of the national interest with their emphasis on the single-minded aggrandizement of national power and wealth and the welfare interests of citizens rather than the generality of humankind. Few advocates for humanitarian intervention were prepared to challenge frontally the privileging of citizens (or at least the sovereign state that notionally serves them). So, rather than appealing primarily to an imagined cosmic compassion, they attempted to show that unremediated butchery in foreign lands adversely affects the interests of people at home. They emphasized material factors like spikes in undocumented immigration caused by persons fleeing persecution and the threat of deadly diseases or international criminal and terrorist organizations able to incubate in anarchic places. Some also invoked immaterial ones such as the need to act abroad in ways that reaffirm the constitutional culture, i.e., the unifying principles of liberal states faced with increasingly diverse populations.

Finally, humanitarian intervention commanded attention because the conditions for which it is sometimes the only plausible response tear at the hearts of the substantial number of influential actors who can identify with suffering outside their family, tribe, nation, or other central reference group. With global media, distance from the Western metropolises no longer fosters the dismissive claim that "these are people of whom we know so little." Ephemerally and arbitrarily to be sure, the media, television in particular, force our participation in other peoples' torments. And often, in part because Manichean structures resonate in our cultural roots, in part because the justifying conditions of humanitarian intervention usually involve radically unequal struggles, the narrative communicated to us has identifiable delinquents as well as sympathetic victims. Most people have been bullied at one time or another. When they happen to live in a nation of unrivaled military power, the possibility of vicariously avenging remembered humiliation is gripping.

Initial challenges by states to the Charter restraints on the use of force

Within a few years of the United Nations' founding, states able to pursue ends (other than immediate self-defense) by means of the threat or use of force began signaling their taste to do so, preferably without openly violating the new normative dispensation. Believing that what was good for the United Fruit Company was good for the United States, in 1954 Washington conducted a proxy invasion of Guatemala to overthrow an elected government encroaching on the imperial prerogatives the company had for decades exercised in that unhappy place.[19] Two years later the Soviet Union asserted its own imperial pretensions by invading Hungary when its people overthrew obedient local satraps of Moscow. Also in 1956 the British and French invaded Egypt from the sea while their co-conspirator, Israel, occupied the Sinai Peninsula. These were challenges in fact to the new normative dispensation, as most scholars construed it, but not altogether in form.

The United States implicitly reaffirmed the rule it was so plainly violating by claiming that authentically indigenous forces had overthrown the Guatemalan Government of Jacobo Arbenz.[20] Moscow relied on a supposed invitation from the Hungarian authorities,[21] although not from the government actually in place at the time of the intervention and backed by the regular armed forces. And Israel invoked a right of self-defense against guerrilla incursions from the Sinai that it packaged conceptually as the "armed attack" which Article 51 of the Charter stipulated as the necessary condition for the exercise of legitimate self-defense.[22] Britain and France, however, relied on a supposed authority to act unilaterally to protect the rights of states, established by treaty and practice, to navigate the Suez Canal, a right they claimed to be threatened by Egypt's government.[23] Speaking for the United States, Secretary of State John Foster Dulles, instigator of the surreptitious US invasion of Guatemala, rejected both the Israeli and Anglo-French rationalizations. Referring to Egypt's previous behavior, he stated:

> We have, however, come to the conclusion that these provocations – serious as they were – cannot justify the resort to armed force. If . . . we were to agree that the existence in the world of injustices which this Organization has so

---

[19] Stephen Schlesinger and Stephen Kinzer, *Bitter Fruit: The Untold Story of the American Coup in Guatemala* (Doubleday, Garden City, NY, 1982).

[20] Ibid.

[21] See UNSCOR, 746th mtg. 4, UN Doc. S/PV.746 (1956), and Rein Mullerson, "Intervention by Invitation," in Lori Fisler Damrosch and David J. Scheffer eds., *Law and Force in the New International Order* (Westview Press, Boulder, 1991).

[22] John Quigley, *Palestine and Israel: A Challenge to Justice* (Duke University Press, Durham, NC, 1990).

[23] D. Kay ed., *The United Nations Political System* (Krieger Publishing Company, Melbourne, Fla., 1967), pp. 264 ff.

far been unable to cure means that the principle of the renunciation of force should no longer be respected, that whenever a nation feels that it has been subjected to injustice it should have a right to resort to force in an attempt to correct that injustice, then I fear that we should be tearing this Charter to shreds . . . [T]he violent armed attack by three Members of the United Nations upon a fourth cannot be treated as anything but a grave error inconsistent with the principles and purposes of the Charter.[24]

As violent transnational incidents began to multiply, a number of distin-guished scholars, virtually all from countries allied with the United States in the Cold War, developed interpretive strategies that could expand the occasions for the legitimate use of force beyond self-defense from armed attack and Security Council enforcement actions. They fell into two juris-prudential camps that I refer to as "classicists" (or "textualists") and "legal realists."[25] The former are conservative in the sense of assuming that words, phrases, and sentences in treaties often have plain meanings and usually have specific and ascertainable original intentions which, consis-tent with the principle of the rule of law, are binding as long as the treaty remains in force. By this means, they seek to conserve elements of order in an anarchic political system. To that end, they privilege indicators of inten-tion closest in time to the text's creation. The latter – the legal realists – pursue the same end by standing the former's premises almost on their heads. Nevertheless, representatives of both schools can find their ways to the same goal of loosening Charter restraints. In this connection, I turn first to the legal realists.

Legal realism's defense of humanitarian intervention

The central strategy of legal realism is to shift the main burden of inquiry about the "meaning" of a law, regulation or treaty from the past to the present once the broad purposes and principles of the text have been clar-ified. It does so supposedly in order that law better fulfill its role as an instrument of public policy. The great virtue of law, which I use here in the sense of official rules, is also its potential vice. Through laws, we translate policies into detailed directions to government officials and private citizens.

---

[24] 1956 UNGA *Records*, 1st Emergency Special sess., 562nd mtg., 23.
[25] "Legal realists" should be distinguished from international relations' "political realists," de-scended in the modern era from Hans Morgenthau but with roots extending back to Thucydides.

They provide a means for securing the more-or-less uniform application of policy over vast reaches of space and time. In other words, they fix the policy response to a societal need.[26]

It is this capacity to fix that constitutes their great virtue but also their potential vice. For we fix by means of texts and texts endure while circumstances – political, technological, economic, intellectual, and moral – change.[27] In theory, the words can be altered to suit circumstances. In practice, particularly in pluralistic political systems, epitomized by the international one, it is often more difficult to amend than to adopt texts, particularly constitutional ones which are usually made peculiarly difficult to amend. Moreover, the change in circumstances may not have made the text as a whole obsolete. It may simply have created a number of unforeseen contexts in which strict application of the rule according to the common literal meaning or the alleged original understanding of its directives may not produce the policy outcome dictated by its main underlying principles and purposes. For fear of exposing the law as a whole to unwanted revision, its greatest current beneficiaries may prefer to live with policy anomalies at what they see as the margin of its applications.[28]

Where a legal order includes courts of general and compulsory jurisdiction, courts can mitigate the problem of fixed words and changing circumstances by making minute adjustments through a stream of judgments applying the rule in varying contexts and subtly calibrating the explanations of their judgments in order to minimize any appearance of breaking loose from a textual anchor. In any event, they are formally authorized to make those judgments and, since they cannot themselves manufacture cases in that they have no executive power, they are relatively unthreatening. In the international system, by contrast, the main sources of rule application, particularly in matters related to international security, are the executive organs of states. Being interested parties, they are incapable of impartial judgment; their authority derives not from common consent but from the sheer state-based organization of international order; and, where they are powerful,

---

[26] For a legal realist view on the use of force, see Anthony C. Arend and Robert J. Beck, *International Law and the Use of Force: Beyond the UN Charter Paradigm* (Routledge, New York, 1993).

[27] See Introduction in W. Michael Reisman and Andrew R. Willard eds., *International Incidents: The Law that Counts in World Politics* (Princeton University Press, Princeton, 1988).

[28] See e.g. Myres S. McDougal and W. Michael Reisman, "Rhodesia and the United Nations: The Lawfulness of International Concern," 62 *American Journal of International Law* (1986), 1, 3.

they are able to manufacture the occasions for decision and then to execute their decisions all for the enhancement of their parochial interests.

In reaction to those features of international law, some scholars seek to uphold the rule of law by clinging to the literal details of the text and such original understandings as they can establish. To legal realists, that is a self-defeating strategy. Powerful states will not be constrained by old texts in dusty books construed in ways that seriously compromise their interests. Rules acquire authority in the international system by prescribing in greater or lesser detail the behavior that, in a particular area of activity, optimally advances the shared interests of major states. They are the outcomes of negotiation among decisive actors within states culminating in decisions to accept a common set of rights and obligations. In part because international legal rules are, among other things, convenient formal summaries of national interests assessed in relative tranquility, they tend to control the regular decision-making agenda within states and may even trump the call to optimize outcomes in a particular case where application of the rule seems likely to produce sub-optimal gains. But, legal realists argue, where, because circumstances have changed or (in any event) the particular constellation of facts was not foreseen, application of a rule in accordance with its common or long-established meaning threatens highly valued interests of important state actors, the meaning will fail to control behavior.

States may openly reject the established meaning or offer a mendacious account of their behavior or simply act without explanation. Whichever tactic they choose may well be read by other states as a sign of provocative purposes[29] requiring a response in fact disproportionate to the initial state's real intention. The result can be an escalation of reciprocal acts immediately threatening to international order. In addition, perceived evasion or avoidance of norms deemed controlling undermines long-term stability by eroding confidence in the value of formal commitments. These are two consequences, legal realist scholars would presumably argue, of a backward-looking epistemology with all its attendant rigidities of perspective. A third is to hobble law in its basic task of facilitating the consistent and extensive direction of public and private behaviors necessary for the realization of public policy in multitudinous conditions.

---

[29] See e.g. Ved Nanda, "US Forces in Panama: Defenders, Aggressors or Human Rights Activists? The Validity of United States Intervention in Panama under International Law," 84 *American Journal of International Law* (1990), 494.

In order to avoid these consequences, governments and legal scholars alike need to focus on the present and seek to clarify and publicize contemporarily demanded or policy-maximizing interpretations of old texts whether of international agreements or of scholarly tomes purporting to summarize and thereby crystallizing past state behavior into rules as specific and binding as the provisions of a treaty. The legal realist ascription of high legal relevance to the actual contemporary interests and preferences of powerful states rather than the formalized summary of interests and preferences evidenced by old texts leads ineluctably to superior status for deeds over words, thereby multiplying the law-making opportunities of states with the power to make precedents.[30]

As I have suggested in earlier writing, adherence to the legal realist canon facilitates interpretations of governing law conducive to the legalization of intervention for humanitarian as well as other purposes.[31] Legal realists have released themselves from the constraining language of particular UN Charter Articles like 2(4), 51 and 53 by means of three related moves. One, available also to classicists, is to insist that the historically unparalleled limits the Charter imposes on self-help as a means of enforcing international law presuppose the operation of an effective collective security system.[32] That system, the details of which are sketched in Charter Articles 43–47, required a high degree of cooperation among the permanent members because the Charter endowed each one with the power to block Security Council action. When, with the advent of the Cold War, cooperation collapsed, the Charter provisions dependent on it were, in effect, suspended. States were remitted to the dictates of customary law with its relatively broad tolerance for the vindication of important legal rights by force, albeit as a last recourse.

With the Cold War reduced to history, cooperation among permanent members is about at the level one would expect among powerful states with imperfectly congruent interests and disparate political cultures, i.e. no worse than the founding states of the United Nations could reasonably have anticipated. If that is a fair statement of the case, then it would seem to follow from the logic of the claim about the contingent character of

---

[30] Anthony D'Amato, "Customary International Law," in *International Law: Process and Prospect* (2nd edn, Transnational Publishers, Dobbs Ferry, 1995). See also Nanda, "US Forces in Panama" and Anthony D'Amato, "The Invasion of Panama was a Lawful Response to Tyranny," 84 *American Journal of International Law* (1990), 520.

[31] Tom J. Farer, "Human Rights in Law's Empire, the Jurisprudence War," 85 *American Journal of International Law* (1991), 117, 121ff.

[32] See e.g. Introduction, in Reisman and Willard, *International Incidents*.

Charter restraints that they are now once again operative. Yes, one could possibly quibble that the details of the Charter's original collective security vision are not yet in place. There is, for instance, no network of agreements between member states and the UN committing the former to second to the Council's order units of their armed forces subject to specified terms and conditions.[33] But that is a patently weaseling argument for sustaining a position that rested on the displacement of envisioned post-war cooperation by a comprehensive and reflexive hostility between the Soviet and American superpowers as they then were, a failure of the system's animating spirit not of the detailed process conceived for its expression.

The quibble, moreover, is hoisted on the legal realist petard. For if we look for legal guidance to contemporary consensus made manifest in the practice of states, we find a consensus that the Security Council should deal with aggression, the traditional core breach of the peace, by authorizing coalitions of the willing under whatever leadership they will accept. This was the lesson of the Council's response to Iraq's invasion of Kuwait.[34] In short, the collective security system worked and without any post facto chorus about the advantages of having the Security Council in future manage as well as authorize and monitor the conduct of defensive wars. We may conclude that Articles 43–47 are defunct. The collective security system largely as envisioned by the founders, albeit modified in its details by practice, is in place. So legal realists still determined to avoid the Charter's detailed strictures on the use of force need to make a much more impressive move.

Michael Reisman, successor to Myres McDougal at the fountainhead of legal realism, the Yale Law School, has proposed one. In order to do it justice, I will quote him at some length:

> Every legal system ... includes a constitutive process, which establishes and maintains the institutions and procedures by which decisions are to be taken ... When a unilateral action occurs, its legal appraisal varies as a function of the constitutive configuration in which it occurs. Four constitutive configurations are relevant: first, constitutive processes without hierarchical institutions of decision; second, constitutive processes in which there are

---

[33] Charter of the United Nations signed 26 June 1945, entered into force 24 October 1945, 59 Stat. 1031, TS No. 993, 3 Bevans 1153 (1969), Articles 43–47.

[34] UN Security Council Resolution 678 had authorized "Member States co-operating with the Government of Kuwait ... to use all necessary means to uphold and implement [the Security Council's resolutions regarding the Iraqi invasion] and to restore international peace and security in the area." SC Res. 678 (29 November 1990), 29 ILM (1990), 1565.

hierarchical institutions which are manifestly ineffective; third, constitutive processes in which the hierarchical institutions are generally effective, but prove to be ineffective for the application of particular norms; and fourth, constitutive processes in which hierarchical institutions are highly effective and in which unilateral actions will simply be characterized as taking the law into one's own hands, and hence delictual, no matter what the explanations and how passionate the justifications proffered.[35]

Having laid that conceptual framework, Reisman begins to make his move. Since the adoption of the Charter, he states, the "international decision process" has been opened for the first time "to broad and effective non-governmental participation" and this development has had profound consequences. Through the influence of non-governmental actors and over the opposition of many state elites, the international human rights code was installed as part of the substance of international law. At first, and as a consequence of the fighting retreat of state elites, the human rights norms enunciated in various formal treaties functioned much less as legal rules than as aspirations falling outside the active responsibilities of the Security Council and even other less puissant UN organs.

> Now, however, the new and expanded international decision process has taken a hitherto normatively uncertain human rights "standard of achievement" [i.e. human rights as aspirations to be progressively realized], refashioned it into the international protection of human rights, and elevated it to an imperative level of international law.[36]

Although human rights now constitute real law supported by widespread demands for enforcement, the only UN organ with real enforcement power is the Security Council. And it cannot discharge its law enforcement task in this area, because the members do not share a consensus on human rights norms like the one prevailing with respect to a traditional case of interstate aggression where the Council is expected to act effectively.[37] Now comes Reisman's clincher.

> [T]he absence of consensus on human rights [among the permanent members] means that [the Council's] remedial action . . . is unlikely [in cases of grave human rights violations requiring a forceful response]. Yet the

---

[35] W. Michael Reisman, "Unilateral Action and the Transformation of the World Constitutive Process: The Special Problem of Humanitarian Intervention," 11 *European Journal of International Law* (2000), 7–8.
[36] Ibid., p. 15.   [37] Ibid.

international legal process's demand for a remedy for grave violations...
has become so powerful and urgent that democratic governments that are
susceptible to non-governmental influence and that have the wherewithal to
effect a remedy are under great pressure to act unilaterally. *Hence, for purposes
of the enforcement of human rights, a constitutive process of the fourth type now
reverts to the third type: enforcement through the Security Council, if it can be
achieved, but enforcement unilaterally if it cannot.*[38]

Reisman frankly concedes that the constitutive regime he perceives, one
that "begins to reserve different legal treatment for different types of unilateral actions, based principally on the purpose or objective of the actions
concerned," is anomalous. He sees as well that, "[s]ince many participants
assume that an ineluctable feature of law is generality of application, this
constitutive regime engenders more normative ambiguity and cognitive
dissonance." Nevertheless, he implies with what I envision as an expressive
shoulder shrug, he can only tell it as it is.[39]

A traditional international lawyer might at this point ask whether
Reisman has proffered here a legal argument or a meta-legal description of
what he takes to be the "real," that is, the operational legal order. The answer,
of course, is that the question misses the legal realist point, namely that the
operational legal order is the only legal order. The traditional "sources" of
the law – principally formal governmental behavior such as the ratification
of treaties or substantive acts like enforcing with warships the claimed limits
of the territorial sea – remain as indicators of the inter-subjective consensus
(or lack thereof) about what actions are legitimate. But governments have
been joined by other actors, non-governmental organizations (important
in themselves and also as proxies for international civil society) "who assess,
retrospectively or prospectively, the lawfulness of international actions and
whose consequent reactions shape the flow of events."[40]

Reisman's is a seductive appeal to all agents in the international system to
transcend an obsessive focus on the supposed plain meaning of authoritative
texts, mainly Articles 2(4) and 51 of the UN Charter. Reisman also urges
us to transcend the conviction that the tight Charter constraints on the

---

[38] Ibid. Emphasis added.

[39] I am reminded of the story about the three baseball umpires chatting over drinks one evening
while vacationing together at a resort. One says to the others: "I call them as I see them." The
second responds: "I call them as they are." The third umpire, a man notorious for his swaggering
toughness, looks challengingly at his two colleagues and declares: "When I call them, they are."

[40] Reisman, "Unilateral Action," p. 13.

use of force must be taken as the operative law until formally amended or displaced by the customary practice of all major states and blocs, including those presently unsympathetic to unilateral humanitarian intervention. The Report of the Independent International Commission on Kosovo illustrates the continuing grip of the classicist perspective. Its authors, prominent persons deeply committed to the effective defense of human rights, felt compelled to conclude that the NATO action could not be fit within the Charter scheme and was therefore in a formal sense illegal. Nevertheless, as an essentially altruistic last-recourse response to horrible violations of fundamental human rights, they found it to be "legitimate."[41]

Legal realists like Reisman provide a conception of the legal process that dissolves the distinction between legality and legitimacy. In effect he is saying to Commission members and other human rights advocates struggling to reconcile respect for law with the protection of humanity: "Chill out! If the great bulk of actors in the widened international decision process regard behavior as legitimate, it is perforce legal." Illegality in the minds of Commission members stemmed from the inability of NATO to satisfy procedural requirements. Legitimacy rested on the satisfaction of substantive ones. Since insofar as human rights are concerned, the prevailing constitutive process, according to Reisman, is the third type, the procedural requirements are not operative legal restraints.

The classicist defense of humanitarian intervention

Classicism, to which government lawyers in particular seem attracted, certainly has not prevented all of its adherents from finding tolerances in the Charter for any number of interventions. Indeed, classicists have worked the Charter for all the ambiguities it can yield. Their hermeneutic strategies have included:

1. Construing Article 2(4)'s prohibition of force or the threat thereof against political independence or territorial integrity as not to cover *temporary* occupation of part or all of a nation's territory for ends allegedly consistent with the principles and purposes of the Charter (such as "promoting and encouraging respect for human rights and for fundamental freedoms" and enforcing respect for the "self-determination of peoples");[42]

---

[41] The Commission was established by the Government of Sweden. Independent International Commission on Kosovo, *Kosovo Report* (Oxford University Press, Oxford, 2000).

[42] Charter of the United Nations, Article 1(2).

2. Claiming that intervention at the request of a recognized government, a contingency not explicitly addressed in the Charter, confirms rather than prejudices the exercise of sovereign discretion protected by Article 2(7);[43]

3. Insisting that Article 53's requirement of Security Council authorization for enforcement action pursuant to regional arrangements can be satisfied by approval after the fact manifested by failure to condemn and/or claiming that the use of force when recommended but not commanded by regional institutions is not "enforcement action,"[44] and ignoring the further question of how, then, it can be reconciled with Article 2(4) where it is not categorized as the collective self-defense against armed attack authorized by Article 51;

4. Insisting that foreign assistance to opponents of a recognized government, even amounting to no more than the provision of weapons and advice, constitutes armed attack within the meaning of Article 51 justifying an armed response either by the object of the attack or by its friends;[45]

5. Claiming that states, like Cyprus in its independence agreement, may barter away a portion of their insulation from intervention and then be held to their bargain.[46]

As Thomas Franck and Jane Stromseth demonstrate in their contributions to this volume, one need not abandon the classical epistemology in order to build a fairly persuasive case for the legality of NATO's intervention.[47] A resolution condemning it was defeated in the Security Council by a vote of twelve to three[48] and that twelve included votes from Asia, Africa, and Latin America, among them Brazil and Malaysia, traditionally very prickly on sovereignty issues and willing to resist pressure from the West. Another

---

[43] See Tom J. Farer, "Harnessing Rogue Elephants: A Short Discourse on Foreign Intervention in Civil Strife," 82 *Harvard Law Review* (1969), 530.

[44] See Tom J. Farer, "The Role of Regional Collective Security Arrangements," in Thomas G. Weiss ed., *Collective Security in a Changing World* (Lynne Rienner Publishers, Boulder, 1993).

[45] See Tom J. Farer, "The Regulation of Foreign Intervention in Civil Armed Conflict," 142 RCADI (1974), 291. But this position was later rejected by the International Court of Justice. See International Court of Justice Decision, *Military and Paramilitary Activities in and Against Nicaragua (Nicar. v. US), ICJ Reports, 1986,* p. 14 (27 June).

[46] See e.g. Tom J. Farer, "The United States as Guarantor of Democracy in the Caribbean Basin: Is there a Legal Way?" 10 *Human Rights Quarterly* (1988), 157.

[47] See Jane Stromseth, "Rethinking Humanitarian Intervention: The Case for Incremental Change," ch. 7 in this volume; and Thomas M. Franck, "Interpretation and Change in the Law of Humanitarian Intervention," ch. 6 in this volume.

[48] S/1999/328, 26 March 1999; S/PV.3989, 3989th mtg., 26 March 1999 at 6.

effort to marshal at least an implicit censure, this time in the form of a Russian draft resolution in the UN Commission on Human Rights calling for "an immediate cessation of the fighting" and attributing (not unreasonably) "victims and casualties amongst the civilian population [to] missile strikes and bombings," also met defeat by a substantial margin.[49] Moreover, the Organization of the Islamic Conference, hardly an organization reflexively supportive of US initiatives, stated that "a decisive international action was necessary to prevent humanitarian catastrophe and further violations of human rights [in Kosovo]." It communicated this view through a letter from the Permanent Representative of the Islamic Republic of Iran to the UN addressed to the President of the Security Council.[50] Furthermore, Sean Murphy notes that the Security Council associated itself with the intervention by authorizing UN participation in the measures called for by the ceasefire agreement coerced from the Serbs. "Security Council action to move forward with conflict management should not be viewed as a wholesale endorsement by all Security Council members of all proceeding actions, but surely Russia and China's willingness to support this new UN 'Trusteeship' suggests some level of ratification."[51]

Sean Murphy, who like Franck and Stromseth finds flexibility in the Charter system without cutting himself loose from the text (without, that is, simply jettisoning the classicist premises), also sees UN behavior in the Kosovo case against the backdrop of the humanitarian interventions in Liberia (1990)[52] and in Sierra Leone (1998)[53] along with the 1991 US-led military operations first in northern Iraq (on behalf of the Kurds) and then a year later in the southern part of that country. The latter operations continue to this day in the form of enforced no-fly zones and periodic

---

[49] UNSCOR, 54th sess., 3989th mtg., UN Doc. S/PV 3989 (1999).

[50] Letter dated 31 March 1999 from the Permanent Representative of the Islamic Republic of Iran to the United Nations Addressed to the President of the Security Council. UN Doc. S/1999/363, annex (1999).

[51] Sean Murphy, "Calibrating Global Expectations Regarding Humanitarian Intervention" (14 December 2000), p. 5, presented at the Harvard University Conference "After Kosovo: Humanitarian Intervention at the Crossroads," 18–19 January 2001.

[52] For a discussion of the AACS intervention in Liberia, see David Wippman, "Enforcing the Peace: ECOWAS and the Liberian Civil War," in Lori F. Damrosch ed., Enforcing Restraint: Collective Intervention in Internal Conflicts (Council on Foreign Relations, New York, 1993).

[53] For a discussion of the AACS intervention in Sierra Leone, see Karsts Nard and Emily W. Schabacker, "The Use of Force to Restore Democracy: International Legal Implications of the AACS Intervention in Sierra Leone," 14 American University International Law Review (1998), 321.

attacks on Iraqi aircraft and air-defense installations. Despite the lack of explicit Security Council authorization in any of these instances, all seemed to enjoy at worst broad tolerance among UN members. Do these cases, taken together, amount to an amendment of the Charter by the practice of states?

Murphy himself is cautious. He says that "perhaps" they can be taken as "suggesting a nascent trend."[54] That is caution squared. His caution, I believe, concerns the dimensions of this evident loosening of attitudes about intervention. In Kosovo, Liberia, and Sierra Leone, intervention was carried out by organizations of states that, under the forgiving practices of the UN, can claim the status of regional organizations within the meaning of Chapter VIII of the Charter.[55] Iraq is an even more special case. Since it has never complied fully with the conditions of the ceasefire approved by the Security Council,[56] it has given the US and its allies a basis for treating the no-fly patrols as continuing pressure for compliance and an ongoing exercise in preemptive defense of neighboring states implicitly threatened by the incorrigible Iraqi regime: an unrepentant and unregenerate aggressor. Even under Milošević, Serbia was never treated as if it were a totally rogue state.

Still, there are facets of the Serbia–Kosovo case, in addition to the fact that this was an instance of intervention by a regional organization composed of normally law-abiding states, which may limit its precedential implications. Among two which Murphy names are: (1) the complicity of the Serbian regime in grave violations of Security Council resolutions, like the one creating safe havens in Bosnia, and in awful violations of human rights (i.e. its track record); and (2) the fact that before the bombing began, "the Security Council had expressly identified actions taken by Serbia in Kosovo as a threat to the peace which could lead to a humanitarian catastrophe."[57] Part of the loosening trend Murphy cautiously suggests are the interventions authorized explicitly by the Security Council in Somalia, Rwanda (perversely after the fact), and Haiti. One might even include East Timor where the government's consent was secured through open economic pressure. In his essay for this volume, Thomas Franck, after marshaling and construing teleologically a host of violent initiatives and the ensuing acts and

---

[54] Murphy, "Calibrating Global Expectations," p. 6.
[55] See Farer, "Role of Regional Collective Security Arrangements."
[56] SC Res. 687 (3 April 1991), 30 ILM (1991), 847.
[57] Quoted in Murphy, "Calibrating Global Expectations," p. 9.

omissions, condemnations and silences, of UN organs, sees growing tolerance of humanitarian intervention as a sub-set of a more general loosening of constraints on uses of force previously deemed illegal under the Charter, including preemptive self-defense, rescue of nationals, and reprisals.

As I noted earlier, the prerogatives of sovereignty shrank considerably over the second half of the twentieth century. As one of the first substantive acts of its very first session in 1946, the UN Human Rights Commission denied itself the authority even to read appeals from private persons allegedly suffering violations of their human rights.[58] Now its special rapporteurs roam the world confronting governments and publicizing delinquencies.[59] For the first three decades after the Universal Declaration of Human Rights, the standard rhetorical response of governments to questions about their treatment of citizens was to brand such questions as intrusions into the reserved domain of domestic jurisdiction. Today this is a rare invocation. Governments drop arguments when they no longer rally support. Humanitarian interventions are the trailing armored tail of the now completed move to make all gross violations of fundamental rights the business of the international community.

The loosening of constraints on humanitarian interventions not authorized by the Security Council raises an obvious question: what is to prevent abuses of this leeway by hegemonic powers or regional organizations controlled by major powers? In deference to the uneasiness of many scholars and the risk of downright flaccidity in the restraints on force, Sean Murphy suggests anchoring the Kosovo precedent in Article 52 of the Charter. In other words, rather than calling interventions by regional agents "enforcement actions" requiring, under the most natural reading of Article 53, Security Council authorization, call them actions "dealing with . . . matters relating to the maintenance of international peace and security as are appropriate for regional action . . . [and] are consistent with the Purposes and Principles of the United Nations."[60] In this way Kosovo along with the humanitarian interventions are made to signify an implicit modification of the procedural requirements of the Charter in order to give *regional agents*

---

[58] See Tom J. Farer and Felice Gaer, "The UN and Human Rights: At the End of the Beginning," in Adam Roberts and Benedict Kingsbury eds., *United Nations, Divided World: The UN's Roles in International Relations* (2nd edn, Clarendon Press, Oxford; Oxford University Press, New York, 1993).

[59] Ibid.   [60] Murphy, "Calibrating Global Expectations," pp. 9–10.

a laissez-passer to effect humanitarian interventions complying with the relevant substantive criteria.

But privileging regional agents and arrangements, particularly as a way of normalizing the Kosovo case, is hardly a panacea. "Regions" are artificial constructions adopted on the basis of intuition, intellectual and bureaucratic convenience, and political interests. The US State Department, for instance, has long had regional bureaus and disputes about which countries go where. Neither of the political organs of the United Nations nor the International Law Commission has ever attempted to define "region" for the purpose of clarifying Chapter VIII. The practices of member states acting independently or through the UN imply acceptance of a highly voluntarist approach, i.e. any groups of states that bind themselves by treaty to some degree of political and economic cooperation are free to regard themselves as having established a "regional arrangement." Conversely, a coalition that spurns the designation, as NATO did at the time of its founding (preferring to call itself a collective self-defense arrangement precisely in order to fall outside the terms of Chapter VIII), is not a Chapter VIII arrangement.[61]

The nub of the matter, then, is that groups of like-minded regimes seem able to form regional mutual protection machines designed to guarantee their survival against domestic as well as foreign opponents. Or one powerful state can pressure weak adjoining regimes into an arrangement that may provide a fig leaf for self-interested interventions. Some would argue that this has already occurred in the case of Russia and the former Soviet Republics in Central Asia and the Caspian area.[62]

The potential for facilitating hegemonic interventions by regional powers, particularly for maintaining docile, collaborative governments, is one cause for concern about a view of Chapter VIII that allows for military coercion without prior Security Council authorization. However, in this respect Murphy's proposed reinterpretation of Article 52 adds little to the existing potential for abuse, the source of which is the traditional license for interventions invited by incumbents clinging to their seats. But in one

---

[61] See Farer, "Role of Regional Collective Security Arrangements."

[62] See James D. Wilets, "The Demise of the Nation-State: Towards a New Theory of the State Under International Law," 17 *Berkeley Journal of International Law* (1999), 193, 200ff. noting that Russian forces have intervened in Tajikistan, Georgia, and Moldova, and that Russian President Boris Yeltsin has suggested that Russia should be granted special powers to stop ethnic conflict in the states under the political sphere of the former Soviet Union.

respect Murphy's proposal does add a potentially significant escape hatch from the Charter's normative order.

It is one thing to recognize the authority of states to limit their sovereignty through treaties in which each licenses all of the others to intervene in defined circumstances through prescribed procedures. At least within very broad limits, this reciprocal (at least in form) diminution of sovereign rights is a prerogative immanent in sovereignty.[63] It is another thing to provide a rationale for intervention by one group of states in another state that is not party to their reciprocal agreement and presumably to their common values, shared interests, and mutual respect. But that is the result of trying to domesticate the Kosovo precedent by anchoring it within Article 52. Serbia, after all, is not a member of NATO. If NATO can legally intervene in a geographically contiguous non-member state, then why should not other regional organizations like the Arab League or organizations yet unformed that one or another regional or sub-regional power may succeed in constructing? Perhaps before conceding authority to Chapter VIII arrangements, it would be desirable to establish within the UN a formal credentialing process for claimants to the status.

Collective interventions and the problem of abuse

Murphy's proposal raises the question of whether, as a matter of law, morality, or policy, collective interventions for allegedly humanitarian purposes or other principles and purposes of the UN should be privileged over unilateral ones. Should collective humanitarian interventions be given a license to act without prior authorization or a presumption of compliance with substantive standards? In his widely admired book on *Just and Unjust Wars*, the political theorist Michael Walzer, writing in defense of India's 1971 invasion of East Pakistan which aborted a genocidal assault by West Pakistan's army on its eastern region, declared:

> Nor is it clear to me that action undertaken by the UN, or by a coalition of powers, would necessarily have had a moral quality superior to that of the

---

[63] Although, where the license is loosely conditioned and temporally unlimited, and particularly where it cannot be withdrawn, it may amount to so great a relinquishment of sovereignty as to be ultra vires under international law. See e.g. Tom J. Farer, "A Paradigm of Legitimate Intervention," in Damrosch, *Enforcing Restraint*; Farer, "The United States as Guarantor of Democracy in the Caribbean Basin," 161; and David Wippman, "Treaty-based Intervention: Who Can Say No?" 62 *University of Chicago Law Review* (1995), 607.

Indian attack. What one looks for in numbers is detachment from particularist views and consensus on moral rules. And for that, there is at present no institutional appeal; one appeals to humanity as a whole. States don't lose their particularist character merely by acting together. If governments have mixed motives, so do coalitions of governments. Some goals, perhaps, are canceled out by the political bargaining that constitutes the coalition, but others are super-added; and the resulting mix is as accidental with reference to the moral issue as are the political interests and ideologies of a single state.[64]

Accidental? For a man whose speculations are for the most part anchored shrewdly in the quiddity of real life, this claim seems to float balloon-like above the evidence of contemporary history. It certainly runs contrary to Murphy's qualified justification of NATO's Kosovo intervention, in which he takes special note of the fact that each of the sixteen member states approved the intervention through a process of democratic deliberation.[65]

Why is the fact that the NATO intervention took place multilaterally, by an organization of democracies, important for present purposes? First, because many of those members are small, incapable by themselves of projecting force, and vulnerable to intervention should relations with their neighbors change. In part, perhaps, for that reason, political culture in most NATO nations is far more permeated by positive attitudes towards international law and the United Nations than is true of NATO's leader, the United States. For instance, even the United Kingdom under Margaret Thatcher, Ronald Reagan's ideological sibling, abstained rather than oppose the General Assembly condemnation of Reagan's intervention in Grenada.[66]

When acting alone, the US has frequently wrapped particularistic interests of an economic or geo-political character in humanitarian garments. Contrast the motives for US behavior when it has acted alone, because it could not secure OAS or UN authorization – Grenada, Panama, Central America in the 1980s – and when it has acted with such authorization (Desert Storm, Somalia, Haiti). Great powers are inevitably more self-regarding, inevitably more resistant to legal constraint than the generality

---

[64] Walzer, *Just and Unjust Wars*, p. 107.
[65] Murphy, "Calibrating Global Expectations," pp. 3–4.
[66] On 2 November, the UN General Assembly voted 108 to 9 with 27 abstentions, in favor of a resolution declaring the "armed intervention" in Grenada a "flagrant violation of international law." See GA Res. 38/7 (2 November 1983). The governments of the UK, Japan, West Germany, and Canada, all of whom had abstained from the vote, made statements publicly condemning the US intervention.

of weak ones. In the cases where the UN has authorized humanitarian interventions, the humanitarian case has been strong. Where it has condemned interventions, the case has been weak if not altogether meretricious. Thus for reasons grounded in theory and practice, one needs to conclude that imputing authorizing power to large coalitions of states in a condition of voluntary association offers a very important guarantee that intervention is not designed to serve interests incompatible with the principles and purposes of the Charter.

One cannot argue persuasively that just-war analysis is properly concerned only with matters of substance rather than process. For the process of authorization has always been part of the formal criteria for a just war. In Saint Thomas Aquinas's classic statement, the first criterion of justness was "that the prince has authorized the war."[67] Thus he sought to limit violence and strengthen order by delegitimating the use of force by lords all up and down the mediaeval hierarchy as well as by outlaw groups – pirates and unemployed mercenaries, for example. In the nineteenth century, the prince became the nation-state and in the twenty-first he arguably morphs into the UN or regional organizations. Within the Western moral tradition, then, procedures do have a place. It is not only outcomes and motives that matter. Moreover, given the recent much less the historical abuse of humanitarian justifications for the use of force, certainly from a consequentialist perspective, multilateralism matters morally. By seeming to claim the contrary, Walzer allows us to say of him in this instance what one wit remarked of Oliver Wendell Holmes: that even when he was clearly wrong, he was wrong clearly.

Enthusiasts for unilateral humanitarian intervention must of course take a comparatively sanguine view of the contemporary risks of abuse. Michael Reisman readily concedes that the past behavior of states, if considered a prologue, is disheartening[68] not because at the high tide of Western imperialism the law was honored in the breach thereof, the use of force to seize territory, wealth, or people being legally permissible then,[69] but rather because of nineteenth-century imperialism's gaseous invocation of civilizing missions and morally educative vocations. The ineffable slaughter of World War I changed all that. In seeking revenge for the cataclysm, despite their own generative roles, the victorious European allies, France and the UK,

---

[67] Quoted in Arthur Nussbaum, *A Concise History of the Law of Nations* (Macmillan, New York, 1947), p. 42.
[68] Reisman, "Unilateral Action," p. 6.   [69] See Farer, "Law and War."

sought to try the German Kaiser for initiating an aggressive war.[70] Suddenly war as just another means for advancing national interests was gone. The allies coincidentally attempted to formalize this transformation of the legal and moral status of violence in the terms of the League of Nations Charter (albeit leaving loopholes that the UN Charter would appear to close).[71]

Referring to the years after the League's establishment, Reisman writes that the "states [that] purported to be acting on the basis of humanitarian intervention were acting quite selectively and usually in circumstances in which national interests unrelated to humanitarian concerns played no small part in the motive for the action."[72] But now, he urges us to believe, "the potential for abuse in humanitarian intervention is considerably reduced."[73] The reason is the incorporation of humanitarian non-governmental organizations and humanitarian values into the constitutive process and what he sees as the coincident attrition of support by security elites, particularly in the United States, for interventions with a strong humanitarian focus.

The relationship between that coincidence and his claim about the reduced risk of abuse is opaque. After all, the history of abuse consisted, as Reisman himself states, of the invocation of humanitarian motives in cases where states were actually pursuing highly particular national interests. So what is the relevance of the fact that in very recent cases where the national interest quotient was low and the humanitarian one high, the impulse to intervene came from non-governmental elites and resistance came from the official security community? The test of the potential for abuse comes when a great power's political and military leaders believe that the proportions are reversed, i.e. that they can advance narrow interests by means of intervention and there is just enough butchery going on to support a plausible claim of humanitarian intervention even as other ends are pursued.

The United States has faced this test not only in the decades immediately following the founding of the League and in the early years of the Cold War but within recent decades in Central America and the Caribbean. And in the judgment of most scholars and governments, including those of NATO allies, and, in the Central American case, of an almost unanimous World Court, it has not infrequently failed. Panama was the last conspicuous failure. Has the constitutive process on which Professor Reisman stakes

---

[70] Peter Maguire, *Law and War* (Columbia University Press, New York, 2000), pp. 71ff.
[71] Reisman, "Unilateral Action," p. 16.   [72] Ibid.   [73] Ibid.

his faith changed so dramatically in so short a time? History has no doubt accelerated in certain respects. But in terms of social change, this would amount to warp speed. Russian peacekeeping operations in the Caucasus, notionally invited (and hence not technically interventions) but under conditions of necessity the Russians themselves are believed to have in some degree contrived,[74] also should encourage caution about heralding a sea change in the behavior of states.

For reasons given above I doubt that the increased influence of nongovernmental actors and the development of a globally ubiquitous and denationalized media are sufficiently potent forces to much reduce by themselves the abusive potential of a license for humanitarian intervention. Nevertheless, it does not follow that a license would add significantly to global disorder. Mendacious invocation of humanitarian intervention would be morally repulsive, but not necessarily very damaging to world order. Such invocation has, as far as I can see, three possible consequences. One is that abuse of an exception for unilateral intervention would generate profound skepticism about allegations of genocide-like crimes and thereby inhibit unilateral and multilateral interventions when they were indeed required to terminate gross delinquencies. A second is that the availability of humanitarian intervention as a recognized exception to the Charter prohibition of force might at least occasionally swing the balance of national decision processes in favor of an illegal intervention. The third is that it would contribute to a more generalized cynicism about legal restraints on the use of force and thereby weaken the normative status of peace.

Mendacious invocation of humanitarian intervention, which is likely, would not be unprecedented. Claims to be helping humanity sounded among the hodge-podge of justifications for Europe's nineteenth-century imperial interventions. And whether removing or exterminating Native Americans, acquiring Cuba, suppressing an independence movement in the Philippines, or making Latin America safe for capitalism, the United States has rarely missed an opportunity to invoke humanitarian ends. Even the lumpen Brezhnev doctrine of the former Soviet Union, justifying interventions in Eastern Europe to maintain "Proletarian Solidarity,"[75] could

---

[74] See John P. Willerton, "Symposium: European Security on the Threshold of the 21st Century: Current Development and Future Challenge: Russian Security Interests and the CIS," 5 *Willamette Journal of International Law and Dispute Resolutions* (1997), 29.

[75] See Modern History Source Book: The Brezhnev Doctrine, 1968. Available at http://www.fordham.edu/halsall/mod/1968brezhnev.html (5 March 2002).

be seen as an effort to mask national interest with claims of service to a wider one. But since abuses of a similar character would not be novel and since the possibility of appeal at least to moral values would remain even if humanitarian intervention never acquired legal status, I find little basis for concluding that legalizing humanitarian intervention is likely to constitute an important new threat to world order.

Reflecting on the natural law approach to ethical issues, Joseph Boyle recalls "[Thomas] Aquinas's view that all practical decision-making is governed by the principles of natural law, but that many decisions and policies do not follow from these principles by a rigorous process of deduction and analytical thought."[76] As a substitute means of ethical guidance, Catholic theologians and other natural law thinkers have developed "the category of practical wisdom or *prudentia* to account for the highly contextualized and contingent character of human decisions."[77]

What is true of natural law is no less true of its secular counterpart. The perceived legitimacy of future interventions to protect people from state or, for that matter, private terrorists can never be a function of some sort of mechanical compliance with general criteria. Despite their differences, many legal realists and classicists converge on this point. Jane Stromseth's chapter in this volume could be seen as a peculiarly persuasive reconciliation of the two jurisprudential schools in the realm of humanitarian intervention. While canvassing the relevant practice, she identifies elements that appear to have influenced positive appreciation of interventions invoking humanitarian concerns. In addition, she reviews the criteria proposed in several codification projects. The result is a checklist of factors that will shape and structure assessments of future cases by the political organs of the United Nations, individual states, and other consequential actors in international affairs.

Her checklist[78] exhaustively captures the elements which have, at least until now, governed judgment about whether to celebrate or castigate intervention. On the threshold of 9/11, interventions which were manifestly a means of last resort to avert or terminate slaughter and ethnic cleansing or deadly famine, which did not risk a much wider war or permanent occupation of alien territory, and which were reasonably calculated to achieve their goal by means themselves consistent with humanitarian norms were likely

---

[76] Joseph Boyle, "Natural Law and International Ethics," in Terry Nardin and David Mapel eds., *Traditions of International Ethics* (Cambridge University Press, Cambridge, 1992), p. 125.
[77] Ibid.   [78] Stromseth, ch. 7 in this volume.

to be deemed legitimate, at least by Western governments and unofficial human rights and humanitarian bodies, even if it was not possible (whether due to time constraint or a prospective veto) to secure prior authorization from the Security Council or a regional organization.

Humanitarian intervention after 9/11

How, if at all, has the war against terrorism triggered by 9/11 affected (or appeared likely to affect over time) the context of ideas, interests, and values in which humanitarian intervention achieved prominence in discourse about foreign policy, if only erratically in foreign policy itself? In private conversations immediately after 9/11, some advocates of humanitarian intervention within the academic community pessimistically concluded that whatever the effect of the counter-terrorist war on terrorism, it would effectively eviscerate humanitarian intervention as an operative element in American foreign policy. Six months after the event, this judgment remains very plausible but just possibly premature. There are at least some grounds – uncertain ones, to be sure – for anticipating more rather than fewer interventions in circumstances arguably justifying humanitarian intervention.

One of the initial incidents of war is the reduced significance of sovereignty and boundaries. Indeed, as between the parties, they lose most if not all of their normative power. For in seeking to destroy each other's forces, each party claims and, to the extent it can, implements the right to seek out those forces in the other state or in a collusive third party or one too weak to prevent belligerent use of its territory.[79] But with the exception of World War II, most wars of the past century, and for at least another century before that in Europe, did not tend to undermine the force of national boundaries. War between two states (as distinguished from war as a supposedly natural and thus permanent incident of life on the planet) was seen as a transient phenomenon at the end of which most things would return to the status quo ante albeit with a somewhat altered division of the world's material and immaterial goods.

The war against terrorism declared by the United States after 9/11 has a very different feel because it has no clear temporal or spatial limit. In his January 2002 State of the Union Address, President George W. Bush reiterated the warning that the war was only beginning and that the threat against

---

[79] Or, of course, in the global commons: the high seas and space.

which it was directed remained dire. That threat, he said, included the terrorists themselves, who were widely dispersed, and states sympathetic to terrorism, particularly those disposed to acquire or further develop weapons of mass destruction.[80]

The subtext of the President's address, construed in light of previous statements by the Bush Administration since 9/11, was that the United States was going to hunt down and eliminate terrorists wherever they might be found, and also to prevent states deemed friendly with terrorism from enhancing their capacities with respect to weapons of mass destruction. And it was prepared to act preemptively rather than simply as a response to an actual or imminent armed attack. What are some of the concrete measures that would seem to fall within this Bush Doctrine? Rather than working through the often slow and unpredictable process of extradition, the United States might parachute troops into countries to seize suspected terrorists or might assassinate them by inserting special forces or employing air strikes. Within Iraq, it might use zones protected by air power to arm and train forces drawn from the Kurd and Shia communities. Then it might launch them, backed by US firepower, against Saddam Hussein's regime in Baghdad. In the case of Iran, it might employ cruise missiles against nuclear reactors or other facilities relevant to the production of nuclear, chemical, or biological weapons; it might blockade the country to force agreement on international weapons inspections or to prevent importation of dual-use technologies.

After 9/11, the Security Council, anticipating the US attack on Al-Qaeda and the Taliban regime, affirmed the right of the United States to act forcefully in its defense.[81] Since Article 51 of the Charter recognizes an *inherent* right of self-defense, affirmation was unnecessary. In this unprecedented case of a large, well-financed transnational organization with demonstrably great destructive capacity and declaredly aggressive ends, the right can reasonably be construed to include seizure of suspected Al-Qaeda members in states unable or unwilling to arrest and either try or extradite them. But it plainly does not encompass the overthrow of regimes with records of aggressive behavior. Nor does it legitimate the use of force against states

---

[80] A transcript of Bush's 29 January 2002 State of the Union Address is available at http://www.cnn.com/2002/ALLPOLITICS/01/29/bush.speech.txt/index.html (5 March 2002).

[81] See S/Res/1373 (2001) reaffirming that acts of international terrorism "constitute threats to international peace and security," and additionally reaffirming "the right of individual or collective self defense."

deemed unfriendly in order to deny them weapons systems already deployed by other sovereign states or to enforce compliance with treaty obligations. At this point, there is simply no cosmopolitan body of respectable legal opinion which could be invoked to support so broad a conception of self-defense. It is in fact reminiscent of the notion of strategic preemption that animated German policy in the early years of the twentieth century. Its key idea is the political justification of assaulting another state in order to block any unfavorable shift, however long term, in the balance of power. Even tactical preemption – for instance, invading a neutral country in time of war in the belief that your opponent is likely to do so at some later point – has, since the adoption of the Charter, been deemed illegal. It was unsuccessfully invoked by the Nuremberg defendants in relation to the German invasion of Norway in 1940.

The Bush Doctrine, *to the extent it implies unilateral action*, simply cannot be contained within the UN Charter norms which have served as the framework of international relations for the past half century. It challenges a root principle of the Charter system, namely the formal equality of states. For this Bush Doctrine purports among other things to concede to some states (e.g. Israel, France, and India) but not others (e.g. Iran) the right to provide for their defense in whatever manner they deem fit. It also implies the erosion of other core features of national sovereignty, including exclusive authority to exercise police and judicial power within recognized frontiers. It arrogates to the United States an unfettered discretion to decide to whom other states can give asylum and whom they are obligated to prosecute or extradite.

The shift in the previously regnant (albeit increasingly tattered) sovereignty paradigm, which the Bush Administration is arguably trying to effect, could be seen as lowering legal and associated psychological and political barriers to the transnational projection of force for all legal ends, in particular for the protection of internationally recognized human rights as well as the protection of states and persons from terrorist acts. In short, events since 9/11 might possibly have initiated a frame-shattering, norm-changing process which will reduce them still further.

The normative consequences of 9/11 are likely to depend on the "what" and "how" of American action. Despite his declared readiness to act unilaterally, President Bush has been soliciting support from consequential states, including China and Russia. Obtaining it will doubtless require compromise in the application of the Bush Doctrine or compensatory side deals or both. If the President secures Security Council authorization for coercive measures to prevent the further proliferation of weapons of mass destruction, *in form* the inherited normative framework survives. For within its broad if not unlimited discretion under the Charter to avert threats to the peace by whatever means it deems useful, the Council can authorize action on a case-by-case basis which has a discriminatory impact, such as denying weapons to one state even though they are deployed by another. But discrimination sustained over time, perhaps only by bare weighted majorities in the Security Council, particularly if it dialectically elicits hostile small-country majorities in the General Assembly, would begin to look like (but might never become) a substantially transformed normative system which could be characterized as shared hegemony or condominium, with the United States *primus inter pares* with respect to the rest of the small group of owners.

One could, of course, argue that certain signs of such a transformation appeared some years ago when the Security Council began selectively authorizing interventions, albeit for humanitarian rather than counter-terrorist reasons. But the cases were, after all, few in number. Moreover, condominium implies agreement on ends and means and active collaboration. In fact, the Chinese merely acquiesced in cases like Somalia and Haiti, declaring them extraordinary exceptions and resisting any effort at codification. And when Kosovo came along, they confirmed the lack of real agreement by joining the Russians in blocking authorization of the NATO intervention. The nub of the matter, then, is that on the eve of 9/11, condominium was little more than a theoretical alternative to a Charter system which had in two original moves reconciled the principle of formal equality with the reality of asymmetric capabilities: it had concentrated enforcement authority in the Security Council; while giving the permanent members a veto, it had required them to secure the votes of four additional states in order to act.

A process of decision-making constitutes a normative system only when those affected believe that in general they have an obligation to obey its results. In other words, compliance with outputs of the process results at least in part from perceptions that it is legitimate. If fear alone secures compliance, I would not call the decision-making process normative although it might possibly be effective for a time. It seems to me likely that a coalition limited to NATO members plus China and Russia might be able episodically to find the four additional votes needed to authorize intervention and other sorts of coercive activity. But the NATO-plus-two coalition might well prove too narrow to maintain the Council's legitimating authority. The Charter frame would then crack and finally shatter. In other words, the formality of Security Council authorization is not enough to maintain the frame. Condominium as a successor normative system would, I believe, require inclusion of certain additional states such as India, Japan, Brazil, and South Africa and at least one Muslim state: Iran or Indonesia. It remains to be seen whether the United States is able or willing to secure the requisite coalition.

If the United States were determined to intervene globally but unable or unwilling to do so in partnership with the requisite states, it would now have the raw power to intervene outside the law recognized by the majority of states. So in theory it could sustain a policy of wide-ranging intervention in the face of opposition from a majority of states generally and from Security Council members in particular. But if, through its conduct of the anti-terrorist war, it catalyzed a hardening of opposition to armed intervention, the political and material[82] costs of intervention would undoubtedly grow. Without access to facilities in Pakistan and other states bordering Afghanistan, US operations would have been much more difficult to sustain. Indeed, without authorization for overflight of adjoining states, legally it could have done little more than pepper the country with missiles. Overthrowing Saddam Hussein without Turkish and Saudi support and replacing him with a stable and relatively benign alternative would be a very expensive feat. Furthermore, a unilateralist policy might gradually strain relations with France, the UK, and Germany, countries on whom the US now relies for help in rebuilding weak or roguish states.

Increased costs would tend to limit intervention to cases given the highest priority. Those cases will inevitably be ones focused on preempting terrorist acts, eliminating terrorist groups, and deterring state action deemed supportive of terrorism. Humanitarian goals might incidentally be advanced in certain instances, but they would not be a principal basis for action. However, they might not be entirely adventitious: in an effort to reduce the internal and external costs of interventions widely perceived to be illegal, the United States might consciously incorporate human rights concerns into its operational goals.

Still, it may seem awfully sanguine to assume that where humanitarian goals do not trigger interventions but are rather a cosmetic applied to

---

[82] The material costs would increase because it would become harder to find partners willing to lend troops, funds, and infrastructure.

counter-terrorist operations, humanitarian intervention will be at least as common a remedy for atrocity as it was before 9/11. For how likely is it that the conditions likely to foster intervention for purposes of counter-terrorism would frequently coincide with latent or actual gross violations of human rights of the kind that have in the recent past fueled calls for humanitarian intervention?

The extent of overlap depends to some degree on the nature of the lens through which the terrorist threat is perceived. Before 9/11, the lens apparently used by the United States had a rather narrow angle. At its focal point were places containing groups capable of transnational violence and with an articulated anti-American agenda. Since then, the angle of vision may have widened to include places where prevailing conditions can foster or facilitate terrorism. The Afghani narrative as it unfolded in the wake of 9/11 could be read as an exemplary tale for United States policy-makers and those in other countries as well. Danger, it seemed to say, can incubate in remote places where central authority is weak and permeable and/or inspired by values deeply inimical to those of the neo-liberal world. Where the state is weak and the society torn by conflict, groups with transnational terrorist agendas can rent safe havens where they can plan, recruit, train, and hide following an operation. And as their power increases or central authority attenuates still further, they may even appropriate part of the territory or colonize the feeble regime. In addition, whether or not there is conflict within them, weak and incompetent and/or profoundly corrupt states impel the evolution of private, clandestine channels for the movement of money, goods, and people. These channels are available to terrorists as well as ordinary people who need such channels to survive or at least to evade the state's extortions.

Not all such states are necessarily venues for massive assaults on human rights. The Cold War Italian state was corrupt, deeply penetrated by mafias and clandestine channels, but still a humane setting for quotidian life, except perhaps for those living in areas largely relinquished by the state to informal Mafiosi governance. Still, this post 9/11 reading of the Afghani text provides a new non-humanitarian angle for visualizing the US stake in places like Somalia, Sierra Leone, Sudan, the Congo, and Liberia. Its relevance to a war against terrorism is not merely theoretical. The Sudan was, after all, home to Osama bin Laden for a number of years following his self-conversion to militant anti-Americanism, and remained a site for some of his businesses even after he was forced to move. Belief in Al-Qaeda penetration of still anarchic Somalia inspires US naval patrols off its coast and threats of intervention.[83] Evidence of Al-Qaeda involvement in the illicit diamond trading associated with the grisly conflicts in Congo, Sierra Leone, and Liberia has recently emerged.[84]

Coincidence is imperfect. Several of the recent objects of, or candidates for, humanitarian intervention have not been weak, poorly organized states. The relative competence of the pre-genocide Rwandan state and the organization of its societal majority made the genocide possible. And the Serbian state which, through its local dependents, pursued ethnic cleansing and perpetrated slaughter in Bosnia and Kosovo was neither risibly weak nor chaotic. Nevertheless, it is not impossible to develop a counter-terrorist rationale for humanitarian intervention in the Balkan and Rwandan abattoirs. In both cases, but most extravagantly in the latter, the internal conflicts together with horrible human rights violations ended up threatening the stability of adjoining states. In fact, the powder train ignited by the Rwandan genocide helped blow what was by then left of the Congolese state virtually out of operational existence. Unfortunately, fear of anarchic conditions might just as easily inspire support for brutish governments and, in the case of civil conflicts, for a quick and decisive victory by the initially more powerful faction, whatever the humanitarian costs.

Conclusion

How, then, should we sum up the normative prospects for humanitarian intervention in the years immediately ahead? *Cautiously!* From this temporal vantage point, a mere half year after 9/11, one sees trails running off initially in several directions. Where they actually lead is considerably less clear.

The United States may ride its self-defense claims a while longer and a bit further without alienating the jury of consequential international actors. How long and how far it may do so will be influenced to some degree by all four of the following factors: first, Washington's ability to demonstrate

---

[83] See e.g. David S. Cloud, "US Navy, Allies Patrol Sea off of Somalia in Search of Fleeing Al Qaeda Fighters," *Wall Street Journal*, 4 January 2002; Robert Tait, "US Sets Sights on Somalia's Training Camps," *The Scotsman*, 26 November 2001, p. 7.

[84] See e.g. Douglas Farah, "Digging Up Congo's Dirty Gems; Officials Say Diamond Trade Funds Radical Islamic Groups," *Washington Post*, 30 December 2001.

previous collusion or current collaboration or even simply harboring Al-Qaeda members or the members of other terrorist groups widely perceived to threaten the United States and to have non-negotiable ends; second, its willingness to use force only as a means of last resort for ending collaboration or securing just punishment of Al-Qaeda members; third, the extent of its efforts at least to consult at a minimum with other permanent members and with states likely to be affected by an intervention whether because of their political and economic ties with the object of intervention or their proximity; fourth, the humanitarian effect of the intervention in terms both of collateral damage during the intervention and, conversely, of positive side effects on the condition of human rights in the country. But even where the final three factors are positive, it is hard to see the self-defense claim independently bearing much weight where the target state cannot be connected to 9/11.

So the United States will quickly face a severe choice if, as now appears likely, it proposes to employ coercion for wider strategic purposes. Either it will set about trying to build an authentic and authentically broad multilateral coalition with all the compromises and side deals that will entail or it will act only with the support of clients. If it chooses the latter course, it will probably be unable (and hence may not even try) to secure Security Council authorization. In the regions where it is most likely to act, either there are no regional systems of legitimation or, where they exist, they are as unlikely as the Security Council to endorse US action.

The US would thus find itself operating flagrantly outside the normative consensus. One, perhaps the most likely, result would be the progressive erosion of the Charter consensus about the use of force and a corresponding loss of normative protection against intervention. But, as I have suggested above, the probable international *political* consequences of aggressive unilateralism would enhance the costs of intervention for various purposes. Costs could rise further if the main response to aggressive unilateralism was a reaffirmation of (rather than generalized departure from) Charter norms in an effort to restrain the exercise of US power and limit the threat to sovereignty whether from the US or lesser countries. Heightened sensitivity to the risk of intervention generally would necessarily undermine justifications for the humanitarian sub-species.

For humanitarian intervention and, more importantly, for humanity, the most sanguine development would be a broad reading of the Afghani text by the Bush Administration and by its counterparts in other major states and, indeed, all states which have on balance been adapting successfully to globalization. Ideally there would grow among them the conviction that the world consists of centers of order which cannot isolate themselves from the centers of disorder. The latter emit poisons of various kinds and will go on doing so until order is "imposed." Not, however, the colonial order of rifle, noose, and theft: in part because it will not command support from the peoples of the West; in part because, while you can hang rulers and shoot conspicuous militants, you cannot cage the vast desperate populations awakened by globalization and set in motion. Order in our time means empowering indigenous figures to replace kleptocracy with political systems that with reasonable impartiality enforce rational laws and produce essential public goods.

Imposing order will require intervention on a scale certainly not imagined before 9/11. As I implied at the outset of this chapter, until then the appeal to human solidarity was sufficient only episodically and then only where people were dying telegenically rather than expiring slowly from all the pathologies of powerlessness and immiseration. To bring the latter hope, it will be necessary, particularly in much of Africa but also in Central Asia and spottily elsewhere in the developing world, to reinvent the state and to insert into its now corrupt and palsied limbs both political and technocratic advisers recruited from the centers of order with financial and coercive resources at their call. These will be trusteeships, in fact if not in name, brought into being by positive inducements, conditional assistance to local agents, and outright force, and executed by summoning the hitherto repressed or marginalized elements of these dystopias to plan for the liberation previously granted in form but denied in fact. Compensating the initial costs of this great project will be a vast long-term increment in the security of the centers of order and a vast expansion of participation in the global system of production and exchange.

For all the dispute about its legality and legitimacy, humanitarian intervention as conceived before 9/11 was a band-aid on a few suppurating wounds in a radically diseased body. Perhaps for that very reason, it could be accommodated, albeit with difficulty, within the scheme of the Charter. To treat the disease, we will have to invent a new scheme of international cooperation, one that, like weapons of mass destruction, has no historical parallel. What Osama bin Laden and his friends may have inadvertently accomplished is to stiffen humanitarianism with the iron of national security and thus to make it interesting to the parochial, narrowly compassionate figures who predominate in the councils of the leading states. Little in their biographies gives grounds for hope that they will face the 9/11 challenge with imagination and generosity no less than fire and sword. Still, one clings to the thought expressed by a fourteenth-century Arab scholar who wrote: "In the time of trouble avert not thy face from hope, for the soft marrow abideth in the hard bone."[85]

[85] Quoted in Rhoda Thomas Trip, *The International Thesaurus of Quotations* (Penguin Books, New York, 1976), p. 285.

PART II

The ethics of humanitarian intervention

3

The liberal case for humanitarian intervention

Introduction

In this chapter I argue that humanitarian intervention is morally justified in appropriate cases. The argument centrally rests on a standard assumption of liberal political philosophy: a major purpose of states and governments is to protect and secure human rights, that is, rights that all persons have by virtue of personhood alone.[1] Governments and others in power who seriously violate those rights undermine the one reason that justifies their political power, and thus should not be protected by international law. A corollary of the argument is that, to the extent that state sovereignty is a value, it is an instrumental, not an intrinsic, value.[2] Sovereignty serves valuable human ends, and those who grossly assault them should not be allowed to shield themselves behind the sovereignty principle.[3] Tyranny and anarchy cause the moral collapse of sovereignty.[4]

I am indebted to the authors of this volume for comments and criticisms on earlier drafts. I especially thank Bob Keohane, Jeff Holzgrefe, Elizabeth Kiss, Allen Buchanan, and Guido Pincione.

[1] I first made the argument in Fernando R. Tesón, *Humanitarian Intervention: An Inquiry into Law and Morality* (2nd edn, Transnational Publishers, Dobbs Ferry, 1997) (hereinafter *Humanitarian Intervention*). In this chapter I expand and refine this argument.

[2] For an extended analysis of this idea, see Fernando R. Tesón, *A Philosophy of International Law* (Westview Press, Boulder, 1998) (hereinafter *Philosophy of International Law*), ch. 2.

[3] Most proponents of humanitarian intervention endorse this claim. See Simon Caney, "Humanitarian Intervention and State Sovereignty," in Andrew Walls ed., *Ethics in International Affairs* (Rowman & Littlefield, Oxford, 2000), pp. 117, 120–21, and authors cited therein. For a more guarded version of the same argument, see Michael Smith, "Humanitarian Intervention: An Overview of the Ethical Issues," 12 *Ethics and International Affairs* (1998), 63, 75–79.

[4] As Saint Augustine said: "In the absence of justice, what is sovereignty but organized brigandage? For what are bands of brigands but petty kingdoms?" *The City of God*, cited by R. Phillips, "The Ethics of Humanitarian Intervention," in R. L. Phillips and D. L. Cady eds., *Humanitarian Intervention: Just War v. Pacifism* (Rowman & Littlefield, London, 1996), pp. 1, 6.

I supplement this argument with further moral assumptions. The fact that persons are right-holders has normative consequences for others. We all have (1) the obligation to *respect* those rights; (2) the obligation to *promote* such respect for all persons; (3) depending on the circumstances, the obligation to *rescue* victims of tyranny or anarchy, if we can do so at a reasonable cost to ourselves. The obligation in (3) analytically entails, under appropriate circumstances, the *right* to rescue such victims – the right of humanitarian intervention. Because human rights are rights held by individuals by virtue of their personhood, they are independent of history, culture, or national borders.

I define permissible humanitarian intervention as the *proportionate international use or threat of military force, undertaken in principle by a liberal government or alliance, aimed at ending tyranny or anarchy, welcomed by the victims, and consistent with the doctrine of double effect.*

I present the argument in the next section. In subsequent sections I consider and reject possible objections: the relativist objection; the argument that humanitarian intervention violates communal integrity or some similar moral status of national borders; the view that governments should refrain from intervening out of respect for international law; and the view that humanitarian intervention undermines global stability. A further section addresses the difficult question of the moral status of acts and omissions. I discuss the conceptual structure of the liberal argument and respond to the objection that humanitarian intervention is wrong because it causes the deaths of innocent persons. I also evaluate the moral status of the failure to intervene and conclude that, depending on the circumstances, it can be morally culpable. I then examine the internal legitimacy of humanitarian intervention. I conclude with a few critical reflections about the non-intervention doctrine.

The liberal argument for humanitarian intervention has two components. The first is the quite obvious judgment that the exercise of governmental tyranny and the behavior that typically takes place in situations of extreme anarchy are serious forms of injustice towards persons. The second is the judgment that, subject to important constraints, external intervention is (at least) morally permissible to end that injustice. I suggest below that the first part of the argument is uncontroversial. For the most part, critics of humanitarian intervention do not disagree with the judgment that the situations that (according to interventionists) call for intervention are morally abhorrent. The situations that trigger humanitarian intervention are acts such as crimes against humanity, serious war crimes, mass murder, genocide, widespread torture, and the Hobbesian state of nature (war of all against all) caused by the collapse of social order.[5] Rather, the disagreement between supporters and opponents of humanitarian intervention concerns the second part of the argument: interventionists claim that foreigners may help stop the injustices; non-interventionists claim they may not. The related claims from political and moral philosophy that I make (that sovereignty is dependent on justice and that we have a right to assist victims of injustice) concern this second part of the argument. If a situation is morally abhorrent (as non-interventionists, I expect, will concede) then neither the sanctity of national borders nor a general prohibition against war should by themselves preclude humanitarian intervention.

This discussion concerns *forcible* intervention to protect human rights. I address here the use and the threat of military force (what I have elsewhere called hard intervention)[6] for humanitarian purposes. However, the justification for the international protection of human rights is best analyzed as part of a continuum of international behavior. Most of the reasons that justify humanitarian intervention are extensions of the general reasons that justify interference[7] with agents in order to help victims of their unjust behavior. Interference and intervention in other societies to protect human rights are special cases of our duty to assist victims of injustice. However, many people disagree that humanitarian intervention is part of a continuum: they treat war as a special case of violence, as a unique case, and not simply as a more violent and destructive form of human behavior that can nonetheless be sometimes justified. They do not regard war as part of a continuum of state action; and do not agree with Clausewitz that war is the continuation of politics (*politik*) by other means. Intuitively, there is something particularly terrible, or awesome, about war. It is the ultimate form of human violence. That is why many people who are committed to human rights nonetheless oppose humanitarian intervention. To them, war is a crime, the most hideous form of destruction of human life, and

---

[5] I believe that forcible intervention to restore democracy may be justified, not on general moral grounds, but on specific grounds such as agreement or the existence of regional norms to that effect – as is the case, I believe, in Europe and the Americas.

[6] See my *Humanitarian Intervention*, pp. 133–36.

[7] For terminological convenience, I use the term "intervention" to refer to forcible action. I refer to other forms of action to protect human rights, ranging from regular diplomacy to economic and other sanctions, as "interference."

so it cannot be right to support war, even for the benign purpose of saving people's lives. Good liberals should not support war in any of its forms.

I am, of course, in sympathy with that view. Who would not be? If there is an obvious proposition in international ethics, it has to be that war is a terrible thing. Yet the deeply ingrained view that war is always immoral regardless of cause is mistaken. Sometimes it is morally permissible to fight; occasionally, fighting is even mandatory. The uncritical opposition to all wars begs the question about the justification of violence generally.[8] Proponents of humanitarian intervention simply argue that humanitarian intervention in some instances (rare ones, to be sure) is morally justified, while agreeing of course that war is generally a bad thing. But it is worth emphasizing here that critics of humanitarian intervention are *not* pacifists. They support the use of force in self-defense and (generally) in performance of actions duly authorized by the Security Council. So their hostility to humanitarian intervention cannot be grounded on a general rejection of war. Part of the task of this chapter is to examine those other reasons.

The liberal argument

As I indicated, the liberal case for humanitarian intervention relies on principles of political and moral philosophy. Political philosophy addresses the justification of political power, and hence the justification of the state. Most liberal accounts of the state rely on social contract theory of some kind to explain and justify the state. Here I follow a Kantian account of the state. States are justified as institutions created by ethical agents, that is, by autonomous persons. The liberal state centrally includes a constitution that defines the powers of governments in a manner consistent with respect for individual autonomy. This Kantian conception of the state is the liberal solution to the dilemmas of anarchy and tyranny. Anarchy and tyranny are the two extremes in a continuum of political coercion. Anarchy is the complete absence of social order, which inevitably leads to a Hobbesian war of all against all. The exigencies of survival compel persons in the state of nature to lead a brutal existence marked by massive assaults on human dignity. This is a case of too little government, as it were. At the other extreme, the

---

[8] The only philosophically coherent (although counterintuitive) argument against humanitarian intervention is the pacifist position, one that opposes all violence. For a spirited defense of that view, see Robert Holmes, *On War and Morality* (Princeton University Press, Princeton, 1989).

perpetration of tyranny[9] is not simply an obvious assault on the dignity of persons: it is a betrayal of the very purpose for which government exists. It is a case of abuse of government – of too much government, as it were. Humanitarian intervention is one tool to help move the quantum of political freedom in the continuum of political coercion to the Kantian center of that continuum away, on the one hand, from the extreme lack of order (anarchy), and, on the other, from governmental suppression of individual freedom (tyranny). Anarchical conditions prevent persons, by reason of the total collapse of social order, from conducting meaningful life in common or pursuing individual plans of life. Tyrannical conditions (the misuse of social coercion) prevent the victims, by the overuse of state coercion, from pursuing their autonomous projects. If human beings are denied basic human rights and are, for that reason, deprived of their capacity to pursue their autonomous projects, then others have a prima facie duty to help them.[10] The serious violation of fundamental civil and political rights generates obligations on others. Outsiders (foreign persons, governments, international organizations) have a duty not only to respect those rights themselves but also to help ensure that governments respect them.[11] Like justified revolutions, interventions are sometimes needed to secure a modicum of individual autonomy and dignity. Persons trapped in such situations deserve to be rescued, and sometimes the rescue can only be accomplished by force. We have a general duty to assist persons in grave danger if we can do it at reasonable cost to ourselves. If this is true, we have, by definition, a *right* to do so. The right to intervene thus stems from a general duty to assist victims of grievous injustice. I do not think that the critic of humanitarian intervention necessarily disagrees with this in a general sense. Rather, his opposition to humanitarian intervention relies on the supposed moral significance of state sovereignty and national borders.

There has been considerable debate about whether or not the concept of a legitimate state requires a thick liberal account. David Copp and John Rawls, among others, have argued that it does not.[12] They claim, in only

---

[9] I use the term "tyranny" as shorthand for gross and widespread human rights abuses. I use the term "anarchy" as shorthand for massive breakup of social order.

[10] See the discussion in Nancy Sherman, "Empathy, Respect, and Humanitarian Intervention," 12 *Ethics and International Affairs* (1998), 103.

[11] See Thomas Pogge, "Cosmopolitanism and Sovereignty," in C. Brown ed., *Political Restructuring in Europe: Ethical Perspectives* (Routledge, London, 1994), p. 89; and Caney, "Humanitarian Intervention and State Sovereignty," p. 121.

[12] See David Copp, "The Idea of a Legitimate State," 28 *Philosophy and Public Affairs* (1999), 1; John Rawls, *The Law of Peoples* (Harvard University Press, Cambridge, Mass., 1999).

slightly different ways, that legitimacy is unrelated to the duty of obedience, and that liberals generally must respect non-liberal states that fulfill some minimal functions.[13] They want to say that there is a layer of legitimacy (presumably banning foreign intervention) stemming from the fact that the government in question fulfills those functions. This is true even if the government does not fare well under liberal principles and thus cannot legitimately command the citizens' allegiance.

That discussion, important as it is for other purposes, is largely irrelevant to the present question.[14] The argument in this chapter is concerned with the conditions for the legitimacy of forcible humanitarian intervention, not with the related but distinct question of which states and governments are members in good standing of the international community. These authors seem at times to conflate these two issues. The collapse of state legitimacy is a necessary but not a sufficient condition of humanitarian intervention. The issue of the justification of humanitarian intervention, therefore, is narrower than the general issue of how liberal governments should treat non-liberal regimes. It is perfectly possible to say (*contra* Rawls and Copp) that a non-liberal government should *not* be treated as a member in good standing of the international community while acknowledging (with Rawls and Copp) that it would be wrong to intervene in those states to force liberal reforms. The situations that qualify for forcible intervention are best described as "beyond the pale" situations. Only outlaw regimes (to use Rawls's terminology) are morally vulnerable to humanitarian intervention. Because I differ with these writers on the question of legitimacy of non-liberal (but not "beyond the pale") regimes, I believe that *non-forcible* interference to increase human rights observance in those societies is morally justified – a view they reject.[15] All regimes that are morally vulnerable to humanitarian intervention are of course illegitimate, but the reverse is not true. For many reasons, it may be wrong to intervene by force in many regimes that are objectionable from a liberal standpoint. Humanitarian intervention is

[13] For Copp, a state is legitimate when it fulfills certain "societal needs": "Idea of a Legitimate State," pp. 36–45. For Rawls, states might be morally objectionable from a liberal standpoint but still legitimate because they are "decent." See Rawls, *Law of Peoples*, pp. 35–44, 59–82.

[14] I believe that the account of international legitimacy offered by Rawls (and, for the same reasons, by Copp) is mistaken, for reasons I have explained elsewhere at length. See my *Philosophy of International Law*, ch. 4.

[15] In my view, non-liberal yet "within the pale" regimes should be treated as if they were "on probation" on their way either to joining the liberal alliance or to collapsing into extreme tyrannies. For a view of international legitimacy similar to the one I defend, see Allen Buchanan, "Recognitional Legitimacy and the State System," 28 *Philosophy and Public Affairs* (1999), 46.

reserved for the more serious cases – those that I have defined as tyranny and anarchy. Again, the illegitimacy of the government is a necessary, not a sufficient, condition for the permissibility of humanitarian intervention.[16]

But if this is correct, it does require amending my original argument. It is no longer possible to ground the legitimacy of humanitarian intervention *solely* on the question of the moral legitimacy of the regime, because there are many cases where the collapse of political legitimacy will not be enough to justify intervention. Still, there are several consequences to the finding of illegitimacy. First, intervention against legitimate regimes is always banned. Second, it may well be that in a particular case it would be wrong to intervene, but the reason will never be the need to respect the *sovereignty* of the target state. Third, the liberal conception of state legitimacy will guide the correct behavior by the intervenor. He must abide by the general duty to promote, create, or restore institutions and practices under which the dignity of persons will be preserved.

I indicated that critics of humanitarian intervention are not pacifists. They object to *this kind* of war, a war to protect human rights. They do not object to wars, say, in defense of territory. This position is somewhat anomalous because it requires separate justifications for different kinds of wars. In contrast, the liberal argument offers a unified justification of war. War is justified if, and only if, it is in defense of persons and complies with the requirements of proportionality and the doctrine of double effect.[17] Take the use of force in self-defense. What can possibly be its moral justification? Very plausibly, this: that the aggressor is assaulting the rights of persons in the state that is attacked. The government of the attacked state, then, has a right to muster the resources of the state to defend its citizens' lives and property against the aggressor. The defense of states is justified *qua* defense of persons. There is no defense of the *state* as such that is not parasitic on the rights and interests of individuals. If this is correct, any moral distinction between self-defense and humanitarian intervention, that is, any judgment that self-defense is justified while humanitarian intervention is not, has to rely on something above and beyond the general rationale of defense of persons.

---

[16] I should have made this point clearer in *Humanitarian Intervention*. I was concerned with refuting the non-interventionist argument from sovereignty, and thus paid insufficient attention to other reasons that might bar humanitarian intervention against illegitimate regimes. In this chapter I attempt, among other things, to remedy that omission.

[17] See below for a discussion of the doctrine of double effect.

The relativist objection

Some object to the very project of using liberal political theory to address humanitarian intervention – or indeed any international question. The argument goes something like this. The world is ideologically and culturally too diverse to apply any one philosophy to a problem that concerns all persons in the globe. Because many people reject liberal principles, attempts to use liberal philosophy are unduly biased.[18] One would have to draw on different ethical traditions in order to analyze international problems. The outcome of liberal analysis might be good for someone who already accepts liberal principles, but not for those who do not. In other words, it might be necessary to do some comparative ethics before addressing these problems in order to identify which, if any, is the content of a global "overlapping consensus."

I have a general answer and a specific answer to this criticism of the liberal case for humanitarian intervention. I have never been able to see merit in relativism as a general philosophical view.[19] If, say, our philosophical judgment that all persons have rights is sound, then it is universally sound. It does not really matter if the *historical origin* of that judgment is Western or something else. Those who object to liberal principles on the grounds that they are Western commit the genetic fallacy. They confuse the problem of the *origin* of a political theory with the problem of its *justification*. The truth (moral or empirical) of a proposition is logically independent of its origin. The liberal can concede that the views he defends are Western, and still maintain that they are the better views. Another way of putting this is that the effort to find a justification for the exercise of political power is not an effort to *describe* the way Westerners think. Philosophical analysis is critical and normative, not descriptive. Of course, liberal views may be right or wrong, but they cannot possibly be right for some and wrong for others. Conversely, if *illiberal* views of politics are correct, then that has to be shown by rational argument, not by merely recognizing that some people, or other people, or many people, believe in them. To be sure, any philosophical justification of political power relies on assumptions, and critics may challenge the liberal justification of political power by challenging the assumptions.

---

[18] See, for example, Bhikhu Parekh, "Rethinking Humanitarian Intervention," 18 *International Political Science Review* (1997), 49, 54–55.

[19] See Fernando R. Tesón, "Human Rights and Cultural Relativism," 25 *Virginia Journal of International Law* (1985), 869.

But that, of course, is philosophical argument. Perhaps the illiberal assumptions are as plausible as the liberal ones, but that will not be because, say, many people in illiberal societies believe in them. If many persons endorse liberal assumptions and many other people endorse inconsistent illiberal assumptions, both sides cannot be right. Liberal analysis must assume that liberal assumptions (such as the importance of individual autonomy) are the better ones, universally. The liberal conception I defend is thus cosmopolitan, and as such rejects attempts at locating political morality in overlapping consensus, or other forms of majority validation. It rejects arguments *ad populum.*

Second, that objection does not seem to reach the first part of the argument: that the situations that warrant intervention – tyranny and anarchy – are morally abhorrent forms of political injustice. I believe that all reasonable religious and ethical theories converge in the judgment that those situations (mass murder, widespread torture, crimes against humanity, serious war crimes) are morally abhorrent. We are not dealing here with differences in conceptions of the good, or with various ways to realize human and collective excellence, or with the place of religion, civic deliberation, or free markets in political life. We are confronting governments that perpetrate atrocities against people, and situations of anarchy and breakdown of social order of such magnitude that no reasonable ethical or political theory could reasonably condone them. And, of course, if there are political theories that condone those situations, too bad for them: they cease to be reasonable or plausible. I do not believe, however, that the critic of humanitarian intervention wants to rely on a moral theory that justifies grievous human rights violations. I hope that I do not need deep studies in comparative ethics and religion to say that under any religious or ethical system the kind of situation that warrants humanitarian intervention is morally intolerable. For example, I doubt that someone who endorses religious or political doctrines that advance communal values and reject liberal reliance on individual autonomy will treat the extreme examples of tyranny or anarchy that warrant humanitarian intervention as morally tolerable or justified.[20]

On the other hand, the *second* part of the argument requires a reliance on conceptions about the justification of states, governments, and borders. As

[20] For the view that there is a considerable overlap on humanitarian intervention among different religious traditions, see Oliver Ramsbotham, "Islam, Christianity, and Forcible Humanitarian Intervention," 12 *Ethics and International Affairs* (1998), 81.

indicated above, I want to say that certain situations are morally abhorrent under any plausible ethical theory, *and* that those situations sometimes justify humanitarian intervention under a liberal conception of politics. Someone may agree with the first proposition but not with the second. He might agree that the situations are morally abhorrent but maintain that humanitarian intervention is still not justified: it is not for foreigners to remedy those wrongs. These other theories might hold particular views about the sanctity of borders, or about the moral centrality of communities, or about the moral relevance of distinctions between nationals and foreigners. Here again, all I can do is offer arguments to reject those views in favor of a more cosmopolitan approach. My point is rather this: to the objection that supporting humanitarian intervention presupposes a (biased) liberal commitment to human rights, the liberal can respond, "But surely you're not saying that under your (non-liberal) view these atrocities are justified. Whatever it is that you value, it cannot be this." The non-liberal critic can then make the following move: "I agree that this is morally abhorrent under my non-liberal principles as well, but those same principles, unlike yours, bar foreign interventions." Thus, non-interventionist views of international ethics attempt to *sever* (unconvincingly, I contend) domestic from international legitimacy. But if the non-liberal agrees that the situation is abhorrent, then the liberal interventionist cannot be biased because he thinks just that. The non-liberal needs reasons beyond his skepticism about rights and autonomy in order to question the legitimacy of humanitarian intervention in cases where he would agree with the liberal that the situation is morally abhorrent. He needs a theory of sovereignty under which foreigners are morally precluded from saving victims of extreme injustice.

The moral relevance of national borders: communal integrity

If the non-interventionist accepts that tyranny and anarchy are morally abhorrent, he might resort to theses of international ethics that place decisive value on sovereignty and national borders. Consider the following case. The provincial government in a federal state is committing atrocities against an ethnic group. Moreover, the provincial army is prepared to resist the federal army, so that a civil war will take place if the federal government tries to stop the massacre. Non-interventionists (like everyone else) will no doubt regret that a civil war will erupt, but surely will not object in principle to the *internal* intervention by federal troops aimed at stopping the massacre. In fact, they will likely praise the intervention.

Yet they will object if those same troops cross an *international* border to stop similar atrocities committed by a sovereign government in a neighboring state. For them, national borders mysteriously operate a *change in the description* of the act of humanitarian rescue: it is no longer humanitarian rescue, but war. (Why aren't massive human rights violations also called war, for example a war of the government against its people? Is it because usually part of the population is an accomplice in the perpetration?) The argument for this distinction has to rely on the moral significance of national borders as a corollary of the principle of sovereignty. But national borders can hardly have moral significance *in this context*. For one thing, national borders are the serendipitous result of past violence and other kinds of morally objectionable or irrelevant historical facts. More generally, a great deal of suffering and injustice in the world derives from the exaggerated importance that people assign to national borders. From ethnic cleansing to discrimination against immigrants, from prohibitions to speak foreign languages to trade protections that only benefit special interests, the ideas of nation, state, and borders have been consistently used to justify all kinds of harm to persons.

In spite of all that, there are surely reasons for respecting national borders, at least as long as one believes that a world of separate states is a desirable thing.[21] Those reasons are, in my view, two, and neither invalidates humanitarian intervention in appropriate cases. The first and most important has to do with the legitimacy of the social contract, as it were. Kant famously wrote, "No state having an independent existence, whether it be small or great, may be acquired by another state through inheritance, exchange, purchase, or gift."[22] The idea here is that a state that is somehow the result of the free consent by autonomous individuals in civil society must be respected. Violating those borders would amount, then, to treating the state and its citizens "as things."[23] This is the liberal premise defended here, that the sovereignty of the state and the inviolability of its borders are parasitic on the legitimacy of the social contract, and thus sovereignty and

---

[21] Separate states might be desirable in order to maximize freedom. See my *Philosophy of International Law*, pp. 17–19.

[22] Immanuel Kant, "Perpetual Peace: A Philosophical Sketch" (1795), in Hans Reiss ed., *Kant: Political Writings* (Cambridge University Press, Cambridge, 1970), p. 94.

[23] Ibid.

borders, too, serve the liberal ends of respecting freedom and human rights. Where half the population of the state is murdering the other half, or where the government is committing massive atrocities against its own citizens, national borders have lost most of their moral strength.[24] At the very least, they are morally impotent to contain foreign acts aimed at stopping the massacres.

Michael Walzer offers the best-known defense of the moral aptitude of national borders to ban humanitarian intervention.[25] According to Walzer, there is a crucial distinction between domestic and international legitimacy. A government may be illegitimate internally, but that does not mean that foreign armies are entitled to intervene to restore legitimacy. Walzer claims that in most cases there is enough "fit" between people and government to make injustice a purely domestic matter from which foreigners are excluded. Only the citizens themselves may overthrow their tyrant. It is only when the lack of fit is *radically* apparent, says Walzer, that intervention can be allowed. That will only occur in cases of genocide, enslavement, or mass deportation. He supports this thesis by communal considerations: nations have histories and loyalties that define their political process, and that process should be protected as such, even if some of its outcomes are repulsive to liberal philosophers. Walzer calls this "communal integrity."

As a preliminary matter, Walzer (unlike other non-interventionists) allows humanitarian intervention in important classes of cases. Yet his rationale for not allowing humanitarian intervention in other cases of tyranny and anarchy is, I believe, deeply wrong. By pointing out that dictators come from the society itself, from its families and neighborhoods, Walzer insinuates that tyranny and anarchy come naturally, as it were; that in some sense the victims are responsible for the horrors they suffer. It also presupposes that there is something morally valuable ("self-determination")

---

[24] They have not lost all their moral strength, though, because tyranny and anarchy do not mean open season for foreigners to invade at will. The guiding liberal principle here is the duty to respect persons. Tyranny and anarchy authorize foreigners to cross national borders to restore respect for persons, not for other purposes. But this will be true in the purely domestic example as well.

[25] See Michael Walzer, "The Moral Standing of States: A Response to Four Critics," 9 *Philosophy and Public Affairs* (1980), 209–29. I criticize his argument at length in *Humanitarian Intervention*, pp. 92–99. See also the discussion (in basic agreement with the view in the text) in Caney, "Humanitarian Intervention and State Sovereignty," pp. 122–23; and Jeff McMahan, "The Ethics of International Intervention," in Anthony Ellis ed., *Ethics and International Relations* (Manchester University Press, Manchester, 1986), pp. 36–49.

in the fortuitous balance of existing political forces in a society.[26] But political processes are not valuable per se. Their value depends on their being minimally consistent with the imperative to respect persons.[27] It is even grotesque to describe the kinds of cases that warrant humanitarian intervention as "processes of self-determination" and suggest, as Walzer does, that unless there is genocide, there is a necessary fit between government and people. David Luban put it best: "The government fits the people the way the sole of a boot fits a human face: After a while the patterns of indentation fit with uncanny precision."[28]

Having said that, there is a kernel of truth in a possible reading of Walzer's argument, best put by John Stuart Mill.[29] Mill argued that humanitarian intervention is always wrong because freedom has no value unless the victims themselves fight for their liberation. People cannot really be free if foreigners do the fighting for them. While this argument is problematic (why isn't freedom valuable if someone else helps us achieve it?), it does make an important point. Citizens of the state ruled by a tyrant (or victimized by warlords in a failed state) have a responsibility to help put an end to their plight. The intervenor has a right to expect their reasonable cooperation in putting an end to tyranny, in shouldering the moral and material costs of intervention, and in building democratic institutions. It is their government, their society. Foreign efforts to help them depend on their cooperation and willingness to build or restore those institutions.

One corollary of Mill's point is the requirement that the victims of tyranny or anarchy welcome the intervention. Walzer and other critics of humanitarian intervention say that in most cases the victims do not really want to be liberated by foreigners, that they would rather put up with

---

[26] See Gerald Doppelt, "Walzer's Theory of Morality in International Relations," 8 *Philosophy and Public Affairs* (1978), 3.

[27] The point I make in the text applies to regimes against whom humanitarian intervention presumably would *not* have been justified on other (mostly consequentialist) grounds. Would anyone say now, for example, that there was anything valuable in the "self-determination" of East Germany, a state created and maintained by terror and violence? Yet at the time most people (academics included) bowed to the realities of political power and proclaimed East Germany a legitimate state, entitled as such to all the privileges and prerogatives associated with statehood. Traditional views of international law, on this as in other matters, suffer, at the very least, from moral blindness.

[28] David Luban, "The Romance of the Nation-State," 9 *Philosophy and Public Affairs* (1980), 395–96.

[29] See John Stuart Mill, "A Few Words on Non-Intervention," in John Stuart Mill, *Dissertations and Discussions* (Spencer, Boston, 1867), vol. III, pp. 171–76.

their tyrants than see their homeland invaded. This is a view influenced by communitarianism. Communitarians contend that persons not only have liberty interests: they also, and more importantly, have communal interests, those that define their membership in a group or community – their social identity. Indeed, for communitarians, liberty interests are parasitic on communal interests or values. On this view, the average citizen in any country (including those ruled by tyrannical regimes) will be wounded in his self-respect if foreigners intervene, even if it is for a good purpose, because such intervention strikes at the heart of his social identity. The corollary seems to be that the average citizen in an oppressive regime *prefers* to remain oppressed than to be freed by foreigners.

I believe that while this situation is empirically possible, it is highly unlikely to occur. For one thing, there is no valid community interest of the citizen who *collaborates* with the abusers. In a society afflicted by tyranny there is a group (sometimes the minority, sometimes the majority) that benefits from the government's persecution of others. These are the rent-seekers of the worst kind, those who capture the machine of horror for their own purposes. To describe this as "community interest" is grotesque. It is also wrong to presume that victims oppose liberating intervention. I would think that the evidence supports the opposite presumption: that victims of serious oppression will welcome rather than oppose outside help. This was seemingly the case in the interventions in Grenada, Iraq, Rwanda, Haiti, and Kosovo, among others.

The only persons whose consent deserves consideration are those who oppose both the regime *and* foreign intervention for moral reasons. They might say that the regime is murderous but that foreign invasion of their homeland is unacceptable, even if undertaken for the purpose of ending the ongoing killings. Should their refusal be decisive? Should prospective intervenors treat the veto by political and civic leaders who oppose the regime as a decisive reason for not intervening? I do not think so, for the following reason: I very much doubt that you can cite *your* communal interests validly to oppose aid to *me*, when *I* am strapped to the torture chamber, even if you are not complicitous.[30] Only *I* (the torture victim) can waive my right to seek aid; only my consent counts for that purpose.

---

[30] In the same sense, see McMahan, "Ethics of International Intervention," p. 41. This is the appropriate response to relativist critics of the US–British efforts in Afghanistan aimed at liberating women. The male Muslim believer, even if innocent, has no standing to object to efforts aimed at saving others.

So, to summarize: in a tyrannical regime the population can be divided into the following groups: the victims; the accomplices and collaborators; and the bystanders. The last group can in turn be subdivided into those who support the regime and those who oppose it. Of these groups, only the first, the victims, have (arguably) a right to refuse aid. The accomplices and bystanders who support the regime are excluded for obvious reasons. Their opposition to intervention does not count. And the bystanders who oppose the regime cannot validly refuse foreign aid on behalf of the victims.

Democratic leaders must make sure before intervening that they have the support of the very persons they want to assist, the victims. Yet the view (suggested by Walzer)[31] that a *majority* of the population must support the intervention is wrong, because the majority may be complicitous in the human rights violations. Suppose the government of a multi-ethnic state tries to exterminate a minority ethnic group. Let us further assume that a history of ethnic animosity leads the majority group to support the genocide. Humanitarian intervention is justified even if the majority of the population of the state opposes it. An intervenor must abide by the duty to restore the rights of persons threatened by tyranny or anarchy. Whether or not these goals will be advanced cannot be decided by simply taking opinion polls in the population of the tyrannical or anarchical society.

Another reason to respect national borders is that they may help secure the stability of social interaction, that is, the mutual expectations of individuals who interact within and across demarcations of political jurisdictions. The reasons for having national borders, then, are analogous to the reasons for respecting the demarcations of property rights. Property owners should be allowed to exclude trespassers because that facilitates the internalization of externalities and thus maximizes the efficiency in the use of resources.[32] Similarly, it might be argued that states must be allowed to exclude foreign "trespassers" who attempt to free ride on the cooperative efforts of the citizens of the state. Giving the state exclusive jurisdiction over its territory maximizes global gains, just as giving farmers exclusive property rights over their land maximizes aggregate wealth. These efficiency considerations become particularly relevant in the aftermath of the intervention. Successful intervenors, unlike internal victors, have little incentive to treat the target

[31] See Walzer, "Moral Standing of States."
[32] See the classic discussion in Harold Demsetz, "Toward a Theory of Property Rights," 57 *American Economic Review Papers* (1967), 347–59.

country as something that is theirs – they lack long-term property rights over the territory.[33] Likewise, internal victors (such as the current ruling group in Afghanistan) in an intervention have a greater incentive to restore the political fabric of their society than do external victors. These reasons point to the need to assign *some* instrumental importance to national borders and counsel prudence on the part of the intervenor. Consequentialist considerations are also crucial for planning the post-intervention stage in order to achieve lasting success in terms of the moral values that justified the intervention.[34]

However, these considerations do not exclude the legitimacy of humanitarian intervention, because the kinds of situations that warrant intervention are of such gravity that they cannot possibly be trumped by the pragmatic considerations just discussed. The protection of national borders is necessary, under this argument, to preserve the glue that binds international society, and as such re-emerges in the post-intervention phase. Yet allowing the atrocities to continue is a much worse dissolver of that glue than the infringement of borders.

I conclude, then, that the right of humanitarian intervention in appropriate cases is unaffected by the existence of national borders. The latter owe their importance to considerations of justice and efficiency. Where these values are grossly assaulted by tyranny and anarchy, invoking the sanctity of borders to protect tyranny and anarchy is, on reflection, self-defeating.

The argument from international law

This chapter is mostly concerned with the moral–political defense of humanitarian intervention. However, I want to consider a popular argument against humanitarian intervention frequently offered by international lawyers. Humanitarian intervention is objectionable, they claim, because states have an obligation to abide by international law. Governments who intervene by force violate a central tenet of the international legal system.[35] This argument, of course, locates the obligation to obey the law outside international law itself: there is a moral reason to comply with international

---

[33] Robert O. Keohane, personal communication (on file with the author).

[34] See Robert O. Keohane, "Political Authority after Intervention: Gradations in Sovereignty," ch. 8 in this volume.

[35] See, among others, Louis Henkin, "The Use of Force: Law and US Policy," in Council on Foreign Relations, *Right v. Might* (Council on Foreign Relations Press, New York, 1991), pp. 37–73.

law even where doing so leads sometimes to undesirable or even immoral outcomes.[36]

This argument is fatally flawed. First, it rests on a highly dubious premise. The view that international law (conceived as anchored in the practice of states) prohibits humanitarian intervention depends upon a reading of state practice informed by state-oriented values. Critics of humanitarian intervention have complained that supporters of the doctrine engage in a subjective, value-oriented analysis of custom and treaty.[37] On their view, objective analysis yields instead an unequivocal verdict against humanitarian intervention. Again, this is not the place for legal debates, but I will say this much: state practice is at the very least ambivalent on the question of humanitarian intervention, so any interpretation of that practice (for or against) has to rely on extra-legal values.[38] There is no such thing as a "state practice" that mechanically yields a legal rule. Diplomatic history has to be interpreted in the light of our moral and empirical assumptions about the purposes of international law. If this is correct, the positivist rejection of humanitarian intervention is far from objective, notwithstanding the claims of international lawyers to the contrary. It is informed by a set of values that privileges the preservation of governments and political regimes over the protection of human rights. The contrast is not between "subjective" interventionist legal analysis and "objective" non-interventionist legal analysis, but between international lawyers who uphold human values and international lawyers who uphold state values. Non-interventionists delude themselves when they accuse interventionists of bias. They have their own bias. Part of their problem is their mistaken belief that legal analysis is conceptually autonomous and that political philosophy and other forms of normative analysis have no place in legal reasoning. In reality, what many

---

[36] Another version of the argument has a consequentialist rather than a deontological flavor: states should not intervene because doing so *undermines* compliance with international law in the long run.

[37] See, for example, Ian Brownlie, "Thoughts on Kind-hearted Gunmen," in Richard Lillich ed., *Humanitarian Intervention and the United Nations* (University Press of Virginia, Charlottesville, 1973), p. 139.

[38] See the summary of the debate in J. L. Holzgrefe, "The Humanitarian Intervention Debate," ch. 1 in this volume. In my view, Allen Buchanan's thoughtful piece, "Reforming the International Law of Humanitarian Intervention," ch. 4 in this volume, unnecessarily concedes that the NATO intervention in Kosovo was illegal because of a lack of Security Council authorization. That prompts him to examine the issue of illegal reform of international law. I do not think that Security Council authorization was required in the Kosovo case; however, Buchanan's analysis remains pertinent for other cases of reform of international law through illegal acts.

international lawyers do is smuggle their statist bias under the guise of autonomous legal analysis.[39] The critic of humanitarian intervention will fare much better if he deals with the applicable moral arguments for and against humanitarian intervention rather than hiding behind the supposed conceptual autonomy of legal reasoning.

There is another answer to this objection. No one disputes that international law prohibits the use of force generally. Yet the kinds of cases that warrant humanitarian intervention disclose *other* serious violations of international law: genocide, crimes against humanity, and so on. The typical situation where we consider intervening is not one where we are contemplating violating international law as opposed to not violating international law. These are cases where whatever we do we will end up tolerating a violation of *some* fundamental rule of international law. Either we intervene and put an end to the massacres, in which case we apparently violate the general prohibition of war, or we abstain from intervening, in which case we tolerate the violation by other states of the general prohibition of gross human rights abuses. The maxim "other things being equal, states must obey international law" can hardly mean "other things being equal, states must obey international law even if doing so allows an ongoing, equally egregious violation of international law." The obligation to abide by international law, then, does not help the non-interventionist. His position now depends either on a dubious judgment that an international war is always worse than tyranny or anarchy, or on an equally dubious distinction between acts and omissions.[40]

The decisive reason for solving this conflict of principles in favor of allowing humanitarian intervention in appropriate cases stems from the realization that the value of sovereignty is problematic unless it is understood as an *instrumental* good, that is, as a means to other more fundamental ends. The gross violation of human rights is not only an obvious assault on the dignity of persons, *but a betrayal of the principle of sovereignty itself*. The non-interventionist faces a dilemma here. Either he believes that state sovereignty is intrinsically valuable, or he concedes that sovereignty is instrumental to the realization of other human values. If the former, he has to say that the prohibition of intervention has nothing to do with respecting persons, in which case he is forced to invoke unappealing (and wholly

[39] For a recent example of this kind of approach, see Simon Chesterman, *Just War or Just Peace? Humanitarian Intervention and International Law* (Oxford University Press, Oxford, 2001).
[40] See the discussion below.

discredited) organicist conceptions of the state.[41] If the latter, he has to demonstrate that the human values served by sovereignty in the long term justify allowing the massacres to continue now – a daunting task.

Readers unpersuaded by my jurisprudential stance will still claim that law and morality are separate and that a positivist reading of international law prohibits humanitarian intervention. Even so, this chapter may be of some use to them: they may take the argument here as a *de lege ferenda* proposal, that is, a proposal for reforming international law. Someone who thinks that a positivist reading of international law prohibits humanitarian intervention yet also thinks the moral argument in this chapter is correct must conclude that international law is morally objectionable and should join in the effort to reform it.

A sovereign state is an institution created by men and women to protect themselves against injustice, and to facilitate mutually beneficial social co-operation. The non-interventionist cannot locate his priority of sovereignty in anything that is *internal* to the target state in these kinds of cases. Therefore, the argument against humanitarian intervention must rely on the importance of sovereignty for ends that are *external* to the target state. To these arguments I now turn.

The objection from global stability

One important objection to humanitarian intervention relies on the need to preserve world order. The idea here is not that there is anything morally important *internally* about the sovereignty of the state. What is important instead is to preserve the stability of the *system of states* in the long run.[42] Humanitarian intervention undermines that stability both by the very act of intervening, and by creating a dangerous precedent that lends itself to abuse by aggressive states.[43] The use of the doctrine of humanitarian intervention rationale by even well-intentioned governments will contribute to generalized chaos, and an unjust order is preferable to chaos. Injustices should be

---

[41] I have called this view "the Hegelian Myth": see my *Humanitarian Intervention*, ch. 3. See also Charles Beitz's classical work, *Political Theory and International Relations* (Princeton University Press, Princeton, 1979), pp. 69–71; and Caney, "Humanitarian Intervention and State Sovereignty," p. 122.

[42] See, for example, Stanley Hoffmann, *Duties Beyond Borders: On the Limits and Possibilities of Ethical International Politics* (Syracuse University Press, Syracuse, 1981), p. 58.

[43] In this sense, see Thomas Franck and Nigel Rodley, "After Bangladesh: The Law of Humanitarian Intervention by Military Force," 67 *American Journal of International Law* (1973), 290.

remedied in ways that do not undermine the stability of the state system, that is, by "peaceful" means. The avoidance of conflict is a prerequisite for world order.

This objection to humanitarian intervention is unconvincing. First, it is open to an important moral rejoinder. Assuming for the sake of argument that the state system is worth preserving, it is highly problematic to *use* the victims of tyranny and anarchy for that purpose. The non-interventionist argument has a decidedly theological flavor. It is analogous to the response of the religious believer to the complaint that God allows things like the Holocaust to happen. The believer claims that God allows the Holocaust because He has a higher purpose that we, as finite beings, cannot possibly grasp. Similarly, the non-interventionist claims that there is a higher global purpose that justifies not interfering with tyranny and anarchy. In this case, however, that higher purpose is not inscrutable: we are told it is the preservation of the state system. I am unconvinced by the believer's response (what higher end can an omnipotent Being possibly have to allow the Holocaust?)[44] Yet while I am willing to give God the benefit of the doubt, that benefit does not extend to academics. The claim seems to me morally unappealing, because whatever the merits of the state system, its preservation cannot surely be achieved at that kind of human cost. It is not even clear that "the preservation of the state system" is much more than a euphemism for the arch-conservative view that incumbent governments and the status quo should be preserved regardless of their value to actual human beings.

The second answer to the argument is the same as I gave in the discussion of the relevance of national borders. Tyranny and anarchy are at least as likely to generate instability and chaos as interventions – perhaps even including in the calculation the harm caused by non-humanitarian interventions.[45] The argument from the stability of world order ignores this crucial fact. The reason for this strange neglect is theoretical: statism treats states as the only relevant units in international relations and ignores what happens between states. This is the anthropomorphic view of the state that has

---

[44] Theological query: if we know that God wants the Holocaust to happen for inscrutable reasons, should we or should we not intervene to stop it?

[45] Have international wars caused more or less suffering than tyranny and anarchy? I do not know the answer. But what seems reasonably certain is that the harm caused by tyranny and anarchy in the world has been much greater than collateral harms caused by humanitarian interventions, even by those that failed.

caused so much harm to persons and confusion in international thinking. As long as there is "order" within states, the non-interventionist thinks that he can safely ignore what happens within them. I do not need to cite here the overwhelming evidence about the causal relation between internal upheaval and international instability. In the face of that evidence, one who is concerned with long-term stability should rationally support a general prohibition of aggressive war *and* a system for protection of human rights that includes a properly limited right of humanitarian intervention.[46]

Finally, the empirical claim that a rule allowing humanitarian intervention will trigger unjustified interventions and will thus threaten world order is implausible. The claim can now be tested, because there have been a number of humanitarian interventions since 1990 or so. The non-interventionist argument, as I understand it, is that allowing these humanitarian interventions will encourage governments and other international actors to over-intervene, often with spurious motives. Governments, it is argued, will find it easier to intervene for selfish motives because they can rely on precedent and offer self-serving humanitarian justifications. But this, quite simply, has not happened. It is true that the end of the Cold War has caused, alongside the spread of democracy and free markets, political instability in certain regions. Yet this had nothing to do with the occurrence of more humanitarian interventions, but rather with ethnic rivalries and similar factors. (Perhaps if we had had a clearly defined and institutionalized rule allowing humanitarian intervention we might have been able to prevent, through deterrence, some of the horrific things that happened in those ethnic conflicts.) I do not think it can be seriously claimed that the interventions in Somalia, Rwanda, Haiti, and Kosovo have shaken the world order beyond recognition.[47] On the contrary, those interventions have improved things on the whole. And when interventions have failed, that merely means that tyranny and anarchy have continued unchecked. Failed humanitarian interventions have not made matters worse. There is an obvious reason why humanitarian interventions are unlikely to produce the chaos that non-interventionists fear: intervention is very costly,

[46] For a general discussion of the relationship between internal political arrangements and international peace, see Michael Doyle, "Liberalism and World Politics," 80 *American Political Science Review* (1986), 1151–70; John Owen, "How Liberalism Produces the Democratic Peace," 19 *International Security* (1994), 87–125; and the discussion in my *Philosophy of International Law*, pp. 1–38.

[47] But see Michael Byers and Simon Chesterman, "Has US Power Destroyed the UN?" *London Review of Books*, 29 April 1999, p. 29.

so governments have a considerable disincentive to undertake *any* intervention. Acting in Kosovo was very costly to NATO – if only in economic terms. In addition, the right of humanitarian intervention can be suitably designed to prevent escalation, perhaps allowing intervention when such risk is minimal.[48] Furthermore, if the system of states breaks down because there are many humanitarian interventions (by definition prompted by tyranny and anarchy) perhaps this collapse is a desirable thing. Just as the surrender of sovereignty by individuals to states need not involve the elimination of their moral autonomy, so the surrender of sovereignty by states to an international *liberal* authority should not necessarily result in universal tyranny.[49] The death of a state is never bad in itself (think of the demise of the Soviet Union or East Germany). Only the deaths of its citizens.

Acts, omissions, and the rights of the innocent

Tyranny or anarchy is a necessary but not a sufficient condition of the legitimacy of humanitarian intervention. As in all moral matters, we have competing reasons of various kinds to guide behavior. It might well be that in a particular case humanitarian intervention in a state would be wrong notwithstanding the fact that the government of that state is itself guilty of serious human rights violations. Sometimes we cannot right the wrong even if it is justified for us to do so. Sometimes intervening is unacceptably costly to us, the intervenor. And sometimes righting a wrong entails harming persons in objectionable ways; that is, in ways and to an extent that would be at least as objectionable as the wrongs we are intending to remedy.

The moral dilemmas of intervention are not well captured by distinctions between deontological and consequentialist approaches to humanitarian intervention, for several reasons. First, philosophical defenses of humanitarian intervention will necessarily combine deontological and consequentialist elements. The liberal case for humanitarian intervention, for instance, contains both deontological elements (a principled commitment to human rights) and consequentialist ones (the requirement that interventions cause more good than harm). Second, military action, including humanitarian intervention, will almost always violate the rights of innocent persons, so under a strict deontological view the intervenor will presumably never be

---

[48] See McMahan, "Ethics of International Intervention," p. 24.   [49] Ibid.

justified, even if his purpose is to protect human rights, and even if it is certain that such will be the result of the intervention. This is because the intervention will violate the rights of innocents. The objection, then, is that, even if successful, the humanitarian intervention would have used innocent persons as a means to an end – something prohibited by a strict deontological approach. There is an interesting paradox here: the liberal argument for humanitarian intervention is rights-based, and as such it has a strong deontological flavor, yet at the same time the liberal interventionist is countenancing the deaths of innocents in apparent violation of deontological constraints.

The reply to this objection is that the strict deontological approach is misguided here. If it were sound, no war or revolution would ever be justified, because the just warriors almost always would have to kill innocents. For example, under that view the Allies would have had no justification to respond to Germany's aggression in World War II, because such response would have resulted (as it did) in the deaths of many innocent persons (such as German children). The strict deontological approach leads to counterintuitive results – at least as far as international politics are concerned.

The liberal argument for humanitarian intervention has a somewhat different conceptual structure. Justified intervention aims to *maximize* human rights observance, but the intervenor is constrained by *the doctrine of double effect*. Thus, humanitarian intervention cannot be simply grounded in what Nozick has called "utilitarianism of rights,"[50] because this may conceivably allow the deliberate targeting of innocent persons if conducive to realizing the humanitarian objective. This is prohibited by the doctrine of double effect.[51] According to this doctrine, an act in which innocents are killed is only legitimate when three conditions are satisfied:

1. The act has good consequences – such as the killing of enemy soldiers in a just war;
2. The actor's intentions are good, that is, he aims to achieve the good consequences. Any bad consequences – such as the killing of non-combatants – are not intended; and

---

[50] See Robert Nozick, *Anarchy, State, and Utopia* (Basic Books, New York, 1974).

[51] For an influential discussion of the doctrine of double effect, see Warren Quinn, "Actions, Intentions, and Consequences: The Doctrine of Double Effect," 18 *Philosophy and Public Affairs* (1989), 334. See also the excellent discussion by Horacio Spector, *Autonomy and Rights* (Oxford University Press, Oxford, 1992), pp. 101–51.

3. The act's good consequences – such as the killing of enemy soldiers –
   outweigh its bad consequences – such as the killing of non-combatants.
   This is called the doctrine of proportionality.[52]

The doctrine of double effect thus distinguishes between actions with intended bad consequences and actions with unintended bad consequences.
The former give rise to moral blameworthiness. The latter may, depending on the circumstances, be excused. Thus proportionate collateral harm
caused by a humanitarian intervention, where the goal is to rescue victims
of tyranny or anarchy, may, depending on the circumstances,[53] be morally
excusable. So on the one hand, humanitarian intervention is not an action
conceptually structured, from the standpoint of the agent, as deontolog-
ically pure behavior where the agent (the intervenor) is absolutely constrained to respect the rights of everybody. It is instead an action intended
to *maximize* universal respect for human rights but morally constrained
by the prohibition of *deliberately* targeting innocent persons. The proportionate *collateral* deaths of innocent persons, while indirectly caused by the
intervenor, do not necessarily condemn the intervention as immoral. The
argument for humanitarian intervention is located midway between strict
deontological approaches and consequentialist ones like utilitarianism. The
latter directs agents to intervene whenever they maximize the good in terms
of the general welfare (often conceived in terms of human lives). The former

---

[52] I follow here a slightly amended version of the classic definition provided by Michael Walzer, *Just
and Unjust Wars: A Moral Argument with Historical Illustrations* (Basic Books, New York, 1977),
p. 153. See a similar definition by Quinn, "Actions, Intentions, and Consequences," p. 334, n. 3.
Walzer, like other just war theorists before and after him, feels compelled to invoke the doctrine
of double effect in order to assert the legitimacy of any war. See also Duane Cady, "Pacifist
Perspectives on Humanitarian Intervention," in Phillips and Cady, *Humanitarian Intervention*,
pp. 38–39; Francis V. Harbour, "The Just War Tradition and the Use of Non-lethal Chemical
Weapons During the Vietnam War" in Andrew Valls ed., *Ethics in International Affairs: Theories
and Cases* (Rowman & Littlefield, Oxford, 2000), p. 50. To be sure, the doctrine has come under
attack. See Alistair McIntyre, "Doing Away with Double Effect," 111 *Ethics* (2001), 219–55. But
one who rejects the doctrine (at least with respect to war) is forced to counterintuitive positions,
such as that no war or revolution is ever justified.

[53] I say "depending on the circumstances" because, as Horacio Spector, following Phillippa Foot,
shows, it is not the case that there is *always* a moral difference between causing an undesirable
result with direct intention and causing it with oblique intention. See Spector, *Autonomy and
Rights*, pp. 104–05 (citing Phillippa Foot, "The Problem of Abortion and the Doctrine of Double
Effect," in Phillippa Foot, *Virtues and Vices and Other Essays in Moral Philosophy* [Blackwell,
Oxford, 1978], p. 20). These discussions show the difficulty of identifying with any precision
when and why the "foreseen–intended" distinction operates. I treat humanitarian intervention as
a case where the distinction does operate, as the opposite conclusion leads to the counterintuitive
result of morally banning all wars. See discussion in the text below.

would forbid intervention that would result in violations of the rights of innocents – even intervention that will certainly maximize universal rights observance. Instead, humanitarian intervention understood as a morally constrained form of help to others accepts that sometimes causing harm to innocent persons is justified as long as one does not *will* such harm in order to achieve, not a greater general welfare, but a goal that is normatively compelling under appropriate principles of morality. The doctrine rejects, as deontological doctrines do, undifferentiated calculations of costs and benefits where justice (as a goal of the intervention) would be just one indicator of good aggregate consequences among many others.

The goal of saving lives and restoring human rights and justice is compelling enough to authorize humanitarian intervention even at the cost of innocent lives.[54] It is not simply that the intervenor is improving the world in a general sense. In typical cases, the intervenor is not just saving lives – although this goal is, indeed, normatively compelling. He is helping to restore justice and rights, the purpose of all justified political institutions – most prominently the state. The goal of restoring human rights and justice thus is more than simply helping people, although of course if it is achieved people will be helped. The goal of restoring minimally just institutions and practices is *normatively privileged* regardless of the advancement of the general welfare. For example, humanitarian *aid* is of course desirable, but it only temporarily relieves some of the symptoms of anarchy and tyranny. Building and restoring democratic, rights-respecting institutions, if successful, not

---

[54] It is tempting to think of the goal of *fighting evil* as an additional morally compelling goal of humanitarian intervention. However, human evil is present only in a subset of the class of cases that qualify for intervention. Many humanitarian disasters are caused by natural events and by simply incompetent or impotent rulers. In cases of tyranny, however, the moral urgency to defeat evil would be, I believe, an additional reason to act. Assuming equal risk, do citizens in liberal democracies have a more stringent duty to intervene to defeat a malevolent tyrant than to intervene to save victims of, say, an earthquake? On evil, see Immanuel Kant, *Religion Within the Limits of Reason Alone* (ed. Theodore M. Greene and Hoyt H. Hudson, Harper, New York, 1960), pp. 34–39. See also the discussion in Robert Sullivan, *Immanuel Kant's Moral Theory* (Cambridge University Press, Cambridge, 1989), pp. 124–26. We seem to lack a theory of evil. For Kant, radical evil is the natural tendency of human beings to follow inclination instead of duty; for Carlos Nino, radical evil is simply an evil of great magnitude: see Carlos S. Nino, *Radical Evil on Trial* (Yale University Press, New Haven, 1999). A more useful distinction, it seems to me, is between *opportunistic* evil and *principled* evil. The opportunistic agent causes evil to advance his self-interest; the principled agent causes evil by following an evil maxim. Which one of these is worse is a matter for debate. Some of the most horrific acts were caused by principled evildoers, persons committed to an evil cause (think about 11 September 2001), yet dictators who murder and torture just to stay in power, like Saddam Hussein, are capable of horrendous things as well.

only means doing the right thing for that society: it also addresses a central cause of the problem.[55] In that sense the justification of humanitarian intervention is both deontological and utilitarian.[56] That is why the loss of lives is not the only indicator of the legitimacy of humanitarian intervention.

This conceptual understanding of humanitarian intervention as an action aimed at maximizing respect for human rights yet constrained by the doctrine of double effect prompts the examination of two related issues. One is the permissibility of killing innocent persons in an (otherwise justified) humanitarian intervention. The other is the moral status of the *failure* to intervene. Interventionists have to explain why the (inevitable) deaths of innocents that occur in any humanitarian intervention are morally justified. After all, such persons do not voluntarily surrender their right to life. Therefore, knowingly causing their deaths is morally problematic, even for a benign purpose. Conversely, non-interventionists have to explain why the *failure* to intervene is justified in cases where a potential intervenor can prevent or end a massacre or similar event at reasonable cost. The two issues are related. As a preliminary matter, the critic of humanitarian intervention needs to say more than that he condemns violence generally. If his opposition to humanitarian intervention is part of his general condemnation of political violence, then presumably he must weigh the moral costs of allowing the massacres against the moral cost of intervening. The scale may tip for or against intervention, but a categorical non-interventionist position cannot be justified by a general abhorrence of violence, since the non-interventionist is taking a position that permits the perpetration of the atrocities. It is hard to see why opponents of humanitarian intervention rarely mention *that* violence while invoking their general condemnation of war. To the charge that failure to intervene may be morally culpable, the non-interventionist replies by making a moral distinction between acts and omissions. He claims that those who intervene will *cause* the bad results

---

[55] I leave aside here the issue of economic assistance and the building of economic institutions. I happen to believe that only effective mechanisms to protect human rights *and* the creation of free markets will help solve societal problems, especially in the developing world. See Fernando R. Tesón, "In Defense of Liberal Democracy for Africa," 13 *Cambridge Review of International Affairs* (1999), 29.

[56] Of course, most successful humanitarian interventions will also benefit most persons in the state in the utilitarian sense. This need not always be so, though: think about a large majority committing atrocities against a small minority. Be that as it may, I here wish to avoid the larger issue of whether utilitarians can successfully recast deontological concerns into consequentialist language.

(deaths of innocents, destruction), whereas those who do not intervene *do not cause* the atrocities (the tyrant does). That position is part of a general view that killing is morally worse than letting die. The argument goes something like this. A government that fails to intervene to stop atrocities in another country (assuming it can do so at reasonable cost to itself) is simply *letting innocent people die*. If that government decides instead to intervene, it will *kill some innocent people* for sure. Because killing is morally worse than letting die, humanitarian intervention should therefore be prohibited.

The question of the moral status of actions and omissions has been extensively discussed in philosophy, but not to my knowledge in international relations or international law. Some of the conclusions that can be drawn from the philosophy literature are relevant here. It seems that it is justified *sometimes* to cause the deaths of some persons in order to save a greater number, even if one rejects a purely utilitarian approach.[57] In other words, killing some to save others does not always amount to *using* the former to save the latter. It seems that we need to know *how* persons are killed and saved, as well as ascertain the nature of the relationship between the greater good and the lesser evil.[58] One solution is along ideal consent lines: the action is justified if all of the persons involved in the event, that is, those who would be sacrificed and those who would be saved (not knowing whether or not they would have been one or the other), would have agreed in advance that the action would have been appropriate.[59]

Now let us recast the problem in terms of humanitarian intervention. The government that intervenes knows that some innocent persons will

---

[57] This is known as "the Trolley Problem." See Judith Jarvis Thomson, "Killing, Letting Die, and the Trolley Problem," in J. M. Fischer and M. Ravizza eds., *Ethics: Problems and Principles* (Harcourt Brace Jovanovich Publishers, Fort Worth, 1991), p. 67. The literature on the Trolley Problem and its variations is abundant. See, inter alia, Spector, *Autonomy and Rights*; Frances Myrna Kamm, "Harming Some to Save Others," 57 *Philosophical Studies* (1989), 229; and now F. M. Kamm, *Morality, Mortality* (Oxford University Press, Oxford, 1996), vol. II; Erick Mack, "On Transplants and Trolleys," 53 *Philosophy and Phenomenological Research* (1993), 163; and Guido Pincione, "Negative Duties and Market Institutions" (unpublished, 2001), pp. 5–35. Thomson herself restates the problem in Judith Jarvis Thomson, *The Realm of Rights* (Harvard University Press, Cambridge, Mass., 1990).

[58] For example, Frances Myrna Kamm has suggested the Principle of Permissible Harm, according to which the greater good *causing* the lesser evil is a *sufficient* condition for moral permissibility of the action. See Kamm, *Morality, Mortality*, vol. II, p. 174. Is humanitarian intervention such a case? Are collateral deaths "caused" by the greater good, that is, the restoration of justice and human rights? The answer will depend on the analysis of the concept of cause – a task well beyond the scope of this essay.

[59] Ibid.

(regrettably) die if it intervenes to save the many victims of tyranny or anarchy. Let us stipulate that the intervention will indirectly[60] cause one-fifth of the innocent[61] casualties that the tyrant will cause. I suggest that the case for the permissibility of humanitarian intervention is *more compelling* than the standard case for the permissibility of killing one person to save five. In the former, those who intervene to stop human rights abuses attempt to *remedy an injustice*.[62] In the latter sort of cases there is no ongoing injustice. Rather, the problem is how to reconcile (1) our intuition that we cannot kill an innocent person in order to save five persons with (2) our intuition that sometimes we are justified in doing so, and (3) our further conviction that the explanation of (2) cannot simply be that it is always justified to kill some people to save more lives (as shown by compelling counterexamples).[63] But in the humanitarian intervention situation, it is not simply a question of saving more than those who are killed by the intervention: as we saw, the intervenor attempts to restore human rights and justice. So if we think that it is sometimes permissible to allow the deaths of innocent persons in order to save others in cases where the beneficiaries suffer no injustice, *a fortiori* it should be permissible to allow (regrettably) the deaths of innocent persons in cases where the agent is attempting to rescue persons from ongoing and serious acts of injustice. As I indicated above, in the typical humanitarian intervention case the situation to be redressed is *normatively qualified* as gross injustice; it is not merely a question of numbers. A crucial related requirement, of course, is that the intervenor avoid as much as possible collateral deaths and damage, and that, where those collateral deaths are unavoidable, the intervenor abide by the doctrine of double effect. Under these doctrines, the just warrior should never *intend* the deaths of innocents. He should centrally intend the restoration of human rights. If, in doing so, he collaterally causes the reasonably proportionate deaths of some innocent persons, the warrior can, depending on the circumstances, be excused for having done so.

Plausibly, humanitarian intervention meets the test of ideal consent as well. Citizens of a state would ideally agree that humanitarian intervention

---

[60] By "indirectly" I mean here that the intervenor does not *will* but simply *foresees* those deaths – the double-effect prescription.

[61] I ignore here the moral significance of killing non-innocent persons.

[62] I am grateful to Guido Pincione for having suggested this point.

[63] One such counterexample is the *transplant* case: we do not intuitively accept that a surgeon is justified in killing an innocent person in order to use his organs to save five dying patients.

should be allowed for those extreme cases of injustice even at the cost
of the deaths of some innocents, and even if some of those citizens will
inevitably be those persons. The parties might agree to humanitarian intervention either by application of John Rawls's *maximin* principle[64] or by a
stronger assumption about the parties' public-spirited commitment to political justice and human rights, or by a combination of both. This test should
not be confused with a similar test of hypothetical consent that we could
employ to determine whether or not ideal *global* contractors would agree to
an international legal *principle* allowing for humanitarian intervention.[65] I
believe the result of that mental experiment is positive as well. In summary,
rational persons *within a state* will agree, I believe, to allow humanitarian
intervention, not knowing what place they will have in that society. These
parties know the state to which they belong. And rational *global* parties
who *do not* know what state they belong to will likewise agree to a general
rule allowing humanitarian intervention in appropriate cases.[66] No rational
person will agree to a blanket sovereignty principle banning intervention
because they may end up trapped as victims of tyranny or anarchy.

What about the possible non-interventionist's claim that failure to intervene cannot be culpable? Even if correct, this would not be an argument
against humanitarian intervention, but only in favor of the *permissibility of
abstaining* from intervening. If the foregoing conclusions are correct, the
supporter of humanitarian intervention has met the objection that intervention is wrong because it is a positive act that results in the deaths of innocents. At the very least, the foreigner who abides by the doctrine of double
effect is not morally precluded from acting by the fact that his behavior may
result in the deaths of innocent persons. He is morally permitted to act.

But more importantly, it is difficult to maintain a coherent and intuitively
acceptable moral distinction between acts and omissions in many cases. The
foreigner who refrains from intervening to stop atrocities may be negligent
or culpable in some cases. Whatever the philosophical differences between

---

[64] "All social primary goods – liberty and opportunity, income and wealth, and the bases of self-
respect – are to be distributed equally unless an unequal distribution of any or all of these
goods is to the advantage of the least favored." John Rawls, *A Theory of Justice* (Belknap Press,
Cambridge, Mass., 1971), p. 303.
[65] See Fernando R. Tesón, "International Obligation and the Theory of Hypothetical Consent,"
15 *Yale Journal of International Law* (1990), 109–20.
[66] See Mark Wicclair, "Rawls and the Principle of Non-intervention," in H. G. Blocker and
E. H. Smith eds., *John Rawls' Theory of Social Justice* (Ohio University Press, Athens, 1980),
pp. 289–308, and the discussion in my *Humanitarian Intervention*, pp. 61–74.

acts and omissions, the agent who refuses to intervene is responsible for not having done things he could have done to stop the atrocities. Even if there is a valid distinction between act and omission, all that it proves is that the actor who refuses to intervene to stop atrocities is not as morally blameworthy as the perpetrator himself. But this fact does not exonerate this actor from the quite distinct charge of having failed to help others.

Consider the genocide committed in Srebrenica in July 1995. Bosnian Serb forces overran the Bosnian town before the eyes of 300 Dutch peacekeepers.[67] The Bosnian Serb forces captured between 7,000 and 8,000 defenseless men and boys and killed almost all of them.[68] The International Criminal Tribunal for the Former Yugoslavia properly decided that this was genocide, and sentenced the field commander, Radislav Krstic, to forty-six years in prison. This is considered one of the worst atrocities committed in any European conflict since World War II.[69] The shock we felt in the face of such evil has perhaps obscured another shocking fact. The area was supposed to be a protected United Nations enclave. However, General Bernard Janvier of France, the overall United Nations commander for Bosnia at the time, ignored repeated warnings by the peacekeepers and vetoed, until the very last minute, NATO air strikes requested by them.[70] He could have saved those 7,000 victims, but chose not to act. Now let us assume that General Janvier is an educated officer of the French Army. Very likely he took international law classes as part of his instruction. If so, very likely he was told that humanitarian intervention is prohibited by international law, by the same people who argue for that proposition today in France and elsewhere. We can say that he is guilty of omission, because he could have acted, and he had the necessary authority and ability to understand the gravity of the situation. To borrow a famous phrase used in Nuremberg, he was capable of moral choice. General Janvier's blameworthiness is not the same as Krstic's, of course, but he is still morally culpable.

Yet we must also blame, I believe, the moral poverty of the principle of non-intervention. Sometimes, those who believe in wrong ideas can

---

[67] See M. Simons, "Tribunal Finds Bosnian Serb Guilty of Genocide," *New York Times*, 3 August 2001.

[68] Ibid.

[69] There are many competitors for that title, however: the events in Bangladesh in 1971, in Cambodia in the mid-seventies, and in Rwanda in 1994 are serious contenders.

[70] Observers have unanimously decried this omission. George Will calls it "criminal incompetence," *Washington Post*, 9 August 2001; the *Los Angeles Times* referred to it as a blot on the West's record, a "sin of omission," 6 August 2001.

cause great harm when they implement them. It is not too farfetched to imagine that General Janvier was implementing his belief in the principle of non-intervention. If interventionists have to explain Somalia, non-interventionists have to explain Srebrenica.

The condemnation of war is part of the condemnation of political violence generally, and thus it should include the condemnation of internal atrocities. The moral issue is *not*: are we prepared to fight a war, with all the bad consequences we know all wars involve? The question is: should we act to stop the internal atrocities, knowing that there will be serious moral costs? Simply put, the non-interventionist has the burden of explaining why the killings that occur across borders are morally distinguishable from the killings that occur within them. As we saw, he has not met that burden.

The internal legitimacy of humanitarian intervention

There is a seldom-discussed yet centrally important aspect of humanitarian intervention: how can a liberal government justify humanitarian intervention *to its own citizens*?[71] Under some liberal justifications of the state, humanitarian intervention is problematic. For example, a liberal might claim that the state is justified as a mere instrument for solving certain inefficiencies that occur in the state of nature (such as those created by the private punishment of wrongs). The state, on this view, would be a mere tool for advancing its citizens' interest. This is what Allen Buchanan calls the "discretionary association" view of the state. Under this view, the government does not have authority to engage the collective resources of the state in a humanitarian intervention because it does not owe any duties to foreigners. The government would be violating its fiduciary duty. Buchanan, rightly in my view, rejects this position and argues for the existence of a natural duty to "contribute to the inclusion of all persons in just arrangements."[72] The discretionary association view endorses a world in which states act properly when they pay no attention to oppression elsewhere, as long as they discharge their fiduciary duty towards their own citizens (Buchanan calls this the "Swiss model"). Such a world is undesirable, so, Buchanan concludes, states should properly be seen also as instruments of justice, and

---

[71] To my knowledge, the only treatment of this issue is by Allen Buchanan, "The Internal Legitimacy of Humanitarian Intervention," 7 *Journal of Political Philosophy* (1999), 71.

[72] Ibid., p. 83.

can and should be used to promote human rights in other societies as long as this is done at a reasonable cost.

Buchanan's point is important because it removes a preliminary philosophical objection to cosmopolitan, pro-human rights, foreign policy. In order to assess the validity of humanitarian intervention, however, the argument needs to be supplemented by considerations related to the legitimacy of the use of *military* resources. Buchanan correctly shows that citizens and their governments have an obligation to *promote* human rights in a general way. For example, citizens must accept that their tax dollars may be used to contribute to the organizations of free elections in foreign countries, or to foreign aid given for democratic purposes, or to the financing of international human rights courts and other liberal international institutions. They can accept – indeed demand – that their government adopt pro-human rights positions in international organizations. But this is consistent with the citizens' opposition to the government using *force* for humanitarian purposes. A state that promotes human rights generally yet refuses to use military force to stop atrocities departs from the Swiss model. Yet the issue of whether or not it is permissible or mandatory for a liberal government to send military forces to end anarchy or tyranny abroad remains intact.

To see this clearly, consider libertarian arguments against humanitarian intervention.[73] According to them, governments do not have the right to compel citizens to fight for the freedom of foreigners. This argument differs, on the one hand, from the one given by international lawyers and some realists,[74] and, on the other, from Buchanan's argument. Unlike lawyers and some realists, libertarians do not believe in the principle of sovereignty and despise tyranny much as liberal interventionists do. For libertarians (as for liberal interventionists), despotic regimes lack legitimacy and are thus not protected by any sovereignty principle. However, libertarians believe that a government cannot legitimately force *its own* citizens to fight for someone else's freedom. This argument has a strong and a weak version. The strong version is that the government can *never* coerce people into

---

[73] See, for example, T. G. Carpenter, "Setting a Dangerous Precedent in Somalia," 20 *Cato Foreign Policy Briefing*, 18 December 1992. Available at www.cato.org (5 March 2002).

[74] I am thinking of realists like Hedley Bull, for whom the principle of non-intervention is crucial to the preservation of the state system. See H. Bull, *The Anarchical Society: A Study of Order in World Politics* (Macmillan, London, 1977). As Buchanan rightly points out, some realists oppose humanitarian intervention with an argument similar to the "discretionary association view," that is, that the government owes duties only to its citizens. See Buchanan, "Internal Legitimacy," pp. 77–79.

fighting wars, even wars in the defense of the person's own society. Persons retain an absolute control over their choices to use violence in self-defense. For libertarians, aggressive force is morally banned, and one legitimate function of the state is to control aggressive violence. But the use of force to repel aggression (defensive force) is not banned: it is morally permitted. If the use of force is morally permitted, not obligatory, then the victim of an attack retains the power to decide whether he will fight for his life, property, or freedom. Others (the government especially) cannot make those choices for him, and especially cannot coerce him into combat. If this is true with respect to force used in one's own defense, it is true *a fortiori* of coercion for the purpose of forcing someone to fight in defense of her fellow citizens, and even more *a fortiori* of coercion to force someone to defend foreigners. In short: the strong libertarian argument contends that a state is worth defending only if citizens rise spontaneously against the aggressor. Those who choose not to fight are within their rights and should be left alone.

The weak version of the libertarian argument holds that coercion to force people to fight in defense of their own state, their fellow citizens (self-defense), is justified, but coercion to force people to fight in defense of the freedom of foreigners is not. This weaker version may rely on the public goods argument. National defense is a public good. If people are allowed to choose individually whether they should contribute to repelling an aggression they will be tempted to free ride on the defense efforts of others. There is market failure with respect to national defense: everyone wants to repel the aggressor, but they hope others will risk their lives to do so. Because everyone reasons in the same way, the public good (defense) is under-produced and the state succumbs to the aggressor. This version of the libertarian argument, then, accepts the government's role in defending the state. It rejects, however, the legitimacy of humanitarian intervention, perhaps because it does not regard foreigners as participants in a coop-erative enterprise (as fellow citizens would be) and thus the public goods problem does not even arise. And the government in a libertarian state surely does not have a mandate to protect the rights of persons other than its own citizens. Both versions of the libertarian critique of humanitarian intervention are consistent with accepting Buchanan's view: libertarians may consistently concede that the government has a prima facie obligation peacefully to promote universal human rights as part of their natural duty of justice, yet claim that the government may not force people *to fight* in order to save foreigners from tyranny.

Libertarians rightly draw our attention to the exaggerated claims that government makes on our freedoms and resources. It is easy for someone who thinks that "something must be done" about, say, the victims in Kosovo, to send *others* to risk their lives to do it. Because of that, libertarians have given a powerful cautionary warning against conscription for fighting foreign wars. What was wrong with Vietnam, on that view, is not that it was an unjust war (an uncertain assertion, perhaps) but that the government was forcing unwilling persons to fight for the freedoms of others. This is an important question of political philosophy: what is the proper role of a liberal government with respect to military efforts? Under what conditions can a liberal government force citizens to fight? The answers to these questions are independent of the answer to the question of the place of sovereignty as a bar to intervention. The questions, however, should be addressed as important questions of democratic theory, and they have a direct bearing on humanitarian intervention. If libertarians are right, humanitarian intervention is wrong, not because dictators are or should be protected by international law, but because governments cannot validly force people to fight in foreign wars.

A possible reply to the libertarian argument is that the duty to assist victims of injustice in other societies raises (as self-defense does) problems of collective action.[75] Just as a government can give a public goods argument to justify coercing its citizens into fighting for national defense, so could a government conceivably give a public goods argument to justify coercing its own citizens to fight for the freedom of foreigners. The argument would go as follows. Humanitarian intervention is risky, so individuals in a liberal society who think it is right to intervene in a neighboring country to end tyranny or anarchy might nonetheless expect that others will make the effort. They free ride on the courage of others. And if enough people think this way, the public good (rescuing foreigners from tyranny or anarchy) is under-produced. Assuming the existence of a natural duty to justice, the power of the government to draft soldiers for humanitarian intervention is necessary in order to block opportunistic moves *ex post*.[76]

I think that the public goods argument justifies humanitarian intervention with the important qualification that the government must send

---

[75] Robert O. Keohane suggested this possibility.

[76] Of course, such a view is only mildly libertarian. The more extreme libertarian either denies that a natural duty to justice is a genuine public good, or denies outright the legitimacy of the state's provision of public goods. I thank Jeff Holzgrefe for drawing my attention to this point.

voluntary soldiers before resorting to conscription. This is because the public goods argument depends on the assumption that the good in question is demanded by a sufficient number of people. Because the demand for national defense is likely to be strong, conscription is needed to eliminate free riders. But, while humanitarian intervention is also a public good in the sense that it allows for opportunistic moves *ex post* (people who would agree *ex ante* to intervene will refuse to fight once the veil of ignorance is lifted), it is not certain that demand for humanitarian intervention will be as strong as demand for national defense. There will be genuine objectors who are not, by definition, opportunistic agents. Therefore, a liberal argument must balance respect for these genuine dissenters with the need to implement the natural duty of justice. In other words, the duty that liberal governments have to promote global human rights is not absolute: it must cohere with other important moral–political considerations, such as the need to respect non-opportunistic exercises of individual autonomy. A way to do this is to resort to voluntary armed forces.

The libertarian cannot oppose the use of a voluntary army. Voluntary soldiers have validly consented to fight in cases where the legitimate government believes there is (a morally) sufficient reason (apart from consent) to fight. The libertarian would have to say that the government is misreading the contract: perhaps the contract contains an implicit clause under which the person inducted into the armed forces only consented to fight in self-defense. I doubt those contracts can reasonably be construed that way.[77] Rather, the draftee has plausibly delegated to the government the right to choose for him whether a war is worth fighting.

Some people might object to this view, saying that consent is tainted, that draftees come from the poorer segments of society and cannot foresee the multifarious ways in which they can be used and manipulated by the powerful party, the government. But whatever the merits of this view, it cannot be held by a libertarian, who insists that revealed consent be honored even if the terms of the contract are otherwise objectionable. The unconscionability objection may be available to someone who objects to humanitarian intervention for other reasons, but not to the libertarian. I am skeptical about the merits of the unconscionability argument anyway, for a number of reasons. First, if one is going to uphold the validity of draft contracts

---

[77] For a typical enlistment contract, see http://www.usmilitary.about.com/pdf/enlistment.pdf (5 March 2002), especially Section 5(b).

one cannot plausibly read into them an implicit clause that devolves on the draftee the power to pick and choose among the wars he wants to fight. This would of course frustrate the very idea of voluntary draft, because the temptation not to fight when the occasion arises is too strong. But more important, I believe that the draftee can reasonably expect that he will be sent to fight for worthy causes, and whether or not a humanitarian intervention is a worthy cause is an open question to be decided on its merits, not on the dubious grounds that the draftee could not plausibly foresee that such occasion (the need to save foreigners from tyranny or anarchy) could arise. Another way of putting this is that the notion of unconscionability is parasitic on the merits of the intended enforcement of the contract. To say that forcing an enlisted member of the armed forces to fight to save Kosovars from genocide is unconscionable is to *decide* that it is outrageous, that the cause does not warrant fighting. But this is surely an independent question to be decided on its merits.

The doctrine of humanitarian intervention simply holds that sometimes such wars are justified. It seems natural to say that enlisted persons have agreed to let the government decide when those wars are justified.

I conclude this section by rejecting the libertarian position insofar as it overlooks the public good argument for humanitarian intervention. I accept, however, an amendment inspired by the libertarian insight: when a government decides to intervene for humanitarian reasons, it must use the standing armed forces first, then call for volunteers, and only as a last resort enact a general draft.

Concluding comment

Non-interventionism is a doctrine of the past. It feeds on illiberal intellectual traditions (relativism, communitarianism, nationalism, and statism) that are objectionable for various reasons and that, where implemented, have caused grievous harm to persons. Neither the assumptions nor the consequences of non-interventionism are defensible from a liberal standpoint. The very structure of the non-interventionist argument belies the spurious pedigree of the doctrine. We are supposed to outlaw humanitarian intervention because that is what most governments say we should do. But, of course, those who wield or seek power over their fellow citizens (incumbent governments and would-be rulers) have an obvious incentive to support non-intervention. We know that governments (even the better

ones) will think about international law and institutions with their priorities in mind, that is, presupposing and affirming state values. But we like
to think that we are not victims of such a perverse structure of incentives.
We have the choice to think about international law and institutions with
human values in mind. Non-interventionists deceptively present their doctrine as one that protects communal values and self-government, yet even
a cursory look at history unmasks non-intervention as the one doctrine
whose origin, design, and effect is to protect established political power
and render persons defenseless against the worst forms of human evil. The
principle of non-intervention denies victims of tyranny and anarchy the
possibility of appealing to people other than their tormentors. It condemns
them to fight unaided or die. Rescuing others will always be onerous, but
if we deny the moral duty and legal right to do so, we deny not only the
centrality of justice in political affairs, but also the common humanity that
binds us all.

4

Reforming the international law of humanitarian intervention

ALLEN BUCHANAN

The need for reform

The deficiency of existing law

The NATO intervention in Kosovo (1999) is only the most recent of a series of illegal interventions for which plausible moral justifications can be given. Others include India's intervention in East Pakistan in response to Pakistan's massive human rights violations there (1971), Vietnam's war against Pol Pot's genocidal regime in Cambodia (1978), and Tanzania's overthrow of Idi Amin's murderous rule in Uganda (1979). Without commenting on what the dominant motives of the intervenors were, it is accurate to say that in each case military action was aimed at preventing or stopping massive human rights violations. All could qualify as instances of humanitarian intervention, which may be defined as follows: humanitarian intervention is the threat or use of force across state borders by a state (or group of states) aimed at preventing or ending widespread and grave violations of the fundamental human rights of individuals other than its own citizens, without the permission of the state within whose territory force is applied.

In all three instances in the 1970s the intervention was, according to the preponderance of international legal opinion, a violation of international law. None was a case of self-defense and none enjoyed UN Security Council authorization.

There is, however, an important difference in the case of the NATO intervention. Unlike the previous interventions, the NATO intervention in

Material from Allen Buchanan, "From Nuremberg to Kosovo: The Morality of Illegal International Legal Reform" appears with permission of the editors of *Ethics* and the University of Chicago Press.

Kosovo and the ensuing debate over its justifiability have focused attention on the deficiency of existing international law concerning humanitarian intervention. In the aftermath of Kosovo, there seems to be a widening consensus that there is an unacceptable gap between what international law allows and what morality requires.

However, this way of stating the deficiency is incomplete. As Kofi Annan emphasized, the impossibility of gaining Security Council authorization for the intervention indicated a disturbing tension between two core values of the international legal system itself: respect for state sovereignty and a commitment to peaceful relations among states, on the one hand, and the protection of basic human rights, on the other.[1] The point is not simply that the intervention, though illegal, was morally justifiable; in addition, it was consonant with one of the most important values of the UN and of the entire system of international law on its most progressive interpretation.[2]

More precisely, the perception is growing that the requirement of Security Council authorization is an obstacle to the protection of basic human rights in internal conflicts. Since the majority of violent conflicts are now within states rather than between them, the time is ripe to consider changing or abandoning a rule of humanitarian intervention that was created for a quite different world.

Three different justifications for illegal interventions

Many who acknowledge the illegality of the humanitarian interventions listed above nevertheless commend them. Plainly, the strongest justification for intervening despite the illegality of doing so is that intervention was morally permissible – or even morally obligatory. The moral principle to which such justification appeals is among the most fundamental: the need to protect basic human rights.

Often the question of the moral justifiability of illegal humanitarian interventions is framed as a simple choice as to which should take priority: fidelity to law or basic moral values. Thus NATO leaders and US State Department officials asserted that the situation in Kosovo was a dire moral

---

[1] Kofi Annan, "Speech to the General Assembly," SG/SM/7136 GA/9569: Secretary-G, 20 September 1999, p. 2.

[2] The charge that the intervention was illegal is based on the most straightforward interpretations of the UN Charter, Articles 2(4) and 2(7). For a full account of the illegality of the NATO intervention, see J. L. Holzgrefe, "The Humanitarian Intervention Debate," ch. 1 in this volume.

emergency that justified acting without Security Council authorization. Let us call this the Simple Moral Necessity Justification, according to which basic moral values can trump the obligation to obey the law.

As I have already suggested, there is a second, more subtle moral justification that was suggested from time to time by the remarks of some public figures during the Kosovo crisis: the intervention was justified (though illegal) because it was necessary if a humanitarian disaster was to be averted *and* was supported by a core value of the international legal system itself. What this second justification adds to the first one is the idea that an act can be *lawful*, though illegal.[3] Unlike the Simple Moral Necessity Justification the Lawfulness Justification clearly expresses a commitment to values embodied in the legal system – not just those of morality – in this case the protection of international legal human rights.

According to a third line of justification NATO's illegal humanitarian intervention was undertaken not only to respond to a dire moral emergency but also with the aim of contributing to the development of a new, morally progressive rule of international law according to which humanitarian intervention without Security Council authorization is sometimes permissible. Let us call this the Illegal Legal Reform Justification. The idea is that existing international law was violated to initiate a moral improvement in the international legal system. In the case of the Kosovo intervention, the needed reform was to make the international legal system do a better job of serving one of its own core values, the protection of human rights.

The Simple Moral Necessity Justification presents the illegal action as morally necessary, without in any way implying that the international legal system as a whole, or even the particular rule that is violated, is in need of improvement. Employing this first justification for illegal humanitarian intervention is fully consistent with believing that the existing rule requiring Security Council authorization is a good rule, even that it is the best rule possible. But the Simple Moral Necessity argument in itself is also neutral as to the value of the rule of law. It might consistently be advanced by someone who rejected the entire enterprise of international law.

The Lawfulness and the Illegal Legal Reform Justifications differ in that regard. They both express a commitment to the rule of law. The Lawfulness Justification is based on the assumption that the fact that the values served

---

[3] This use of the term "lawful" is borrowed from Jane Stromseth: see her "Rethinking Humanitarian Intervention: The Case for Incremental Change," ch. 7 in this volume.

by the intervention are core values of the legal system matters, normatively speaking, adding weight to the justification of moral necessity. The Illegal Legal Reform Justification validates the illegal intervention as an act directed towards reforming the legal system.

There is a difference between the Lawfulness and Illegal Legal Reform Justifications, however: the latter, but not the former, implies that the existing rule requiring Security Council authorization is not optimal, and that a new norm of humanitarian intervention, according to which Security Council authorization is not always needed, is morally preferable. The Lawfulness Justification, in contrast, is compatible with the view that even though it is necessary in exceptional cases to break a particular law in the name of a core value embodied in the system, attempts to change the law would make things even worse.

My focus in this chapter is on the third type of justification, the justification of illegal acts of humanitarian intervention by appeal to the goal of legal reform. However, much of what I say will also be applicable to the Lawfulness Justification as well.

Although I believe that *illegal* acts directed towards reform may bear a special burden of justification, at least for those who profess to value the rule of law, I will argue that in some cases that burden can be met. My more general interest, however, is in the morality of attempts to reform the international law of humanitarian intervention, whether they involve illegality or not.

Although the Kosovo intervention has stimulated consideration of the need for reform, there has been both a lack of clarity regarding the full range of options for how that reform might come about and an almost total neglect of the question of which paths towards reform are morally preferable. My aim in this chapter is to remedy both these deficiencies. What follows is offered as a contribution to that part of the moral theory of international law that addresses the morality of legal reform.

Why illegal action may be necessary for international legal reform

The sources of international law

The prospect that illegal acts may be necessary in order to achieve significant improvements in the international legal system arises because of the difficulty of achieving reform through purely legal means. The ways in which international law can be made significantly limit the options for achieving meaningful reform through legal means alone.

There are two chief sources of international law: treaty and custom. If the target of moral improvement is the development of a norm prohibiting some form of behavior engaged in by more than a few states or the creation of a new norm that allows behavior that previously would have been a violation of the rights of sovereignty that all states enjoy, reform by treaty may be a very slow process if it occurs at all.

Suppose that the goal of reform is to establish a rule of international law that not only requires states to "promote" human rights within their own borders and to supply periodic reports on their progress in doing so to some international body (as the major human rights covenants stipulate), but that also obligates, or at least permits, the signatories to intervene to halt massive violations of human rights that occur in domestic conflicts in other states when less intrusive means have failed. Many states will refuse to sign such a treaty. Others may sign but postpone ratification indefinitely. Some may sign and ratify, but weaken the force of the treaty by stating "reservations" regarding some clauses (thereby exempting themselves from their require-ments) or by stating "understandings" which interpret burdensome clauses in ways that make them less inimical to state interests.

As an avenue for moral improvements that are both significant and timely, the process by which international *customary* law is formed is per-haps somewhat more promising, but still very difficult and uncertain. In briefest terms, a new norm of customary law is created as the result of the emergence of a persistent pattern of behavior by states, accompanied by the belief on the part of state actors that the behavior in question is legally required or legally permissible (the *opinio juris* requirement).

There are several aspects of this process that substantially limit the efficacy of the customary route towards system improvement. First, international law allows states to opt out of the new customary norm's scope by consis-tently dissenting from it. Second, how widespread the new pattern of state behavior must be before a new norm can be said to have "crystallized" is not only disputed but probably not capable of a definitive answer. Third, even if a sufficiently widespread and persisting pattern of behavior is established, the satisfaction of the *opinio juris* requirement may be less clear and more subject to dispute. Pronouncements by state leaders may be ambiguous or mixed, in some cases indicating a recognition that the behavior in question is legally required or permissible, in other cases appearing to deny this.

Given these limitations, the efforts of the state or states that first attempt to initiate the process of customary change are fraught with uncertainty. If the new norm they seek to establish addresses a long-standing and widespread pattern of state behavior, and one in which many states profess to be legally entitled to persist, other states may not follow suit. Or, if other states follow suit, they may do so for strictly pragmatic reasons and may attempt to ensure that a new customary rule does not emerge by officially registering that they do not regard their behavior as legally required (thus thwarting satisfaction of the *opinio juris* condition).

The point is that new customary norms do not emerge from a single action or even from a persistent pattern of action by one state or a group of states. Thus the initial effort to create a new customary norm is a gamble. A new norm is created only when the initial behavior is repeated consistently by a preponderance of states over a considerable period of time and only when there is a shift in the legal consciousness of all or most states as to the juridical status of the behavior. At any point the process can break down. For example, if one powerful state dissents from an emerging norm, other states may decide it is prudent to register dissent as well or to refrain from pronouncements that would otherwise count towards satisfying the *opinio juris* requirement. For all these reasons, significant and timely reform through the creation of new customary norms of international law is difficult and uncertain.

In fact it appears that significant change through the development of new customary law will usually, if not always, require illegality. For example, the first acts designed to help create a new norm that limits sovereignty in the name of protecting human rights or redressing inequities in the distribution of wealth between developed and less developed countries will violate the existing rules that define sovereignty. Some would go further, arguing that customary legal change always involves illegality in the early stages of the process. At the very least it appears that significant and expeditious customary law reform without illegality is unlikely.

It has long been recognized that reliance on change through the establishment of new custom is a formidable obstacle to fundamental social change. All of the great proponents of the modern state – the state with legislative sovereignty – from Bodin and Hobbes to Rousseau recognized the severe constraints that adherence to the evolution of customary law imposed on the possibilities for reform. They argued that only the power to issue and enforce rules that can overturn even the most deeply entrenched customary norms in domestic society would suffice; thus their insistence on legislative sovereignty.

But in the international system there is nothing approaching a universal legislature.[4] To summarize: heavy reliance on customary law, absence of a sovereign universal legislature, and the obvious limitations of the treaty process together result in a system in which reform without illegality is more difficult than in domestic systems.[5]

Progress through illegality: historical cases

Indeed, it can be argued that some of the more fundamental moral improvements in the international legal system have resulted, at least in part, from illegal acts. Consider one of the great landmarks of reform: the outlawing of genocide. To a large extent this was an achievement of the Nuremberg War Crimes Tribunal (though at the time the term "genocide" was not part of the legal lexicon). However, a strong case has been made by a number of respected commentators that the "Victor's Justice" at Nuremberg was illegal under existing international law. In particular, it has been argued that there was no customary norm or treaty prohibiting what the Tribunal called "crimes against humanity" at the time World War II occurred. But quite apart from this, it has been argued that even if (contrary to what some commentators say) aggressive war was already prohibited at the time World War II began, there was no international law authorizing the criminal prosecution of individuals for waging or conspiring to wage aggressive war.

There is no denying that the Nuremberg Tribunal contributed to some of the changes in international law that we regard as epitomes of progress – not just the prohibitions of genocide and aggressive war but also the recognition of the rights of human subjects of medical experimentation.[6]

---

[4] The UN Charter can be amended but the prospects for amendment that would result in a rule of humanitarian intervention not requiring Security Council authorization are poor because ratification of an amendment requires a two-thirds majority vote in the Security Council which must include all the permanent members.

[5] The foregoing picture of international law's limited resources for lawful moral reform is, of course, a sketch in broad strokes. There are more subtle modes by which international law can be changed. For example, judicial bodies (such as the International Court of Justice) or quasi-judicial bodies (such as the UN Human Rights Committee) can achieve reforms under the guise of interpreting existing law. However, as a broad generalization it is fair to say that these modes for effecting moral improvements are both limited and slow.

[6] The Nuremberg Code, which prohibits experimentation on human subjects without consent, was drafted as a direct result of the prosecution of the Nazi doctors for their inhumane experiments on unwilling human subjects. See German Territory under Allied Occupation, 1945–55:

Nevertheless, it can be argued that some of the punishments meted out at Nuremberg were illegal.

One could also make the case that a series of illegal actions over several decades played a significant role in one of the other most admirable improvements in the international legal system: the prohibition of slavery. In the late eighteenth and early nineteenth centuries Britain used the unrivaled power of its navy to attack the transatlantic slave trade.[7] Britain's overall strategy included legal means, in particular the forging of a series of bilateral treaties; but it also undertook illegal searches and seizures of ships flying under the flags of states that had not entered into these treaties, as well as attempts to get other countries to enforce their own laws against commerce in human beings. It is probable that what success Britain had in persuading other states to cooperate in efforts to destroy the slave trade was due in part to its willingness to use illegal force. The destruction of the slave trade was a milestone in the development of a growing human rights movement that eventually issued in the international legal prohibition of slavery, but which also expanded to include other human rights.

Once the role of such illegal acts is acknowledged, it is unwarranted to assume that continued progress will be achieved with reasonable speed and without illegality. On the contrary, given the system's limited resources for change by legal means – and the fact that it is still a state-dominated system in which many of the most serious defects calling for reform lie in the behavior of states – the question of the morality of illegal legal reform is inescapable. Yet discussions of the morality of illegal humanitarian intervention have generally failed to distinguish between justifications that appeal to the goal of legal reform and those that appeal either only to the necessity of doing what is morally right (the Simple Moral Necessity Justification) or to the idea that what is morally right is also supported by values embodied in the existing legal system (the Lawfulness Justification).

US Zone, Control Council Law No. 10, *Trials of War Criminals before the Nuremberg Military Tribunals* (US Government Printing Office, Washington, DC, 1949), vol. II, pp. 181–82; William J. Bosch, *Judgment on Nuremburg: American Attitudes toward the Major German War-crimes Trials* (University of North Carolina Press, Chapel Hill, 1970).

[7] Alfred P. Rubin, *Ethics and Authority in International Law* (Cambridge University Press, Cambridge, 1997), pp. 97–130; Reginald Coupland, *The British Anti-slavery Movement* (Oxford University Press, London, 1993), pp. 151–88. Note that in adducing this example, I am not assuming that the motives of the British Government were pure, only that a justification for the forcible disruption of the transatlantic slave trade that could have been given was that these illegal actions would contribute towards a moral improvement in the international legal system. Whether those who instigated the policy of disrupting the transatlantic slave trade were motivated by humanitarian concerns or not is irrelevant.

The main alternatives for reforming the law of humanitarian intervention

New treaty law – within or outside the UN system?

Attempts to create a new international legal rule allowing humanitarian intervention without Security Council authorization through treaty might take either of two very different forms. The first, which has been suggested by the Independent International Commission on Kosovo, is to work for reform through treaty *within* the UN system. This might be accomplished by a General Assembly Resolution specifying a new rule of intervention combined with amendments to the UN Charter (Articles 2(4) and 2(7)) to make the latter consistent with the former.[8] This route towards reform has two attractions: it would require no illegalities and it would be a broadly democratic or majoritarian reform, issuing from a broad base of support in the international community.

However, for the foreseeable future this strategy is extremely unlikely to be realized. Given how jealous states tend to be about infringements on their sovereignty and given how many states wish to have a free hand to oppress dissenting groups within their borders, it is doubtful that the majority of the members of the UN would vote for such a resolution. Even if the needed two-thirds majority in the General Assembly were mustered, a two-thirds majority of the Security Council that includes all the permanent members is also required for amendment. The same veto power on the part of the permanent members that results in a failure to authorize humanitarian interventions would most probably block such a constitutional change.

If reform through treaty within the UN system is unworkable, proponents of reform should consider the possibility of a treaty-based approach that simply bypasses the UN system.[9] The most likely and morally defensible version of this alternative would be a coalition of liberal–democratic states, bound together by a treaty that would specify some well-crafted criteria that must be satisfied for intervention to be permissible in the absence of Security Council authorization. The constraining criteria would presumably include familiar elements of just war theory, such as proportional force and protection of noncombatants, but might also make a limited concession

---

[8] Independent International Commission on Kosovo, *Kosovo Report* (Oxford University Press, Oxford, 2000).

[9] I am indebted to Jeff Holzgrefe for impressing upon me the importance of taking this strategy seriously.

towards the UN system by requiring General Assembly or Security Council resolutions condemning the human rights violations that provoke the need for intervention. This strategy for reform might be undertaken either as a result of coming to the conclusion that the UN system is unworkable or in an attempt to spur reform in the UN. In either case, it would involve illegality, since the actions to be undertaken by the liberal–democratic coalition would violate existing UN-based law on humanitarian intervention. The hope would be that what was first an intervention treaty among a small number of states would eventually gain wider participation.

The phrase "UN-based law" is chosen deliberately. Proponents of reform through the creation of a liberal–democratic coalition for humanitarian intervention would stress that the UN is not identical with international law. Rather, it is only one, historically contingent, institutional embodiment of the idea of an international legal system. International law existed before the UN and may exist after the UN's demise. A probing investigation of the possibilities for reforming international law concerning humanitarian intervention should evaluate, not simply grant, the assumption that reform must be achieved within the framework of the UN system. This is especially true given the rather dim prospects for reform-through-treaty within the UN framework.

One cannot assume without argument that the only alternative for responsible reform efforts is to work within the UN system because only in this way can reform be legitimate. First, the legitimacy of the UN system itself is open to dispute, chiefly because it rests on state consent under conditions in which many, perhaps most, states are not sufficiently democratic to be able to claim to represent their citizens. Unless states represent their citizens, it is something of a mystery as to why one should think that state consent in itself (read: the consent of undemocratic state leaders) should carry so much normative weight as to be the sole source of legitimacy, especially in a system that is as deficient from the standpoint of substantive justice as the existing international legal system. Second, it should not be assumed that legitimacy is an absolute value. In the case of extremely imperfect legal systems, the need for substantive reform – at least when this involves strengthening protection for basic human rights – could sometimes trump legitimacy. In the next section, I will explore these deeper issues of legitimacy and justice in more detail. Here I only want to indicate that it is a mistake simply to dismiss out of hand the possibility that treaty-based reform might be undertaken in a way that bypasses the UN system.

Reform through the creation of a new customary rule of humanitarian intervention

Some who recognize the need to reform the law of humanitarian intervention, including Jane Stromseth, advocate a gradualist, case-by-case process that will eventually result in a new rule of customary international law that would not require Security Council authorization in all cases.[10] Those who hold this view see the NATO intervention as an important step in the process and also intimate that this adds weight to its justification.

As the NATO intervention illustrates, the reform-through-new-custom approach, like the attempt to create the possibility of intervention without Security Council authorization through treaty that bypasses the UN system, will almost certainly involve illegality. At least the initial state actions that contribute towards the creation of a new customary rule that allows intervention without Security Council authorization will violate Articles 2(4) and 2(7) of the Charter.

In the remainder of this chapter I will focus mainly on reform through the creation of new custom, for three reasons. First, the NATO intervention did not involve any attempt to create a new treaty-based right of humanitarian intervention. Instead, it is best viewed, if we attempt to understand it as an act directed towards legal reform, as a step in the process of creating a new customary norm. Second, if forced to make a prediction, I would speculate that at present reform through the emergence of new customary law is more likely than reform through treaty outside the UN. For these reasons I will turn shortly to an examination of the morality of efforts at reform through the creation of new customary law concerning humanitarian intervention, focusing on the NATO intervention in Kosovo for concreteness.

It might be argued that there is one final reason to concentrate on reform through the creation of new custom. At least at first blush, it appears that the customary law route to reform enjoys a comparative advantage from the standpoint of legitimacy over the option of creating new treaty law outside the UN system: state action only creates a new rule of customary international law if a preponderance of states come to regard that type of action as legal. In other words, the *opinio juris* requirement does something to ensure that new customary law enjoys the support of states other than those actually engaging in the intervention, and surely this contributes to

---

[10] See Jane Stromseth, ch. 7 in this volume.

the legitimacy of an intervention, helping to counterbalance the stigma of illegality. Later I will challenge this assertion, arguing that under current conditions, when so many states are flawed by basic injustices and are so undemocratic that they cannot be viewed as representing their peoples, support by a majority of states does little to assure legitimacy.

Legal absolutism: the blanket condemnation of illegal acts

Two objections to conscientious law-breaking

Some prominent legal scholars, including J. S. Watson and Alfred Rubin, roundly condemn illegal acts done in the name of morality, including those done for the sake of morally improving the international legal system.[11] Unfortunately, such critics tend to assume rather than argue convincingly that illegalities in the name of system reform are not morally justified.

It appears that the condemnation of illegal acts of reform stems from two complaints: one is that those who commit them fail to show proper fidelity to law; the other is that they are guilty of moral hubris or moral imperialism, being too willing to impose their own views of what is right on others.[12] It will prove helpful, therefore, to distinguish two distinct questions: (1) what is the moral basis of the commitment to bringing international relations under the rule of law? And (2) under what conditions, if any, can an agent's judgments about what justice requires count as good reasons for attempting to impose rules on others? In order to answer the first question, we need an account of *fidelity to law* that enables us to determine how a would-be reformer should weigh the fact that his proposed action is illegal. In order to answer the second question, we need an account of *moral authority* (what Rawls calls legitimacy) that enables us to determine if the would-be reformer is justified in imposing on others a norm to which they have not consented and which they might reject. My strategy will be to construct and evaluate arguments that can be employed to articulate these two complaints.

---

[11] Rubin, *Ethics and Authority*, esp. pp. 70–206; J. S. Watson, "A Realistic Jurisprudence of International Law," in *The Yearbook of World Affairs* (London Institute of World Affairs, London, 1980).

[12] My account of the bases of the complaint of those who condemn illegal acts of reform is somewhat reconstructive.

The simple fidelity to law argument

Consider first an argument to show that illegal acts of reform are not justifiable because they betray a failure to show a proper fidelity to the law.

1. One ought to be committed to the rule of law in international relations.
2. If one is committed to the rule of law in international relations, then one cannot consistently advocate (what one recognizes to be) illegal acts as a means of morally improving the system of international law.
3. Therefore, one ought not to advocate illegal acts as a means of morally improving the system of international law.

The first step is to clarify the phrase "the rule of law" in the argument in order to understand just why honoring the commitment to the rule of law is important. There are in fact two quite different ways in which critics of illegal reform may be understanding "the rule of law" in the Fidelity Argument. According to the first, "the rule of law" refers to a normatively rich ideal for systems of rules. According to the second, "the rule of law" means something that may be much less normatively demanding, namely, a system of rules capable of preventing a Hobbesian condition of violent chaos. Let us see how the Fidelity Argument reads under these two interpretations.

Fidelity to the ideal of the rule of law

According to the first interpretation, the rule of law is an ideal composed of several elements: laws are to be general, public, not subject to frequent or arbitrary changes, and their requirements must be reasonably clear and such that human beings of normal capacities are able to comply with them.[13] These requirements help ensure that a system of law provides a stable framework of expectations, so that individuals can plan their projects with some confidence and coordinate their behavior with that of others.

There is another element of the rule of law as a normative ideal which on some accounts is of special importance: the requirement of equality before the law. The precise import of this requirement is, of course, subject to much dispute, but the core idea is that the law is to be applied and enforced impartially.

---

[13] Lon L. Fuller, *The Morality of Law* (Yale University Press, New Haven, Conn., 1964), pp. 33–39.

If we read "the rule of law" in the Fidelity Argument as referring to this normatively demanding ideal, as including the requirement of equality before the law, then the argument is subject to a serious and obvious objection. The difficulty is that the international legal system falls short of the requirement of equality before the law. The most powerful states (such as China, the United States, and the Russian Federation) not only play an arbitrarily disproportionate role in the processes by which international law is made and applied but also are often able to violate the law with impunity.

According to the first interpretation of the Fidelity Argument, it is our moral allegiance to the rule of law as a normative ideal that is supposed to be inconsistent with advocating or committing what we believe to be illegal acts even if they are directed towards reforming the system. But to the extent that the existing system falls far short of the ideal of the rule of law in one of its most fundamental elements, the requirement of equality before the law, allegiance to the ideal exerts less moral pull towards strict fidelity to the rules of the existing system. Indeed, allegiance to the rule of law as an ideal might be thought to make illegal acts *morally obligatory* in a system that does a very poor job of approximating the requirements of the ideal. More specifically, a sincere commitment to the rule of law might be a powerful reason for committing illegal acts directed towards bringing the system closer to fulfillment of the requirement of equality before the law, if there is no lawful way to achieve this reform.[14]

The point is that one cannot move directly from the commitment to the rule of law as an ideal to strict fidelity to existing law. Whether a commitment to the rule of law as an ideal precludes illegal reform actions will depend in part upon the extent to which the existing system approximates the ideal.

Notice also that the critics' second complaint has little force against illegal acts of reform directed towards making the system better satisfy the requirements of the ideal of the rule of law, especially that of equality before

---

[14] The problem of achieving greater equality among states is a complex one. One cannot assume that the best or only way to achieve greater equality is by greater democratic participation in the making and application of international law. One alternative would be a system of constitutional checks on actions of more powerful states. For example, international norms specifying when humanitarian intervention is justified might be crafted to reduce the risk that powerful states would abuse them, in two ways: by requiring very high thresholds of human rights abuses before intervention was permitted, and by requiring international monitoring of the process of intervention to facilitate *ex post* evaluation of whether the requirement of proportionality was met, etc. I am indebted to T. Alexander Aleinikoff and David Luban for emphasizing this point (personal communication).

the law. To say that the core accepted elements of the rule of law are merely the personal moral views of the reformers, and that it would therefore be illegitimate to impose them on others, would be extremely inaccurate. Not only are they widely accepted, but unless they are assumed to be highly desirable it is hard to make sense of the idea of fidelity to the law as a moral ideal. In the next subsection we will see that the illegitimacy issue – the question of when an agent is morally justified in imposing moral standards on those who do not accept them – has more bite when the moral principles motivating illegal acts of reform are more controversial.

Substantive justice

There is another reason why a simple appeal to the ideal of the rule of law cannot show that illegal reform acts are not morally justifiable: the extent to which a system of rules exemplifies substantive principles of justice affects the strength of the pull towards compliance. Approximation of the ideal of the rule of law is a necessary, not a sufficient, condition for our being obligated to comply with legal norms, even if a deep commitment to the ideal of the rule of law is assumed. A system might do a reasonably good job of exemplifying the elements of the rule of law and still be seriously defective from the standpoint of substantive principles of justice. For example, the system might be compatible with, or even promote, unjust economic inequalities, depending upon the content of the laws of property and the extent to which the current distribution of wealth is the result of past injustices. Similarly, the elements of the ideal might be satisfied, or at least closely approximated, in a system that failed to meet even the most minimal standards of democratic participation. The elements of the rule of law prevent certain kinds of injustices and help ensure the stability and predictability that rational agents need, but they do not capture the whole of justice. And if justice is to enjoy the kind of moral priority that is widely thought to be essential to the very notion of justice, then one cannot assume that illegal acts directed towards eliminating grave injustice in the system are always ruled out by fidelity to the ideal of the rule of law. Since many, indeed perhaps most, extant theories of justice include more than the requirements of the rule of law, it would be very misleading to assume that any illegal action for the sake of reforming the international legal system by making it more just must be the imposition of the reformer's subjective view of morality or merely personal views.

Nevertheless, a more subtle form of the moral authority issue remains: even if it is true that most or even all understandings of justice take it to include more than an approximation of the ideal of the rule of law, there is much disagreement about what justice requires, and it is appropriate to ask what makes it morally justifiable for an actor to try to impose on others the conception of justice she endorses. I take up the moral authority issue below.

Earlier I suggested that an appropriate conception of the ideal of the rule of law would include the requirement of equality before the law. Some might disagree, limiting the ideal of the rule of law to the other elements listed above. If they are right, then this is further confirmation that the rule of law is not the only value that is relevant to assessing the weight of our commitment to fidelity to law. For if equality before the law is not to be included in the ideal of the rule of law, then there is a strong case for including it among the most basic and least controversial principles of justice, at least for those who value the role that law can play in securing justice. But, if so, then whether it is morally permissible to violate a law to improve a legal system must surely depend in part on how unjust the system is.

The legitimacy of the international legal system

The international legal system not only tolerates extreme economic inequalities among individuals and among states, it legitimizes and stabilizes them in manifold ways, not the least of which is by supporting state sovereignty over resources.[15] In addition, the international legal system is characterized by extreme political inequality among the primary members of the system (states). As already noted, a handful of powerful states wield a disproportionate influence over the creation, and above all the application and enforcement, of international law. Indeed, it is not implausible to argue that the extreme and morally arbitrary political inequality that characterizes the society of formally equal states robs the system of legitimacy. By a legitimate legal system I mean one whose institutional structures provide a framework within which its authorized actors are morally justified in making, applying, and enforcing laws.

---

[15] Henry Shue, *Basic Rights* (2nd edn, Princeton University Press, Princeton, 1980), pp. 131–52; Thomas Pogge, "An Egalitarian Law of Peoples," 23 *Philosophy and Public Affairs* (1994), 195–224.

To make a convincing case that these defects deprive the international legal systems of legitimacy would require articulating and defending a theory of system legitimacy.[16] That task lies far beyond the scope of the present discussion. However, this much can be said: the more problematic a system's claim to legitimacy, the weaker the moral pull of fidelity to its laws, other things being equal. Neither Watson nor Rubin addresses the issue of whether illegal acts of reform may be justified if they hold a reasonable prospect of significantly improving the legitimacy of a system whose legitimacy is at the very least subject to doubt. However, we shall see later that there is a way of understanding their opposition to illegal reform as resting on a conception of system legitimacy that emphasizes adherence to the state consent supernorm, the principle that to be international law, a norm must enjoy the consent of states.

Given the existing international legal system's deficiencies from the standpoint of what is either a cardinal element of the ideal of the rule of law or a basic, widely shared principle of justice, namely, equality before the law, and from the standpoint of a fairly wide range of principles of distributive justice, and given that the extreme political inequality among the states poses a serious challenge to the legitimacy of the system, it is implausible to assert that a commitment to the rule of law, as a moral ideal, rules out all illegal action for the sake of reform. The very defects of the system that provide the most obvious targets for reform weaken the moral pull of strict fidelity to its laws.

So far my analysis shows only that there is no simple inference from allegiance to the ideal of the rule of law to the moral unjustifiability of illegal acts directed to system reform. It does not follow, of course, that everything is morally permissible in a system as defective as the international legal system so long as it is done in the name of reform. An important question remains: given that a commitment to the ideal of the rule of law does not

---

[16] There are two quite different conceptions of legitimacy that are often confused in the writing of political theorists. The first, weaker, conception is that of being morally justified in attempting to exercise a monopoly on the enforcement (or the making and enforcement) of laws within a jurisdiction. The second, stronger, conception, often called "political authority," includes the weaker condition but in addition includes a correlative obligation to obey the entity said to be legitimate on the part of those over whom jurisdiction is exercised. I have argued elsewhere that it is the former conception, not the latter, that is relevant to discussions of state legitimacy in the international system. I would also argue that this is true for legitimacy of the system. Allen Buchanan, "Recognitional Legitimacy and the State System," 28 *Philosophy and Public Affairs* (1999), 46–78.

categorically prohibit illegal acts of reform, under what conditions are which sorts of illegal acts of reform morally justified? As a first approximation of an answer, we can say that, other things being equal, illegal acts are more readily justified if they have a reasonable prospect of contributing towards (a) bringing the system significantly closer to the ideal of the rule of law in its most fundamental elements, (b) rectifying the most serious substantive injustices supported by the system, or (c) ameliorating defects in the system that impugn its legitimacy.

The rule of law as necessary for avoiding violent chaos

Our first interpretation of "the rule of law" in the Fidelity Argument understood that phrase in a normatively demanding way: to be committed to the rule of law is to respect and endeavor to promote systems of rules that satisfy or seriously approximate the various elements of this ideal. We saw that on this interpretation the connection between being committed to the rule of law and refusing to violate existing international law is more tenuous and conditional than the critics of illegal reform assume.

The second interpretation of "the rule of law" as it occurs in the Fidelity Argument owes more to Hobbes than to Fuller. The idea is that even if international law falls far short of exemplifying some of the key elements of the ideal of the rule of law and even if it is seriously deficient from the standpoint of substantive justice and legitimacy, it is all that stands between us and violent chaos.[17] On this interpretation of the Fidelity Argument, we are presented with an austere choice: abstaining from illegal acts of reform or risking a Hobbesian war of each against all in international relations.

This is a false dilemma. As a sweeping generalization, the claim that illegal acts of reform run an unconscionable risk of violent anarchy is implausible. It would be more plausible if two assumptions were true: (a) the existence of the international order depends solely upon the efficacy of international law and (b) international law is a seamless web, so that cutting one fiber (violating one norm) will result in an unraveling of the entire fabric.

---

[17] Watson can perhaps be interpreted as endorsing this version of the Fidelity Argument. He strongly emphasizes that international law will only be effective in constraining the behavior of states if it is consensual and rejects illegal acts of reform as being incompatible with the requirement of consent (Watson, "Realistic Jurisprudence," pp. 265, 270, 275). The chief difficulty with this line of argument is that, while it would be extremely implausible to say that there must be perfect compliance with the law for it to be effective, Watson does nothing to indicate either what level of compliance is needed for effectiveness or what counts as effectiveness.

The first assumption is dubious. It probably overestimates the role of law by underestimating the contributions of political and economic relations and the various institutions of transnational civil society to peace and stability in international relations. But even if the first assumption were justified, the second, "seamless web," assumption is farfetched. History refutes it. As we have already noted, there have been illegal acts that were directed towards, and that actually contributed to, significant reforms, yet they did not result in a collapse of the international legal system.

Respect for the state consent supernorm

Some critics of illegal reform, including Watson and Rubin, are especially troubled by the willingness of reformers to violate what these critics believe is an essential (constitutional) feature of the existing international legal system: the state consent supernorm, a secondary rule (in Hart's sense of that term) according to which law is to be made and changed only by the consent of states.[18] (As was noted earlier, the requirement of state consent here is understood in a very loose way to be satisfied either by ratification of treaties or through conformity to norms that achieve the status of customary law.) The question, then, is this: why is the state consent supernorm of such importance that illegal acts of reform that violate it are never morally justified? There appear to be three answers worth considering: (1) only if the state consent supernorm is strictly observed will violent chaos be avoided, because only state consent can render international law effective; (2) state consent is the only mechanism for creating effective norms of peaceful relations among states that is capable of conferring legitimacy upon international norms; or (3) the state consent supernorm ought to be strictly adhered to because doing so reduces the risk that stronger states will prey on weaker ones.

Thesis (1)

The general claim that compliance with legal norms can only be achieved if those whose behavior is regulated by the norms consent to them is clearly false. In the case of domestic legal systems, virtually no one would assert that consent to every norm is necessary for effectiveness. So if the importance

---

[18] Rubin, *Ethics and Authority*, pp. 190–91, 205, 206; Watson, "Realistic Jurisprudence," pp. 265, 270, 275.

of consent is to supply a decisive reason against acts of reform that violate the state consent supernorm in international law, it must be because there is something special about the international arena that makes consent necessary if law is to be effective enough to avoid violent chaos.

If the realist theory of international relations were correct, it would provide an answer to the question of what that something special is. According to the realist theory, the structure of international relations precludes moral action except where it happens to be congruent with state interest. The importance of creating norms by state consent, on this view, is that it provides a way for states, understood as purely self-interested actors, to promote their shared long-term interests in peace and stability. Unless realism is correct, it is hard to see why we should assume that consent is necessary for effective law in the international case, while acknowledging, as we must, that it is not necessary for effectiveness in domestic systems.

Realism has been vigorously attacked, most systematically by contributors to the liberal theory of international relations. Because I believe these attacks are telling, I will not reenact now all too familiar argumentative battles between realists and their critics. Instead, I will focus on the second and third versions of the argument that a proper appreciation of the consensual basis of existing international law precludes justifiable acts of illegal reform.[19]

Thesis (2)

This is the view that what is morally attractive about the existing international legal system is not just that it avoids the Hobbesian abyss, but that it does so by relying upon the only mechanism for creating and changing norms of peaceful interaction that can confer *legitimacy* upon norms, given the character of international relations.[20] (A legitimate norm, here, is understood as one that it is morally justifiable to enforce.)

---

[19] The literature exposing the deficiencies of the various forms of realism in international relations is voluminous. Of particular value are Charles Beitz, *Political Theory and International Relations* (Princeton University Press, Princeton, 1979), pp. 3–66; and writings on the liberal theory of international relations by Anne-Marie Slaughter, "International Law in a World of Liberal States," 6 *European Journal of International Law* (1995), 503–38; and Andrew Moravcsik, "Taking Preferences Seriously: A Liberal Theory of International Politics," 51 *International Organization* (1997), 513–53.

[20] Terry Nardin, *Law, Morality, and the Relations of States* (Princeton University Press, Princeton, 1983), pp. 5–13; John Rawls, *The Law of Peoples* (Harvard University Press, Cambridge, Mass., 1999), pp. 51–120.

The underlying assumption is that the members of the so-called community of states are moral strangers, that the state system is a mere association
of distinct societies that do not share substantive ends of a conception of
justice, rather than a genuine community.[21] In the absence of shared substantive ends or a common conception of justice, consent is the only basis
of legitimacy for a system of norms. Within domestic societies, there are
moral–political cultures that are "thick" enough to fund shared substantive
ends or conceptions of justice and hence to provide a basis for legitimacy
without consent; but not so in international "society." But if state consent
is the only basis for legitimacy in the international system, then illegal acts
of reform that violate the state consent supernorm, such as illegal interventions to support democracy or to prevent massive violations of human
rights in ethnic conflicts within states, strike at the very foundation of international law and hence are not morally justifiable, at least for those who
profess to be committed to reforming that system.[22]

The most obvious defect of this line of argument is that its contrast between international society as a collection of moral strangers and domestic
society as an ethical community united by a "thick" culture of common
values is overdrawn. Especially in liberal societies, which tolerate and even
promote pluralism, whatever it is that legitimates the system of legal rules,
it cannot be shared substantive ends or even a shared conception of justice.
What Thesis (2) overlooks is that democratic politics in liberal domestic
societies includes deliberation – and heated controversy – over which substantive ends to pursue, not simply over which means to use to pursue
shared substantive ends.

In particular, liberal domestic societies often contain deep divisions as to
conceptions of distributive justice, with some citizens espousing "welfare-
state" conceptions and others "minimal state" or libertarian conceptions.
Yet such societies somehow manage to avoid violent chaos and also appear
to be capable of having legal systems that are legitimate.

An advocate of Thesis (2) might respond, relying on Rawls's views in
Political Liberalism and *The Law of Peoples*, that the members of liberal societies do share what might be called a core conception of justice – the idea

---

[21] Nardin acknowledges that states do share some ends, e.g. the flourishing of international trade,
but his view seems to be that what is distinctive about international law is that it binds states
together in the absence of shared substantive ends.

[22] Watson, "Realistic Jurisprudence," p. 268.

that society is a cooperative venture among persons conceived as free and equal – but that there is no globally shared core conception of justice.[23] Hence adherence to the state consent supernorm is necessary in international law, but not in domestic law.

There are three difficulties with this response. First, divisions within liberal domestic societies, especially concerning distributive justice, may be so deep that we must conclude either that (a) there is no shared core conception of justice or that (b) if there is, it is so vague and elastic that it cannot serve as a foundation for a legitimate system of legal norms. (Even if it is true that welfare-state liberals and libertarians both hold that society is a cooperative endeavor among "free and equal" persons, their respective understandings of freedom and equality diverge sharply.) Second, and more important, even if it is, or once was, true, that value pluralism among states is much deeper than within them, there is evidence that this may be changing. As many commentators have stressed, international legal institutions, as well as the forces of economic globalization, have contributed to the development of a transnational civil society in which a culture of human rights is emerging. This culture of human rights is both founded on, and serves to extend, a shared conception of basic human interests and a conception of the minimal institutional arrangements needed to protect them.[24] Moreover, the canonical language of the major human rights documents indicates a tendency towards convergence that may be as good a candidate for a core shared conception of justice as that which Rawls attributes to liberal societies: the idea that human beings have an inherent equality and freedom. So even if it is true that a system of legal norms can be legitimate only if it is supported by a common culture of basic values or a shared core conception of justice, it is not clear that international society is so lacking in moral consensus that state consent must remain an indispensable condition if norms are to be legitimate.

There is a third, much more serious, objection to the proposition that illegal acts of reform that violate the state consent supernorm are morally unjustifiable because they undermine the only basis for legitimacy in the

---

[23] Rawls, *Law of Peoples*, pp. 51–120; John Rawls, *Political Liberalism* (Columbia University Press, New York, 1993), pp. 89–172.

[24] For a valuable exposition and defense of the idea of a global culture of human rights, see Rhoda E. Howard, *Human Rights and the Search for Community* (Westview Press, Boulder, 1995), p. 120.

international legal system: due to the very defects at which illegal acts of reform are directed, the normative force of state consent in the present system is morally questionable at best.

What is called state consent is really the consent of state leaders. But in the many states in which human rights are massively and routinely violated and where democratic institutions are lacking, state leaders cannot reasonably be regarded as agents of their people.[25] Where human rights are massively violated, individuals are prevented or deterred from participating in processes of representation, consultation, and deliberation that are necessary if state leaders are to function as agents of the people capable of exercising authority on their behalf.

But if state leaders are not agents of their people, then it cannot be said that state consent is binding because it expresses the people's will. How, then, can the consent of individuals who cannot reasonably be viewed as agents of the people they claim to represent confer legitimacy? Illegal acts directed towards creating the only conditions under which state consent could confer legitimacy cannot be ruled out as morally unjustifiable on the grounds that they violate the norm of state consent.

This is not to say that the requirement of state consent, under present conditions, is without benefit or that the benefits it brings are irrelevant to the question of whether the system is legitimate. It can be argued, as I have already suggested, that adherence to the state consent supernorm has considerable instrumental value, quite apart from the inability of state consent as such to confer legitimacy on norms. This is the point of the third thesis about the importance of the state consent requirement.

Thesis (3)

This account of why the state consent supernorm is so important as to preclude illegal acts of reform that violate it is much more plausible than the first two. It does not assume that any violation of the norm of state consent poses an unacceptable risk of violent chaos, nor that state consent is supremely valuable because only it can achieve peace through norms that are legitimate. The proponent of Thesis (3) can cheerfully admit that law can be effective without consent and that under existing conditions

---

[25] Fernando R. Tesón, *A Philosophy of International Law* (Westview Press, Boulder, 1998), pp. 39–41.

state consent is in itself incapable of conferring legitimacy on the norms consented to. Instead, her point is that adherence to the state consent supernorm is so instrumentally valuable for reducing predation by stronger states upon weaker ones that it ought not to be violated even for the sake of system reform. Thesis (3) relies on the empirical prediction that if the international legal system fails to preserve the formal political equality of states by adhering to the state consent supernorm, the material inequalities among states will result in predatory behavior and in violations of individual human rights as well as rights of self-determination which predation inevitably entails.[26]

It is no doubt true that the state consent supernorm provides valuable protection for weaker states. But even if this is so, it does not follow that acts of reform that violate the state consent supernorm are never morally justifiable. Acts of reform that are very likely to make a significant contribution to making the system more egalitarian – that contribute to increasing the substantive political equality of states, thereby reducing the risk of predation – may be morally justified under certain circumstances, even if they violate the state consent supernorm.

Another way to put this point is to note that the instrumental argument for strict adherence to the state consent supernorm is very much a creature of non-ideal theory. At least from the standpoint of a wide range of theories of distributive justice, the existing global distribution of resources and goods is seriously unjust. But presumably these injustices play a major role in the inequalities of power among states. If the system became more distributively just, the inequalities of power that create opportunities for predation would diminish, and with them the threat of predation and the instrumental value of the state consent supernorm.

What this means is that there is nothing inconsistent in both appreciating the value of adherence to the state consent supernorm as a way of reducing predation and being willing to violate it in order to bring about systemic changes that will undercut the conditions for predation. The difficulty for the responsible reformer lies in determining when the prospects for actually achieving a significant reform in the direction of greater equality or justice are good enough to warrant undertaking an action that may have the effect of weakening what may be the best bulwark against predation the system

---

[26] Benedict Kingsbury, "Sovereignty and Inequality," 9 *European Journal of International Law* (1998), 599–625.

presently possesses. While the instrumental (antipredation) argument may be powerful enough to create a strong presumption – for the time being – against violating the state consent supernorm, it is hard to see how it can provide a categorical prohibition on illegal acts of reform.

Furthermore, observing the state consent supernorm is not the only mechanism for reducing the risk of predation. The theory and practice of constitutionalism in domestic legal systems offer a variety of mechanisms for checking abuses of power. For example, a norm requiring that individual states or groups of states may intervene in domestic conflicts to protect human rights only when explicitly authorized to do so by a supermajority vote in the UN General Assembly would provide a valuable constraint on great power abuses.

The results of this section can now be briefly summarized. I have argued that the notion of fidelity to law cannot provide a decisive reason for refraining from committing illegal acts directed towards reforming the international legal system. A sincere commitment to the ideal of the rule of law is not only consistent with illegal acts of reform; it may in some cases make such acts obligatory. Further, it is not plausible to argue that illegal acts of reform always constitute an unacceptable threat to peace and stability. Finally, I have argued that being willing to commit an illegal act of reform need not be inconsistent with a proper appreciation of the need to provide weaker states with protection against predation. I now turn to the other main challenge to illegal international legal reform: the charge that reformers wrongly impose their own personal or subjective views of morality upon others.

Moral authority

The charge of subjectivism

Opponents of illegal reform, such as Watson and Rubin, heap scathing criticism on those who would impose their own personal or subjective views of morality or justice on others. The suggestion is that those who endorse violations of international law, and especially those who disregard the state consent supernorm, are intolerant ideologues who would deny to others the right to do what they do. It is a mistake, however, to assume, as these critics apparently do, that the only alternatives are subjectivism or strict adherence to legality.

Internalist moral criticism of the system

An agent who seeks to breach international law in order to initiate a process of bringing about a moral improvement in the system need not be appealing to a subjective or merely personal view about morality. Instead, she may be relying upon moral values that are already expressed in the system and, to the extent that the system is consensual, upon principles that are widely shared. In fact, it appears that some who were sympathetic to NATO's intervention in Kosovo, including UN Secretary-General Kofi Annan, believed that this intervention was supported by one of the most morally defensible fundamental principles of the international legal system, the obligation to protect human rights, even though it was inconsistent with another principle of the system, the norm of sovereignty understood as prohibiting intervention in the domestic affairs of the Former Yugoslav Republic.[27] To describe those who supported the intervention by appealing to basic human rights principles internal to the system as ideologues relying on a merely personal or subjective moral view is wildly inaccurate.

Two views of moral authority

Since the appearance of Rawls's book *Political Liberalism* there has been a complex and spirited debate about the nature of what I have called moral authority. Two main rival views have emerged. According to the first, which Rawls himself offers, moral authority, understood as the right to impose rules on others, is subject to a requirement of reasonableness. It is morally justifiable to impose on others only those principles that they could reasonably accept from the standpoint of their own comprehensive conceptions of the good or of justice, with the proviso that the latter fall within the range of the reasonable.[28] Rawls has a rather undemanding notion of what counts as a reasonable conception of the good or of justice: so long as the view is logically consistent or coherent and includes the idea that every person's good should count in the design of basic social institutions, it counts as reasonable. As I have argued elsewhere, Rawls's conception of moral authority counts as reasonable grossly inegalitarian societies, including those

---

[27] Kofi Annan, "Speech to the General Assembly," SG/SM/7136 GA/9569: Secretary-G, 20 September 1999, p. 2.
[28] Rawls, *Political Liberalism*, pp. 136–37.

that include systematic, institutionalized racism or caste systems or systems that discriminate systematically against women.[29]

Grossly and arbitrarily inegalitarian social systems count as reasonable on Rawls's view because the requirement that everyone's good is to count is compatible with the good of some counting very little. To that extent Rawls's conception of reasonableness is at odds with some aspects of existing international human rights law, including the right against discrimination on grounds of gender, religion, or race.

The root idea of the Rawlsian conception of moral authority is respect for persons' reasons in the light of what Rawls calls "the burdens of judgment." To acknowledge the burdens of judgment is to appreciate that, due to a number of factors, reasonable people can disagree on the principles of public order. Like Rubin and Watson, Rawls is concerned about those who assume that their belief that certain moral principles are valid is sufficient to give them the moral authority to impose those principles on others. In that sense, Rawls's reasonableness condition is an attempt to rule out the imposition of purely personal or subjective moral views.

However, Rawls's reasonableness criterion does not rule out imposing moral standards that others do not consent to. What people can reasonably accept, given their moral views, and what they actually do accept or consent to may differ. So, according to the Rawlsian conception of moral authority (or, in his preferred term, legitimacy), acts of reform that violate the state consent supernorm are not necessarily unjustifiable, even if we slide over the problem of inferring the consent of persons from the consent of states.

Rawls's conception of moral authority focuses almost exclusively on one aspect of being reasonable, or of showing respect for the reasons of others: humility in the face of the burdens of judgment. Rawls's only acknowledgment that reasons must be of a certain quality to warrant respect and toleration is the very weak requirement of logical consistency or coherence.

A quite different conception of moral authority acknowledges the burdens of judgment and also affirms that part of what it is to respect persons is to respect them as beings who have their own views about what is good and right but places more emphasis on what might be called "epistemic responsibility" as an element of reasonableness.[30] According to this view, respect

---

[29] Allen Buchanan, "Justice, Legitimacy, and Human Rights," in Victoria Davion and Clark Wolf eds., *The Idea of Political Liberalism* (Rowman & Littlefield, Lanham, Md., 2000), pp. 73–89.

[30] Thomas Christiano, "On Rawls's Argument for Toleration" (unpublished paper); Allen Buchanan, *Justice, Legitimacy, and Self-determination: Moral Foundations for International Law* (Oxford University Press, New York, forthcoming).

for persons' reasons does not require that we regard as reasonable any moral view that meets Rawls's rather minimal requirements of logical consistency or coherence and of taking everyone's good into account in some way. In addition, to be reasonable, and hence worthy of toleration, a moral view must be supportable by a justification that meets certain minimal standards of rationality.

In other words, to be worthy of respect moral views must be supported by reasons and reasoning that is of a certain minimal quality that goes beyond logical consistency or coherence. In particular, it must be possible to provide a justification for a moral view that does not rely on grossly false empirical claims about human nature (or about the nature of blacks, or women, or "untouchables") and which does not involve clearly invalid inferences based on grossly faulty standards of evidence. The intuitive appeal of this more demanding conception of what sorts of views are entitled to toleration lies in the idea that respect for persons' reasons requires that those reasons meet certain minimal standards of rationality, the underlying idea being that it is respect for persons' reasoning, not their opinions, that matters. Also according to this conception of moral authority, it is a mistake to assume that anyone who tries to reform the international legal system by performing acts that are violations of its existing norms is thereby imposing on others her purely personal or subjective moral views. The charge of subjectivity should be reserved for those views that do not meet the minimal standards of epistemic responsibility. Different versions of this view would propose different ways of fleshing out the idea that epistemic responsibility requires more than mere logical consistency or coherence.

My aim here is not to resolve the debate about what constitutes moral authority (though I have argued elsewhere that the epistemic responsibility view is superior to the Rawlsian view).[31] Instead, I have introduced two rival conceptions of moral authority, in order to show that both create a space between rigid adherence to existing consensual international law and the attempt to impose purely subjective, personal moral beliefs in violation of existing law. So even though it is correct to say that purely subjective or merely personal moral views cannot provide a moral justification for illegal acts of reform, it does not follow that anyone who breaks the law is merely acting on a subjective or personal view.

---

[31] Buchanan, "Justice, Legitimacy, and Human Rights" and *Justice, Legitimacy, and Self-determination*.

Watson and Rubin are quite correct to question the moral authority of proponents of illegal reform. Merely believing that one is right in itself is not a sufficient reason for doing much of anything, much less for violating the law or trying to initiate a process that will result in imposing laws on others without their consent. But they are mistaken to assume that those who advocate illegal acts of system reform must lack moral authority, and they offer no account of moral authority to show that illegal reformists must, or typically will, lack moral authority.

In addition, as I have already argued, quite apart from whether either the Rawlsian conception of moral authority or the epistemic responsibility conception is correct, those who brand all proponents of illegal reform "subjectivists" entirely overlook the fact that in some cases, perhaps most, the reformer's justification is internalist, appealing to widely shared moral principles already expressed in the system. It does not follow that these internal values of the system are beyond criticism, but they are not purely subjective or merely personal; instead, they are widely held, systematically institutionalized values. In appealing to the internal values of the system in order to justify an illegal act, the reformer is doing precisely what reformers (as opposed to revolutionaries) do: trying to see that the system does a better job of realizing the values it already embodies and is supposed to promote. The proper lesson to draw from Watson and Rubin's worries about moral subjectivism is that the justification of illegal acts of reform must rest upon a conception of moral authority, not that no justification can succeed.

Towards a theory of the morality of international legal reform

The need for a moral theory of reform

Assuming that the international law of humanitarian intervention is in need of reform, critical and systematic thinking is needed to determine how reform would best be achieved. Plainly, any proposal for reform should score well on the requirement of feasibility, but that is not sufficient. In addition, proposals for reform must pass the test of moral evaluation. In this section I propose a set of guidelines that those embarking on reform efforts should take into account.

I focus on illegal acts directed towards reform because I believe it is illegal acts that encounter the most resistance and that a special burden of justification must be borne by anyone who proposes to violate existing law in the name of legal reform. In the next section I focus on special criteria for evaluating the morality of acts directed towards reform through the creation of a new customary law of intervention that applies due to peculiarities of the customary process, in particular the satisfaction of the *opinio juris* requirement.

Guidelines for determining the moral justifiability of illegal acts of reform

The problem of illegal reform is located in the part of non-ideal normative theory of international law that deals with how we are to move towards the institutional arrangements prescribed by ideal theory. We are now in a position to articulate some of the key considerations that such a non-ideal theory would have to include. My aim here is not to offer a developed, comprehensive theory of the morality of transition from non-ideal to ideal conditions, but only to sketch some of its broader outlines so far as it addresses the problem of illegal acts of reform directed towards the creation of new international law concerning humanitarian intervention. To do this I will articulate and support a set of guidelines for assessing the morality of proposed illegal acts directed towards the moral improvement of the system of international law.

The guidelines are derived from the preceding analysis of the objections to illegal acts of reform. While none of those objections rules out the moral justifiability of illegal acts of reform, they do supply significant cautionary considerations that a responsible agent would take into account in determining whether to engage in an illegal act aimed at reforming the system. I will then clarify the import of the guidelines and demonstrate their power by applying them to the recent NATO intervention in Kosovo.

An important limitation of the guidelines should be emphasized: they are not designed to provide comprehensive conditions for the justification of humanitarian intervention. Instead, they are to be applied to proposals for illegal interventions directed towards legal reform once the familiar and widely acknowledged conditions for justified intervention are already satisfied. Among the most important of these familiar conditions is the principle of proportionality, which requires that the intervention not produce as much harm (especially to the innocent) as, or more harm than, the harm it seeks to prevent. Much of the criticism of NATO's intervention in Kosovo focuses on the failure to satisfy this requirement.

My concern, however, is with the special justificatory issues raised by the illegality of an act of intervention that is directed towards system reform. To respond to these justificatory issues, I offer the following guidelines.

1. Other things being equal, the closer a system approximates the ideal of the rule of law (the better job it does of satisfying the more important requirements that constitute that ideal), the greater the burden of justification for illegal acts.
2. Other things being equal, the less seriously defective the system is from the standpoint of the most important requirements of substantive justice, the greater the burden of justification for illegal acts.
3. Other things being equal, the more closely the system approximates the conditions for being a legitimate system (i.e., the stronger the justification for attempts to achieve enforcement of the rules of the system), the greater the burden of justification for illegal acts.
4. Other things being equal, an illegal act that violates one of the most fundamental morally defensible principles of the system bears a greater burden of justification.
5. Other things being equal, the greater the improvement, the stronger the case for committing the illegal act that is directed towards bringing it about; and if the state of affairs the illegal act is intended to bring about would not be an improvement in the system, then the act cannot be justified as an act of reform.
6. Other things being equal, illegal acts that are likely to improve significantly the legitimacy of the system are more easily justified.
7. Other things being equal, illegal acts that are likely to improve the most basic dimensions of substantive justice in the system are more easily justified.
8. Other things being equal, illegal acts that are likely to contribute to making the system more consistent with its most morally defensible fundamental principles are more easily justified.

The rationale for the guidelines

The basic rationale common to all the guidelines is straightforward. They provide a way of gauging (a) whether any given illegal act can accurately be described as being directed towards reform of the system and, if so, (b) whether committing it is compatible with a sincere commitment to

bringing international relations under the rule of law. The guidelines articulate the considerations that an ideal agent who is committed to pursuing
justice through legal institutions, but cognizant of the deficiencies of the
existing system, would take into account in determining whether to commit
or endorse an illegal act of legal reform. This characterization of such an
agent is intended to abstract, allowing for the fact that different agents may
have different views about what justice requires. Thus the guidelines are
intended to provide concrete guidance without presupposing a particular
theory of justice.

Guideline 1 captures the idea that, for those who are committed to the
ideal of the rule of law, the fact that a system closely approximates that ideal
provides a presumption in favor of compliance with its rules. Guideline 2
is a reminder that satisfying the formal requirements of the ideal of the
rule of law is not sufficient for assessing the moral quality of a legal system
and hence for determining the weight of the presumption that we ought to
comply with its rules. In addition to satisfying or seriously approximating
the ideal of the rule of law, a legal system ought to promote justice. The
elements of the rule of law supply important constraints on the sorts of rules
that may be employed in pursuit of the goal of substantive justice, but they
are not the only factor relevant to assessing the moral quality of the system –
how well the system promotes the goal of substantive justice also matters. In
the case of the international legal system, it is relatively uncontroversial to
say that the most widely accepted human rights norms constitute the core
of substantive justice (to call this a subjective or purely personal view would
be bizarre). To the extent that the protection of human rights is an internal
goal of the international legal system, the appeal to substantive justice is an
appropriate consideration in determining whether illegal action is morally
justifiable and cannot be dismissed as the imposition of purely personal or
subjective moral views.

Guideline 3 rests on the assumption that the conditions that make the
system legitimate, including preeminently its capacity to promote substantive justice within the constraints of the ideal of the rule of law, give us moral
reasons to support it and that consequently we should be more reluctant,
other things being equal, to violate its rules if it scores well on the criterion
of legitimacy.

Guideline 4 follows straightforwardly from the fundamental commitment to supporting the international legal system as an important instrument for achieving justice. The reformer, by definition, is someone who is

striving to bring about a moral improvement in the system. Accordingly, she must consider not only the improvement that may be gained through an illegal act, but also the need to preserve what is valuable in the system as it is.

Guideline 5 is commonsensical, stating that the justifiability of the illegal act of legal reform depends upon whether, and if so to what extent, the state of affairs the act is intended to bring about would constitute an improvement in the system. In the case of an illegal act intended to help create a new customary norm, this means that the new norm must actually be an improvement over the status quo.

Guideline 6 acknowledges a fundamental tension in the enterprise of trying to develop a morally defensible system of law: on the one hand, a person who seeks to reform a legal system, qua reformer (as opposed to revolutionary), values the indispensable contribution that law can make to protecting human rights and serving other worthy moral values; on the other hand, she appreciates that the enterprise of law involves the coercive imposition of rules and that for this to be justified the system must meet certain moral standards. What this means is that the project of trying to develop the legal system to achieve the goal of justice must be accompanied by efforts to ensure that the system has the features needed to make the pursuit of justice through its processes morally justifiable. Thus guideline 6 acknowledges the distinction between justice and legitimacy and emphasizes that anyone who is committed to working within the system to improve it should take the legitimacy of the system itself as an important goal for reform.

Guideline 7, like guideline 3, emerges from my criticism of those opponents of illegal reform who make the mistake of thinking that conformity with the ideal of the rule of law is all we should ask of a legal system. There I argued that whether a legal system achieves, or at least is compatible with, the substantive requirement of justice is relevant to determining the system's moral pull towards compliance. My discussion of alternative views of moral authority showed that, while Watson and Rubin are correct to condemn those who would attempt to impose subjective, that is, purely personal, conceptions of substantive justice on the legal system, illegal reform for the sake of improving the substantive justice of the system is compatible with recognizing a reasonable requirement of moral authority and hence with acting from moral commitments that are not subjective in any damaging sense.

Guideline 8 is also intuitively plausible. A reformer who commits an illegal act that can reasonably be expected to make the system conform better to its own best principles is acting so as to support the system and, to that extent, the presumption against acting illegally that supporters of the system should acknowledge is weakened.

A word of caution is in order. The guidelines proceed on the assumption that content can be given to the idea of improving the system morally and they employ the notion of justice. However, they are intended neither to provide a comprehensive moral theory nor to supply content for the notion of justice. They are designed to provide guidance for a responsible actor who values the rule of law in international relations and is aware of both the system's need for improvement and the difficulties of achieving expeditious change by strictly legal means. It is inevitable that different agents may reach different conclusions about whether a particular illegal act directed towards system reform is morally justifiable, just as conscientious individuals can disagree as to whether a particular act of civil disobedience in a domestic system is morally justified. In some cases these different conclusions will be the result of different understandings of justice. But without having settled all disputes about what justice is, it is still possible to show that an actor who is sincerely committed to the rule of law in international relations, and who believes the existing system is worthy of efforts to reform it, can consistently perform or advocate illegal acts of reform. And it is possible to develop guidelines for responsible choices regarding illegal acts of reform.

NATO intervention in Kosovo: a test case

The guidelines must be abstract if they are to cover a wide range of possible illegal acts of reform. To appreciate their value and to clarify their meaning, I will apply them to NATO's intervention in Kosovo. I will assume (following what I believe to be the preponderance of informed legal opinion) this was an illegal act. I noted in the first section that three quite different types of justifications could be given for the intervention. My concern in this chapter is with the third type, the Illegal Legal Reform Justification. So the question is: how does this illegal act, justified in this way, fare with regard to the eight guidelines for assessing the moral justifiability of illegal acts of system reform?

It would be difficult to argue that guidelines 1, 2, or 3 weigh conclusively against NATO's intervention in Kosovo. As I have already noted, the existing system of international law departs seriously from the ideal of the rule of law, at least so far as this includes the principle of equality before the law, falls short of satisfying substantive principles of justice, including those, such as human rights norms, that are internal to the system, and can be challenged on grounds of legitimacy because of the morally arbitrary way in which international law is often selectively applied in the interest of the stronger.

From the standpoint of guideline 4, the intervention in Kosovo initially looks problematic, simply because of the charge that its illegality consisted in the violation of one of the most fundamental principles of the system, the norm of sovereignty articulated in Articles 2(7), 2(4), and Chapter VII of the UN Charter, which forbid armed intervention except in cases of self-defense or Security Council authorization. However, guideline 4 refers to the most morally defensible fundamental norms of the existing legal system. If the new customary norm of intervention that the illegal act is intended to help establish would in fact constitute a major improvement in the system, it would do so by restricting sovereignty, and this implies that the norm of sovereignty in its current form is not fully defensible. In other words, the reformist rationale for acting in violation of the existing norms of sovereignty so as to help establish a new customary norm of intervention is that the existing norm of sovereignty creates a zone of protected behavior for states that is too expansive, at the expense of the protection of human rights. The more dubious is the moral defensibility of the principle of the system that the illegal act violates, the less force guideline 4 has as a barrier to illegal action. In cases where the establishment of a new norm through illegal action would constitute a major improvement because the existing norm that is violated is seriously defective, guideline 4 poses no barrier to illegal action. So whether guideline 4 counts for or against NATO's intervention in Kosovo depends upon whether the change the illegal act is aimed at producing would in fact be a major moral improvement in the system, which is addressed in guidelines 5–8.

Consider next guideline 5. Recall that the act in question is aimed at the establishment of a new customary norm and that the process by which new customary norms are created is a complex, multistaged one in which there are many opportunities for failure. Above all, it is important to remember that whether a new customary norm of intervention will arise will depend not just upon what NATO did in this case but upon whether a stable pattern of similar interventions comes about, upon whether states persistently dissent from the propriety of such interventions, and upon whether those who contribute to establishing a stable pattern of similar interventions do so in a way that satisfies the *opinio juris* requirement. Given these inherent uncertainties of the effort to bring about moral improvement through the creation of a new customary norm, an actor contemplating an illegal act of reform of this sort should be on very firm ground in judging that the new norm would in fact be a major improvement. In the next subsection I will argue that this condition was not met in the case of NATO's intervention in Kosovo.

It is tempting to assume that, from the standpoint of substantive justice, the Kosovo intervention scores high because the establishment of a norm authorizing intervention into internal conflicts to prevent massive human rights violations would constitute a major improvement in the system. Moreover, the charge of subjectivism (lack of moral authority) rings hollow in this sort of case because, as Kofi Annan suggested, the protection of human rights is a core value that is internal to the system. However, whether or not the NATO intervention can be described as an act of illegal reform that would, if successful, bring about a major improvement in the system depends upon the precise character of the norm that this illegal act is likely to contribute to the establishment of – and upon whether a norm of this character would be likely to be abused.

What sort of new norm of intervention?

From the standpoint of its justifiability as an illegal act directed towards improving the system, just how the illegal act is characterized matters greatly. It is not sufficient to characterize the NATO intervention as an act directed towards establishing a new norm of humanitarian intervention in domestic conflicts. Such a characterization misses both what makes the act illegal and what is supposed to make it an act directed towards improving the system by helping to establish a new norm of intervention: the fact that it was undertaken without UN authorization. Those who endorse the act, not simply as a morally justifiable act but as an act of reform calculated to contribute to the creation of a new norm, are committed to the assertion that the requirement of Security Council authorization is a defect in the system. And the fact that the intervention proceeded without Security Council authorization is the chief basis for the widely held view that the intervention was illegal.

For purposes of evaluating the justifiability of the NATO intervention as an illegal act directed towards reforming the system, then, the characterization of the act must at least include the fact that it occurred without Security Council authorization. But something else must be added to the characterization: the fact that the intervention was undertaken by a regional military alliance whose constitutional identity is that of a pact for the defense of its members against aggression. Those who undertook the intervention and their supporters emphasized that it was conducted by NATO, presumably because they thought that this fact made the justification for it stronger than would have been the case had it been undertaken by a mere collection of states.

Note that this appeal to the status of NATO as a regional defensive organization recognized by international law cannot refute the charge of illegality. According to Article 51 of the UN Charter, military action, including action by regional organizations as identified in Article 52, is permissible without Security Council authorization only in cases of the occurrence of armed attack against a state or a member of such an organization.[32] So the question remains: would a new customary norm permitting intervention by regional military organizations, or those that qualified as such under Article 52, be a moral improvement in the international legal system?

The answer to this question is almost certainly negative. A military alliance such as NATO is not the sort of entity that would be a plausible candidate for having a right under international law to intervene without UN authorization. The chief difficulty is that such a norm would be too liable to abuse. To appreciate this fact, suppose that China and Pakistan formed a regional security alliance and then appealed to the new norm of customary law whose creation NATO's intervention was supposed to initiate to justify intervening in Kashmir to stop Hindus from violating Muslims' rights in the part of that region controlled by India.[33]

It is one thing to say that NATO's intervention was morally justified as the only way of preventing massive human rights violations under conditions in which Security Council authorization was not obtainable. It is quite another to claim that the intervention was justified as an act directed towards legal reform. The former justification makes no claims about the desirability of

[32] Barry E. Carter and Phillip R. Trimble, *International Law: Selected Documents* (Little, Brown, Boston, 1995), pp. 14–15.
[33] This example was suggested to me by Hurst Hannum.

a new rule concerning intervention and is quite consistent with the view that, despite its defects, the rule requiring Security Council authorization is, all things considered, desirable under present conditions. The justification we are concerned with makes a stronger and much more dubious claim, namely that the current rule requiring Security Council authorization ought to be abandoned and replaced with a new rule empowering regional defense alliances to engage in intervention at their discretion. Perhaps the current rule of intervention ought to be rejected, but it is very implausible to hold that adopting this new rule would be an improvement.

Defenders of the NATO intervention might reply, however, that there is a great difference between the members of NATO, on the one hand, and China and Pakistan, on the other. Unlike China and Pakistan, all members of NATO are liberal–democratic countries, with free presses and a political culture that questions government actions. In that respect NATO is much more accountable and therefore less likely to abuse the right to intervene than an alliance of repressive, unaccountable states.[34] This reply certainly strengthens NATO's case, but it does not go far enough. The problem is that an action such as the intervention in Kosovo does not wear a unique description on its sleeve. How the action is characterized by the majority of states will make a difference as to what it serves as a precedent for. There is all the difference in the world between regarding NATO's intervention as an intervention by a military alliance and as an intervention by a military alliance of liberal–democratic states, with the accountability that this implies. If NATO's leaders were concerned to take the first step towards a new, more enlightened customary norm of intervention, they should have done more to emphasize their own democratic accountability and thereby reduce the chance that their action would be viewed as a precedent for more dangerous intervention by military alliances whose members were not accountable. In other words, by failing to do all it could have to *specify* the principle it was acting on, NATO ran the risk that its action would come to be viewed as a precedent for a change in customary law that would not in fact be an improvement over the current requirement of Security Council authorization. In the next section I argue that there is an interesting relationship between the problem of specification and the satisfaction of the *opinio juris* condition for the emergence of a new customary norm.

---

[34] This point is due to Robert Keohane.

Taking the *opinio juris* condition seriously

The eight guidelines stated above are quite general. They apply to illegal acts directed towards reforming any legal system, not just international law. And, as I have argued, at least one of them, guideline 5, calls into question the adequacy of appealing to the need for reform to justify the illegal NATO intervention in Kosovo. But precisely because they are so general, the guidelines fail to make clear something that is crucial for the evaluation of illegal acts directed towards reform through the creation of new customary international law, namely the fact that any such acts must be undertaken in a way that reflects the importance of satisfying the *opinio juris* requirement.[35]

In other words, a conscientious reformer must act in such a way not only so as to help ensure that a morally defensible new pattern of state behavior will emerge regarding humanitarian intervention, but also so as to contribute to a shift in consciousness regarding the legal status of such actions. What sorts of actions might the intervenor undertake that could reasonably be expected to contribute to such a shift?

My suggestion is that, in the case of the NATO intervention, there are at least two dimensions of what I referred to earlier as *lawfulness* which, if taken into account by the intervenors during and after the intervention, could reasonably be expected to contribute towards satisfaction of the *opinio juris* requirement. The first has to do with the nature of the intervening entity. As I noted earlier, NATO does not appear to be the sort of entity that could reasonably be authorized to intervene without UN authorization. The point is not simply that NATO is a self-defense pact and that none of its members was under attack. More important, NATO's charter does not include clear statements committing it to the role of being an impartial protector of universal human rights, dedicated to supporting and, where necessary, supplementing other international legal agencies that have the responsibility for protecting human rights.[36] Had NATO begun an open, publicized process of transforming its juridical character in this way at the time of the intervention and carried through on it in the immediate aftermath, this would have made it much more likely that other states would come to regard humanitarian interventions by entities

---

[35] I am indebted to Jeff Holzgrefe for suggesting this important point.

[36] Omar Dahour, "Self-determination and Just War in Kosovo," 2 *Radical Philosophy Review* (1999), 14.

of *that sort* to be legally permissible, even when they lack Security Council authorization.

Without this public effort to transform its identity, NATO's action is likely to be regarded simply as a morally excusable violation of international law (as many regarded the interventions in East Pakistan and Uganda), rather than as a prototype for a new, defensible legal norm regarding humanitarian intervention. What sorts of actions come to be regarded as legally required or permitted depends in part upon whether the agents performing them are the sorts of entities that could lawfully do so. NATO lacked the juridical character that could be expected to contribute to satisfaction of the *opinio juris* requirement.

Second, if, after the intervention was concluded, NATO had taken a leadership role in orchestrating an inclusive, public deliberation to develop consensus on a better international legal norm and procedures for humanitarian intervention, this too would have increased the probability of a shift in consciousness regarding the possibility of legal interventions without Security Council authorization. In fact, as I have already noted, the Independent International Commission on Kosovo, not NATO, embarked on this constructive path by suggesting several options for reform that would be an improvement on the current requirement of Security Council authorization.

These options were offered as ways of bringing about the needed reform without illegality. However, the Independent Commission did not go so far as to pronounce that successful reform would occur by strictly legal means. Instead, it suggested that NATO's illegal intervention itself might have played a beneficial role as an insistent "wake-up" call, motivating the international community to explore legal options for legal reform.[37]

My point is that, if NATO's goal was not simply to prevent a particular humanitarian disaster but to begin a process of legal reform, then it should have taken steps after the intervention to increase the probability that a new norm would emerge which states could reasonably regard as a legally binding norm, thus satisfying the *opinio juris* requirement. To accomplish this, NATO should have done at least two things. First, it should have begun the process of transforming itself into an entity of the sort that would be authorized to intervene under a norm of the sort that states would be likely

---

[37] See Independent International Commission on Kosovo, *Kosovo Report*, and Michael Perry, personal communication.

to come to regard as legally binding. Second, it should have facilitated an inclusive, legitimacy-conferring process of international deliberation to devise ways of using or modifying existing international legal procedures and institutions to achieve a responsible specification of the content of the norm, in order to provide appropriate safeguards in the absence of Security Council authorization. A new pattern of state action that is seen to conform to a norm that has been specified by such a lawful process is clearly more likely to come to be regarded as a legal norm.

Stromseth might object that such a process of deliberation about how to codify a new rule of humanitarian intervention is doomed to failure at the present time. However, even if she is correct, there may be considerable value in *attempting* to achieve codification. Even if only a limited consensus emerges from such efforts, this may contribute to the eventual emergence of a new customary norm. In other words, Stromseth may be wrong in assuming that the choice is between efforts to codify and the development of new custom.

To engage in a responsible act of illegal legal reform, then, is not simply to perform an action that under some true description of it or another provides the template for a superior norm. It is also necessary to perform the action, to justify it publicly, and to follow through on it in such a way as to facilitate the satisfaction of the *opinio juris* requirement. NATO failed to do this. Whether or not NATO's action was justified simply as a violation of international law for the sake of moral principle, it was not credible as an act directed towards reform of the international law of humanitarian intervention.

Reform through treaty that bypasses the UN

The preceding analysis shows that the strategy of trying to reform international law regarding humanitarian intervention through the creation of new customary law is a high-risk option, a process that may derail at any number of points or perhaps result in a new norm that is not an improvement over the old one. Given these risks and uncertainties, an agent that initiates the process of customary change ought to act in such a way as to maximize the chances that a new norm will eventually emerge and that it will be specified in such a way as to constitute an improvement over the status quo. But the process can go awry or not come to fruition, even if the initiator does everything that should be done, because whether a new norm emerges and what its character turns out to be depends upon the responses of the majority of states.

The majoritarian dimension of the process – the fact that a majority of states must change their behavior and their attitude towards the legality of intervention without Security Council authorization – makes this route to reform vulnerable to the deficiencies of the majority. The same pessimism noted earlier regarding the prospects for reform by treaty within the UN system therefore seems to attach to reform by new custom. In a world in which many states cleave resolutely to their power to abuse their own minorities, achieving reform of the law of humanitarian intervention through the emergence of new custom may be a precarious, or at least a very slow, path towards progress. To overlook this obvious point would be to make the mistake of assuming that the only serious obstacle to reform is the regressive behavior of certain permanent members of the Security Council. The problem goes much deeper.

A sober appreciation of the risks and uncertainties of reform through the creation of new custom requires us to consider the option of change through treaty among liberal–democratic states, outside the UN system. The crucial point is that it is a mistake to assume that support by a majority of states, either through treaty or in the process of customary change, is a necessary condition for efforts to achieve reform to be morally justifiable. State-majoritarianism, under current conditions in which many states are not democratic, cannot be viewed as having the same legitimacy-conferring power as the consent of individuals. At most, state-majoritarianism has normative weight as a device for constraining abuses by more powerful states.

However, it is not at all obvious that the only way, or even the best way, to constrain powerful states is by subjecting the process of reforming humanitarian intervention to state-majoritarianism. Instead, the needed constraint might be achieved in a treaty-based coalition among liberal–democratic states by a combination of two factors: first, treaty specification of a fairly demanding set of necessary conditions for intervention; second, the democratic accountability between and within participating liberal–democratic states discussed earlier. And even if it could be shown that state-majoritarianism provides a more effective constraint against great power abuses, reducing the risk of abuse is not an absolute value. Not just the harm, but also the good that a liberal–democratic coalition could do must be considered.

Earlier I suggested that the morality of international legal reform is complicated because, under current conditions, there may be a conflict between the need to achieve gains in substantive justice, namely, better protection of basic human rights, on the one hand, and legitimacy, on the other. I now want to suggest that it is inaccurate to say that pursuing reform through a treaty-based coalition for intervention outside the UN, and hence without the support of a majority of states, offends against the value of legitimacy in the name of substantive justice. State-majoritarianism, as I have just argued, has little to recommend it from the standpoint of legitimacy: the consent of state leaders who do not represent their citizens does not itself confer legitimacy. Instead, under current conditions, state-majoritarianism has normative weight only to the extent that it helps curb great power abuses in intervention. But I have also argued that attempts to reform the law of humanitarian intervention that require support from the majority of states (whether through constitutional amendment to the UN Charter or through the creation of new custom) do not hold great promise for success. The real issue, then, is whether the commitment to making the system substantively more just is best honored by paths to reform that attempt to check great power abuses through state-majoritarianism or by relying upon devices for constraint that can be built into a liberal–democratic coalition for humanitarian intervention.

Conclusions

My chief aim in this chapter has been to identify, and to begin the task of developing a solution for, an important but neglected problem in the non-ideal part of the normative theory of international law: the morality of attempts at legal reform. I have focused on illegal acts aimed at developing a new, morally superior norm of humanitarian intervention, for the simple reason that their illegality creates a special burden of justification for the reformer, given his commitment to the rule of law. However, much of my discussion has implications for broader issues of reform whether it involves illegality or not.

I have also shown the inadequacy of a simple and common response to the problem – the Legal Absolutist charge that such acts are impermissible because they are inconsistent with a sincere commitment to the rule of law or betray a willingness to act without moral authority by imposing purely personal or subjective views of morality on others. By exploring the array of factors that are relevant to determining whether an illegal act of reform is morally justified, I hope to have vindicated the concerns of those such as Watson and Rubin that such illegalities bear a serious burden of justification, while at the same time showing that to reject illegal reform wholesale is to fail to appreciate the complexities of the issues.

My analysis demonstrates that the moral evaluation of an illegal act of humanitarian intervention is more complex than is ordinarily assumed. A responsible agent confronted with the possibility of preventing a humanitarian disaster but aware that doing so is illegal under existing international law will ask not only whether there is a sound moral principle that allows or requires him to violate the law, but also whether he should act so as to try to bring about a change in the law. If the answer to the latter question is affirmative, the burdens of responsible agency are extensive. In particular, in the case of attempting reform through the creation of new customary law, acting responsibly requires more than ensuring that the illegal action can, under some favorable description of it, provide the template for an improved norm of intervention. In addition, the agent of illegal acts of reform must act in such a way as to promote satisfaction of the *opinio juris* condition. Doing this may require actions that go far beyond the intervention itself.

I have also articulated a vexing and momentous issue at the heart of the problem of reform: is better protection of human rights through a rule-governed practice of intervention best achieved through working within the UN-based system of law, or by creating a treaty-based regime of constrained intervention outside of it?

Facing the problem of justifying illegal legal reform head-on, rather than by pretending that reform efforts are legal by stretching the concept of legality, forces us to probe the morality of attempts to create new customary law, to examine what it is to honor the commitment to the rule of law in an imperfect system, to examine critically the assumption that legitimacy requires endorsement of new norms by the majority of states, and to ponder the nature of the international legal system and the conditions for its legitimacy.

PART III

Law and humanitarian intervention

5

Changing the rules about rules?
Unilateral humanitarian intervention
and the future of international law

MICHAEL BYERS AND SIMON CHESTERMAN

In the course of NATO's 1999 air campaign in Kosovo, most international lawyers remained conspicuously silent on the strict legality of the intervention. Of those who gave on-the-record comments, many couched their opinions in terms of "traditional international law," observing that it provided no clear basis for the intervention but usually refraining from condemning the intervention as illegal.[1] Subsequent legal analysis has seen less ambiguity – and greater divergence of opinion. Authors with more or less similar understandings of the factual situation in Kosovo in the early months of 1999 – widespread and escalating persecution of the non-Serb population by a government and army with a history of mass atrocities elsewhere – arrive at sometimes starkly different conclusions, both on the law as it stood at the outset of the intervention, and on the potential for legal change.[2]

---

[1] See, for example, N. Lewis, "The Rationale: A Word Bolsters Case for Allied Intervention," *New York Times*, 4 April 1999; W. Branigin and J. Goshko, "Legality of Airstrikes Disputed in US, UN – China Condemns 'Blatant Aggression',," *Washington Post*, 27 March 1999; C. Greenwood, "Yes, But Is the War Legal?" *Observer*, 28 March 1999.

[2] See, for example, R. Wedgwood, "NATO's Campaign in Yugoslavia," 93 *American Journal of International Law* (1999), 828; T. Franck, "Lessons of Kosovo," 93 *American Journal of International Law* (1999), 857; B. Simma, "NATO, the UN and the Use of Force: Legal Aspects," 10 *European Journal of International Law* (1999), 1; A. Cassese, "*Ex iniuria ius oritur*: Are We Moving towards International Legitimation of Forcible Humanitarian Countermeasures in the World Community?" 10 *European Journal of International Law* (1999), 23; N. Krisch, "Unilateral Enforcement of the Collective Will: Kosovo, Iraq, and the Security Council," 3 *Max Planck United Nations Yearbook* (1999), 59; M. Kohen, "L'emploi de la force et la crise du Kosovo: vers un nouveau désordre juridique international," 32 *Revue Belge du droit international* (1999), 122; S. Sur, "Le recours à la force dans l'affaire du Kosovo et le droit international," 20 *Les notes de l'ifri* (2000), 1. See also Independent International Commission on Kosovo, *Kosovo Report*

Normally, when academic lawyers come to starkly different conclusions, this indicates that the questions of law are difficult ones on which experts reasonably can disagree. On the basis of traditional approaches to the interpretation of treaties and the analysis of customary rules, however, the Kosovo intervention was clearly illegal, and regarded as such by enough states that it could not possibly have contributed to a change in the law. It is therefore tempting to dismiss those who come to any other conclusion as mistaken or opportunistic in their interpretation.

But the debate over the Kosovo intervention may be seen in the broader context of changes in the nature of international legal argument more generally. Those authors who believe that the Kosovo intervention was legally justified and/or an important precedent arrive at their conclusions because they reject – if oftentimes implicitly or unconsciously – traditional approaches to the interpretation and application of international rules, and instead adopt new assumptions and procedures.[3]

In this chapter we seek to recast the debate on "unilateral humanitarian intervention" by shedding some light on these underlying issues.[4] First, we sketch out the underlying rules and procedures according to which international law has traditionally been interpreted, developed, and changed, and explain why a right of unilateral humanitarian intervention does not yet exist and is unlikely to develop, at least through the operation of the traditional rules about rules. We then explore how the underlying rules and procedures might themselves be undergoing change as a result, in part, of the Kosovo intervention and the ensuing debates over its legality. This leads to a consideration of the impact such changes to the rules about rules might have on the international legal system as a whole.[5]

Crucially, we argue that in order to take seriously the arguments of those scholars who defend the legality of unilateral humanitarian intervention, one must assume a radical change in the international legal system – a

(Oxford University Press, Oxford, 2000). Available at http://www.kosovocommission.org (5 March 2002).

[3] An insightful and thought-provoking exception to this trend is Thomas M. Franck, "Interpretation and Change in the Law of Humanitarian Intervention," ch. 6 in this volume.

[4] By "unilateral humanitarian intervention" we mean an armed intervention, by one or more states, conducted without the express authorization of the Security Council, and justified on the basis of humanitarian need.

[5] For an evaluation of change in the international legal system drawing on moral theory, see Allen Buchanan, "Reforming the International Law of Humanitarian Intervention," ch. 4 in this volume.

change that is, in our view, as unwarranted as it is unsound. Perhaps recognizing this, most of the acting states in situations of alleged unilateral humanitarian intervention have avoided using the term. The position adopted here is that an alternative approach – exceptional illegality – is both more consistent with the positions of states, and in keeping with principles of international law. In addition to being more realistic, however, it also reflects the fact that debate over the legality of humanitarian intervention is too often divorced from the political and moral questions that provide its impetus. Quite apart from the fact that achieving consensus on rules governing such interventions (unless the manner of creating such rules is radically changed) is likely to prove impossible, the debate detracts from, and may undermine, the significant advances over the past half century in the fields of human rights and conflict prevention. Moreover, any advance in that debate would likely be at the cost of principles fundamental to the development of an international rule of law.

Rules about rules

There are two principal sources of international law. Customary international law is an informal, unwritten body of rules that derives from the practice of states together with *opinio juris* – a belief, on the part of governments, that the practice is required by law or is at least of relevance to its ongoing evolution. Most rules of customary international law apply universally, which means that all states contribute to their development, maintenance, or change. As far as any particular putative rule or change to a rule is concerned, states can actively support it through their practice or statements, passively support it by doing nothing, or actively oppose it through contrary practice and protests. Only if most states support, and none or only a few oppose, it can the desired new or changed rule become a binding rule of customary international law.[6]

Treaties are quasi-contractual written instruments entered into by two or more states and registered with a third party, usually the UN Secretary-General. They are interpreted on the basis of agreed rules that are

---

[6] On customary international law, see generally M. Akehurst, "Custom as a Source of International Law," 47 *British Yearbook of International Law* (1974–75), 1; G. Danilenko, *Law-making in the International Community* (Martinus Nijhoff, Dordrecht, 1993); M. Byers, *Custom, Power and the Power of Rules: International Relations and Customary International Law* (Cambridge University Press, Cambridge, 1999).

conveniently set out in a treaty of their own, the 1969 Vienna Convention on the Law of Treaties, which has long been accepted, even by non-parties, as an accurate codification of the customary international law of treaties.[7] The most important rule concerning interpretation is set out in Article 31(1): "A treaty shall be interpreted in good faith in accordance with the ordinary meaning to be given to the terms of the treaty in their context and in the light of its object and purpose."

The relationship between the two principal sources of international law is similar to the relationship between domestic statutes and the common law. As between the parties to a treaty, an unambiguous provision of the treaty prevails over a conflicting rule of customary international law. One treaty – the UN Charter – even states explicitly that it prevails over all other treaties. This quasi-constitutional instrument, adopted in 1945, has since been ratified by 189 (virtually all) states.[8]

The picture is complicated somewhat by the existence of a few non-treaty rules of a "peremptory" character that have the ability to override conflicting, non-peremptory rules. Peremptory rules, which are similar to "public policy" rules in some national legal systems, include the prohibitions on genocide, torture, and the aggressive use of force. Referred to as *jus cogens*, they are considered by most international lawyers to be customary in origin and thus the result of a process of development similar to that of customary international law. They therefore require the support of most, if not all, states, as expressed through their active or passive support, coupled with a sense of legal obligation. Given the public policy and peremptory character of these rules, the threshold for their development is necessarily very high: higher than that for other customary rules.[9]

---

[7] 1155 UNTS 331; 8 ILM (1969), 679. Available at http://untreaty.un.org (5 March 2002). The most important non-party is the United States. President Nixon, when submitting the Convention to the Senate for its consent to ratification, stated that it "is an expertly designed formulation of contemporary treaty law and ... is already generally recognized as the authoritative guide to current treaty law and practice." Senate Executive Document L, 92nd Congress, 1st sess. (1971) 1. See also *Namibia Advisory Opinion, ICJ Reports, 1971*, p. 67.

[8] On the relationship between treaties and customary international law, see generally R. Baxter, "Treaties and Custom," 129 *Recueil des cours* (1970–71), 25; O. Schachter, "Entangled Treaty and Custom," in Y. Dinstein ed., *International Law at a Time of Perplexity: Essays in Honour of Shabtai Rosenne* (Martinus Nijhoff, Dordrecht, 1989), p. 717; Byers, *Custom, Power and the Power of Rules*, pp. 166–80.

[9] On *jus cogens*, see generally Vienna Convention on the Law of Treaties, Arts. 53, 64; L. Hannikainen, *Peremptory Norms (Jus Cogens) in International Law* (Lakimiesliiton Kustannus, Helsinki, 1988); S. Kadelbach, *Zwingendes Völkerrecht* (Dunker and Humblot, Berlin, 1992); Byers, *Custom, Power and the Power of Rules*, pp. 183–203.

International law and the Kosovo intervention

Against this backdrop, any analysis of the legality of the Kosovo intervention must begin with an interpretation of the relevant treaty – the UN Charter – in accordance with the rules on interpretation laid out in the Vienna Convention, especially Article 31(1).[10] The critical provision of the Charter is Article 2(4):

> All Members shall refrain in their international relations from the threat or use of force against the territorial integrity or political independence of any State, or in any other manner inconsistent with the Purposes of the United Nations.

The ordinary meaning of Article 2(4) is clear: the use of force across borders is simply not permitted. This meaning is supported by the UN Charter's context, object, and purpose – a global effort to prohibit unilateral determinations of the just war by vesting sole authority for the non-defensive use of force in the Security Council.[11]

The Charter sets out only two exceptions to the Article 2(4) prohibition, neither of which applies to the Kosovo intervention. First, the Security Council may authorize the use of force if it does so explicitly through a resolution adopted under Chapter VII.[12] No such authorization to use force for humanitarian ends was provided in any of the resolutions concerning Kosovo. The last resolution before the intervention, Resolution 1203 of 24 October 1998, specifically "affirms that, in the event of an emergency, action may be needed to ensure their [the OSCE Verification Mission's] safety and freedom of movement." It makes no mention of humanitarian intervention and concludes by stating that the Council remains "seized of the matter." It was thus made clear that any decision to engage in a humanitarian intervention was to be made by the Council alone, at a subsequent meeting.[13]

---

[10] For the text of Art. 31(1), see above, p. 180.

[11] See O. Schachter, "The Legality of Pro-democratic Invasion," 78 *American Journal of International Law* (1984), 646.

[12] Article 42 of the Charter states that the Security Council "may take such action by air, sea, or land forces as may be necessary to maintain or restore international peace and security."

[13] The previous resolution on Kosovo had been more specific, stating that the Council decided, "should the concrete measures demanded in this resolution and resolution 1160 (1998) not be taken, to *consider further action* and additional measures to maintain or restore peace and stability in the region": SC Res. 1199 (1998), para. 16 (emphasis added).

Military action commenced without subsequent involvement by the Council. The Council's first act was to consider a draft resolution, submitted by Russia shortly after the bombing began, which sought to condemn NATO's actions as illegal. Although the draft resolution was defeated – in part because five NATO members then on the Council voted against it[14] – this did not constitute the positive authorization required by the Charter.[15] Nor was such an authorization provided by Resolution 1244 of 10 June 1999, which was limited to establishing an international security presence and civilian administration to deal with the consequences of the intervention.[16] Much as Resolution 687 in no way validated Iraq's invasion of Kuwait, Resolution 1244 in no way validated NATO's actions in Yugoslavia.

The second exception to the Article 2(4) prohibition is the right of self-defense. This right is contingent upon an armed attack on the state asserting the right, and limited to acts taken in self-defense that are both necessary and proportionate. Self-defense was not available as a justification for the Kosovo intervention because it was never suggested that Yugoslavia was planning to attack any NATO states. Nor did NATO consider the people of Kosovo capable of having their own right of self-defense, and inviting assistance on that basis. Kosovo was not itself a state, which is a basic requirement for self-defense under international law.[17]

Having determined that there was no legal justification for the Kosovo intervention within the UN Charter, one may then ask whether a right to intervene had developed in customary international law. But since clear treaty provisions prevail over customary international law, an ordinary customary rule allowing intervention would not have been sufficient to override Article 2(4). Nor could any deficiencies in the UN system have enabled NATO to fall back on any such customary rule. When, in the 1949 *Corfu Channel* case, the United Kingdom sought to justify an intervention in Albanian territorial waters on the basis that nobody else was prepared

---

[14] The five NATO members were Canada, France, the Netherlands, the United Kingdom, and the United States. Argentina, Bahrain, Brazil, Gabon, Gambia, Malaysia, and Slovenia also voted against the draft resolution: UN Press Release SC/6659 (26 March 1999). See J. Miller, "Russia's Move to End Strike Loses: Margin Is a Surprise," *New York Times*, 27 March 1999.

[15] S. Chesterman, *Just War or Just Peace? Humanitarian Intervention and International Law* (Oxford University Press, Oxford, 2001), p. 213.

[16] SC Res. 1244 (1999).

[17] On self-defense, see generally UN Charter, Art. 51; I. Brownlie, *International Law and the Use of Force by States* (Clarendon Press, Oxford, 1963); B. Simma ed., *The Charter of the United Nations: A Commentary* (Oxford University Press, Oxford, 1994), p. 676.

to deal with the threat – mines planted in an international strait – the International Court of Justice rejected the argument:

> The Court cannot accept this line of defence. The Court can only regard the alleged right of intervention as a policy of force, such as has, in the past, given rise to the most serious abuses and such as cannot, whatever be the present defects in international organization, find a place in international law.[18]

Under traditional understandings of international law, the only way the Kosovo intervention could have been legal was if a right of unilateral humanitarian intervention had somehow achieved the status of *jus cogens* and thus overridden conflicting treaty provisions.[19] In determining whether these legal developments had occurred as of 24 March 1999, one must first consider the practice of states in the decades preceding the intervention. Had the preponderance of state practice – and accompanying *opinio juris* – indicated a change towards a right of humanitarian intervention in the absence of Security Council authorization?

The history of the second half of the twentieth century is one of non-intervention for humanitarian purposes. The few interventions that might have been justified on a humanitarian basis – Bangladesh, Cambodia, Uganda – were justified on other terms, while interventions in Liberia, Somalia, Bosnia, Haiti, and Rwanda were conducted on the basis of Security Council authorizations,[20] and in some cases also at the invitation of the targeted state.[21] Added to this, states have repeatedly and often unanimously affirmed the principle of non-intervention through resolutions and declarations of organs such as the UN General Assembly.[22] The only credible precedent – the 1991 creation of a no-fly zone in northern Iraq – was itself

[18] *ICJ Reports, 1949*, p. 4 at p. 35.

[19] The prohibition of the use of force is itself frequently cited as a rule of *jus cogens*. In the *Nicaragua* case the ICJ quoted with approval the following statement by the UN International Law Commission: "[T]he law of the Charter concerning the prohibition of the use of force in itself constitutes a conspicuous example of a rule in international law having the character of *jus cogens*." *ICJ Reports, 1986*, p. 14 at p. 100 (para. 190).

[20] See generally Chesterman, *Just War or Just Peace?*

[21] See generally G. Nolte, *Eingreifen auf Einladung – Zur völkerrechtlichen Zulässigkeit des Einsatzes fremder Truppen in internen Konflikt auf Einladung der Regierung (Intervention upon Invitation – Use of Force by Foreign Troops in Internal Conflicts at the Invitation of a Government under International Law [English summary])* (Springer, Berlin, 1999).

[22] See, for example, 1970 United Nations Declaration on Friendly Relations, UNGA Res. 2625 (XXV) (unanimous) (for example, "No State or group of States has the right to intervene, directly or indirectly, for any reason whatever, in the internal or external affairs of any other State").

explicitly justified on the basis of a new right of unilateral humanitarian intervention by only one of the three intervening states.[23] The development of a new rule of customary international law, especially one with peremptory status, requires considerably more than a single partial exception in a half-century of non-intervention on humanitarian grounds.

In addition, on the basis of these same traditional understandings of international law, the Kosovo intervention could not even contribute to the future development of such a right. International reaction to the intervention was at best mixed: Russia, China, and India all spoke out strongly against it, as did Namibia (which voted in the Security Council to condemn the bombings), Belarus, Ukraine, Iran, Thailand, Indonesia, and South Africa.[24] Following the intervention, the 133 developing states of the G77 twice adopted declarations unequivocally affirming that unilateral humanitarian intervention was illegal under international law.[25]

All that said, could we be so certain of our conclusions if the traditional rules concerning the interpretation of treaties and the formation of custom were themselves changing, as the result of at least some states and authors adopting new assumptions and procedures? What if Article 31(1), for instance, no longer reflected the current state of the customary international law on treaty interpretation?

Changing the rules about rules: treaty interpretation

At the 1968–69 Vienna Conference on the Law of Treaties, Myres McDougal, the head of the United States delegation, proposed that a purposive approach be adopted as the preferred method of interpretation in international

---

[23] A. Aust, Legal Counsellor, FCO, statement before HC Foreign Affairs Committee, 2 December 1992, *Parliamentary Papers*, 1992–93, HC, Paper 235-iii, p. 85, reprinted in 63 *British Yearbook of International Law* (1992), 827. This was one of a number of rationales given for the action. See Chesterman, *Just War or Just Peace?*, pp. 196–206.

[24] See Krisch, "Unilateral Enforcement," pp. 83–84.

[25] See Ministerial Declaration, 23rd Annual Meeting of the Ministers for Foreign Affairs of the Group of 77, 24 September 1999, available at http://www.g77.org/Docs/Decl1999.html (5 March 2002), paragraph 69 of which reads, *inter alia*: "The Ministers . . . rejected the so-called right of humanitarian intervention, which had no basis in the UN Charter or in international law"; Declaration of the Group of 77 South Summit, Havana, Cuba, 10–14 April 2000, available at http://www.g77.org/Docs/Declaration_G77Summit.htm (5 March 2002), paragraph 54 of which reads, *inter alia*: "We reject the so-called 'right' of humanitarian intervention, which has no legal basis in the United Nations Charter or in the general principles of international law." The 133 states in question included 23 Asian states, 51 African states, 22 Latin American states, and 13 Arab states.

law. The approach would have emphasized a comprehensive examination of the context of the treaty aimed at ascertaining the common will of the parties – as that common will evolved over time.[26] McDougal's proposal generated considerable opposition and was rejected in favor of the textually oriented, hierarchical series of rules now set out in Articles 31 and 32 of the Vienna Convention.[27]

Today, however, the United States, some of its allies, and an increasing number of authors are reasserting a preference for a broadly gauged purposive approach. For example, in June 2000, lawyers from the State Department, the Defense Department and the National Security Council concluded that the 1972 Anti-Ballistic Missile Treaty between the United States and Russia (as the successor to the Soviet Union's treaty obligations) could be interpreted so as to allow construction work, including the pouring of concrete, to be carried out on a proposed anti-ballistic missile radar station in Alaska.[28] They came to this conclusion notwithstanding the terms of Articles 1(2) and 2(2)(b) of the Treaty, which read:

1. (2) Each Party undertakes not to deploy ABM systems for a defense of the territory of its country and not to provide a base for such a defense, and not to deploy ABM systems for defense of an individual region . . .
2. (2) The ABM system components . . . include those which are: (b) undergoing construction; . . .[29]

---

[26] UN Conference on the Law of Treaties, Official Records (1st sess., 1969), pp. 167–68.

[27] Ibid., pp. 168–85. The US proposal was rejected by 66 votes to 8, with 10 abstentions. Tom Farer has described the selection of interpretive approach as involving a choice between a textually oriented "classical view" and a more malleable approach that he terms "legal realism." As Farer explained, the classical view presumes that the parties to a treaty "had an original intention which can be discovered primarily through textual analysis and which, in the absence of some unforeseen change in circumstances, must be respected until the agreement has expired according to its terms or been replaced by mutual consent." In contrast, supporters of the "legal realist" approach regard "explicit and implicit agreements, formal texts, and state behavior as being in a condition of effervescent interaction, unceasingly creating, modifying, and replacing norms. Texts themselves are but one among a large number of means for ascertaining original intention. Moreover, realists postulate an accelerating contraction in the capacity and the authority of original intention to govern state behavior. Indeed, original intention does not govern at any point in time. For original intention has no intrinsic authority. The past is relevant only to the extent that it helps us to identify currently prevailing attitudes about the propriety of a government's acts and omissions." Farer, "An Inquiry into the Legitimacy of Humanitarian Intervention," in L. Damrosch and D. Scheffer eds., Law and Force in the New International Order (Westview Press, Boulder, 1991), p. 186.

[28] E. Schmitt and S. Myers, "Clinton Lawyers Give a Go-Ahead to Missile Shield," New York Times, 15 June 2000.

[29] 944 UNTS 13. Available at http://fletcher.tufts.edu/multi/texts/abm.txt (5 March 2002).

Applying Article 31(1) of the Vienna Convention, the ordinary meaning of the term "under construction" clearly includes the pouring of concrete.[30] Yet a White House spokesman felt able to assert:

> The treaty, itself, does not provide a definition of what constitutes a so-called "breach," but it's prudent for us to examine what the possible interpretations of the ABM Treaty would be as we continue with our development effort. There are a range of interpretations available, but we have made no decision.[31]

Another example of purposive interpretation arose during the Kosovo crisis, when efforts to reinterpret the UN Charter reached almost farcical dimensions. As James Rubin has explained:

> There was a series of strained telephone calls between Albright and Cook, in which he cited problems "with our lawyers" over using force in the absence of UN endorsement. "Get new lawyers," she suggested. But with a push from Prime Minister Tony Blair, the British finally agreed that UN Security Council approval was not legally required.[32]

A final example of purposive interpretation involves the attempt, by a few US authors and the Belgian Government, to argue that unilateral humanitarian intervention does not contravene Article 2(4) of the UN Charter because it is not directed against the "territorial integrity or political independence of any State."[33] Two decades ago, Oscar Schachter dismissed this argument as requiring an "Orwellian construction" of those terms; in other words, it ran directly contrary to the ordinary meaning, as well as to the clear object and purpose of the UN Charter.[34] But what if the rules concerning interpretation have since changed, or are perhaps in the process of changing?

---

[30] See *Concise Oxford English Dictionary* (8th edn, Oxford University Press, Oxford, 1990), p. 246, where the verb "construct" is defined as "make by fitting parts together; build, form (something physical or abstract)."

[31] Press Briefing by J. Siewert and P. J. Crowley, 15 June 2000. Available at http://www.usinfo. state.gov/topical/pol/arms/stories/00061505.htm (5 March 2002).

[32] J. Rubin, "Countdown to a Very Personal War," *Financial Times*, 30 September 2000.

[33] See, for example, A. D'Amato, "The Invasion of Panama was a Lawful Response to Tyranny," 84 *American Journal of International Law* (1990), 520; F. Tesón, *Humanitarian Intervention: An Inquiry into Law and Morality* (2nd edn, Transnational Publishers, Dobbs Ferry, 1997), pp. 150–62. See also W. M. Reisman, "Coercion and Self-determination: Construing Charter Article 2(4)," 78 *American Journal of International Law* (1984), 645 ("In the construction of Article 2(4), attention must always be given to the spirit of the Charter and not simply to the letter of a particular provision"). For the arguments of Belgium, see *Legality of Use of Force Case* (Provisional Measures) (ICJ, 1999), pleadings of Belgium, 10 May 1999, CR 99/15 (uncorrected translation).

[34] Schachter, "Legality of Pro-democratic Invasion," p. 649. The argument also runs contrary to numerous statements by the UN General Assembly and the International Court of Justice.

The rules of treaty interpretation apply as rules of customary international law for those states that have not ratified the Vienna Convention, including the United States.[35] And even the meaning of Article 31(1) could conceivably change as a result of the practice of states with regard to treaty interpretation.[36] How other states react to reassertions of the purposive approach therefore matters in terms of evaluating whether the content of these rules has changed in the last three decades.

Although most states have not evinced support for new interpretive rules, that may not be the end of the inquiry. It may also matter how one evaluates the reactions, or lack of reactions, to reassertions of the purposive approach. In other words, is the accepted approach to evaluating different kinds of state practice, and the state practice of different states, itself perhaps also undergoing change? For if the rules concerning customary international law are changing, the rules concerning interpretation will themselves have become more open to change.

Changing the rules about rules: customary international law

Numerous authors point to the Kosovo intervention as state practice supportive of a new customary rule, with statements by the United States and several of its allies articulating humanitarian motives presented as evidence of an accompanying *opinio juris*.[37] As indicated above, however, this is insufficient to bring about a change in customary international law as it is traditionally understood. In order to be taken seriously, these arguments

---

See, for example, 1970 United Nations Declaration on Friendly Relations; *Nicaragua Case, ICJ Reports, 1986*, p. 14 at p. 134 (para. 268) ("while the United States might form its own appraisal of the situation as to respect for human rights in Nicaragua, the use of force could not be the appropriate method to monitor or ensure such respect").

[35] 1155 UNTS 331; 8 ILM (1969), 679. Available at http://untreaty.un.org (5 March 2002).

[36] See Vienna Convention, Art. 31(3)(b) ("There shall be taken into account together with the context . . . any subsequent practice in the application of the treaty which establishes the agreement of the parties regarding its interpretation"). It may also be possible – if difficult – actually to modify a treaty obligation by way of customary international law. See generally Danilenko, *Law-making*, pp. 162–72; Byers, *Custom, Power and the Power of Rules*, pp. 172–80.

[37] See, for example, President Clinton's speech on 24 March 1999: "In the President's Words: 'We Act to Prevent a Wider War'," *New York Times*, 25 March 1999 ("We act to protect thousands of innocent people in Kosovo from a mounting military offensive"); Lewis, "The Rationale" (quoting a spokesman for the US National Security Council as well as Abram Chayes, Diane Orentlicher, Michael Reisman, Ruth Wedgwood, and Thomas Franck); and the statement of the UK delegate to the UN Security Council on 24 March 1999: S/PV.3988 (1999) 12 ("Every means short of force has been tried to avert this situation. In these circumstances, and as an exceptional measure on grounds of overwhelming humanitarian necessity, military intervention is legally justifiable").

must be interpreted as implying that the rules concerning the formation of custom have themselves changed, or are in the process of changing. For example, are acts, as opposed to statements, today accorded more weight than previously? Does the practice of the powerful now count for more, as compared to the practice of the weak? Or does a lower threshold now exist with regard to the development of customary rules of a humanitarian or human rights character? The widespread acceptance among many Western governments that the Kosovo intervention was not clearly illegal suggests that, at least from the perspective of one sector of international society, changes of these kinds may indeed be under way.[38]

The development of customary international law has long been a matter of some disagreement among states – and among academic lawyers. One contested issue concerns the character of state practice. Some authors, such as Anthony D'Amato, Mark Weisburd, and Karol Wolfke, have insisted that only physical acts count as state practice, which means that any state wishing to support or oppose the development or change of a rule must engage in some sort of act, and that statements or claims do not suffice.[39]

Numerous authors have opposed this position.[40] One reason for their opposition is that, insofar as this approach concerns the change of rules, it would seem to require violations of customary international law. In short, acts in opposition to existing rules constitute violations of those rules, whereas statements in opposition do not. Consequently, this approach is, in Michael Akehurst's words, "hardly one to be recommended by anyone who wishes to strengthen the rule of law in international relations."[41] But this approach does more than reduce the space for diplomacy and peaceful persuasion; it also provides a substantial advantage to powerful states in developing customary international law.

The polarization between those who think that only acts constitute state practice and those who support a broader conception is perhaps most

[38] That said, the similarly widespread view that the intervention was "illegal but legitimate" suggests a degree of uncertainty with this position. See Independent International Commission on Kosovo, *Kosovo Report*. It may also support an alternative approach. See discussion below.

[39] A. D'Amato, *The Concept of Custom* (Cornell University Press, Ithaca, 1971); D'Amato, "Invasion of Panama"; M. Weisburd, *Use of Force: The Practice of States since World War II* (Pennsylvania State University Press, University Park, 1997); K. Wolfke, *Custom in Present International Law* (2nd rev. edn, Martinus Nijhoff, Dordrecht, 1993).

[40] See, for example, Akehurst, "Custom as a Source of International Law"; I. Brownlie, "Remarks," in "Comparative Approaches to the Theory of International Law," 80 *American Society of International Law Proceedings* (1986), 154; N. Onuf, "Book Review: Karol Wolfke, *Custom in Present International Law* (2nd rev. edn)," 88 *American Journal of International Law* (1994), 556.

[41] Akehurst, "Custom as a Source of International Law," p. 8.

evident in the debate over whether, and how, resolutions of international bodies such as the UN General Assembly contribute to customary international law. Since the 1960s, developing states and a significant number of authors have asserted that resolutions are important instances of state practice which are potentially creative, or at least indicative, of rules of customary international law.[42] In the 1986 *Nicaragua* case the International Court of Justice reinforced this view by accepting that a series of General Assembly resolutions played a role in the development of customary rules prohibiting intervention and aggression.[43] That decision was condemned by the United States, which, along with a significant number of primarily American authors, has resisted any effort to recognize resolutions as state practice.[44] This resistance has had some success: today, General Assembly resolutions play a markedly less important role in debates over customary international law than they did just twenty years ago. For example, the literature on NATO's 1999 intervention in Kosovo, much of which considers the possibility of a customary right of unilateral humanitarian intervention, contains almost no references to the relevant General Assembly resolutions, including the 1970 Declaration on Friendly Relations.[45]

Statements by individual states or groups of states are also accorded significantly less weight. During the 1960s, '70s, and '80s, the views of the G77 were treated as being of considerable relevance to any assessment of customary international law. The same cannot be said of the statements issued by that same group following the Kosovo intervention, expressing the view that unilateral humanitarian intervention is illegal.[46] A review of the subsequent literature turns up scarcely a mention of those statements, especially in articles and books published in the United States.[47]

---

[42] See, for example, R. Higgins, *The Development of International Law through the Political Organs of the United Nations* (Oxford University Press, Oxford, 1963), pp. 5–7; O. Asamoah, *The Legal Significance of the Declarations of the General Assembly of the United Nations* (Martinus Nijhoff, The Hague, 1966), pp. 46–62; Jorge Castaneda, *Legal Effects of United Nations Resolutions* (trans. Alba Amoia) (Columbia University Press, New York, 1969), pp. 168–77.

[43] *Nicaragua Case, ICJ Reports, 1986*, p. 14 at pp. 97–100 (paras. 183–90).

[44] See, for example, G. Arangio-Ruiz, "The Normative Roles of the General Assembly of the United Nations and the Declaration of Principles of Friendly Relations," 137 *Recueil des Cours* (1972-III), 455–59; S. Schwebel, "The Effect of Resolutions of the UN General Assembly on Customary International Law," 73 *American Society of International Law Proceedings* (1979), 301; D'Amato, "Invasion of Panama" and *Concept of Custom*; Weisburd, *Use of Force*.

[45] UNGA Res. 2625 (XXV).   [46] See above, p. 184, n. 25.

[47] Exceptions include Krisch, "Unilateral Enforcement"; I. Brownlie, 95 *American Society of International Law Proceedings* (2001), 13, 14.

The novel conception of international law that is being constructed and reinforced by a limited group of Anglo-American international lawyers is possible only by ignoring the wider circle of states and international lawyers around the world. A broader analysis, in contrast, reinforces traditional assumptions and procedures – and thus leads to very different conclusions on issues such as unilateral humanitarian intervention.[48] To many commentators in Africa, for example, the debate over Kosovo-style interventions simply misses the point.

When the Organization of African Unity (OAU) was created in 1963, a defining feature was the extent to which state sovereignty was privileged. Of the seven core principles affirmed by the OAU Charter, four sought to prohibit any form of interference – let alone intervention – in the internal affairs of member states. Military adventures by Western colonial powers had made Africa's new leaders wary of any form of intervention across borders.[49]

Even if there has been some evidence of a shift in views since the end of the Cold War, the term "humanitarian intervention" remains particularly controversial in Africa.[50] At least three questions are prominent in the

---

[48] See, for example, just some of the rich writings on unilateral humanitarian intervention in other languages: Kohen, "L'emploi de la force et la crise du Kosovo"; Sur, "Le recours à la force dans L'affaire du Kosovo"; N. Ronzitti, "Raids aerei contro la Repubblica federale di Iogoslavia e Carta delle Nazioni Unite," 82 *Rivista di diritto internazionale* (1999), 481; D. Thürer, "Die NATO-Einsätze in Kosovo und das Völkerrecht," *Neue Zürcher Zeitung*, 3–4 April 1999; Christian Tomuschat, "Völkerrechtliche Aspekte des Kosovo-Konflikts," 74 (1–2) *Friedens-Warte* (1999), 33; G. Nolte, "Kosovo und Konstitutionalisierung: zur humanitären Intervention der NATO-Staaten," 59 *Zeitschrift für ausländisches öffentliches Recht und Völkerrecht* (1999), 941.

[49] See A. Adebajo and C. Landsberg, "The Heirs of Nkrumah: Africa's New Interventionists," 2(1) *Pugwash Occasional Papers* (2001), 1.

[50] A more interventionist posture has been adopted by Africa's "new interventionists" – including Muammar Qaddafi, Yoweri Museveni, Paul Kagame, Charles Taylor, and Blaise Compaoré – who have been willing to violate the non-intervention and territorial integrity clauses of the OAU Charter. Most notably, South African President Nelson Mandela articulated a broad defense of intervention at the 1998 OAU summit in Ouagadougou: "Africa has a right and a duty to intervene to root out tyranny . . . we must all accept that we cannot abuse the concept of national sovereignty to deny the rest of the continent the right and duty to intervene when behind those sovereign boundaries, people are being slaughtered to protect tyranny." Address of the President of the Republic of South Africa, Nelson Mandela (Summit Meeting of the OAU Heads of State and Government, Ouagadougou, Burkina Faso, 8 June 1998). Available at http://www.oau-oua.org/oau_info/burkdoc/mandela.htm (5 March 2002). Meanwhile, the OAU and other regional organizations such as the Economic Community of West African States (ECOWAS), the Southern African Development Community (SADC), and the Inter-Governmental Authority on Development (IGAD) have demonstrated a willingness to play a more active role in regional peace and security.

African context. First, does "intervention" refer solely to military intervention, or can it encompass other forms, ranging from the provision of aid to the relief of debt? The OAU's role in providing election observers, for example, exhibits a preparedness to accept international supervision that previously would have been regarded as unacceptable interference. Second, what significance is to be attributed to consent, and how might that consent be determined? Numerous colonial interventions were undertaken with the "consent" of a pliant local regime. Third, is the adjective "humanitarian" appropriate on a continent that has been the target of a great many interventions directed at other ends? Referring to certain military actions as "humanitarian" may conceal their true nature. Moreover, military action may be a poor substitute for preventative measures addressing the economic and social problems that lead to humanitarian crises.

These issues are of more than lexicological interest. A widespread view among African commentators is that debate on this topic has become mired in the question of Kosovo-style interventions. Such a model is simply inappropriate to the African context, not least because the West has demonstrated that it is now unwilling to commit the resources to fight such a high-tech war (or, indeed, virtually any war) on African soil. The failure to intervene to stop the Rwanda genocide is but one case in point. In the absence of such a commitment, a focus on purely military solutions to humanitarian problems is at best diversionary, at worst inflammatory.[51]

The views from African and other developing states are frequently overlooked by Anglo-American authors.[52] It is true that the practice of developing states is generally less well documented than that of relatively developed states, and less likely to be available electronically and in English.[53]

---

[51] See "Humanitarian Intervention: Perspectives from Africa." Available at http://www.ipacademy. org (5 March 2002) (summarizing a consultation on humanitarian intervention held by the International Peace Academy in Gabarone, Botswana, December 2000). See further F. Olonisakin and J. Levitt, "Regional Security and the Challenges of Democratisation in Africa: The Case of ECOWAS and SADC," 13 *Cambridge Review of International Affairs* (1999), 66.

[52] Important but frequently overlooked works include U. O. Umozurike, "Tanzania's Intervention in Uganda," 20 *Archiv des Völkerrechts* (1980), 301; J. Farrokh, "Unilateral Humanitarian Intervention: Some Conceptual Problems," in Rafael Gutiérrez Girardot et al. eds., *New Directions in International Law: Essays in Honour of Wolfgang Abendroth* (Campus, Frankfurt, 1982), p. 459; *Le droit d'ingérence est-il une nouvelle légalisation du colonialisme?* (Publications de l'Académie du Royaume du Maroc, Rabat, 1991); N. Chadrahasan, "Use of Force to Ensure Humanitarian Relief – A South Asian Precedent Examined," 42 *International and Comparative Law Quarterly* (1993), 664.

[53] See Byers, *Custom, Power and the Power of Rules*, pp. 37–38, 153.

However, when it comes to statements such as those by the G77 on human-itarian intervention, none of these explanations pertain. The adoption of these particular documents was reported in the press and the documents themselves are easy to find, in English, on the Internet.[54]

And even those who consider the views of the less powerful often forget that such states may be pressured into supporting the positions of the "leading" states. For example, the United States made various promises to resume normal trade relations, provide aid, support World Bank loans, and exclude certain states from international conferences in order to secure the adoption of Security Council Resolution 678 in November 1990 and thus greater legitimacy for Operation Desert Storm.[55] In itself, the use of carrots and sticks to encourage support for a desired course of action is not unusual in international relations. But it distorts our assessments of what governments really think – the *opinio juris* of customary international law.[56] Moreover, the application of economic and political pressure by a powerful state – especially the single superpower – in one situation can also create a reputation for throwing its weight around that is helpful to it in other, subsequent situations. It is well known that Yemen lost US $70 million in annual aid from the United States because of its vote against Resolution 678.[57] It seems probable that other recipients of US aid would now at least think twice before voting against the United States within the Security Council.

It is possible, however, that we are witnessing something more than just a continued effort to degrade the influence of resolutions, the relative weight of statements as opposed to acts, and thus the law-making contributions of the less powerful. The United States, and at least some authors, may also be seeking a degree of *formal* recognition for the greater influence of the actions and opinions of powerful states in the formation of customary international law.

[54] See above, p. 184, n. 25. It is noteworthy that neither of the G77 statements were deemed worthy of reproduction in *International Legal Materials*, the widely used compilation regularly published by the American Society of International Law.

[55] See B. Weston, "Security Council Resolution 678 and Persian Gulf Decision Making: Precarious Legitimacy," 85 *American Journal of International Law* (1991), 523–24.

[56] On the role of power in *opinio juris*, see B. Stern, "La coutume au coeur du droit international," in *Mélanges offerts à Paul Reuter* (Pedone, Paris, 1981), p. 479 (approved English translation at 11 *Duke Journal of Comparative and International Law* [2001], 89).

[57] See J. Miller, "Mideast Tensions: Kuwaiti Envoy Says Baker Vowed 'No Concessions' to Iraqis," *New York Times*, 5 December 1990.

It is true that powerful states have always had a disproportionate influence on customary law-making, in large part because they have a broader range of interests and activities and consequently engage in more practice than other states. But paying less attention to some states is one thing: having a legal justification for doing so is another. It is possible that the legal principle of sovereign equality is now, quietly but resolutely, under attack. In the US literature, in particular, analyses and arguments concerning customary international law increasingly make reference to "leading" and "major" states or nations – words that suggest that some states matter more than others in a manner significant to the formation of custom.[58]

Ian Brownlie identified this tendency in his 1995 General Course at the Hague Academy:

> The *modus operandi* for the formation of customary law supposes an equality of States and also a principle of majoritarianism. A certain amount of contracting out is possible but the generality of States are permitted by their conduct to develop customary rules...
>
> This approach to international law creates problems for those who hold that inequalities of power between States should be reflected in the way in which the law is made and applied, and this involves what may be called the hegemonial approach to law-making. The hegemonial approach to international relations may be defined as an approach to the sources which facilitates the translation of the difference in power between States into specific advantages for the more powerful actor. The hegemonial approach to the sources

---

[58] Richard Falk, for example, refers to "leading states" ("The Complexities of Humanitarian Intervention: A New World Order Challenge," 17 *Michigan Journal of International Law* [1996], 491; "Re-framing the Legal Agenda of World Order in the Course of a Turbulent Century," 9 *Transnational Law and Contemporary Problems* [1999], 451). According a special role to "powerful states" is also increasingly common. See, for example, J. Yoo, "UN Wars, US War Powers," 1 *Chicago Journal of International Law* (2000), 355 ("Achieving the progressive goals of international law – ending human rights violations, restoring stability and peace based on democratic self-determination – often requires powerful nations to violate international law norms about national sovereignty and the use of force"). These efforts to differentiate between states are, it should be noted, not the same thing as assigning particular importance to the practice of "specially affected states," an approach deemed proper by the International Court in the 1969 *North Sea Continental Shelf Cases*, *ICJ Reports, 1969*, p. 3 at p. 42 (para. 73). Although the broader range and greater frequency of activities of powerful states are more likely to make them "specially affected" by any particular legal development, up to now there has been, in Gennady Danilenko's words, "no indication that their special status in customary law-making is recognized as a matter of law." Danilenko, *Law-making*, p. 96.

involves maximizing the occasions when the powerful actor will obtain "legal approval" for its actions and minimizing the occasions when such approval may be conspicuously withheld.[59]

It is clear that, as the number of less powerful states increases and the economic and military gap between the weak and the strong grows, powerful states, and authors from powerful states, do have an interest in altering the principle of sovereign equality – a principle which operates, in a multitude of contexts, to constrain the law-making influence of the powerful.[60]

We may also be witnessing efforts to reduce the time necessary for the development of customary international law. Much of the literature concerning unilateral humanitarian intervention focuses on the decade following the end of the Cold War. There is an assumption, implicit in this literature, that the geopolitical shifts of 1989–91 rendered previous practice of little relevance to determining the contemporary balance of influence and interests – and thus the current state of customary law. This assumption is made notwithstanding the fact that the interests of most states have not changed on many issues, including the use of force in international relations. As the G77 made clear after the Kosovo intervention, weak states still attach considerable importance to the existence of legal protections against the use of force.[61] Since the capacity of the United States and its allies to influence law-making is much greater today than it was a decade ago, a reduction in the time involved in the formation of customary international law, by discounting long-established practice, disfavors weak states and favors the single superpower.[62]

---

[59] I. Brownlie, "International Law at the Fiftieth Anniversary of the United Nations," 255 *Recueil des Cours* (1995-I), 49.

[60] The principle of sovereign equality ensures that all states are entitled to participate in law-making in bodies such as the UN General Assembly which operate on the basis of one state – one vote, in the negotiation and conclusion of treaties, and in the formation of customary international law. But though the participation of the weak imposes some limits on the law-making influence of the powerful, differences in influence can still be substantial. See generally Byers, *Custom, Power and the Power of Rules.* Cf. A. Buchanan, "From Nuremberg to Kosovo: The Morality of Illegal International Legal Reform," 111 *Ethics* (2001), 683–86 (considering the curious argument that equality before the law will be improved by allowing certain powerful states to act illegally to reform the law).

[61] See above, p. 184, n. 25.

[62] The Kosovo intervention raises a host of additional issues concerning customary international law and, more particularly, possible changes to the manner in which customary rules are made and changed. What weight should be accorded to arguments in the alternative as potential contributions to the development of customary rules? The putative right of unilateral humanitarian

Exceptional legality?

The United States has always been reluctant to subject its national interests to multilateral structures. But this tendency has advanced to new levels under the Administration of President George W. Bush, which has opposed the conclusion and implementation of multilateral instruments on, among other things, climate change, arms control, and international crimes.[63] Individually, these actions suggest the traditional United States suspicion of international regulation. Taken together they suggest a more general opposition to any form of multilateral constraints on its behavior – that is, an opposition to international law as such, at least insofar as it binds the United States.

Perhaps what we are seeing, then, is not so much an effort to change all of international law as an effort to create new, exceptional rights for the United States alone, not only with regard to treaties, but also with regard to treaty interpretation and customary international law – and thus to the use of force. Similar exceptional rights have been created by other states in the past, albeit on a much more limited basis. In 1984, for example, the Federal Republic of Germany abandoned its claim to a three-mile territorial sea within the specific confines of the German Bight and claimed a new limit

---

intervention was not the principal justification advanced by most NATO states for the Kosovo intervention; in most cases it was advanced – if at all – only in ambiguous terms. With regard to the two states that articulated such a claim most clearly at the time – the Netherlands and the United Kingdom – the additional question arises of whether one state, in this case a partner in the relevant act, can express the *opinio juris* for other states' practice.

A related issue concerns the weight to be accorded to academic writing that advances legal arguments to justify governmental actions that the governments themselves have not articulated. Most of the support for a right of unilateral humanitarian intervention has been generated by authors who have attached legal arguments to policy decisions that may in fact have been made in disregard – if not conscious violation – of international law. Similarly, what weight, if any, should be accorded to expressions of opinion by the media and non-governmental organizations on this and other legal issues?

Is it the case, also, that a lower threshold now exists with regard to the development of customary rules of a humanitarian or human rights character? Suggestions to this effect have certainly appeared in the literature, and may be bolstered by recent debates concerning possible differences between human rights and other rules with regard to their effects on reservations to treaties, and on the law of state succession.

[63] See, for example, Associated Press, "US Won't Follow Climate Treaty Provisions, Whitman Says," *New York Times*, 28 March 2001; D. Sanger, "Bush Flatly States US Will Pull Out of Missile Treaty," *New York Times*, 24 August 2001; B. Crossette, "Effort by UN to Cut Traffic in Arms Meets a US Rebuff," *New York Times*, 10 July 2001; B. Crossette, "US Opposition to Tribunal Worries European Supporters," *New York Times*, 14 July 2001.

on the basis of a sixteen-mile box defined by geographical co-ordinates.[64] The new claim, which was explicitly designed for the limited purpose of preventing oil spills in those busy waters, met with no public protests from other states. This was perhaps because the position and interests of Germany in that situation were different enough that other states were prepared to allow for the development of a prescriptive right as an exception to the general rule.

The same might be said of the position and interests of the single super-power in the post-Cold War period, in which case the development of exceptional rules would depend on the responses of other states to the exceptional claims. Given the potentially substantial political, military, and economic costs of opposing the United States in any particular law-making situation, acquiescence might well occur – at least with regard to those claims that are not specifically contrary to the vital interests of other states. Most importantly, acquiescence may also be likely with regard to the advancement of new approaches to the interpretation of at least some treaties and the identification and assessment of at least some forms of state practice and expressions of *opinio juris*. It is this pattern of assertion and acquiescence in exceptional claims and new approaches that might, in turn, eventually lead to the development of one set of legal processes for the single superpower and another set for all other states.[65]

We do not believe that any of these fundamental changes to the international legal system have, in fact, taken place. The views of the international society of states are, in our opinion, a much more important factor in the development and change of international law than many Anglo-American authors believe them to be. To borrow an insight from Daniel Warner, the rules according to which international law is interpreted, developed, and changed are not the billiard balls of classical realism, but rather the table upon which the game is played.[66] The rules about rules are, as a result, the most deeply ingrained of rules, and thus the most resistant to change.[67] Customary international law, in particular, is derived to a considerable

[64] See Decree of 12 November 1984, reproduced in 7 *Law of the Sea Bulletin* (1986), 9–22; Byers, *Custom, Power and the Power of Rules*, p. 95.
[65] For a similar view, see G. Symes, "Force Without Law: Seeking a Legal Justification for the September 1996 US Military Intervention in Iraq," 19 *Michigan Journal of International Law* (1998), 616.
[66] See D. Warner, "The Nuclear Weapons Decision by the International Court of Justice: Locating the *raison* behind *raison d'état*," 27 *Millennium: Journal of International Studies* (1998), 320–24.
[67] See Byers, *Custom, Power and the Power of Rules*, pp. 147–62.

extent from shared understandings of legal relevance and a collectivity of law-making design, not the behavior of actors whose conceptions of self and the good are somehow hermetically sealed from their relations with the outside world.[68] Ironically, the basic claim of those commentators who believe in the existence of new rules about rules is that the new system deprivileges the views of governments, only to privilege the views of commentators.

In addition to representing an unwarranted attempt to revise by stealth the fundamental principles of international law, however, such radical change would also be undesirable. Most obviously, providing a formal exception for a powerful state (or states) to violate rules that continue to apply to all other actors severely undermines respect for a particular rule and for international law more generally. It would probably also encourage violations of the law – at least insofar as the capacity to violate the law and get away with it was the benchmark of being a "leading state." As indicated above, this is not a recipe for strengthening the rule of law.[69]

Even the United States does not advocate such an approach. It is possible that this may stem from a reluctance to engage in *any* legal discussions that might constrain its behavior in future.[70] But it also appears that the US recognizes that its broader interests are protected by continued engagement – even, at times, only on a formal level – with international legal processes, and that institutions such as the UN Security Council may often prove vital to its own national interests.

This selective engagement seems to have been demonstrated by the US response to the terrorist attacks on New York and Washington, DC, on 11 September 2001. Though it obtained a series of strongly worded resolutions from the Security Council, the US (together with the United Kingdom) engaged in a protracted military action that came to stretch the stated justification of self-defense.[71] The action was, however, supported by an extraordinarily broad coalition of states – due in part to the singular unpopularity of Afghanistan's Taliban regime. Nevertheless, initial hopes that the US

---

[68] See P. Haggenmacher, "La doctrine des deux éléments du droit coutumier dans la pratique de la cour internationale," 90 *Revue générale de droit international public* (1986), 5; S. Toope, "Emerging Patterns of Governance and International Law," in M. Byers ed., *The Role of Law in International Politics* (Oxford University Press, Oxford, 2000), p. 91; Byers, *Custom, Power and the Power of Rules*, pp. 147–64, cf. J. Goldsmith and E. Posner, "A Theory of Customary International Law," 66 *University of Chicago Law Review* (1999), 1113.

[69] Akehurst, "Custom as a Source of International Law," p. 8.   [70] See above, p. 195, n. 63.

[71] See M. Byers, "Terrorism, the Use of Force and International Law after 11 September," 51 *International and Comparative Law Quarterly* (2002), 401.

had abandoned unilateralism *tout court* were unfounded. Though it ceased actively opposing measures such as the Kyoto Protocol on climate change and the International Criminal Court, it gave no indication of submitting itself to either regime.

An alternative approach: exceptional illegality

The picture sketched out here may be unduly pessimistic. But it is important that those who support the development of a right of unilateral humanitarian intervention recognize the collateral damage of such a radical change to the international legal order. Moreover, such a change is not the only alternative to condoning slaughter, as the ethical dilemma is too often presented.[72]

If, instead of advancing potentially destabilizing legal claims, states were to admit – explicitly or implicitly – that they were violating international law, the effect would be to strengthen, rather than weaken, the rules governing intervention.[73] In the *Nicaragua* case, the International Court of Justice said:

> The significance for the Court of cases of State conduct *prima facie* inconsistent with the principle of non-intervention lies in the nature of the ground offered as justification. Reliance by a State on a novel right or an unprecedented exception to the principle might, if shared in principle by other States, tend towards a modification of customary international law.[74]

It follows that, if the intervening state admits that it is violating international law, the intervention itself will not undermine the existing rules, while the admission of illegality may in fact serve to strengthen them.

It might be argued that such an approach would undercut political support for an otherwise ethically sound action – states are generally reluctant to admit that they are violating international law. This would be especially the case during a controversial military action. But is it so different from the approach adopted in relation to Kosovo? NATO states have been far more

---

[72] See Chesterman, *Just War or Just Peace?*, ch. 6.

[73] *Contra* Buchanan, "From Nuremberg to Kosovo," p. 675. Buchanan argues that "a person who breaks the law with the aim of improving the legal system thereby shows that he values the contribution that a system of law can make to justice."

[74] *Nicaragua, ICJ Reports, 1986*, p. 14 at p. 109 (para. 207).

reluctant to suggest that they acted on the basis of clear legal principles than their more enthusiastic academic supporters.[75]

For example, then Foreign Minister Klaus Kinkel, in explaining his support for the NATO action in October 1998, identified the situation in Kosovo as a "humanitarian catastrophe" but made clear his desire that any intervention not constitute a precedent for further action.[76] Two weeks before the air campaign, Bruno Simma endorsed this position, noting that "only a thin red line separates NATO's action in Kosovo from international legality" but arguing that it should remain exceptional.[77]

The desire to avoid setting a precedent was also evident in subsequent statements by NATO members. Secretary of State Madeleine Albright stressed in a press conference after the air campaign that Kosovo was "a unique situation *sui generis* in the region of the Balkans," concluding that it is important "not to overdraw the various lessons that come out of it."[78] Prime Minister Tony Blair, for his part, first suggested that such interventions might become more routine, stating that "[t]he most pressing foreign policy problem we face is to identify the circumstances in which we should get actively involved in other people's conflicts."[79] He subsequently retreated from this position, however, and emphasized the exceptional nature of the air campaign.[80]

This retreat was consistent with the more considered UK statements on the legal issues.[81] Indeed, the Foreign Affairs Committee inquiry into the Kosovo intervention concluded its examination of customary international law by stating that one of the experts who had argued that a right of unilateral humanitarian intervention existed was

---

[75] See Buchanan, "From Nuremberg to Kosovo," p. 675 (noting that the chief justification given by NATO states for the Kosovo intervention presented the illegal action as a "necessary exception"). Buchanan concludes that the NATO intervention is "extremely doubtful" as a case of illegal act of reform of the current international system: ibid., p. 704.

[76] Deutscher Bundestag, Plenarprotokoll 13/248, 16 October 1998, 23129. Available at http://dip.bundestag.de/parfors/parfors.htm (5 March 2002).

[77] Simma, "NATO, the UN and the Use of Force," p. 22.

[78] US Secretary of State Madeleine Albright, Press Conference with Russian Foreign Minister Igor Ivanov, Singapore, 26 July 1999. Available at http://secretary.state.gov/www/statements/1999/990726b.html (5 March 2002).

[79] C. Brown, "Blair's Vision of Global Police," *Independent*, 23 April 1999.

[80] See, for example, UK Parliamentary Debates, Commons, 26 April 1999, col. 30 (Prime Minister Blair).

[81] See, for example, UK Parliamentary Debates, Lords, 16 November 1998, WA 140 (Baroness Symons); reaffirmed in UK Parliamentary Debates, Lords, 6 May 1999, col. 904 (Baroness Symons).

too ambitious in saying that a new customary right has developed. We conclude that, at the very least, the doctrine of humanitarian intervention has a tenuous basis in current international customary law, and that this renders NATO action legally questionable.[82]

If this alternative approach of exceptional illegality were adopted, the focus of inquiry would shift to the consequences of the delict, with arguments of "legitimacy" being more properly seen as pleas in mitigation.[83] There are a number of examples of mitigating circumstances being taken into consideration in international law. In the *Corfu Channel* case, mentioned above, the ICJ held that a declaration of illegality was itself a sufficient remedy for the wrong perpetrated by the United Kingdom.[84] And after Israel abducted Adolf Eichmann from Argentina to face criminal charges, Argentina lodged a complaint with the Security Council, which passed a resolution stating that the sovereignty of Argentina had been infringed and requesting Israel to make "appropriate reparation." Nevertheless, "mindful" of the concern that Eichmann be brought to justice, the Security Council clearly implied that "appropriate reparation" would not involve his physical return to Argentina.[85] The governments of Israel and Argentina subsequently issued a joint communiqué resolving to "view as settled the incident which was caused in the wake of the action of citizens of Israel which violated the basic rights of the State of Argentina."[86]

In accordance with such an approach, the human rights violations that prompted a unilateral humanitarian intervention would have to be considered, and to some degree weighed against the actions of the intervening state, in any determination as to whether compensation for violating the rules concerning the use of force is required. Given the fundamental character

---

[82] Foreign Affairs Committee (United Kingdom), Fourth Report – Kosovo (23 May 2000), para. 132 (referring to Christopher Greenwood). Available at http://www.fas.org (5 March 2002).

[83] An alternative approach, of arguing necessity, is discussed by Thomas Franck, "Interpretation and Change in the Law of Humanitarian Intervention," ch. 6 in this volume and was argued, briefly, by Belgium before the International Court of Justice to justify its involvement in the NATO air strikes against Yugoslavia. See Chesterman, *Just War or Just Peace?*, pp. 213–14.

[84] *ICJ Reports, 1949*, p. 4 at p. 36.   [85] S/4349 (1960); SC Res. 138 (1960).

[86] Joint Communiqué of the Governments of Israel and Argentina, 3 August 1960, reprinted in 36 ILR 59. As the prohibition of the use of force is an obligation *erga omnes*, however, a simple waiver by the target state – particularly a waiver by a regime put in power by the intervening state, as in the case of the US invasion of Panama in 1989 – would not avoid the need to explain the action to the larger international community. See S. Chesterman, "Rethinking Panama: International Law and the US Invasion of Panama, 1989," in G. Goodwin-Gill and S. A. Talmon eds., *The Reality of International Law: Essays in Honour of Ian Brownlie* (Oxford University Press, Oxford, 1999), p. 57.

of the rights violated when mass atrocities occur, and the *erga omnes* character of the concomitant obligations, the intervening state might fare quite well in any such after-the-fact balancing of relative violations. Moreover, if the possibility of having to pay compensation were sufficient to deter an intervention, one would have to question the motives of the state wishing to intervene, and the true extent of its humanitarian concern.

An alternative criticism is that the approach advanced here holds an intervening state to a higher standard than a target state – why should intervenors admit the illegality of their actions if alleged violators of human rights do not admit the illegality of their abuses? The answer is that intervenors in such situations take the law into their own hands, and even most supporters of a moral right of humanitarian intervention argue that those hands should be clean. The position here is that this includes an admission of the lack of a legal basis for the intervention, and an ongoing special obligation to make amends for its consequences.[87]

Conclusion

In a provocative speech on humanitarian intervention to the UN General Assembly in September 1999, Secretary-General Kofi Annan stressed that "it is important to define intervention as broadly as possible, to include actions along a wide continuum from the most pacific to the most coercive."[88] This attempt to shift debate away from a focus on NATO's alleged "humanitarian intervention" in Kosovo was repeated in a speech delivered at a seminar in November 2000, when Annan suggested that the term "humanitarian" be dropped or confined to non-forcible actions:

> [T]he humanitarians among us are those whose work involves saving lives that are in imminent danger, and relieving suffering that is already acute. They are people who bring food to those threatened with starvation, or medical help to the injured, or shelter to those who have lost their homes, or comfort to those who have lost their loved ones.[89]

---

[87] Cf. Independent International Commission on Kosovo, *The Follow-up of the Kosovo Report: Why Conditional Independence?* (September 2001). Available at http://www.kosovocommission.org (5 March 2002).

[88] See Press Release, SG/SM/7136, 20 September 1999. This and other speeches on intervention have been collected in K. Annan, *The Question of Intervention: Statements by the Secretary-General* (United Nations Department of Public Information, New York, 1999).

[89] K. Annan, Opening Remarks at the Symposium on Humanitarian Action (International Peace Academy, New York, 20 November 2000). Available at http://www.ipacademy.org (5 March 2002).

From an international legal perspective, this dilution of the term "humanitarian intervention" – dropping the qualifying "humanitarian" and redefining "intervention" to mean anything from dropping food to dropping cluster bombs – might be seen as evidence of woolly thinking on the legal issues involved. But shifting the debate away from a simple question of the legality of unilateral humanitarian intervention, strictly speaking, also served two distinct policy goals.

First, it acknowledged that the legal debate is sterile and unhelpful. It is extremely unlikely that workable criteria for a right of humanitarian intervention without Security Council authorization will ever be developed to the satisfaction of more than a handful of states. Any criteria general enough to achieve broad agreement would be unlikely to satisfy any actual examples of allegedly humanitarian intervention. Indeed, it seems clear from the statements of NATO leaders during and after the Kosovo campaign that they themselves would not want the air strikes to be regarded as a model for dealing with future humanitarian crises.[90] The alternative – a select group of states (such as Western liberal democracies, or perhaps the United States alone) agreeing on criteria amongst themselves – would seriously undermine the current system of international law. It would also greatly undermine the position of the United Nations as an effective organization in the field of peace and security, after the decade in which, despite some obvious failures, it achieved more than in the previous half-century.[91]

More importantly, however, the Secretary-General's position highlights the true problem at the heart of this ongoing debate. States are not champing at the bit to intervene in support of human rights around the globe, prevented only by an intransigent Security Council and the absence of clear criteria to intervene without its authority. The problem, instead, is the absence of the will to act at all. In such circumstances, the primary goal must be to encourage states to see widespread and systematic human rights violations as their concern too – as part of their "national interest" – and to act and act early to prevent them, stop them, or seek justice for them.

These ends are not served by distorting the international legal regime to validate retrospectively actions by one state or group of states, particularly

---

[90] See discussion above, pp. 198–200.
[91] See S. Chesterman and M. Byers, "Has US Power Destroyed the UN?" *London Review of Books*, 29 April 1999, Cf. Buchanan, "From Nuremberg to Kosovo," pp. 703–4 (concluding that, despite the defects in the current system, the current rule requiring Security Council authorization is, all things considered, desirable under present conditions).

when the cost of doing so may include the integrity of the legal order itself. The impetus to bring Kosovo within the neat categories of international law is understandable but misplaced. Indeed, the greatest threat to an international rule of law lies not in the occasional breach of that law – laws are frequently broken in all legal systems, sometimes for the best of reasons – but in attempts to mould that law to accommodate the shifting practices of the powerful.

Interpretation and change in the law of humanitarian intervention

THOMAS M. FRANCK

The letter killeth, but the spirit giveth life

St. Paul's Epistles, 2 Corinthians 3.6

Non-lawyers tend to have greater reverence for the law than do lawyers, perceiving it in almost Hammurabic or Mosaic terms: written in stone and authored by supreme authority. In this, they may reflect the views of those seventeenth- and eighteenth-century legal philosophers who regarded law as the inspired human embodiment of divine wisdom and morality or of those nineteenth-century positivists who understood law to be the commands of supreme rulers.

Beginning in the twentieth century, however, law has come to be understood in less absolute and more dynamically transactional terms, as a system of norms constantly engaged in a process of challenge, adaption, and reformulation. This more contingent view of law may be merely another manifestation of the transformation of the command structure of social order that has come about as a result of political liberalization.

International law has not escaped this changing ethos. Indeed, as law in general has come to be understood less as an ineluctable command and more as part of liberal discourse – and as only one of many instruments of social stabilization and change – so, too, has the perception of international law changed. In the twenty-first century, it has become professionally respectable for practitioners of both domestic and international law, when asked whether a proposed course of conduct is lawful, to reply that, well, sometimes it is, sometimes it isn't, and sometimes it both is and isn't. A lot depends on the specific context in which the act occurs. This essay is intended to elucidate the proposition that law is rarely static and that its evolutionary response to changing circumstances may deliberately be to purchase a degree of contextual reasonableness at some cost to its absolute, one-size-fits-all, certainty.

The Charter as law and law as change

The proposition enunciated in the preceding paragraphs could be developed by recourse to examples from any field of positive law. Indeed, a nuanced understanding of the role of law in the international system requires some analogy to the role of law in national systems, and this essay will draw on this context. Primarily, however, my point of reference will be the UN Charter and, in particular, those parts of the Charter that regulate the use of force by states for purposes of *humanitarian intervention*: is it, or isn't it, lawful?

The UN Charter is, at once, a freeze-frame of historically validated norms and also the foundation for a dynamic political and administrative institution.

At the center of the freeze-frame is Article 2(4) of the Charter, which prohibits states' recourse to force except in self-defense against attack or with prior authorization by the Security Council. That, however, is only part of the Charter. Much of the rest of it establishes a continually dynamic, evolving institution imbued with a spirit of relevance, one in which the emphasis is on practical problem-solving rather than formal doctrinal exegesis.

Thus, while the normative framework of the Charter is self-consciously static, it is also intended to be perpetually evolving as the seemingly static norms are applied to practical situations through an essentially political process operating to solve real crises, instance by instance. The principal UN organs deal with, and try to diminish, the incidence and consequences of humankind's seemingly incorrigible proclivity for violence. To this end, they implement the processes and procedures spelled out in the Charter and, in doing so, adjust and adapt its text to respond to the exigencies of each challenge to good order.

This is not unintended. In 1945, at San Francisco, it was decided that

[in] the course of the operations from day to day of the various organs of the Organization, it is inevitable that each organ will interpret such parts of the Charter as are applicable to its particular functions. The process... will

be manifested in the functioning of such a body as the General Assembly, the Security Council, or the International Court of Justice.[1]

It is significant that this statement by drafters of the Charter presciently predicts the course of Charter adaption, but also that it makes the practice of political bodies co-equal to the Court in construing Charter text. From this, Professor (Judge) Rosalyn Higgins has deduced "that the authority to decide upon disputed questions of the interpretation of the Charter belongs to the organ charged with their application."[2]

Thus, each organ functions as arbiter of its own competence and *modus operandi*. It need not have been that way. Greece, at San Francisco, had proposed that the International Court be designated the sole interpreter of the Charter's meaning. Although that proposal obtained the support of seventeen of the thirty-one states represented on the drafting committee, this was not the two-thirds majority needed to amend the text drawn up by the Powers at Dumbarton Oaks.[3] Consequently, it may be said – with only mild overstatement – the Charter *is* what the principal organs *do*.

What they do tends to be governed, in part, by their concern for institutional effectiveness and relevance, but, perhaps even more, by the self-interest of the member states. This, then, is not the judicial process, with its formal focus on impartiality and principled consistency.

But the process, if not judicial, is also not that of a rabble applying the "law" of the jungle. The diplomats representing governments at the UN, although mostly not lawyers, nevertheless are acutely aware that what they do in fact affects the system's normative parameters. There is, thus, an incongruous yet not inappropriate tendency in the UN's political organs to talk legalese, to justify actions pursued for political ends by elaborately construing what the Charter says, or ought to mean. In this way, lawyer-like diplomats seek to manage two palpable tensions: (1) between short-term national self-interest and the longer-term stake each state has in the credibility and integrity of the system's normative grid; and (2) between what, in a specific political context, may be the sensible or moral course of action and its potential doctrinal consequences. States, even while exercising their political prerogatives in the institutional forums, realize that each action

---

[1] Statement of Committee IV/2 of the San Francisco Conference, UNCIO Doc. 933, IV/2/42(2), at 7; 13 UNCIO Docs. at 703, 709.

[2] Rosalyn Higgins, *The Development of International Law through the Political Organs of the United Nations* (Oxford University Press, Oxford, 1963), p. 66.

[3] Ibid., p. 66, n. 27.

they take, or do not take, has an afterlife as (that most legal of concepts!) a *precedent*.

The Secretary-General has recently addressed this tension between what needs to be done and the normative constraints on doing it. In the aftermath of the genocide perpetrated against 800,000 persons in Rwanda, he has asked: suppose there had been a coalition of the willing able to act pre-emptively, but consent for such rescue had been blocked by the opposition of a permanent member of the Security Council. Had there been a choice, would it have been better to sacrifice the Charter rules if it were possible thereby to save a multitude? Or, would it have been better, at least in the long run, to sacrifice those lives in order more firmly to uphold the letter of the law? What would be the costs to the system of allowing the rules to be bent or, in Secretary Annan's words, of "setting dangerous precedents for future interventions without clear criteria to decide who might invoke those precedents and in what circumstances?"[4] What, on the other hand, would have been the cost to the credibility of the normative system were strict adherence to the laws to have been the proximate cause of a mass slaughter of innocents?

Annan's preference, in this dilemma, is to search for new criteria that would make the rules more responsive to contemporary challenges without altogether abandoning the Charter's normative constraints on the use of force. Although it has lately taken on greater urgency, this is not a new quest. Already in 1945, at the San Francisco Conference, France had proposed an amendment to the draft Charter that would have authorized states to intervene in another nation, even without authorization of the Security Council, when "the clear violation of essential liberties and of human rights constitutes a threat capable of compromising peace."[5] This was rejected as too broad and vague an exception to Article 2(4)'s core "no violence" principle. As an exception to that rule, it lacked clear standards and procedures for deciding who might invoke it and in what circumstances.

The dilemma was not resolved at San Francisco and it remains largely unaddressed, although not – thanks to Secretary Annan's efforts – unrecognized.[6] Understandably, since diplomats, politicians, and civil servants are not legal philosophers, governments have been reluctant to broach

---

[4] Report of the Secretary-General, 54 GAOR, 4th plen. mtg., 20 September 1999, A/54/PV.4, at 2.
[5] 12 UNCIO, Commission II, Committee 2, Doc. 207, III/2/A/3, 10 May 1945, 179 at 191.
[6] See e.g. B. Crossette, "Canada Tries to Define Line Between Human and National Rights," *New York Times*, 14 September 2000.

the subject, recognizing it as potentially divisive and fearing the creation of a "slippery slope." And yet the practical conundrum – whether in any particular crisis to enforce the strict letter of the Charter or accommodate an exception – arises repeatedly in UN deliberations and is addressed often, helter-skelter, obliquely, through myriad little decisions and indecisions, actions and inactions, whenever a state claims a right to use force for what it asserts to be justifiable ends without obtaining the prior UN authorization required by the Charter.

The key to that conundrum cannot be found in the simplistic choice between either sacrificing people to preserve consistent adherence to strict rules, or sacrificing the law to do the moral and sensible thing. But the conundrum must be addressed, however strong the temptation to pretend that it does not exist.

The lady or the tiger: managing impossible choices

Some lawyers seek to escape from the conundrum by strictly separating law from other policy considerations such as justice, morality, or even good sense. Law, they say, does not need to produce good – that is, moral, just, or sensible – results to fulfill its role, which is to organize a peaceable kingdom. Peace may, at times, be incompatible with these other social desiderata, which then cannot always be accommodated by the law. In particular, the argument continues, Western civilization's progress towards freedom rests on the historic severance of morality from law because state-enforced morality is incompatible with the democratic underpinnings of the rule of law. What we call civil liberties derive from the emancipation of public notions of legality from views of moral justification that are (thank heaven!) increasingly being relegated to the private sphere. Legal positivism, which defines law as normative texts deriving their legitimacy from the processes of duly constituted sovereignty – legislatures, executives, and judiciaries – leaves little room for moral absolutes because it rejects the autocratic processes by which moral absolutes are divined and implemented.[7] It does this by constructing a fire-break between secular law and notions of morality.[8]

---

[7] For a classical discussion see H. L. A. Hart, "Positivism and the Separation of Law and Morals," 71 *Harvard Law Review* (1958), 593.

[8] Lon L. Fuller has complained that many different concepts are exiled from real "law" with the stigma of "morality" or "ought-law." Lon L. Fuller, "Positivism and Fidelity to Law: A Reply to Professor Hart," 71 *Harvard Law Review* (1958), 630, 635.

For most of Western history, however, this separation of moral from legal norms was quite alien. In ancient Rome, despite there being one concept – the *jus civile* – for the laws proclaimed by the sovereign and another – the *jus gentium* – for rules generated by common intuition, or human nature, the two were supposed to be symbiotic parts of a single legal system. Although, in the thirteenth century, Thomas Aquinas claimed that the *jus civile*, reformulated as the *jus naturale*, proceeded from God and was thus entitled to priority over the law of the sovereign – a view still shared by Jean Bodin in *De Republica* (1576) and Blackstone in the introduction to his *Commentaries* (1765) – the two systems of rules were mostly seen as symbiotic.[9]

In due course, this uneasy mutual accommodation between positive and natural or divine law ceased. The Reformation undermined the credibility of the Church as legitimate expostulator of the moral aspect of legal systems. Instead, sovereigns bent on secular supremacy encouraged a historic shift to legal positivism. In keeping with this new secularism, natural law, from the time of Thomas Hobbes, began to be exiled from the law libraries. In *Leviathan* (1651) Hobbes argued that might, the prerogative of sovereigns, was the only valid source of commands binding on the subject and that it was thus absolute and illimitable. Taken up by Vattel and transposed to international law in his *Law of Nations* (1758), this legal positivism laid the foundation for a universal system of norms in which such notions as "right reason" and "common moral sense" were banished to the theology schools.[10] International law, like national law, became exclusively defined by the will and expressed commands of sovereigns. In this view, there could only be law among states to the extent their sovereigns chose to make commitments to its strictures. International law, far from being the expression of a universal *jus gentium* or *jus naturale*, was now recognized as essentially a voluntarist system of positive law legitimized by sovereign consent and sovereign power, however much or little those sovereigns might agree to abide by common rules.

In modern times, this view of law as an emanation of secular power continued to inform the work of most jurisprudence, notably the work of John Austin, who, in *The Province of Jurisprudence Determined* (1832), defined law as nothing more nor less than the enforced command of a

---

[9] *Blackstone's Commentaries: With Notes of Reference* (ed. St. George Tucker, William Young Birch and Abraham Small, Philadelphia, 1803) vol. V, p. 42.

[10] Emer de Vattel, *The Law of Nations* (7th Amer. edn by Joseph Chitty, 1849), p. lxvi.

sovereign to a subject. In this, Austin's view was not very different from that of Karl Marx and Friedrich Engels in *The German Ideology* (1859). In none of these power-based views of law (domestic or international) is there any role for norms autonomously validated by God, nature, or a common sense of right and justice.

By the end of World War II, however, the monopoly of the legal positivists was being challenged. At the Nuremberg Trials, it was apparent that some of the most heinous crimes committed by the Nazi defendants had been carried out in accordance with German law as defined positivistically. In the early 1940s, Harvard professor Lon Fuller, seeking to narrow the gap between what was widely perceived as right or just and that which was mandated by positive law, reintroduced a rationalist version of natural law rooted in what he argued was a sociologically demonstrable universal sense of right and wrong.[11]

At almost the same time, a certain skepticism began to gnaw at the roots of legal positivism. Words in legal texts, it was argued, had no fixed meaning. They needed always to be interpreted, and interpretation must inevitably introduce a degree of value subjectivity. Where does this subjectivity look for its inspiration, if not to a common intuition of natural justice? In Britain, Professor J. L. Brierly challenged strict legal positivism with the contention that law

> is not a meaningless set of arbitrary principles to be mechanically applied by the courts, but . . . exists for certain ends, though those ends may have to be differently formulated in different times and places . . . This is so because the life with which any system of law has to deal is too complicated, and human foresight too limited, for law to be completely formulated in a set of rules, so that situations perpetually arise which fall outside all rules already formulated. Law cannot and does not refuse to solve a problem because it is new and unprovided for; it meets such situations by resorting to a principle, outside formulated law . . . appealing to reason as the justification for its decisions.

This "appeal to reason," Brierly explains, "is merely to appeal to a law of nature."[12]

While most modern lawyers may not be quite so willing to see the law of nature reinstated as consort to the majesty of positive law, there is no doubt that rulers, judges, and administrators, in international as in national legal

---

[11] Lon L. Fuller, *The Law in Quest of Itself* (Foundation Press, Chicago, 1940), pp. 12ff.
[12] J. L. Brierly, *The Law of Nations* (4th edn, Clarendon Press, Oxford, 1949), p. 24.

systems, while nowadays still recognizing legality and morality as distinct social regulators, have also come to accept that the power of positive law is diminished if the gap between it and the common sense of values – justice, morality, good sense – is allowed to become too wide. Such dissonance, aside from its philosophical implications, undermines law in a purely utilitarian sense. The capacity of the law to pull towards compliance those to whom it is addressed depends first and foremost on the public perception of its fairness, its reification of a widely shared notion of what is right. The law's self-interest, therefore, demands that a way be found to bridge any gap between its own institutional commitment to consistent application of formal rules and the public sense that order should not be achieved at too high a cost in widely shared moral values.

When law permits or even requires behavior that is widely held to be unfair, immoral, or unjust, it is not only persons but also the law that suffers. So, too, if law prohibits that which is widely believed to be just and moral. Consequently, it is in the law's self-interest to narrow the gap between itself and the common sense of what is right in a specific situation.

A simple illustration may be helpful.

Tom and Jerry are chums. They are each ten years old, children of families living in adjacent houses. One day, Tom and Jerry's fathers quarrel and Tom's father orders him "never to have anything to do with Jerry again."

The next morning, Tom, on his way to school, passes a small lake and sees that Jerry has fallen into it. Tom, unlike Jerry, knows how to swim and so rescues his friend.

On learning of this, Tom's father severely thrashes him for having disobeyed orders.

It must be all but impossible to find any reader of this scenario who would not agree to the following propositions:

1. Punishing Tom for rescuing Jerry is morally wrong;
2. Interpreting the paternal injunction "never to have anything to do with Jerry again" as requiring Tom to abandon his drowning friend profoundly undermines the father's parental authority, marking him as unfit to exercise it. The punishment thus is also counterproductive of the respect the father seeks to inculcate in his son.

The reader might also agree that Tom's father should have understood that his authority would have been better preserved had he, given these circumstances, *not* enforced the injunction to his son "never to have anything to do with Jerry again." To his objection: "OK, but if I didn't enforce my orders, Tom would never respect me again," would we not reply that by enforcing his order in these circumstances he had seriously undermined, rather than reinforced, his authority?

Law – or, in this example, parental authority – does not thrive when its implementation produces *reductio ad absurdum*: when it grossly offends most persons' common moral sense of what is *right*.

Necessity and mitigation as ways out of the conundrum

This insight is relevant to all law, whether international or domestic. An example from domestic law may illustrate the point. In two famous cases before domestic courts, *Regina* v. *Dudley and Stephens*[13] in Britain and *US* v. *Holmes*[14] in America, the courts have dealt with situations in which the strict letter of the law of murder collided with the common sense of justice and morality. In both cases, persons cast into a hopeless predicament at sea killed one of their number to save the rest. In the British case, persons starving and adrift in a lifeboat stayed alive by eating one of their shipmates. In the US case, crew on an overloaded lifeboat jettisoned passengers to prevent its sinking. These actions, of course, were strictly unlawful. Yet, in both instances the legal process, while it did not condone the killings, responded with utmost leniency.[15] In the English case, although the defendants were convicted and sentenced to death, Lord Coleridge, for the unanimous court, commended them "most earnestly to the mercy of the Crown," which, acting on the advice of the Home Secretary, commuted the sentences to six months' imprisonment, most of which had already been served.[16] In the American case, the penalty of six months' imprisonment was subsequently remitted.[17]

Put another way, in neither case was necessity treated as an exculpating defense to a charge of murder. The judges went out of their way to ensure that this remained a crime, even in circumstances of extreme necessity. But the specific, unusual circumstances were not simply ignored to preserve the law's literal consistency. Rather, they effectively mitigated the penalties

---

[13] 14 QBD 273 (1884).   [14] 26 Fed. Cas. 360, 1 Wall Jr. 1 (1842).

[15] For an excellent discussion of this distinction in the *Dudley and Stephens* litigation, see A. W. Brian Simpson, *Cannibalism and the Common Law* (University of Chicago Press, Chicago, 1984), pp. 225–70.

[16] Ibid., p. 247.   [17] 26 Fed. Cas. 360 at 369.

imposed on those whose acts were found to have been illegal but, also, in the extreme circumstances, justifiable. Necessity for action mitigated the consequences of acting illegally, although neither, on the one hand, fully exculpating the actors, nor, on the other, rendering the law nugatory.

It is integral to most national legal systems that an action may be regarded as illegal but that the degree of that illegality should be determined with due regard for extenuating or mitigating factors. Most criminal codes make some kind of distinction between *unlawfulness* – in the sense of an act violative of positive law – and *culpability*, with the latter connoting what Professor George Fletcher artfully describes as "the nature of crime as a moral or value-based category."[18] Similarly, Professor H. L. A. Hart states that in "the criminal law of every modern state responsibility for serious crimes is excluded or 'diminished' by some … 'excusing conditions.' "[19] To whatever extent law seeks to deter or to punish acts it will often also create a category of justification or mitigation that takes into account evidence that, in particular circumstances, the act was less culpable. For example, section 3.02 of the 1985 US Model Penal Code provides: "Conduct that the actor believes to be necessary to himself or to another is justifiable, provided that … the harm or evil sought to be avoided by such conduct is greater than that sought to be prevented by the law defining the offense charged."[20] This, in one form or another, has been influential with some state courts. In a recent New York decision, environmentalists obstructed vehicular traffic as a way of demonstrating against the closing of a bicycle lane. They were acquitted of disorderly conduct on the basis of the "necessity defense [which] is fundamentally a balancing test to determine whether a criminal act was committed to prevent a greater harm. The common elements of the defense," the Court held, "in virtually all common-law and statutory definitions include the following: (1) the actor has acted to avoid a grave harm, not of his own making; (2) there are no adequate legal means to avoid the harm; and (3) the harm sought to be avoided is greater

---

[18] George Fletcher, "Introduction from a Common Lawyer's Point of View," in A. Eser and G. P. Fletcher, *Justification and Excuse: Comparative Perspectives* (Transnational Juris Publications, Dobbs Ferry, 1987), pp. 9, 10. See also M. L. Corrado ed., *Justification and Excuse in Criminal Law* (Garland Publishing, New York, 1994).

[19] H. L. A. Hart, "Legal Responsibility and Excuses," in Corrado, *Justification and Excuse*, p. 31.

[20] See, for a practical application of this "greater harm" principle, *The People of the State of New York v. John Gray*, 571 NYS 2d 851 (NY City Crim. Ct. 1991); Thomas Franck, *The Power of Legitimacy Among Nations* (Oxford University Press, New York, 1990), pp. 73–75; Thomas Franck, "Break It, Don't Fake It," 78 *Foreign Affairs* (1999), 116–22.

than that committed." New York, the judge said, imposes the additional requirements that the "harm must be imminent" and "the action taken must be reasonably expected to avert the impending danger."[21]

In one formulation or another, legal systems worldwide accept the need for some such way out of the conundrum in which good law, strictly enforced, conduces to a result which opens an excessive chasm between law and the common moral sense. There may be differences between national systems as to whether necessity excuses a crime or merely mitigates its consequences, but all recognize the obligation of the law to make available one or the other way to resolve – or at least to manage – the conundrum.[22]

Managing the conundrum in the context of the law of humanitarian intervention

International law, like domestic law, also has begun gingerly to develop ways to bridge the gap between what is requisite in strict legality and what is generally regarded as just and moral. That it still has difficulty in doing so is illustrated by the reaction of some states and international lawyers to NATO's action against Yugoslavia in 1999.

As we have seen, the positive law – that is, the UN Charter's Articles 2(4), 42, and 51 – prohibits states from using force "against the territorial integrity or political independence of any state" except in two circumstances: *first*, "in self-defence if an armed attack occurs against a Member of the United Nations" or, *second*, if the Security Council approves the use of force "to maintain or restore international peace and security." In the Kosovo instance, there was no armed attack against a UN member and there was no decision by the Security Council to authorize the use of force. Indeed, some members, including at least two with the power of veto, openly – although with diminishing vigor[23] – opposed any rescue of the Kosovars that would

---

[21] *Gray*, 571 NYS 2d 851 at 853.

[22] I am indebted to an excellent research essay by Devika Hovell, "Necessity: The Mother of In(ter)vention?," written to meet LL M requirements. Fall 2000, New York University.

[23] Russia "displays traces of a shifting attitude" to the intervention and to humanitarian intervention in general. Robert Legvold, "Foreword," in Pugwash Study Group on Intervention, Sovereignty and International Security, 2(1) *Pugwash Occasional Papers* (2001), p. 8. See also to the same effect, Vladimir Baranovsky, "Humanitarian Intervention: Russian Perspectives," ibid., pp. 12ff.; also, Chu Shulong, "China, Asia and Issues of Sovereignty and Intervention," ibid., pp. 39ff. Legvold points out, however, that Russian and Chinese consent to humanitarian intervention "comes with a huge proviso. If coercion is to be used to preempt or end the

involve deployment of military force. After the event, the Ministers of Foreign Affairs of the Group of 77 baldly "rejected the so-called right of humanitarian intervention" saying that it "had no basis in the UN Charter or in international law."[24]

Still, before NATO acted, the Council had already decided that events in Kosovo were creating a threat to peace, the very thing the UN system had been established to ameliorate.[25] The record of Serb forces' genocide in Bosnia, a few years earlier, made that threat palpable. Yet the UN's Charter-designated system of preventive response – Security Council action under Charter Chapter VII – was paralyzed by the threat of a veto. Thus, NATO decided to use force and, in so doing, violated strict Charter legality. It acted, instead, in reliance on mitigating circumstances and moral justification.

So: what is a lawyer to make of NATO's decision to use force?

In his seminal 1991 work, *International Law in Theory and Practice*, Oscar Schachter seems to have preconfigured a convincing answer to this issue. He prefers, of course, that a humanitarian rescue operation be endorsed by the Security Council, if possible, or the General Assembly. Failing that, however, "in the absence of such prior approval, a State or group of States using force to put an end to atrocities when the necessity is evident and the humanitarian intention is clear is likely to have its action pardoned."[26]

A decade later, faced with an actual instance of such atrocities, the Independent (Goldstone) Commission on Kosovo concluded that NATO's action, while not strictly legal, was legitimate. It called for the applicable international law to be interpreted to make it more congruent with "an

---

egregious acts of government, it must occur under the auspices of the United Nations." Ibid., p. 9. Even this caveat may be overstated: the Soviet Union vigorously supported India's intervention in Pakistan to free Bangladesh and, as Professor Alain Pellet has pointed out, the Soviets voted for Security Council Resolution 1244 (1999), making it "inconceivable" that they, or any of the other eleven supporters of the resolution, could have thought unlawful or criminal an action by NATO to which they thereby implicitly gave their blessing. Alain Pellet, "State Sovereignty and the Protection of Fundamental Human Rights: An International Law Perspective," in Pugwash Study Group on Intervention, Sovereignty and International Security, 1(1) *Pugwash Occasional Papers* (1999), p. 42.

[24] Ministerial Declaration on the South Summit, adopted at the twenty-third annual meeting of the Ministers of Foreign Affairs of the Group of 77, 24 September 1999. Circulated by letter dated 29 September 1999 by Ambassador S. R. Insanally of Guyana, Chairman. A/54/432 at 18. UN Press Release GA/SPD/164, 18 September 1999.

[25] S/RES/1199 (1998) and S/RES/1203 (1998).

[26] Oscar Schachter, *International Law in Theory and Practice* (Martinus Nijhoff, Boston, 1991), p. 126.

international moral consensus"[27] and in such a way as to bridge the gap – so starkly revealed by that crisis – between legality and legitimacy, between strict legal positivism and a common sense of moral justice.

Humanitarian intervention in institutional practice

It is undeniable that such a gap exists.

The UN Charter makes no provision for – and indeed, in Article 2(4) appears to forbid – states' use of force at their own discretion to alleviate even the most severe humanitarian crises and deprivations of human rights. It also creates no specific authorization for UN recourse to Chapter VII powers in response to catastrophic human deprivations arising within a state, as opposed to those resulting from actions by one state against another.

Yet, in practice, UN-authorized forces increasingly have been deployed – for example, in Haiti, Somalia, and Bosnia – to redress catastrophic humanitarian deprivations even when, occurring domestically, they have had little or no international consequences. There have also been a few instances in which states, on their own, have engaged in humanitarian interventions in other states. The reactions of the UN system to such "off-Charter" uses of force may be bellwethers of evolution in Charter interpretation.

As in domestic cases of "extreme necessity," it appears that evidence, facts, and process trump absolute legal principles, at least within a narrow, but significant, margin of flexibility. In 1971, India invaded East Pakistan after military repression against separatists in that province had escalated to the point where a million persons had died and 8 million had fled to India.[28] The facts of that disaster were authoritatively confirmed in evidence adduced by the UN Secretary-General.[29] Once India attacked, the invaders quickly defeated Pakistani Government forces and thereby enabled the birth of an independent Bangladesh. India justified its action as lawful self-defense against the floods of refugees unleashed by Pakistan's brutality. More quietly, it invoked the necessity of stopping genocidal violations of human rights.[30] India's UN representative emphasized the absence of alternatives. The UN's

---

[27] Independent International Commission on Kosovo ("The Goldstone Commission"), *Kosovo Report: Conflict, International Response, Lessons Learned* (Oxford University Press, Oxford, 2000), pp. 4, 163–98.

[28] 1971 UNYB 137.   [29] A/8401/Add.1, 21 September 1971, at 7–8, paras. 177–91.

[30] UNSCOR (XXVI), 1608th mtg., 6 December 1971, at 7, para. 70. These events are described in Jane Stromseth, "Rethinking Humanitarian Intervention: The Case for Incremental Change," ch. 7 in this volume.

system, he charged, had "seemed paralyzed and did not take any action to prevent the massive extinction of human rights and genocide."[31]

The Security Council was convened to debate a resolution calling for immediate withdrawal of Indian forces. Eleven states, including all third-world members, voted for it. The Soviets, with Poland, opposed it and the resolution thus failed.[32] Three days later, the General Assembly, by a lopsided majority of 104 to 1 with 10 abstentions, passed essentially the same text.[33] Resentment towards India was strong, and did not abate quickly. Only three years later, however, Bangladesh was admitted to UN membership.[34]

There is no doubt that the humanitarian disaster in East Bengal created an extreme necessity of which there was ample proof. With Moscow backing India and Beijing supporting Pakistan, the UN itself could do nothing to preempt or halt the slaughter, despite urgent pleas by the Secretary-General. Had India not acted, the tragedy undoubtedly would have been compounded. Most states understood this. Yet, a large majority – including most of the small and middle powers of the third world that normally looked to India for direction – refused to ratify India's action. They felt directly threatened: not by the action itself, which elicited widespread sympathy, but by a precedent that appeared to condone the invasion of a country by a more powerful one. Many were deeply troubled by the notion that one state could sit in judgment on another's compliance with human rights and humanitarian law. Probably more decisive was New Delhi's failure to pass the "clean hands" test. Despite its protestations of disinterested humanitarianism, states could see clearly how India's national interest was advanced by the division of its arch-enemy, Pakistan, into two mutually antagonistic states.

The same considerations seemed to shape the UN's response when Vietnam invaded Cambodia, in 1978, to rid it of a Khmer Rouge regime responsible for the deaths of at least 1 million people.[35] Vietnam claimed to be acting in self-defense against armed border incursions by forces directed by the Khmer Rouge.[36] However, Hanoi seemed to realize that this excuse

---

[31] UNSCOR (XXVI), 1608th mtg., 6 December 1971, at 15, para. 165.
[32] S/10416. UNSCOR (XXVI), 1606th mtg., 4 December 1971, at 33, para. 371. Britain and France abstained.
[33] GA Res. 2793 (XXVI) of 7 December 1971.
[34] S. Res. 351 (1974) of 10 June 1974 and GA Res. 3203 (XXIX) of 17 September 1974.
[35] The events and citations in support of facts are detailed in Stromseth, ch. 7 in this volume.
[36] UNSCOR (XXXIV), 2108th mtg., 11 January 1978, at 12, para. 115.

was hardly credible, or, even if credible, that its response would be seen as wildly disproportionate to the threat posed by Cambodian incursions. Accordingly, the Vietnamese authorities sought to portray their actions as humanitarian support for a popular uprising against a regime which, Hanoi said, had turned Cambodia into "a living hell."[37]

However, such a veiled suggestion that military intervention might be justified by reference to the Cambodian Government's massive human rights abuses merely heightened states' concern, which, as in the case of India's invasion of East Bengal, was sometimes voiced with immoderation and with indifference to the fates of the victims of extreme repression. France's representative to the Council, for example, thought an "extremely dangerous"[38] precedent had been set. Similar fears were voiced in the Security Council by representatives of Norway, Bolivia, Sudan, Gabon, Portugal, Malaysia, Singapore, New Zealand, Indonesia, Australia, the UK and, of all places, Bangladesh. The United States was almost alone in balancing concern for sovereignty and non-intervention with care for principles of human rights.[39]

Although a Chinese resolution vehemently condemning the invasion was not put to a vote,[40] a milder version sponsored by seven of the non-aligned called for the withdrawal of Vietnamese forces. It was vetoed by the Soviet Union, but was supported by thirteen of the fifteen Council members.[41] For a decade, the Assembly annually rejected the credentials of the regime installed by Hanoi.[42] States' focus was not on whether the invasion had been good or bad for Cambodia but, rather, on the precedent that would be set if Vietnam's action were condoned. Perhaps an even more decisive factor, for many, was their suspicion of Vietnam's motives. Not until 1988 did the invaders show any signs of leaving Cambodia. Moreover, Hanoi's own human rights record was less than admirable, and the leader installed in Phnom Penh was too evidently no paragon of humanitarianism, having been the deputy commander of the murderous Khmer Rouge.

For most states, therefore, the choice was between two contending Cambodian regimes, one of which was a surrogate of Soviet, the other of

---

[37] Ibid., at 5, para. 56.   [38] UNSCOR (XXXIV), 2109th mtg., 12 January 1979, at 4, para. 36.
[39] UNSCOR (XXXIV), 2110th mtg., 13 January 1979, at 6–7, paras. 65–72.
[40] S/13022, 11 January 1979.
[41] S/13027, 15 January 1979. Only Czechoslovakia sided with Moscow.
[42] GA Res. 34/2A of 21 September 1979. See also 1979 UNYB 291. New credentials were finally accepted in 1988: 1988 UNYB 183; GA Res. 43/10A of 18 October 1988.

Chinese, interests. Neither could credibly claim to represent stellar humanitarian values. In those circumstances, many states seem to have concluded
that their interests were best served by giving priority to the Charter principle of non-intervention even at the cost of applying the law with indifference
to moral values.

That priority, however, is not inevitable. It was not apparent, for example,
in 1978 when Tanzania invaded Uganda to topple the murderous regime
of Field Marshal Idi Amin. Some 300,000 deaths had been attributed to a
rule[43] which, like that of the Khmer Rouge in Cambodia, had horrified and
embarrassed the world. The difference, in this instance, was that there was
far less reason to suspect ulterior motives or strategic designs behind the
invasion, which was greeted in the UN system with unstated but unmistak-
able satisfaction. Although Uganda (seconded by Libya) tried to protest to
the UN Secretary-General and demanded action by the Security Council,
they were unsuccessful in getting that organ even to meet on the issue.[44]
Tanzanian troops, unlike the Vietnamese in Cambodia, remained only for
two years and that at the request of a legitimately elected government.[45]

It is these facts and political circumstances which explain UN acquiescence in the occupation of Uganda by Tanzania. Amin was universally
notorious, Tanzania's President Julius Nyerere widely respected. There was
palpable joy within Uganda at being rid of a cruel dictator whose excesses
had been globally noted. Tanzanian diplomats, nevertheless, studiously
refrained, at least on the record, from claiming to be acting on behalf of
human rights lest their action arouse fears of setting a precedent legitimating a general right of states to engage in humanitarian intervention.
Instead, they relied for cover on the legally far weaker justification of self-
defense against armed border incursions, even though their occupation of
all of Uganda would have had to be seen as vastly disproportionate to the
claimed provocation. Nevertheless, it cannot have escaped the attention of
states, whatever Tanzania's formal pretext, that the action did constitute a
very significant humanitarian intervention to which the UN system had
responded with mute, but evident, satisfaction.

---

[43] S/13228. Letter from the representative of Uganda to the Security Council, 5 April 1979.
[44] See e.g. S/13087. Letter from Libya to Secretary-General. These events are discussed in Stromseth,
ch. 7 in this volume.
[45] See e.g. the Heads of Government communiqué of 4 March 1979, which spoke only of self-
defense against the "unprovoked and premeditated war of aggression launched by Idi Amin
against the United Republic of Tanzania." S/13141 of 5 March 1979.

There are other instances of such acquiescence. In September 1979, France participated in the overthrow of Emperor Jean-Bédel Bokassa of the Central African Empire. The UN greeted this obvious violation of Article 2(4) with silence. The Quai d'Orsay secured immediate African recognition of the new regime,[46] carefully avoiding any claim to be exercising a right of humanitarian intervention; indeed, at first denying any involvement at all. It withdrew its forces quickly after the success of the coup had been ensured.[47]

This does not mean, however, that states were unaware of the issues or the facts. The evidence of Bokassa's massive violations of human rights was well documented. Just before the French intervention, a high-level jurists' commission of the Organization of African Unity had established that the ruler had ordered and participated in the killing of a hundred school children, capping a series of bizarre atrocities. It is in this context that UN acquiescence can be understood.

The UN also acquiesced in silence when British, French, and US forces were sent to the Kurdish regions of Northern Iraq in 1991. This followed vigorous Security Council condemnation of Iraqi actions that had generated a massive flow of Kurdish refugees into neighboring Turkey and Iran. Invoking Chapter VII, the Council declared Iraqi repression to be a threat to international peace and security,[48] although it proved impossible to line up the five permanent members in support of remedial military action.

Again, the specific facts seem to explain the lack of reaction to the unauthorized tripartite intervention. Three million Kurdish refugees had fled towards Turkey and Iran, their misery amply covered on television. British, French, and US troops quickly engaged in feeding and protecting 700,000 displaced persons and in facilitating their safe return to Iraq. By late May, these forces began to be withdrawn, as soon as they could be replaced by UN Guards sent to carry on the mission under an agreement between the UN and Baghdad.[49]

While the three-power action was sought to be justified as a reasonable application of the Council's 5 April finding that Iraq's repression of the Kurds constituted a threat to international peace, this text authorized no such intervention. Indeed, the three-power action drew strong Chinese and Russian condemnation. The acquiescence of the silent majority of UN states,

---

[46] *New York Times*, 23 and 24 September 1979.
[47] *Le Monde*, 25, 26, 28, and 30 September 1979.
[48] S/RES/688 of 5 April 1991.   [49] S/22663, 30 May 1991.

if such there was, is best understood not in normative but in specifically contextual terms: the evident, extreme humanitarian crisis, the operation's limited objectives, and its rapid winding-down.

Similar acquiescence was evident when West African (ECOMOG) regional forces intervened in the vicious civil wars raging in Liberia and Sierra Leone between 1989 and 1999. These conflicts had killed or maimed hundreds of thousands by the time the first 15,000 ECOMOG troops entered Liberia in 1990.

ECOMOG, too, had not followed the rule laid down by Charter Article 2(4). It had not obtained Security Council authorization before engaging in a regional enforcement action, as required by Article 53. Six months after the beginning of the Liberian intervention, however, the Council issued a Presidential Statement that "commended" the West African efforts to secure a peaceful settlement of the dispute. Still, that statement did not actually endorse ECOMOG or its military involvement as required by strict textuality.[50] Almost two more years then elapsed before the Council, at last imposing an embargo on military shipments to the warring factions, cautiously referred to ECOWAS in the context of Chapter VIII Charter-based regional initiatives in a resolution which, however, still refrained from endorsing or authorizing military action.[51] By mid-1993, after a peace agreement between the factions had been brokered, the Council agreed to create a UN presence in Liberia alongside ECOMOG, thereby seeming *retroactively* to endorse the operation's legitimacy.[52]

In 1994, the Assembly, by consensus, approved a Declaration on the Enhancement of Cooperation between the United Nations and Regional Arrangements or Agencies in the Maintenance of International Peace and Security.[53] Prepared by the Assembly's legal (sixth) committee, it painstakingly reiterates the norm that the "Security Council shall, where appropriate, utilize such regional arrangements or agencies for enforcement action under its authority, but no enforcement action shall be taken under regional arrangements or by regional agencies without the authorization of the Security Council."[54] It is difficult to reconcile that restatement of the applicable legal principle with the Security Council's precedent in retroactively endorsing a regional enforcement action that it had not authorized at its inception. One may seek to finesse the dissonance between principle and

---

[50] S/22133, 22 January 1991.   [51] S/RES/788 of 19 November 1992.
[52] S/RES/856 of 10 August 1993; S/RES/866 of 22 September 1993.
[53] GA Res. 49/57 of 9 December 1994.   [54] Ibid., para. 1(d).

practice by asserting that ECOMOG was using military force to intervene in Liberia's civil war on the invitation of that nation's government and, thus, not engaging in enforcement. That position is difficult to maintain, however, if only because the authorities purportedly issuing the invitation to ECOMOG at the time controlled almost no part of Liberia except bits of the capital, Monrovia. Professor Gray notes that "there was considerable uncertainty" whether the ECOMOG action could be said to have been legitimated by the consent of the Liberian authorities. She adds that there was "absence of clear consent from the government and...[that] the government was no longer effective" when it purportedly consented.[55] Besides, the argument that a protracted regional intervention in a nation's civil war does not constitute "intervention" in the context of the prohibition in Article 53(1) if it is undertaken at the invitation of the government may itself constitute a radical reinterpretation of the Charter's text, creating a different but equally evident adaption of principle to respond to practice.

When ECOWAS intervened again, this time in Sierra Leone in 1997, it essentially replicated the Liberian experience. The initial presence of the Nigerian and Guinean forces to counter insurgents was with the consent of the democratically elected President who, however, was soon overthrown in a coup by the Sierra Leone military. Months after the start of the ECOWAS operation, the Council issued a cautious Presidential Statement[56] which welcomed ECOWAS's mediation efforts but did not specifically endorse its resort to military force. Even in October 1997, in imposing an embargo on military supplies to the junta,[57] the Council only commended – but did not expressly authorize – ECOWAS's armed intervention.[58] Nevertheless, the resolution did authorize ECOWAS forces to ensure the halt in shipment of supplies to the junta. The resolution, in this connection, referred to both Chapters VII and VIII of the Charter.

Almost four months later, the Council further supplemented its relations with the ECOWAS forces by authorizing a token Observer Mission of its own,[59] thereby arguably ratifying the intervention retroactively. Formal Council authorization of ECOWAS's action did not come, however, until

---

[55] Christine Gray, *International Law and the Use of Force* (Oxford University Press, New York, 2000), p. 219. See also Georg Nolte, "Restoring Peace by Regional Action: International Legal Aspects of the Liberian Conflict," 53 *Zeitschrift für ausländisches öffentliches Recht und Völkerrecht* (1993), 603.

[56] S/PRST/1997/36.   [57] S/RES/1132 (1997) of 8 October 1997.

[58] See also Press Release, Presidential Statement, SC 6481, 26 February 1998.

[59] S/RES/1181 of 13 June 1998.

October 1999,[60] at the same time as the Council authorized UNAMSIL, its own "coalition of the willing," acting under Chapter VII, to assist ECOMOG.[61] By December, as ECOMOG's dominant Nigerian contingent was "rehelmetted,"[62] UNAMSIL became the force responsible for peace-keeping under the terms of the Lomé Agreement[63] between the combatants, which set terms for ending the civil war, an aspiration soon dashed by new fighting.

These events in Liberia and Sierra Leone could be interpreted as supporting two propositions. First, a regional military initiative taken without prior UN authorization may be *tolerated* where the emergency is palpable, there is no prospect of a UN-led military operation, and the regional organization appears to be acting with clean motives and not solely to advance its members' national ambitions. Second, a humanitarian intervention, even if it has not been authorized by the Council in strict compliance with the terms of the Charter, may later be retroactively *validated* by the Council. This approval may be expressed explicitly, or implicitly through a "commendation" followed by the Council authorizing a UN presence to cooperate with the intervening force.

It is certainly possible to challenge this interpretation of the Council's actions by focusing primarily on what states *said* (or did not say) rather than on what they *did* (or did not do). The ECOMOG interventions in both Liberia and Sierra Leone can also be explained away as actions requested, at least initially, by those embattled governments and, much later, by reference to those forces' exercise of their right to self-defense, as well as to the implementing of various peace agreements.[64] The reality, however, is simpler. It was clear to all that, through the unauthorized ECOMOG intervention, Nigeria was leading its junior partners into a military action to prevent (or to end) dire chaos in two West African states. "Necessity was the mother of intervention."[65] ECOMOG's actions, even if taken in technical non-compliance with Articles 2(4) and 53, were humanitarian necessities in emergencies the UN itself had been unprepared to address.

[60] S/RES/1270 of 22 October 1999.
[61] Ibid. This force has now been authorized at a level approximating that of the former ECOWAS. S/RES/1289 of 7 February 2000; S/RES/1299 of 19 May 2000.
[62] Third Report of the Secretary-General on UNAMSIL, S/2000/186, UN Press Release SC/6821.
[63] S/1999/1073. By S/RES/1289 of February 2000, the size of UNAMSIL was established at 11,000 personnel and it was given increased powers.
[64] Cf. Gray, *International Law and the Use of Force*, p. 233.
[65] I have borrowed this felicitous characterization from Devika Hovell.

The most recent instance of pleading humanitarian intervention to justify unauthorized use of force is NATO's attack against Yugoslavia. That crisis began in 1989, when the Government of Serbia rescinded Kosovo's autonomous provincial status by abolishing its regional self-governance and revoking the official status of the Albanian language spoken by 90 percent of its population. Nine years later, as tensions heightened into violence, the Security Council condemned Serbia's recourse to "excessive force" and called for restoration of Kosovo's autonomy.[66] It promised to consider "additional measures" if these steps were not taken. It reimposed the arms embargo that had been lifted after the Dayton Accords.[67]

All this was to no avail. By September 1998, Yugoslav forces had torched 300 Kosovar villages and displaced 300,000 persons. The Council expressed "deep alarm"[68] and condemned specific large-scale atrocities,[69] but could not achieve consensus to authorize collective military measures due to opposition from Russia and China.

In mid-March 1999, after Yugoslavia had rejected a compromise agreement proposed by a Five-Power Contact Group at Rambouillet, NATO launched air strikes. By that time, 600,000 Kosovars had fled into neighboring states and a further 850,000 were internally displaced.[70] At the UN, India argued that, even if the unauthorized use of force were meant to stop violations of human rights, that "does not justify unprovoked military aggression. Two wrongs do not make a right."[71] The representative of Slovenia countered with a bitter reminder of India's justification, in similar circumstances, for intervening in Bangladesh in 1971.[72]

A resolution proposed by Russia would have condemned NATO's "flagrant violation" of the Charter and demanded an immediate end to the intervention. It was defeated by an impressive majority of three to twelve. Argentina, Bahrain, Brazil, Canada, France, Gabon, Gambia, Malaysia, the Netherlands, Slovenia, the UK and the US voted against it.[73] They seemed to accept the British Ambassador's view that NATO's intervention was "justified as an exceptional measure to prevent an overwhelming humanitarian catastrophe."[74]

---

[66] S/RES/1160 of 31 March 1998.   [67] S/RES/1199 of 23 September 1998.
[68] S/RES/1203 of 24 October 1998.   [69] S/PRST/1999/2, 19 January 1999.
[70] "The Balkans 2000," paper prepared for a Ditchley Foundation Conference by the Conflict Management Group (1999), p. 6. See also Independent International Commission on Kosovo, *Kosovo Report*, pp. 29–84.
[71] UNSCOR (LIV), 3988th mtg., 24 March 1999, at 4.   [72] Ibid., at 7.   [73] Ibid., at 12.
[74] Sir Jeremy Greenstock, ibid., at 8.

In May, Yugoslavia agreed to a cease-fire brokered primarily by Russian Prime Minister Viktor Chernomyrdin.[75] Immediately, the Council, adopting Resolution 1244 of 10 June, approved its terms. These included withdrawal of all Yugoslav forces and administrators from Kosovo, as well as their replacement by troops from NATO and Russia and by civic administrators supplied by the UN and the OSCE.[76] The resolution invoked Chapter VII on behalf of those being stationed in the province.[77] As Professor Alain Pellet has observed, this cannot but be construed as tacit acceptance that the NATO action was not unlawful in the specific circumstances. Otherwise, by authorizing UN civil governance in Kosovo, states would be eating the fruit of a poisonous tree by partaking in the regime brought about by NATO's aggression.[78]

Again, the UN's response appears to have been shaped primarily by factual evidence and the existential context in which the crisis had arisen. It is possible to see in these events a form of retroactive endorsement by the Security Council of NATO's intervention. Especially telling is the Council's resounding rejection of the Russian resolution and its later assumption of a central role in implementing the settlement ending the conflict. That this could be construed as retroactive validation, as with ECOMOG's actions, appears also to have occurred to China, which abstained from the otherwise unanimous Council approval of the settlement ending the conflict and establishing the UN's new role in administering the peace. Its ambassador warned that the Council, by adopting this resolution, was choosing to elevate "human rights over sovereignty" and promoting "hegemonism under the pretext of human rights."[79] Nevertheless, China chose not to exercise its veto.

The Chinese prognosis, however, is too far-reaching. While the Council may indeed be said in Resolution 1244 to have retroactively endorsed NATO's action, such endorsement is probably better explained in pragmatic, rather than in doctrinal, terms. Kosovo's extreme humanitarian crisis had been well covered by the media and was widely apparent from abundant credible evidence. The Council itself had already determined that Serb

[75] S/199/649. See also S/RES/1244 of 10 June 1999, annex 2.
[76] S/RES/1244 of 10 June 1999.   [77] Ibid.
[78] Pellet says "it is inconceivable" that the UN organ entailed with "the primary responsibility for the maintenance of international peace and security" could have "recognised as lawful the situation created by [a] crime" since "if unlawful, the NATO action could only be described as a crime of aggression." Pellet, "State Sovereignty," p. 42.
[79] UNSCOR (LIV), 4011th mtg., 10 June 1999, at 9.

repression threatened to engender a breach of the peace within the meaning of the Charter's Chapter VII. The UN system's ability to do what it should to alleviate what it had identified as a threat to the peace was blocked not by the will of the members but by threat of a veto. This was also evidently not seen as a case of several states flouting the will, as well as the law, of the UN in order to serve their self-interest in unwarranted circumstances.

In context, the operation met several tests. Extreme necessity had been established factually, by credible on-the-ground international monitors and by the media. The immediacy of the need for action was demonstrated by UN reports of increasing atrocities, the large scale of flight by victims, and by the startling similarity between events in Kosovo and the ethnic-cleansing that only recently had occurred in other parts of the former Yugoslavia. The "clean hands" of participants in NATO's action was unassailable, in the sense that its members evidently had no territorial designs on Kosovo and appeared to be fighting a war for purely humanitarian objectives and (mostly) with means calibrated to avoid excessive and collateral damage. Probably it was these considerations that moved the UN members to adopt Resolution 1244, rather than any grand theory prioritizing human rights above sovereignty. Most of the states voting for that resolution probably did not intend to usher in a broadly permissive new rule legalizing autonomous regional humanitarian intervention in general, but one mitigating the consequences of an action which, while formally illegal, was evidently legitimated by the circumstances as understood by the international "jury."

Was the NATO action unlawful? Yes and no. *Yes*, in the sense that the prohibition in Article 2(4) cannot be said to have been repealed in practice by the system's condoning of NATO's resort to force without the requisite armed attack on it or prior Security Council authorization. Such a repeal is not supported by the members of the global system at this time. *No*, in the sense that no undesirable consequences followed on NATO's technically illegal initiative *because, in the circumstances as they were understood by the larger majority of UN members*, the illegal act produced a result more in keeping with the intent of the law (i.e. "more legitimate") – and more moral – than would have ensued had no action been taken to prevent another Balkan genocide. In other words, the unlawfulness of the act was mitigated, to the point of exoneration, in the circumstances in which it occurred.

When may a law be broken and who decides?

The practice of UN organs indicates a significant margin of flexibility in deciding whether or not, and to what extent, to indict violators of the law when the violation occurred in situations of extreme necessity. In notable instances, such sanctioning[80] has been waived in reliance on the credibility of the evidence adduced in support of extenuating facts, on the perceived "clean" motives of those resorting to force, on the immediacy and gravity of the challenge to world peace and common humanitarian values that an intervention sought to avert, and on the proportionality and appropriateness of the measures taken. In the international legal system, as in domestic counterparts, the cost of unlawful conduct has risen or fallen in relation to how these variables operated in each contextual instance. That is not some peculiar weakness of the international regime, or evidence of a "double standard." Rather, it is law's strength that it strives to be not merely consistent but also fair. It is precisely to protect this quality of contextual flexibility, for example, that our domestic legal system features trial by jury and allows judges and juries to consider pleas in mitigation and evidence of extenuating circumstances.

The UN system, too, facilitates a sort of trial by jury and pleas in mitigation. This ensures due attention to the appropriate situational variables and brings into play contextual, textured – not absolute or simple – standards. The onus of demonstrating to the "jury" of UN members that recourse to force in any particular instance is necessary and appropriate rests on those having extraordinary recourse to an unlawful remedy to prevent a much greater wrong. The facts adduced must justify any relaxation of an important general principle in conformity with an urgent and palpable common moral sense that, but for the unlawful action, a greater wrong would have occurred.

When absolute principles are relaxed to permit nuanced exceptions, it is evidence of the specific contextual facts that becomes crucial. The UN system, like most national legal systems, sometimes accommodates and responds to such special pleading. In the relevant UN organs, evidence for and against making an exception is usually adduced by the fact-gathering

---

[80] The term "sanctioning" is used here to denote the imposition of negative consequences ranging from resolutions deploring a transgressor's conduct, through diplomatic and economic embargoes, all the way to authorizing a remedial military response to the transgression.

agencies of national governments and presented to these institutions
by foreign ministries. But, increasingly, intergovernmental and non-
governmental agents also play an important role. The Secretary-General
and UN agencies have reliable reporters in the field,[81] even if they are not always used well. The "Brahimi Report"[82] has recently emphasized the urgent
need for "more effective collection and assessment of information at United
Nations Headquarters"[83] and called for "more frequent use of fact-finding
missions to areas of tension" under the auspices of the Secretary-General.[84]
The problem of inadequate fact-finding, the Report concludes, goes "to the
heart of the question" of peacekeeping[85] and, it may be added, of the other
uses of force. Although the Security Council has authorized the Secretary-
General to conduct specific fact-finding missions, the practice still remains
too episodic and *post hoc*.[86] Yet others, outside the UN system, are also
becoming important contributors to fact-finding. Media with global reach
and non-governmental organizations engaged in humanitarian efforts increasingly play a part.

Adducing evidence is different from assessing its weight and credibility:
the "jurying" function. Where, in the international system, is the "jury of
peers" that may waive strict application of law in reliance on mitigating
circumstances? There are essentially three forums in which such weighing
may be said to occur. One is the International Court of Justice. Another is the
international political forums – the Security Council and General Assembly.
A third "jury" is the court of public opinion, informed and guided by global
television, radio, and the new force of non-governmental organizations as
well as the Internet.

Although the UN secretariat and agencies, the media, and NGOs play
a powerful role in influencing the assessment process, it is the foreign

---

[81] There are several examples of the Secretary-General engaging in fact-finding on the basis of the
office's independent powers under Charter Article 99, or by agreement of the parties to a dispute.
In 1983, in the midst of the war between Iran and Iraq, Iran alleged that Iraq had resorted to
the use of chemical weapons. In his role as finder of fact and acting on his own authority,
the Secretary-General dispatched several missions to the front and was able to confirm that,
despite Iraqi denials, such weapons had been used: S/20060 of 20 July 1998 and references to
earlier reports therein. In 1986, New Zealand and France asked the Secretary-General to render
a binding opinion on the acrimonious *Rainbow Warrior* dispute. For the Secretary-General's
opinion, see 81 *American Journal of International Law* (1987), 325.

[82] Comprehensive review of the whole question of peacekeeping operations in all their aspects,
A/55/305-S/2000/809, 21 August 2000.

[83] Ibid., at 1, para. 6(d).   [84] Ibid., at 54, Annex III, para. 1(b).   [85] Ibid., at 6, para. 32.

[86] See S/RES/620 of 26 August 1988; S/RES/780 of 6 October 1992; S/RES/792 of 30 November
1992; S/RES/872 of 5 October 1993; S/RES/935 of 1 July 1994; S/RES/968 of 16 December 1994.

ministries of states that have ultimate responsibility for deciding what to make of evidence of varying credibility, probity, and significance: the core jurying function. It is up to them to decide whether a persuasive case has been made for an exception to the rules intended to control and inhibit states' recourse to force; or, to put it another way, whether to waive the penalties for a legitimate breach of legality. That responsibility is now habitually exercised, in large part, through the UN political forums: by what states in these organs *say* (or do not *say*) to validate an action and by what they *do* (or refrain from *doing*) in response to a breach of strict legality when it is sought to be justified as necessitated by the extreme consequences of inaction.

It is true, of course, that foreign ministries that determine the policies carried out by their representatives in the Security Council and General Assembly are not bound by the precise scruples underpinning the objectivity of judges and juries. If judges and juries can be trusted to bend the law now and then, to do the "right thing" in cases of extreme necessity, it is not necessarily reasonable to place similar trust in international political forums populated by officials responsible for advancing the national interest.

There are two ways to address these legitimate concerns. One is to point out that these institutions are the principal available means for making a credible determination of the legitimacy of a plea of necessity and that the foreclosure of all such pleas of necessity, on grounds of institutional inadequacy, is morally unacceptable as well as undermining of the law itself. The other is that these institutions have actually been doing a pretty good job of sorting out the chaff (of special pleading) from the wheat (of legitimate pleas of extreme necessity).

It is inconceivable that the world is ready to create a real court-and-jury system that would have sole authority to make the crucial calls as to when the strictures of the Charter may be suspended to permit interventions by regional or mutual defense organizations, let alone by states acting alone. If so, it is surely far better to have the global "jurying" function performed by the legitimate political institutions of the international system than either to preclude all institutional recourse to the moral compass or to permit the moral direction to be set unilaterally by any state acting alone in accordance with its own sense of the situational requisites. This is not only the conclusion to be drawn from common sense but also from practice. Few are the fastidious champions of strict legality that have had the icy stamina to insist in actual humanitarian crises that the law must always trump the common moral instinct. Most foreign offices know that such a rigid insistence that the law be enforced would garner little support even at a hortatory level and none in practice. What nation, for example, would try to compel the proposed Union of African States – had it been in a position to use force to save the Rwandan Tutsis – to refrain from doing so in compliance with the negative vote of one permanent member of the Security Council?

In this sense, the international system does have a "jury," albeit a political one. It is evident from the practice briefly herein described that the UN political organs have been quite perceptive in picking their way between, for example, the special pleading of humanitarian necessity advanced by the Soviets to justify the invasion of Czechoslovakia and, on the other hand, the same justification advanced by the nations of ECOWAS to justify their interventions in Liberia and Sierra Leone. In the face of most situations in which a population is threatened with massive killings or humanitarian deprivations, most states have acted in accordance with a high degree of objectivity in determining whether a situation of extreme necessity has arisen and whether an unlawful humanitarian intervention was, indeed, the lesser wrong. Most states have also sought to balance fairly the system's stake in law that prohibits interventions and its stake in preventing genocide and other massive crimes against humanity. Such balancing is a necessary part of any good legal system.

When the UN political organs are called upon to exculpate or mitigate a breach, it seems that fundamentalist adherence to the literal letter of the Charter text does not alone determine states' verdict. Practice also demonstrates that the jury of states has not rescinded Charter Article 2(4) or replaced it with an understanding that, now, "anything goes." States do not accept that any unilateral, unauthorized use of force for an allegedly "humanitarian" purpose is per se acceptable. They do not operate in the belief that there are no rules. In weighing evidence of extreme necessity, they do not agree that facts cannot be distinguished from lies, or humane altruism from greedy self-interest.

For a state seeking to invoke the law's margin of flexibility, there are hard tests, requiring sophisticated pleading backed by relevant and highly probative evidence: the sort of evidence, for example, the US could not adduce before the General Assembly to support its claim to be rescuing its citizens from lethal danger in Grenada.

"Hard cases," as every law student knows, "make bad law." We do not need bad law made for good cause. Rather, hard cases should facilitate the making of sensible exceptions: the sort exemplified by the rule that an unlawful act shall not be penalized when it can be demonstrated that obeying the law, in the instance, would have led to a far worse result.

Obviously, pleas of necessity are amenable to abuse. The appropriate systemic response to any plea of extreme necessity is extreme caution, but also extreme diligence in promoting synthesis and synergy between legality and legitimacy: between what is lawful and what is right.

7

Rethinking humanitarian intervention: the case for incremental change

JANE STROMSETH

For years to come, NATO's military intervention in Kosovo will shape international attitudes towards the use of force in response to human rights atrocities. In contrast to US military action in Afghanistan in self-defense against terrorist attacks[1] or UN-authorized interventions in Haiti, Bosnia, and Somalia, the legal basis for NATO's intervention in Kosovo remains contested. NATO's action and its aftermath are, in many respects, the latest development in a long-standing historical debate over "humanitarian intervention." Whether the use of force for humanitarian purposes is lawful or otherwise justified in the absence of state consent or United Nations authorization is a question that has long vexed international lawyers and philosophers. What makes the Kosovo case exceptional is the extent to which this question has transcended the pages of scholarly journals and become a preeminent focus of diplomatic discourse and public debate.

UN Secretary-General Kofi Annan made the issue of intervention the centerpiece of his address to the UN General Assembly in September 1999. He focused on the tragic dilemma confronting the international community when the UN Charter's rules regarding the lawful use of force are in tension with human rights imperatives in concrete situations such as Kosovo. On the one hand, as Annan has stressed, military intervention without Security

I would like to thank the editors and contributors to this volume who provided helpful comments on an earlier draft of this chapter, as well as James Schear, Walter Stromseth, David Wippman, and the participants in Georgetown University Law Center's Faculty Workshop for their constructive suggestions.

[1] In its report to the UN Security Council, the United States made clear that it was exercising its right of self-defense in response to the attacks of 11 September. S/2001/946, 7 October 2001. The Security Council, moreover, affirmed the inherent right of self-defense and condemned the terrorist attacks in two resolutions. S/RES/1368 of 12 September 2001; S/RES/1373 of 28 September 2001.

Council authorization may erode the legal framework governing the use of force and undermine the Council's authority by setting potentially dangerous precedents. On the other hand, the Council's failure to act in the face of horrific atrocities betrays the human rights principles of the Charter and erodes respect for the UN as an institution. To avoid such problems in the future, the Secretary-General has emphasized the need to ensure that the Security Council can rise to the occasion and agree on effective action in defense of human rights. Indeed, he has argued that the "core challenge to the Security Council and to the United Nations as a whole in the next century" is "to forge unity behind the principle that massive and systematic violations of human rights – wherever they take place – should not be allowed to stand."[2] Governments, commissions, foreign affairs institutes, non-governmental organizations, and scholars have taken up the Secretary-General's challenge, generating a rich and varied set of reflections on the difficult issues raised by Kosovo and by failures to act in other desperate situations.[3]

This essay argues that the legal status of humanitarian intervention without Security Council authorization remains uncertain after Kosovo and that this, in fact, is a good thing. The uncertain legality of humanitarian intervention puts a very high burden of justification on those who would intervene without UN authorization. Yet this very ambiguity is also fertile ground for the gradual emergence of normative consensus, over time, based on practice and case-by-case decision-making. Moreover, while public debate over guidelines for intervention serves some useful purposes, efforts to formalize or codify legal criteria for a right of humanitarian intervention will be counterproductive, irrespective of whether the criteria govern Security Council action or non-authorized interventions. The most promising path for the future does not involve a formal doctrinal framework that attempts in advance to reconcile human rights principles and the

---

[2] Kofi Annan, Address to the 54th Session of the UN General Assembly, 20 September 1999, reprinted in Kofi A. Annan, *The Question of Intervention: Statements by the Secretary-General* (United Nations Department of Public Information, New York, 1999), p. 39.

[3] The recent literature on this topic is voluminous. I have benefited especially from Adam Roberts, "The So-called 'Right' of Humanitarian Intervention," 3 *Yearbook of International Humanitarian Law* (2000), 3–51; *The Responsibility to Protect: Report of the International Commission on Intervention and State Sovereignty* (International Development Research Centre, Ottawa, 2001), available at http://www.iciss-ciise.gc.ca (5 March 2002); and the Danish Institute of International Affairs, *Humanitarian Intervention: Legal and Political Aspects* (Danish Institute of International Affairs, Copenhagen, 1999).

Charter's non-intervention norms. Instead, it lies in identifying patterns and common elements in recent practice as guidance for the future and in strengthening the capacity of the UN and of regional organizations to work with local actors to prevent and respond to human rights atrocities. In this process of normative evolution and capacity building, the question of the effectiveness of using force for humanitarian purposes must receive greater attention.

To make my case, I will first examine the Kosovo intervention, including the international response to NATO's decision to use force. Next, I will discuss four different approaches to humanitarian intervention in the aftermath of Kosovo. In particular, I will focus on the possible gradual emergence of a normative consensus regarding humanitarian intervention in contrast to attempts to formally codify a legal right to intervene. Finally, I will examine how public debate over guidelines for intervention can contribute to incremental change in attitudes and to improving prospects for effective action to protect victims of atrocities in the future.

The Kosovo dilemma

NATO's use of force in Kosovo raised an acute legal dilemma. On the one hand, NATO's military action did not fit within the two clear legal bases for using force under the UN Charter. It was neither an exercise of the right of individual or collective self-defense in response to an armed attack, nor was it authorized by the UN Security Council. Nor did NATO states try to argue that NATO's intervention fitted within one of these accepted legal bases. While a number of NATO states stressed the implications of the Kosovo crisis for regional stability, a claim of self-defense on these facts would have set a problematic, open-ended precedent that the allies did not wish to establish. Nor would a claim of Security Council authorization, implicit or otherwise, be persuasive in the face of clear Russian and Chinese opposition to the use of force.

On the other hand, NATO states could point to numerous factors that supported the legitimacy of military action. For one, the Federal Republic of Yugoslavia (FRY) flatly refused to comply with Security Council resolutions enacted under Chapter VII of the UN Charter.[4] These included

---

[4] Bruno Simma, "NATO, the UN and the Use of Force: Legal Aspects," 10 *European Journal of International Law* (1999), 1–22; Catherine Guicherd, "International Law and Kosovo," 41 *Survival* (1999), 27–28.

Resolution 1199, which called on the FRY to halt hostilities, take immediate steps to avert an "impending humanitarian catastrophe," and cease action by security forces against the civilian population of Kosovo.[5] NATO states also noted with great concern Secretary-General Annan's report warning of a dire humanitarian disaster in Kosovo, and, like the Security Council itself, NATO members viewed the deteriorating situation in Kosovo as a serious threat to peace and security in the region.[6] NATO's concerns about the desperate humanitarian predicament of Kosovar Albanians escalated after the FRY refused to honor commitments affirmed in Security Council Resolution 1203 and continued to engage in repressive action against the civilian population.[7] Yet, despite the deteriorating situation, a Security Council resolution authorizing force could not be obtained, given the views of several permanent members. In the end, in light of FRY conduct and the Security Council's resolutions, NATO governments concluded – in tandem, though not in unison – that NATO military action was justified even if not technically authorized.

NATO members clearly would have preferred a Security Council authorization had that been possible, but they were prepared to act without it in the extraordinary circumstances in Kosovo. What is striking, however, is the evident reluctance of most NATO states to claim any general "right" of humanitarian intervention in the absence of UN authorization. France, for example, focused on FRY non-compliance with Resolutions 1199 and 1203, and argued that "the legitimacy of NATO's action lies in the authority of the Security Council."[8] Germany emphasized the humanitarian disaster that made military intervention necessary and argued that NATO's action, though unauthorized by the Security Council, was nevertheless consistent with the "sense and logic" of Council resolutions.[9] The United States made no reference to "humanitarian intervention" as a legal concept. Instead, US officials focused on the particular factual circumstances at hand, including "Belgrade's brutal persecution of Kosovar Albanians, violations of international law, excessive and indiscriminate use of force, refusal to negotiate to resolve the issue peacefully, and recent military build-up in Kosovo – all of

---

[5] S/RES/1199 of 23 September 1998.
[6] Ibid.; Simma, "NATO, the UN and the Use of Force," p. 7.
[7] S/RES/1203 of 24 October 1998.
[8] Press Release, French Foreign Ministry, 25 March 1999. I am grateful to my research assistant, David Tallman, for his translation of the French sources used in this essay.
[9] Simma, "NATO, the UN and the Use of Force," p. 12.

which foreshadow a humanitarian catastrophe of immense proportions."[10]
The United States also stressed the implications of the developing refugee
crisis for regional security and invoked the Security Council resolutions
that called the situation a threat to peace and security. In this context, in the
face of Belgrade's persistent refusal to honor its commitments or negotiate a
peaceful solution, the United States ultimately concluded that NATO military action was "justified and necessary to stop the violence and prevent an
even greater humanitarian disaster."[11] Other NATO states likewise avoided
any general doctrinal justification for NATO's action and emphasized instead both the extraordinary circumstances surrounding the intervention
and the Security Council's resolutions.[12]

Britain came the closest in March 1999 to invoking humanitarian intervention as a distinct legal basis for NATO's military action. Six months
earlier Britain had circulated a note to NATO allies arguing that force could
be justified "on the grounds of overwhelming humanitarian necessity" without Security Council authorization, but that certain criteria "would need
to be applied."[13] By March 1999, Britain concluded that force was needed
to avert an imminent humanitarian catastrophe; otherwise continued repression would result in large-scale displacement of civilians and further
loss of life. Britain's Ambassador to the United Nations, Jeremy Greenstock,
argued that "[i]n these circumstances, and as an exceptional measure on
grounds of overwhelming humanitarian necessity, military intervention is
legally justifiable."[14] Other British statements, however, linked the justification for NATO's military action more directly to purposes articulated in
UN Security Council resolutions. As Prime Minister Tony Blair stated in
April 1999:

> Under international law a limited use of force can be justifiable in support
> of purposes laid down by the Security Council but without the Council's
> express authorization when that is the only means to avert an immediate and

---

[10] Statement of Ambassador A. Peter Burleigh to the Security Council, 24 March 1999, S/PV.3988,
3988th mtg., at 4.

[11] Ibid., at 5.   [12] Guicherd, "International Law and Kosovo," pp. 26–28.

[13] UK Foreign and Commonwealth Office note of 7 October 1998, "FRY/Kosovo: The Way Ahead;
UK View on Legal Base for Use of Force," quoted in Adam Roberts, "NATO's 'Humanitarian
War' Over Kosovo," 41 *Survival* (1999), 106. The criteria discussed in this note are quite similar
to those articulated earlier in the decade by Mr. A. Aust, Legal Counsellor, Foreign and Commonwealth Office, in invoking "humanitarian intervention" as a legal basis for the intervention
in northern Iraq to protect the Kurds after the Gulf War. See *British Yearbook of International
Law 1992* (1993), p. 828.

[14] Statement of Sir Jeremy Greenstock to the Security Council, 24 March 1999, in S/PV.3988,
at 12.

overwhelming humanitarian catastrophe. Any such case would in the nature of things be exceptional and would depend on an objective assessment of the factual circumstances at the time and on the terms of relevant decisions of the Security Council bearing on the situation in question.[15]

Britain, in short, was cautious and arguably a bit ambivalent about staking out a general right of humanitarian intervention.

Belgium was prepared to take a few more steps down this road in proceedings before the International Court of Justice. Defending against FRY charges of illegality, Belgium argued in May 1999 that NATO's action was a "lawful armed humanitarian intervention."[16] NATO acted, Belgium contended, to protect fundamental *jus cogens* values, such as the right to life and physical integrity, and to forestall a humanitarian catastrophe acknowledged by the Security Council. Belgium argued further that NATO's action was "compatible" with Article 2(4) of the UN Charter because it was directed against neither the territorial integrity nor the political independence of the FRY.[17] Instead, NATO's action was supported by precedents, including prior interventions that were not condemned by relevant UN bodies. While thus defending NATO's intervention as "entirely legal," Belgium also argued, in the alternative, that NATO's action was excusable under "a state of necessity . . . which justifies the violation of a binding rule in order to safeguard, in face of grave and imminent peril, values which are higher than those protected by the rule which has been breached."[18] Belgium, in short, was prepared to go farther than other NATO states in publicly defending NATO's military action as "lawful armed humanitarian intervention" but also displayed a certain caution in doing so.

Given that NATO's use of force did not fit clearly within the two established legal justifications under the UN Charter, one might have expected a sharply critical response from the Secretary-General of the United Nations and from the Security Council. On the contrary, the Secretary-General was remarkably supportive of NATO's decision in this situation. Annan and many of his top advisers had experienced directly the horrific consequences of UN neutrality in Bosnia in the face of systematic ethnic cleansing and

---

[15] Prime Minister Tony Blair, Written Answer for House of Commons, 29 April 1999, *Hansard*, col. 245.

[16] Argument of Belgium before the International Court of Justice, 10 May 1999, at 7. Available at http://www.icj-cij.org (5 March 2002).

[17] Ibid. Article 2(4) of the UN Charter prohibits "the threat or use of force against the territorial integrity or political independence of any state, or in any other manner inconsistent with the Purposes of the United Nations."

[18] Argument of Belgium, before the ICJ, 10 May 1999, at 8.

recurring atrocities. A similar posture in Kosovo was unacceptable. Instead, the Secretary-General concluded that there "are times when the use of force may be legitimate in the pursuit of peace."[19] Moreover, in a strong speech in Geneva before the UN Commission on Human Rights, the Secretary-General made clear that "ethnic cleansers" and those "guilty of gross and shocking violations of human rights" will find no justification or refuge in the UN Charter.[20] At the same time, the Secretary-General also stressed the Security Council's primary responsibility for maintaining peace and security and the urgent need for unified, effective Council action in defense of human rights in the future.[21]

The UN Security Council also refused to condemn NATO's action. By a vote of three in favor and twelve against, the Council decisively rejected a Russian resolution calling NATO's intervention a flagrant violation of the UN Charter and a threat to peace and security.[22] To be sure, Russia and China – two of the Council's permanent members – emphatically condemned NATO's intervention as contrary to the Charter's provisions governing the use of force. But they secured the support of only one other Council member – Namibia. All the other Council members – from every region of the world, including countries large and small – essentially concurred in NATO's conclusion that force was necessary in these exceptional circumstances. Many states deeply regretted the Security Council's failure to act, but many also concluded that allowing FRY actions to go unchecked would lead to a humanitarian catastrophe and would condone "systematic and brutal violations" of the Council's resolutions.[23] In short, most Council members reached the same conclusion NATO reached: that in these extraordinary circumstances, force was necessary and justified even if it did not fit comfortably within the strictures of the UN Charter's provisions governing force.

Implications for the future

Where NATO states broke ranks – quite dramatically – is in the conclusions they reached about the normative implications of the Kosovo experience

---

[19] Annan, *The Question of Intervention*, p. 33.
[20] Kofi Annan, Address to the United Nations Commission on Human Rights, 7 April 1999, reprinted in ibid., p. 22.
[21] Annan, *The Question of Intervention*, p. 33.
[22] S/1999/328, 26 March 1999; S/PV.3989, 3989th mtg., 26 March 1999, at 6.
[23] Statement by Danilo Turk, Permanent Representative of Slovenia, in S/PV.3988, 24 March 1999, at 6.

for the future. At one end of the spectrum, some allies adopted a kind of "never again" stance, stressing that Kosovo established no precedent but was rather a completely special case. Germany's Foreign Minister argued, for example, that NATO's decision "must not become a precedent" and that "we must avoid getting on a slippery slope" concerning the Security Council's "monopoly on force."[24] French Foreign Minister Védrine likewise stressed that NATO's Kosovo intervention "must remain an isolated case and not constitute a precedent."[25] Yet Vedrine also left the door open a crack:

> [T]he way in which we intervened is an exception, not a precedent. As much as possible, the framework established by the United Nations Charter in Chapter VII must remain the rule. If another exceptional situation arises, we'll take a look at it.[26]

Nevertheless, France insisted during NATO's fiftieth anniversary summit that in the future NATO should refrain from using force without Security Council authorization in non-self-defense situations. The United States drew a quite different conclusion from the Kosovo experience, namely that Security Council authorization is always preferred but not always required.[27] At the same time, the United States declined to embrace a doctrine of humanitarian intervention in light of its open-endedness and potential for abuse. Washington prefers instead to consider the facts and the circumstances of concrete cases rather than opening up a new legal basis for the use of force. At the other end of the spectrum, some NATO states, notably Belgium and the Netherlands, seem willing to argue for humanitarian intervention as a legal basis for action in the future if the Security Council is unable or unwilling to authorize force in compelling situations.[28]

The British response to Kosovo is, in many respects, the most noteworthy. Prime Minister Tony Blair delivered a speech during the Kosovo conflict arguing that the "most pressing foreign policy problem we face is to identify the circumstances in which we should get actively involved in other people's

---

[24] Simma, "NATO, the UN and the Use of Force," p. 13.

[25] Commentary of Foreign Minister Hubert Védrine, *Le Monde Diplomatique*, 1 December 2000.

[26] Interview with Foreign Minister Hubert Védrine, *La "Lettre de la Rue Saint-Guillaume,"* No. 122–123, July 2001, p. 43.

[27] Interview with former US State Department official.

[28] See above, p. 237; Opening Remarks of HE Mr. Jozias van Aartsen, Foreign Minister of the Kingdom of the Netherlands, in International Peace Academy, *Humanitarian Action: A Symposium Summary*, 20 November 2000, pp. 12–13.

conflicts," and he suggested five issues to consider in deciding when and whether to intervene.[29] Yet, despite Britain's strong emphasis on the necessity of responding to the unfolding humanitarian catastrophe in Kosovo, Britain has pulled back a bit from articulating a legal concept of humanitarian intervention in general terms. Despite moves in this direction both during the Kosovo conflict and earlier in the decade when assisting the Kurds in the aftermath of the Gulf War,[30] Britain also linked its justification for military action to purposes and objectives laid down in Security Council resolutions.[31] What is different today is Britain's general interest in articulating political guidelines for humanitarian intervention – inspired no doubt by the Prime Minister himself. A decade earlier, after the Gulf War, the British Foreign Office eschewed the value of criteria for humanitarian intervention, warning that "application of a set of criteria would inhibit the decision making process and limit the flexibility of our response."[32] Since the Kosovo intervention, however, and since Blair's speech, British Foreign Office officials have actively promoted guidelines for humanitarian intervention that aim to identify the circumstances in which *the Security Council* should be prepared to act. The purpose of this exercise, argue the British, is to make unified, effective Council action more likely in the future.[33] Britain has encountered a mixed response to its guidelines initiative even among its NATO allies: some, like the Dutch, actively support this effort, while others, like the United States, have raised questions about the utility of this approach to the subject of humanitarian intervention. In short, NATO allies remain divided on how best to approach the question of humanitarian intervention in the future.

---

[29] Prime Minister Tony Blair, "Doctrine of the International Community," speech in Chicago, 22 April 1999. Available at http://www.number-10.gov.uk (5 March 2002). The five factors Blair identified include: "First, are we sure of our case? War is an imperfect instrument for righting humanitarian distress, but armed force is sometimes the only means of dealing with dictators. Second, have we exhausted all diplomatic options? . . . Third, on the basis of a practical assessment of the situation, are there military operations we can sensibly and prudently undertake? Fourth, are we prepared for the long term? . . . And, finally, do we have national interests involved?"

[30] For official British responses regarding the legal basis for the intervention to protect the Kurds, see the materials quoted in the *British Yearbook of International Law 1992* (1993), pp. 826–28.

[31] Written Answer of Prime Minister Tony Blair, 29 April 1999, *Hansard*, col. 245.

[32] *British Yearbook of International Law 1992*, p. 826.

[33] See below, pp. 262–65 (discussing British initiative spearheaded by Foreign Secretary Robin Cook).

Four approaches to humanitarian intervention

Whether NATO's military intervention in Kosovo ultimately proves to be a unique case or whether it establishes a significant precedent for lawful humanitarian intervention remains to be seen. In the meantime, most states clearly would prefer to secure UN authorization before using force for humanitarian purposes. Moreover, most states probably would agree that the Security Council, acting under Chapter VII, can authorize military action in response to severe atrocities and other humanitarian emergencies that it concludes constitute a threat to peace and security.[34] The difficult issue arises when the Security Council is unable or unwilling to authorize effective action in such circumstances. If unified Council action is not possible, states will again confront the dilemma that arose in Kosovo in which human rights imperatives were pitted against the Charter's rules governing use of force.

Four distinct attitudes or approaches to humanitarian intervention in the absence of Security Council authorization can be identified.[35] Each has pros and cons. First is the status quo approach. This view categorically affirms that military intervention in response to atrocities is lawful only if authorized by the UN Security Council or if it qualifies as an exercise of the right of self-defense. Proponents of this view regard NATO's intervention in Kosovo as a clear violation of Article 2(4) that should not be repeated

---

[34] Under Article 39 of the UN Charter, the Security Council has legal authority to "determine the existence of any threat to the peace, breach of the peace, or act of aggression" and to decide on appropriate measures "to maintain or restore international peace and security." Moreover, the Charter's drafters declined to limit or constrain the Council's authority by defining these terms. Instead, after considerable discussion, they deliberately left the terms "threat to the peace, breach of the peace, or act of aggression" undefined to give the Security Council flexibility in responding to new and unforeseen circumstances. Ruth Russell, *A History of the United Nations Charter* (Brookings Institution, Washington, DC, 1958), pp. 464–65; Benjamin B. Ferencz, *Defining International Aggression* (Oceana Publications, Dobbs Ferry, 1975), vol. I, p. 352. This reality has been affirmed over the years, moreover, in Security Council practice.

[35] Like the study by the Danish Institute of International Relations, *Humanitarian Intervention*, I describe four distinct positions regarding humanitarian intervention unauthorized by the Security Council. My first and second approaches are quite similar to those of the Danish Institute, but my third approach differs. Though a superb report, I find the Institute's third and fourth approaches to be somewhat confusing and hard to differentiate from each other. My framework highlights a third distinctive approach and argues its merits in contrast to the others. The Danish Institute favors an approach it calls "the ad hoc strategy," which is similar to the second approach discussed in this essay.

in the future. Defenders of this position include a number of states, most notably Russia and China.[36]

Proponents of this approach point to the literal text of the UN Charter and to widespread understandings of Article 2(4). They also stress the lack of a consistent practice of humanitarian intervention that might otherwise suggest a customary international law "gloss" on the basic treaty text.[37] Moreover, strict interpretation of the Charter's rules on non-intervention can serve important objectives. By placing a high burden of justification on a party using force, the Charter aims to minimize resort to force as a means of conflict resolution and thereby promote stability. In addition, the high threshold for Security Council authorization of force, including non-opposition by any of the five permanent members, is designed to promote consensus as well as stability by ensuring at least a basic acceptance of military action among key states. Finally, the Charter's rules regarding force aim to protect state sovereignty and the political communities within states from violent external interference.

Yet, after Kosovo, it is hard to take a rigid status quo approach. NATO responded to urgent humanitarian circumstances in a situation recognized as a threat to the peace by the Security Council. Furthermore, neither the Council nor the Secretary-General were prepared to condemn NATO's action. On the contrary, the Security Council rejected a resolution labeling NATO's action a Charter violation. Secretary-General Annan recognized the acute dilemma posed by NATO's non-authorized use of force, but he also emphasized that the UN Charter provides no refuge for those who

---

[36] See Statements by Russia and China on 24 March 1999, in S/PV.3988, at 2–4 (Russia); 12–13 (China). For a scholarly critique of NATO's intervention as a violation of the UN Charter, see Mary Ellen O'Connell, "The UN, NATO, and International Law After Kosovo," 22 *Human Rights Quarterly* (2000), 57, 88–89 ("NATO and its peer organizations are required under international law to have Security Council authorization when using force, except in collective self-defense").

[37] For helpful discussions of past practice by scholars who nevertheless reach differing conclusions regarding humanitarian intervention, see Simon Chesterman, *Just War or Just Peace? Humanitarian Intervention and International Law* (Oxford University Press, Oxford, 2001); Sean D. Murphy, *Humanitarian Intervention: The United Nations in an Evolving World Order* (University of Pennsylvania Press, Philadelphia, 1996); Fernando R. Tesón, *Humanitarian Intervention: An Inquiry into Law and Morality* (2nd edn, Transnational Publishers, Irvington-on-Hudson, 1997); Nicholas J. Wheeler, *Saving Strangers: Humanitarian Intervention in International Society* (Oxford University Press, Oxford, 2000); Tom J. Farer, "An Inquiry into the Legitimacy of Humanitarian Intervention," in L. Damrosch and D. Scheffer eds., *Law and Force in the New International Order* (Westview Press, Boulder, 1991); Thomas M. Franck and Nigel S. Rodley, "After Bangladesh: The Law of Humanitarian Intervention by Military Force," 67 *American Journal of International Law* (1973), 275.

commit atrocities. In short, the international reaction to NATO's intervention suggests that deviation from the strict letter of the UN Charter will be tolerated in exceptional circumstances.

This leads to the "excusable breach" approach to humanitarian intervention. Under this second approach, humanitarian intervention without a UN mandate is technically illegal under the rules of the UN Charter but may be morally and politically justified in certain exceptional cases.[38] In short, it is a violation of the Charter for which states are unlikely to be condemned or punished. The Danish Institute of International Affairs calls such action a justified or legitimate "emergency exit" from the rules of the Charter.[39] But since an "excusable breach" of existing law is justified by extraordinary necessity, the factors justifying such breaches in the future are difficult to specify in advance. Some defenders of this approach thus prefer not to engage in efforts to develop criteria for "emergency exits" from the law on the grounds that "necessity knows no law."[40] Instead, the extraordinary circumstances of each situation must be confronted and addressed case by case.

The excusable breach approach has some distinct benefits. It highlights the truly exceptional nature of legitimate non-authorized humanitarian intervention. It contemplates no new legal rules governing the use of force. On the contrary, the existing legal framework, with its various benefits, is affirmed. Yet, in those extraordinary cases that produce a tension between the rules governing the use of force and the protection of fundamental human

---

[38] What I call the "excusable breach" approach to humanitarian intervention differs somewhat from criminal law concepts of "excuse" and may be closer, though not completely analogous, to justification defenses as understood in criminal law. See Joshua Dressler, *Understanding Criminal Law* (3rd edn, Mathew Bender/Irwin, New York, 2001), sections 16.03, 16.04, 17.05. I use the term "excusable breach" to emphasize that, under this view, the intervention violates the legal norms contained in the UN Charter but that the intervenor should not be sanctioned for doing so. My third approach, "customary law evolution of a legal justification," involves a clearer justification for intervention that ultimately may result in a new legal norm permitting humanitarian intervention in certain circumstances.

[39] Danish Institute, *Humanitarian Intervention*, p. 127.

[40] For a defense of this position, see Chesterman, *Just War or Just Peace?*, p. 230 ("the circumstances in which the law may be violated are not themselves susceptible to legal regulation"). In contrast, for an analysis that favors development of criteria for evaluating "emergency exits" from the law, see the Dutch study on humanitarian intervention: Advisory Council on International Affairs and Advisory Committee on Issues of Public International Law, *Humanitarian Intervention* (The Hague, April 2000), pp. 27–28. Available at http://www.aiv-advice.nl/E1000AD/E113/E113SA.htm (5 March 2002) (hereinafter "Dutch Study").

rights, a "safety valve" is opened.[41] States intervening in such situations are unlikely to be condemned as law-breakers; but they act at their own risk in full awareness that they are violating the rules for a higher purpose.

This approach has evident drawbacks as well, however. For one thing, it is unsatisfying to label as "illegal" action that the majority of the UN Security Council views as morally and politically justified. If such situations were to recur, the tension between legality and legitimacy would yield problems over time. The legitimacy of the legal rules themselves would be called into question. Second, the justifications offered by states – and the international responses to state action – are more nuanced than the "excusable breach" approach. NATO states did not argue "we are breaking the law but should be excused for doing so." Instead, NATO states, in sometimes differing ways, explained why they viewed their military action as "lawful" – as having *a legal basis within the normative framework of international law*. That framework includes fundamental human rights norms as well as resolutions adopted by the Security Council under Chapter VII of the Charter, which in this case called upon the FRY to cease its repressive actions. Furthermore, the international responses to NATO's intervention, including the reactions of the UN Security Council and the Secretary-General, were more complex than the excusable breach approach implies.

This leads to a third approach: customary law evolution of a legal justification for humanitarian intervention in rare cases. This approach looks to both Security Council and broader international responses to instances of non-authorized humanitarian intervention to ascertain patterns, consistency of rationales, and degrees of acceptance, reflected in practice, if certain conditions are met. This approach asks whether an emerging norm of customary international law can be identified under which humanitarian intervention should be understood not simply as ethically and politically justified but also as legal under the normative framework governing the use of force. The strong non-intervention presumption at the Charter's core is affirmed, but this approach allows for a narrow, evolving legal exception and justification for humanitarian intervention in light of concrete circumstances, and in light of the reasons that states and the UN Security Council find persuasive over time, rather than calling such action flatly illegal or an "excusable breach" of the UN Charter.

The advantages of this approach are considerable and, as I will argue, it offers a more promising path for the future than the alternatives. Nevertheless,

---

[41] Danish Institute of International Affairs, *Humanitarian Intervention*, p. 128.

the ambiguities inherent in this approach have led some to advocate a fourth, more explicit, approach to humanitarian intervention. Advocates of this fourth approach favor codification of a clear legal doctrine or "right" of humanitarian intervention. Proponents argue that such a "right" or "doctrine" should be established[42] through some formal or codified means such as a UN Charter amendment or a UN General Assembly declaration. The idea is that humanitarian intervention should be a distinct legal basis for using force on a par with the right of self-defense, with fixed criteria or principles spelled out in advance governing legitimate appeal to the right. Although states have been extremely reluctant to advocate a legal right of humanitarian intervention in the absence of Security Council authorization, a number of scholars, as well as the Independent International Commission on Kosovo, have made the case for establishing such a right or doctrine with specified criteria to guide assessments of legality.[43] The case for codifying a right of humanitarian intervention rests on a normative attitude towards such interventions, a view about the impact of codification on the legitimacy of international law, a position concerning the role of formalization in curbing abuses, and a view about the relative benefits of clarity versus open-endedness in the evolution of international legal norms. The pros and cons of this approach are examined below, where I argue that codification of a "right" of humanitarian intervention is problematic and would be counterproductive at this time.

The incremental development of normative consensus

Attitudes towards the use of force in response to atrocities and other severe humanitarian emergencies have been evolving over the past few decades.[44] During the 1990s, the Security Council authorized the use of force in situations that many states previously would have viewed as strictly "internal"

---

[42] It is hard to argue that such a "right" already exists as a matter of international law. Self-defense and UN authorization are the only legal bases for force clearly provided in the text of the UN Charter. With the possible exception of Britain, moreover, no NATO states invoked any general right of humanitarian intervention at the onset of the Kosovo conflict. But see Tesón, *Humanitarian Intervention*, for a thoughtful moral and legal argument on behalf of a right of humanitarian intervention.

[43] See e.g. Michael L. Burton, "Legalizing the Sublegal: A Proposal for Codifying a Doctrine of Unilateral Humanitarian Intervention," 85 *Georgetown Law Journal* (1996), 417; Independent International Commission on Kosovo, *Kosovo Report* (Oxford University Press, Oxford, 2000), 187–98.

[44] See Wheeler, *Saving Strangers*.

conflicts.[45] In several instances, moreover, groups of states have intervened with force, without advance authorization from the Security Council, at least in part in response to extreme violations of basic human rights. Recent examples include the intervention after the Gulf War to protect the Kurds in northern Iraq as well as NATO's intervention in Kosovo.

Rather than view such interventions as flatly illegal or as "excusable breaches" of the UN Charter, the third approach asks whether a norm of customary international law is beginning to emerge under which humanitarian intervention could be understood as lawful in rare cases under certain circumstances. This approach looks to both Security Council and broader international responses to specific interventions to identify any emerging patterns in the circumstances surrounding the interventions and in the legal justifications that states and the Security Council found persuasive.

This approach has a number of advantages. First, it appreciates the nuances of responses and the evolution of thinking reflected in recent practice. Practice has always been understood as relevant to interpretation of treaty texts, and it is particularly relevant in understanding the UN Charter's legal norms governing the use of force, where the Security Council plays such a central role in addressing international peace and security. This approach focuses on the Security Council's central role as "jury" (to use Thomas M. Franck's term) in calibrating the international community's response to uses of force that do not fall clearly within classic self-defense or UN-authorized military action.[46] Second, this approach takes seriously the legal justifications offered by states and the responses of the international community. In explaining their decision to use force in Kosovo, NATO states argued that their action had a legal basis and they offered reasons why military force in these exceptional circumstances was justified. Furthermore, states committed to following the rule of law will – and should – identify and articulate legal bases for their actions as part of the process of accountability.[47] Humanitarian justifications – particularly the claim of necessary action in

---

[45] Lori Fisler Damrosch ed., *Enforcing Restraint: Collective Intervention in Internal Conflicts* (Council on Foreign Relations, New York, 1993).

[46] Thomas M. Franck, "Interpretation and Change in the Law of Humanitarian Intervention," ch. 6 in this volume, pp. 227–31.

[47] For an insightful analysis of how law shapes decision-making regarding the use of force, including the process of justifying action as consistent with relevant legal norms, see Abram Chayes, *The Cuban Missile Crisis: International Crises and the Role of Law* (Oxford University Press, New York, 1974). Chayes argues that international law operates in three ways to shape and orient decision-making regarding the use of force: (1) law as constraint; (2) law as justification; and (3) law as organization. Law is only one factor, among many, that influences the consideration

the face of humanitarian catastrophe – have become more central, more-over, to how states justify and evaluate military actions.[48] Third, this ap-proach keeps the Charter's non-intervention presumption front and center, but is open to a customary law evolution and acceptance of humanitarian intervention as lawful, based on concrete cases and precedents. Over time, a normative consensus regarding humanitarian intervention that goes be-yond the literal text of the Charter is likely to be reflected in practice – and this approach strives to identify the elements of that emerging consensus in a nuanced and forward-looking way that takes account of subtle but discernible trends in state behavior and in normative judgments.

At present, the normative status of humanitarian intervention is arguably in a state of evolution somewhere between the second and third approaches described above. Some view Kosovo as an example of an "excusable breach" of the Charter's rules governing use of force. Others defend it as a lawful ac-tion in defense of victims of atrocities and ethnic cleansing that should not be understood as a violation of Article 2(4) because of the exceptional circumstances involved.[49] Still others emphasize the Security Council's refusal to condemn NATO's action after the fact as essential to the action's legality.[50] In short, the exact contours of the norm that may be emerging are not yet clear.[51] This should not be surprising: as customary international law norms develop, there are often periods in which the old norm is fraying

of options. As part of a state's decision-making process regarding use of force, law can shape and "constrain" choices not by dictating conduct in any black and white sense, but rather by "orient[ing] deliberation, order[ing] priorities, guid[ing] within broad limits." Ibid., p. 102. Law as justification involves a process of showing that a decision can be reconciled with a set of applicable norms; this process of justification helps to legitimize an action to relevant publics. Moreover, knowledge that an action must be justified can have important effects on the decision-making process itself: "the requirement of justification suffuses the basic process of choice." Ibid., p. 103. Finally, law as organization involves the organizational setting in which a decision occurs, including the allocation of jurisdiction and decision-making power among different actors such as states, regional organizations, and international organizations. As Chayes put it: "institutional structures that are the product of law can be as important as rules, and more so, in organizing and channeling decision." Ibid., p. 102.

[48] Wheeler, *Saving Strangers*.

[49] See, for example, the Belgian argument discussed above, p. 237.

[50] See Thomas M. Franck, ch. 6 in this volume, at pp. 214–15, for a careful analysis of the Security Council's response and its implications for the legal status of NATO's Kosovo intervention.

[51] A norm permitting humanitarian intervention in extraordinary circumstances without advance Security Council authorization could emerge without requiring a change in the Charter's express language. Some scholars have suggested, for instance, that a new gloss on the meaning of Article VIII of the UN Charter governing regional organizations may be developing. See e.g. Sean Murphy, "The Intervention in Kosovo: A Law-shaping Incident?" 94 *Proceedings of the Annual Meeting of the American Society of International Law* (2002), 302, 304; Sean Murphy, "Calibrating

at the edges while a new norm is struggling to be born. Indeed, an extended period of "excusable breaches" may precede the development of a new legal norm.

Still, a good case can be made that elements of a normative consensus in favor of humanitarian intervention in truly exceptional cases may gradually be developing. To be sure, thoughtful scholars will differ on the degree to which they find any consensus emerging from recent practice and on how they characterize the parameters of any developing norm.[52] Nevertheless, in my view, a careful examination and comparison of the Kosovo intervention and the earlier intervention to protect the Kurds following the Gulf War at least suggest the contours of a possible emerging norm. The common elements reflected in these two cases include the following.

Threshold / triggering conditions: In both situations, severe violations of fundamental human rights involving loss of life were occurring. In the case of the Kurds, Iraqi gunships attacked desperate Kurds fleeing into mountains and neighboring territory. In Kosovo, "ethnic cleansing" and military action against Kosovar Albanians was accelerating, against a backdrop of similar conduct in Bosnia. In both Iraq and Kosovo, the territorial government was perpetuating the human rights violations and showed no willingness to stop.

UN Security Council unable to authorize action: In both cases the UN Security Council was unable to authorize military action because one or more permanent members would have vetoed it. *Yet, the intervenors nevertheless maintained a close relationship to the Council.* In both cases, relevant Security Council resolutions existed calling the situation a threat to peace and security, and the military action undertaken was at least consistent with purposes and aims articulated by the Security Council.[53] *In neither*

Global Expectations Regarding Humanitarian Intervention," paper dated 4 December 2000, pp. 9–10; Louis Henkin, "Kosovo and the Law of 'Humanitarian Intervention,'" 93 *American Journal of International Law* (1999), 824, 827–28.

[52] For a helpful discussion, see Antonio Cassese, "*Ex iniuria ius oritur*: Are We Moving towards International Legitimation of Forcible Humanitarian Countermeasures in the World Community?" 10 *European Journal of International Law* (1999), 23–30; Antonio Cassese, "A Follow-up: Forcible Humanitarian Countermeasures and *Opinio Necessitatis*," 10 *European Journal of International Law* (1999), 791–99.

[53] Regarding Kosovo, see the discussion above, pp. 234–38. In the case of northern Iraq, the relevant Security Council resolution was S/RES/688 (1991). For a discussion of this resolution, see Jane Stromseth, "Iraq's Repression of its Civilian Population: Collective Responses and Continuing Challenges," in Damrosch, *Enforcing Restraint*, pp. 85–92; and Wheeler, *Saving Strangers*, pp. 141–52.

case, moreover, did the Security Council criticize or condemn the action undertaken. Furthermore, in both cases, the intervening forces turned the follow-on operation over to the United Nations at the first realistic opportunity and did not seek to maintain a long-term military presence absent UN authority. In Iraq, armed UN guards were deployed to northern Iraq with the consent (albeit compelled) of Iraq, while allied forces maintained no-fly zones overhead to assure overall security. In Kosovo, a UN-authorized mission under a Special Representative of the Secretary-General operates, with NATO forces providing the security backbone for the civilian operation.

Force necessary to stop atrocities: In both cases, force was necessary to stop the severe human rights violations perpetrated by government forces. In each case, the Security Council had called upon the relevant government to stop its abusive action, to no avail. Diplomatic alternatives to the use of force had been tried and had failed. In short, both interventions occurred in a political context in which the intervening states had good reason to believe that further diplomatic negotiations would not result in the government in question halting the ongoing atrocities and, as a consequence, that people would continue to die if no military action was taken.

Proportionality: In both cases, the military actions undertaken were proportional to the end of stopping the atrocities. In Iraq, international military forces established safe havens and thereby facilitated delivery of humanitarian relief and deterred further Iraqi military action. In Kosovo, NATO forces aimed to stop the ethnic cleansing and restore political stability to Kosovo by halting the ability of the FRY military forces and security apparatus to continue a policy of repression against Kosovar Albanians. While some have criticized the nature of NATO's military campaign, NATO states took great pains to comply with the law of armed conflict, and a special Report to the Prosecutor of the International Criminal Tribunal for the former Yugoslavia (ICTY) subsequently found no convincing evidence of war crimes.[54] Moreover, the duration of NATO's action was limited and the overall operation was placed under UN authority within a reasonable period. In Iraq, the military presence on the ground in northern Iraq was of short duration, with UN armed guards soon replacing allied forces. Monitoring of Iraqi airspace by allied air forces has continued, however, because

[54] Final Report to the Prosecutor by the Committee Established to Review the NATO Bombing Campaign against the Federal Republic of Yugoslavia, para. 90–91, available at http://www.un.org/icty (5 March 2002).

of reasonable concerns about the Kurdish population's long-term security in the absence of such monitoring.

The impact on political independence and territorial integrity in both cases is a more complicated issue. In the case of Kosovo, for example, it was not possible to stop the ethnic cleansing and accompanying atrocities without a significant impact upon FRY governmental authority structures (and a de facto effect on territorial integrity), even as UN Security Council Resolution 1244 subsequently attempted to balance these considerations and the rights of Kosovars by calling for "substantial autonomy and meaningful self-administration for Kosovo," while affirming the "sovereignty and territorial integrity" of Yugoslavia and other states in the region.[55] While Kosovo has de facto autonomy, its future status remains unresolved. In Iraq, the government's political control over northern Iraq has been reduced and the Kurdish areas have a degree of de facto autonomy, but the future remains uncertain and Kurdish leaders continue to disagree among themselves regarding negotiations with Baghdad. In short, any simple conclusions regarding the impact of these interventions on "political independence" and "territorial integrity" are difficult to reach, but both interventions arguably were proportionate in relation to the underlying humanitarian aim of assisting a civilian population at grave risk. Nevertheless, the aspirations of the Kurds and the Kosovar Albanians for self-determination add a dimension of complexity to these cases that may not be present in other situations of urgent humanitarian distress.

Humanitarian purpose and effect: Both interventions were motivated to a substantial degree by humanitarian concerns for victims of severe human rights violations. Other strong motivations were clearly present in both cases as well, such as concern for regional stability and for the stability of allied states. Concern about NATO's credibility in the Balkans was also cited by NATO states as a consideration in deciding to act.[56] While the motivations were multifaceted both in Iraq and Kosovo, the military intervention in each case focused on stopping the atrocities, protecting vulnerable individuals, and stabilizing a situation that risked further humanitarian catastrophe. This reinforces the contention that the *nature and purpose* of the action undertaken, and its effects, are more significant than the motive, which will always be multifaceted.

---

[55] S/RES/1244 (1999) of 10 June 1999.

[56] See e.g. Statement by British Foreign Secretary Robin Cook, quoted in Roberts, "NATO's 'Humanitarian War'," p. 109.

Collective action: Both interventions were collective in that a coalition of states acted together: the United States, Britain, and France established safe havens in Iraq; NATO acted in Kosovo. As a result, the intervenors had to justify their action not only to their domestic publics but also to their allies (in this case, democratic allies) and to the larger international community.

Legal justification offered: In both cases, the intervening states argued that force was necessary to stop immediate, serious harm to civilian populations and that a legal basis existed for using force in such circumstances. They expressed, to use Antonio Cassese's term, *opinio necessitatis*.[57] In the case of Kosovo, NATO states invoked both fundamental human rights norms as well as Security Council resolutions adopted under Chapter VII of the Charter – resolutions that characterized the situation as a threat to peace and security and demanded that the FRY cease repressive actions, even though the resolutions did not technically authorize the use of force in response. NATO states, in short, did not argue that they were breaking international law and should be excused for doing so, but instead argued that NATO's action should be understood as *lawful* in the extraordinary factual circumstances at hand. Moreover, although NATO invoked neither UN authorization nor the right of self-defense, the Security Council and the Secretary-General refused to call NATO's action a violation of the UN Charter. Likewise, the states intervening to protect the Kurds argued that a legal basis existed for using force for humanitarian purposes in the exceptional circumstances that existed. In particular, they argued that their actions were consistent with Security Council Resolution 688, which insisted that Iraq allow access to its territory for humanitarian relief purposes and also called upon states to assist in these relief efforts.[58] Moreover, although Resolution 688 did not expressly authorize force, the Security Council did not condemn the allied military action taken.

Two additional elements were present in both cases as well. Both interventions were welcomed by the population that was bearing the brunt of the atrocities. And finally, both interventions had a reasonable prospect of success in achieving their humanitarian objectives. To put it another way, based on what the intervenors knew at the time they decided to commit their forces, both interventions had a reasonable prospect of doing more

---

[57] Cassese, "Follow-up," p. 797.

[58] S/RES/688 (1991). For a discussion of the legal justifications offered, see Stromseth, "Iraq's Repression of its Civilian Population," pp. 85–90, 100; Wheeler, *Saving Strangers*, pp. 141–46, 152–55, 166–69; *British Yearbook of International Law 1992*, pp. 826–28.

good than harm in assisting a desperate civilian population at risk. (I will discuss this challenging issue more fully below.)

In sum, a number of common elements were present in the intervention to protect the Kurds and the intervention in Kosovo, neither of which was condemned by the UN Security Council. It is too early to say with confidence that a positive legal norm is emerging under which humanitarian intervention, under these conditions, unambiguously can be deemed lawful.[59] The most we can safely conclude at this time is that the Security Council is not prepared to say that humanitarian intervention in such circumstances is unlawful. Moreover, in light of the Council's clear refusal to label actions such as NATO's intervention in Kosovo unlawful, and its decision to establish and authorize a follow-on mission in Kosovo, it would be highly problematic if NATO's decision to use force were held illegal by other bodies, such as international judicial tribunals. Even if the legal status of non-authorized humanitarian intervention remains ambiguous as a general matter, a normative consensus may nevertheless emerge over time out of concrete situations such as the interventions in northern Iraq and Kosovo. Other recent interventions that also warrant full examination and comparison include the intervention of the Economic Community of West African States (ECOWAS) in Liberia in the early 1990s and, more recently, in Sierra Leone.[60] In short, the most promising approach for the future is to be open to a possible, gradual acceptance of humanitarian intervention as lawful in certain circumstances, based on concrete cases and precedents.

This incremental approach, which looks to customary law evolution of a legal justification for humanitarian intervention, has important benefits. Like the excusable breach approach, it recognizes both the value of the UN Charter's restraints on force and the Security Council's central role in authorizing military actions other than those taken in self-defense. Yet the

[59] Scholars differ in the degree of specificity with which they articulate elements or criteria reflected in recent practice. They also differ, not surprisingly, over whether that practice should be said to represent the emergence of a new legal norm in favor of humanitarian intervention in exceptional cases. For thoughtful analysis, see Cassese, "*Ex iniuria ius oritur*" and "Follow-up"; Murphy, "Intervention in Kosovo" and "Calibrating Global Expectations."

[60] International Commission on Intervention and State Sovereignty, *Responsibility to Protect*, p. 16. For a discussion of the ECOWAS intervention in Liberia, see David Wippman, "Enforcing the Peace: ECOWAS and the Liberian Civil War," in Damrosch, *Enforcing Restraint*, pp. 157–203. On Sierra Leone, see Lee Berger, "State Practice Evidence of the Humanitarian Intervention Doctrine: The ECOWAS Intervention in Sierra Leone," 11 *Indiana International and Comparative Law Review* (2001), 605.

customary law approach is also open to the emergence of a legal norm that would permit states to intervene for humanitarian purposes in truly urgent and compelling circumstances if the Security Council is simply unable to rise to the challenge. The customary law approach, moreover, encourages states to explain the legal basis and justification for their action forthrightly and, as a result, is more likely to contribute to the development of a normative consensus regarding the circumstances in which humanitarian intervention should be understood as lawful than the excusable breach approach, which instead views each case as an exceptional, unique, and "ad hoc" breach of the Charter.

The customary law approach has some drawbacks, however. Relatively few cases exist to provide data points, making it hard to say definitively that a new norm is developing or what its precise contours are. Also, states taking military action may not explain as clearly as they could – or should – the legal justification for their action, particularly the reasons why they believe intervention for humanitarian purposes should be deemed legal and in what circumstances. As a result, ambiguities and differences of view about the legality of humanitarian intervention will continue, with states sometimes taking quite divergent positions. Some states thus may be deterred from acting, even in compelling cases, because of their uncertainty about the lawfulness of humanitarian intervention. Moreover, any erosion of the traditional rules governing the use of force may lead other states to act opportunistically and to take military action that the Security Council ultimately would reject. In other words, an incremental approach could be abused by powerful states, including dominant states within particular regions of the world.

Still, safeguards against abuse exist within the customary law approach. First, the uncertain legality of unauthorized humanitarian intervention places an appropriately high threshold of justification on those who would intervene without a Security Council mandate. They will be acting with a clear risk of condemnation by the Council after the fact. The non-intervention norm remains central, with a strong presumption that intervention should be authorized in advance by the Security Council. This keeps the focus where it should be – on encouraging greater Council consensus and willingness to act in truly compelling cases. At the same time, if states engage in humanitarian intervention without Council authorization and claim humanitarian intervention as their legal justification, the *opinio juris* requirement involved in the development of customary international law serves as some constraint on abuse, as Allen Buchanan argues.[61] Specific interventions will hold value as precedents for an emerging norm of humanitarian intervention (as opposed to being simply violations or excusable breaches) to the extent that states explain and justify their actions in ways that contribute to broad acceptance of their legality. If states decline to provide such justifications, we may remain in the world of excusable breaches for a longer time rather than moving towards a developing consensus on a new norm regarding humanitarian intervention. But states that are prepared to contribute to the development of a new norm will have an incentive to articulate a justification for their action in a clear and generalizable way.

All things considered, the customary law approach holds out greater promise and has fewer drawbacks than the alternatives. Like the status quo and excusable breach approaches, it welcomes efforts to develop a greater Security Council consensus on responses to humanitarian emergencies in order to minimize the likelihood that states will feel compelled to engage in unauthorized humanitarian intervention. However, the customary law approach better protects the human rights of victims of atrocities by being open to an emerging norm of humanitarian intervention if the Security Council is unable or unwilling to respond in truly compelling cases. If states do act in such situations, moreover, this approach carefully assesses state practice, state legal justifications, and the responses of the Security Council and the broader international community in order to identify emerging elements of consensus – a process that should, over time, yield a clearer legal status for humanitarian intervention. The *opinio juris* requirement for the development of a new legal norm, coupled with the high threshold of justification facing any state engaging in humanitarian intervention, moreover, provide safeguards against abuse. Finally, the customary international law approach allows for learning as we go. Rather than attempting prematurely to institutionalize a legal right of humanitarian intervention without Security Council authorization and to specify in advance the precise circumstances in which such a right can be invoked, the customary law

---

[61] Allen Buchanan, "Reforming the International Law of Humanitarian Intervention," ch. 4 in this volume, at pp. 133–37. Although some NATO states could indeed have been clearer in explaining their legal justification for the use of force in Kosovo and in articulating the principle they were prepared to generalize, I do not find persuasive Buchanan's argument that taking *opinio juris* seriously requires NATO to transform its charter if it is to engage legitimately in humanitarian intervention in the future.

approach looks to practice over time as a better means to build consensus and achieve agreement on the parameters of a norm of humanitarian intervention. In so doing, it avoids the downsides of a codification strategy, to which I will now turn.

The drawbacks of premature codification

Advocates of the fourth approach contend that a legal right or doctrine of humanitarian intervention should be established formally, on a par with the legal right of self-defense. Most proponents of this position advocate an explicit agreement – or codification – of criteria or principles that specify when humanitarian intervention should be deemed lawful in the absence of Security Council authorization. Such criteria would guide assessments of legality both *ex ante* and *ex post* and would be established through a formal instrument such as a UN General Assembly declaration[62] or even a UN Charter amendment. The Independent International Commission on Kosovo, for example, advocates a three-stage process for formalizing a "doctrine" of humanitarian intervention.[63] First, the Commission advocates a "framework of principles" for humanitarian intervention, which includes threshold principles that must be satisfied as well as contextual principles that bear on the degree of legitimacy of an intervention. Next, the Commission urges formal adoption of its proposed framework by the UN General Assembly in the form of a Humanitarian Intervention Declaration, followed by amendment of the UN Charter to put humanitarian intervention on a firmer basis.

Fundamentally, the case for establishing a formal or codified right of humanitarian intervention without Security Council authorization rests on a normative view about the merits of such interventions and an empirical view of their likely frequency. The Kosovo experience affirmed for many the notion that sometimes humanitarian intervention without Security Council authorization is morally and politically justified. If such situations are likely to be extraordinarily rare – and if the Security Council in future cases is more willing to authorize collective action – the case for carving out

---

[62] See e.g. Burton, "Legalizing the Sublegal."

[63] Independent International Commission on Kosovo, *Kosovo Report*, pp. 187–98. The Commission's framework allows for humanitarian intervention without Security Council authorization in exceptional cases, but most of the principles would apply to interventions mandated by the Council as well.

a new legal right or basis for action is less compelling. On the other hand, if future predicaments like Kosovo are likely to arise with some frequency – that is, if the Security Council is likely to be immobilized often in the face of severe and widespread human rights atrocities – the case for formalizing a legal right of humanitarian intervention is stronger. Even then, however, the case is less attractive than the alternative of allowing a legal basis to emerge through practice and precedent, over time, case by case.

One major argument advanced for codifying a legal right of humanitarian intervention is that this would enhance the legitimacy of international law. According to this view, the current legal regime accords such interventions a corrosive "sub-legal" status that provides insufficient protection to human rights principles and perpetuates a gap between legality and morality that ultimately undermines respect for international law.[64] A codified right of humanitarian intervention is offered as a solution that "resolves" the tension between legality and legitimacy as well as the tension between human rights and sovereignty principles contained in the UN Charter.

Yet such a solution to these dilemmas is problematic and premature. Any decision to intervene with force for humanitarian purposes inevitably will involve a delicate and context-specific balancing of principles – the principle of non-use of force, the central role accorded the Security Council and the reasons behind it, the importance of protecting fundamental human rights. The goal of resolving conflicts between such principles abstractly in advance in a doctrinal formulation, and thus delineating a legal right of intervention, is in tension with the usually messy, complicated, and uncertain way in which conflicts actually present themselves. Indeed, the historical record of humanitarian intervention is sufficiently ambiguous that it argues for humility regarding efforts to specify in advance the circumstances in which states can use force, without Security Council authorization, against other states to protect human rights.[65]

Rather than attempt prematurely to codify legal criteria for humanitarian intervention, it is better to continue the gradual process of normative evolution under the UN Charter framework. Over time, as the cases of the Kurds and Kosovo suggest, the elements of a normative consensus regarding

---

[64] For an articulation of this position, see Burton, "Legalizing the Sublegal," at 426–32; and Independent International Commission on Kosovo, *Kosovo Report*, p. 186.

[65] For an argument that humanitarian intervention is best viewed as a "tragic choice" in which competing principles are balanced in the light of unique circumstances, see Roberts, "So-called 'Right' of Humanitarian Intervention."

intervention for humanitarian purposes gradually may develop. In this process, any conflicts between the non-intervention norm and the human rights principles at the heart of the UN Charter can be addressed and resolved in concrete situations. Indeed, an international consensus on when humanitarian intervention should be deemed both legitimate and lawful is more likely to emerge over time from the international community's assessment of concrete interventions such as these than from an exercise in codification. Perhaps some day, if sufficient consensus develops, it might be possible to achieve codification on some aspects of humanitarian intervention, but any such effort would be more promising if it were built on a solid foundation of consensus developed through a process of incremental change.

Advocates of codification now, however, reject such a case-by-case development of legal norms as a recipe for abuse. In their view, formal adoption of a legal doctrine of humanitarian intervention with specified criteria would lessen the prospect of unwarranted, pretextual interventions while encouraging legitimate interventions. But the issue of curbing abuse and encouraging desirable action is far more complex. States' willingness to engage in meritorious interventions is likely to be influenced as much by considerations of feasibility and national interest as by codified criteria for legality, though at the margin agreed criteria could have some influence on state decision-making. On the question of curbing unwarranted interventions, a risk exists that creating a clear legal right of humanitarian intervention would encourage more frequent resort to the practice in less compelling circumstances than at present by creating an additional doctrinal basis for justifying the use of force. Under the current legal regime, states engaging in humanitarian intervention know that they have an extraordinarily high burden of justification. Establishing an additional legal basis for resort to force, albeit with criteria attached, would provide another theory under which states determined to use force can seek to justify their actions – a theory arguably less constrained by objective circumstances than the right of self-defense. (Indeed, even in that context it is not surprising that the International Court of Justice has articulated more demanding requirements for exercise of the right of *collective* self-defense lest states invoke such a right without a clear request for help from the state they are aiding.)[66] To be sure, *if* clear criteria or principles governing humanitarian intervention could be agreed and codified, this could help to curb abuse

---

[66] ICJ, *Nicaragua Case*, para. 199.

by providing an internationally accepted framework of evaluation. Yet it is doubtful that such criteria setting forth the parameters for lawful intervention without Security Council authorization could be codified – at least not in the foreseeable future. The conceptual and practical difficulties involved in codifying criteria for humanitarian intervention are formidable.

The difficulties of codification

Conceptually, there is a certain convergence in the criteria scholars and non-governmental organizations have identified for lawful humanitarian intervention. These criteria generally include: a threshold or triggering set of circumstances (such as severe human rights abuses leading to loss of life on a large scale, and an unwillingness or inability of the state in question to halt the abuses); a requirement that the Security Council be unable or unwilling to take action; a requirement that force be necessary to halt the abuses; that the force used be proportionate to the end of halting the atrocities; and that the law of armed conflict be complied with. To guard against abuse, additional criteria sometimes (though not always) are articulated, including that the intervention be multilateral, perhaps by a regional organization; and that the motivation (or at least the goals and the effects) be primarily humanitarian in nature.

Yet identifying possible criteria and actually codifying them are very different matters. It is one thing to offer a list of factors that ought to guide decision-making on intervention; it is quite another to reach agreement on codifying those criteria in a formal way as part of a legal right of humanitarian intervention. Codification would require a high degree of precision and agreement in spelling out the content of the relevant criteria. Yet, despite many common elements in the various lists of criteria that have been advanced for lawful humanitarian intervention, little prospect for agreement currently exists even among like-minded international lawyers. For instance, some scholars would limit the triggering conditions to genocide and crimes against humanity involving substantial loss of life, while others would include a broader spectrum of humanitarian emergencies. Some would include imminent threat of atrocities among the triggering conditions, while others would not. Some would require a strict exhaustion of non-forcible alternatives while others take a more flexible approach on this issue depending on the circumstances at hand. Some would require submission (and rejection) of an authorizing resolution to the Security Council and then submission of a resolution to the General Assembly; others would not. Some would require a primarily humanitarian motivation, while others emphasize that conduct and effects, not motive, is what counts. Some would require collective action by more than one state; others would not. Some would require "even stricter adherence to the laws of war and international humanitarian law than in standard military operations";[67] others would not. Given these differences, any agreed criteria inevitably would be general in nature, papering over real differences under a superficial consensus, and thus be of limited utility in guiding or assessing conduct. Alternatively, criteria conceivably could be so specific that they would constrain or rule out interventions in as yet unforeseen but compelling situations in the future. In other words, a codification strategy has risks in both directions: if the right is defined narrowly (e.g. only in cases of genocide), it may constrain desirable interventions in other urgent and compelling circumstances. Furthermore, perpetrators of atrocities may calibrate their behavior to fall just below the threshold. But if the right is defined too broadly, and the criteria are too vague, it may be used by opportunistic states to justify a host of undesirable interventions.

This is not to disparage efforts to identify principles and criteria that ought to guide decision-making on humanitarian intervention.[68] Rather, it is to dispute the merits of attempting to codify a legal "right" of humanitarian intervention without Security Council authorization by trying to forge agreement in advance on a list of principles or criteria that spell out the precise contours of that right. Indeed, the practical obstacles to formalizing a legal right of humanitarian intervention are enormous, regardless of how the operative criteria are spelled out.

First, for the foreseeable future, no possibility of achieving agreement among states on such an initiative exists. The vast majority of UN member states would adamantly oppose such a development. As the G77 proclaimed in March 1999: "We reject the so-called 'right' of humanitarian intervention, which has no legal basis in the UN Charter or in the general principles of international law."[69] Russia has actively pursued an initiative through the G8

---

[67] Independent International Commission on Kosovo, *Kosovo Report*, p. 195.

[68] A particularly thoughtful recent effort is contained in ch. 4 of International Commission on Intervention and State Sovereignty, *Responsibility to Protect*, which I discuss more fully below, pp. 265–66.

[69] Final Statement of G77 Ministerial Conference, Cartagena, 8–9 April 2000, para. 263. Available at http://www.nam.gov.za (5 March 2002).

to affirm that any use of force other than in self-defense must be authorized by the UN Security Council. Moreover, while some states in Asia, Africa, and Europe have shown a greater openness to the subject of humanitarian intervention recently, it remains a highly divisive subject internationally.[70]

Second, pursuit of an initiative to formalize a legal right of humanitarian intervention would be counterproductive for those who want to move in this direction. States that otherwise might support humanitarian interventions in concrete cases (tacitly or otherwise) would actively oppose any formal adoption of such a doctrine or right. Indeed, a substantial risk exists that any diplomatic conference convened to address the issue would be dominated by states with the strongest views on the question, namely, those adamantly opposed to any military intervention for humanitarian purposes without the express consent of the UN Security Council. Any declaration or resolution that might emerge would likely reflect a more categorical position than states might take in concrete situations. At best, a bland document reflecting the lowest common denominator or highest common platitude would emerge. Even then, states would simply interpret it in different ways, as the experience with the 1974 General Assembly Definition of Aggression suggests.[71] At worst, a document severely restrictive of any future humanitarian interventions would emerge. Indeed, formalizing criteria – even general criteria – would lead some states to argue that no action should be taken – even in new and unanticipated situations – unless all the criteria are met, which could constrain reasonable responses in the future.[72] In short, the human rights principles at the core of the Charter are not necessarily advanced – nor normative tensions best "resolved" – by seeking to codify a right that most member states would view as contrary to core principles of the UN system.

---

[70] For a helpful discussion of differing perspectives on the issue of humanitarian intervention, see Pugwash Study Group on Intervention, Sovereignty and International Security, 2(1) *Pugwash Occasional Papers* (2001).

[71] "Definition of Aggression" Resolution, GA Res. 3314, UN Doc. A/9631 (1974).

[72] Some commentators advocate a General Assembly resolution on the conditions for humanitarian intervention as a "compromise between the advantages of codification and the political impediments to recognizing a doctrine of unilateral humanitarian intervention." Burton, "Legalizing the Sublegal," p. 448. The Independent International Commission on Kosovo also advocates a General Assembly resolution as the second of three steps towards establishing a doctrine of humanitarian intervention: *Kosovo Report*, p. 187. But such an approach might well be the worst of all worlds. It would not create a clear legal basis for action; it would generate intense diplomatic discord and animosity; and it might be used politically to constrain action in concrete cases of human rights abuses in the future.

This does not mean that efforts to identify the elements of a possible normative consensus on humanitarian intervention are of no value. On the contrary, clarifying the extent to which common elements are present in concrete situations where force has been used for humanitarian purposes, both with and without Security Council authorization, is essential for two purposes: first, to evaluate the degree of international assent to such practices, and second, to assess whether an international law norm in support of such interventions can be said to be emerging. A normative consensus on humanitarian intervention is far more likely to emerge over time from this type of "positivist" exercise – which looks for common elements and practical precedents in recent practice – than from a contentious exercise in codification. Furthermore, recent efforts to encourage more unified and effective Security Council responses to humanitarian emergencies should not be overlooked.

The value of discussions of criteria for incremental change

Ideally, if the Security Council were able to agree on effective responses to human rights atrocities in the future, the acute dilemmas confronted in Kosovo would not arise and any need for a right of humanitarian intervention would be diminished. Thus, a number of recent efforts to articulate criteria for humanitarian intervention aim not at establishing a *legal* basis for unauthorized military action but rather at encouraging *political* consensus to respond to atrocities. The overriding aim of these efforts is to make unified Security Council action more likely in the future by forging agreement on the circumstances in which collective intervention is warranted.

UN Secretary-General Kofi Annan took the lead on this issue when he made the topic of intervention the centerpiece of his 1999 address to the UN General Assembly.[73] Annan has referred on numerous occasions to a "developing international norm in favor of intervention to protect civilians from wholesale slaughter" and to an emerging "international norm against the violent repression of minorities that will and must take precedence over

---

[73] When Annan challenged the UN and the international community to "forge unity behind the principle that massive and systematic violations of human rights ... should not be allowed to stand," he was calling not only for greater political agreement within the Security Council on responses to atrocities. He was also attempting then, and in numerous other speeches and initiatives, to refocus international attention on protecting victims of conflict and to galvanize a greater and more consistent commitment of resources to assist those victims. Annan, *The Question of Intervention*, p. 39.

concerns of State sovereignty."[74] In these and other public addresses, the Secretary-General has sought to reorient thinking about the meaning of sovereignty, reinvigorate commitment to the human rights norms at the very heart of the UN Charter, and put perpetrators on notice that they cannot hide behind the Charter if they commit atrocities.

Annan has worked tirelessly to encourage greater political consensus within the Security Council to respond effectively to human rights atrocities. He has argued, for example, that the Security Council should be prepared to act under Chapter VII of the UN Charter if the parties to a conflict "commit systematic and widespread breaches of international humanitarian and human rights law, causing threats of genocide, crimes against humanity and war crimes."[75] Moreover, in order to encourage appropriate enforcement action by the Council and "to reinforce political support for such efforts, enhance confidence in their legitimacy and deter perceptions of selectivity or bias toward one region or another," the Secretary-General has urged the Council to consider a range of factors before acting. These include: the scope and nature of the breaches of international law and the number of people affected; the inability or unwillingness of local authorities to halt the breaches; "the exhaustion of peaceful or consent-based efforts to address the situation"; the Security Council's ability to monitor actions taken; and "the limited and proportionate use of force, with attention to repercussions upon civilian populations and the environment."[76] In response both to Secretary-General Annan and to Prime Minister Blair, Britain has made pursuit of political guidelines for humanitarian intervention along these lines a central diplomatic initiative.

Britain has focused on developing an agreed set of understandings to guide Security Council decision-making in response to massive violations of human rights and humanitarian law. Foreign Secretary Robin Cook argued that a "set of pragmatic understandings on action in response to humanitarian crises" would help the Council "to reach consensus when such crises occur, thus ensuring effective and timely action by the international community."[77] Cook articulated these understandings on various

---

[74] Ibid., pp. 44, 24.

[75] Report of the Secretary-General to the Security Council on the Protection of Civilians in Armed Conflict, S/1999/957, 8 September 1999, at 21.

[76] Ibid., at 22.

[77] Foreign Secretary Robin Cook, Written Answer to Parliamentary Question, 31 January 2000, reprinted in British Embassy Press Release, International Intervention in Humanitarian Crises.

occasions as part of a public campaign tracking Britain's diplomatic efforts to persuade Security Council members of the value of such an exercise. For example, in July 2000, Cook articulated six "principles" on which to build a "framework to guide intervention by the international community."[78] These include, first, a greater commitment to prevention. As Cook put it: "any intervention, by definition, is an admission of failure of prevention" and "a strengthened culture of conflict prevention" is needed.[79] Second, intervention can take many different forms, but "armed force should only be used as a last resort." Third, "the immediate responsibility for halting violence rests with the state in which it occurs."[80] Cook's fourth principle focuses on the circumstances in which intervention is necessary. "[W]hen faced with an overwhelming humanitarian catastrophe, which a government has shown it is unwilling or unable to prevent or is actively promoting, the international community should intervene," he stressed. However, "there must be convincing evidence of extreme humanitarian distress on a large scale, requiring urgent relief," and "[i]t must be objectively clear that there is no practicable alternative to the use of force to save lives."[81] In short, Cook contended, "we need to strike the correct balance between the sovereign right of states and the humanitarian right of the international community to intervene where necessary." Cook's fifth principle focuses on issues of proportionality and effectiveness:

> [A]ny use of force should be proportionate to achieving the humanitarian purpose and carried out in accordance with international law. We should be sure that the scale of potential or actual human suffering justifies the dangers of military action. And it must be likely to achieve its objectives.[82]

Sixth, and finally, "any use of force should be collective." No single country, Cook argued, can act on behalf of the international community. Britain's own preference is that "wherever possible, the authority of the Security Council should be secured."[83]

Britain has sought to formalize agreement within the Security Council on guidelines along these lines. If agreement were reached, it could be reflected in a Statement by the President of the Security Council on the Council's behalf. The British initiative, while actively supported by the Dutch, has met with little enthusiasm on the larger Security Council, however. Russia

---

[78] Speech by UK Foreign Secretary Robin Cook, "Guiding Humanitarian Intervention," American Bar Association Meeting, 19 July 2000. Available at http://www.fco.gov.uk (5 March 2002).
[79] Ibid., at 3.   [80] Ibid., at 4.   [81] Ibid.   [82] Ibid.   [83] Ibid.

and China prefer to reiterate and affirm existing Charter norms governing the non-use of force. The United States has expressed skepticism about the wisdom or utility of articulating criteria in advance with respect to situations that, in its view, are best assessed in light of their particular circumstances.

Given such resistance, what could the British proposal realistically accomplish in the near term? Not a clear agreement on the circumstances in which the Security Council should be prepared to authorize intervention in response to future Kosovos. Any guidelines acceptable to the entire Security Council likely would be so general that they would provide little in the way of concrete guidance. As a result, it is hard to see how they would help produce consensus in specific crises in the face of deep political disagreements among Council members. Alternatively, if guidelines are too specific, they run the risk of being a possible straitjacket for future action. Even the British prefer to call their approach a set of "understandings" or "guidelines" (rather than "criteria") and to formulate their ideas in fairly general terms to avoid over-constraining future responses by the Security Council. Yet the very process of negotiating and formalizing Security Council guidelines runs a risk of hardening the attitudes of some Council members who otherwise may show flexibility and reach practical accommodations in concrete cases. In short, though well intentioned, the British initiative is not likely to generate consensus on the Security Council regarding the circumstances warranting intervention, at least not any time soon.

Still, the British effort may have some utility if it is understood as part of a longer-term effort to reinforce changing attitudes towards the protection of victims of conflict. During the past decade, for example, the Security Council has shown a greater willingness to consider internal conflicts with severe human rights and humanitarian consequences as threats to peace and security, subject to Security Council action under Chapter VII.[84] The British and Dutch hope, not unreasonably, that their effort to articulate Security Council guidelines can reinforce this trend in favor of viewing severe atrocities as a proper subject of Security Council action under Chapter VII. The nature of Security Council action, moreover, can take many forms, with military action being only one of a wide range of potential responses.

Secondly, and perhaps most important, the British and Dutch hope that articulating guidelines for Security Council action will make it more difficult – or at least more awkward – for permanent members of the

---

[84] See e.g. Damrosch, *Enforcing Restraint*.

Security Council to exercise their vetoes in the face of future humanitarian emergencies like Kosovo or Rwanda. In this spirit, the French have proposed that the Council's permanent members should commit not to exercise their veto to impede interventions in response to humanitarian crises in agreed circumstances.[85] Although other permanent members are unlikely to agree to tie their hands in advance in this way, the French could make an explicit declaration regarding their own intentions that could, in turn, put some political pressure on the other permanent members to at least abstain, rather than veto collective action, in future Kosovo-like situations. Non-permanent members could also declare that they are prepared to support Security Council authorization of humanitarian intervention when certain conditions exist.

Regional organizations could pursue such initiatives as well. For instance, states in a particular regional organization – or even groups of states that span regions – could agree that they would support *Security Council action* in response to severe humanitarian crises in certain circumstances and – even better – would be willing to provide some *resources* to help. The best possibility for developing this concept at present is within the European Union. By identifying at least some circumstances in which member states would be prepared to support Security Council action, such an initiative would aim to reinforce the prospects of unified action under the Charter regime, while keeping open the possibility of support in other compelling situations that may arise in the future.

Innovative efforts to reconceptualize the responsibilities of sovereign states can also contribute to changing attitudes incrementally. Most notable here is the International Commission on Intervention and State Sovereignty's new report, *Responsibility to Protect*, which argues that sovereignty entails a responsibility to protect citizens from atrocities and other humanitarian emergencies, with the state having the primary responsibility. If this responsibility to protect is not met, however, and efforts at prevention fail, the international community has a responsibility to react

---

[85] Interview with Foreign Minister Hubert Védrine, *La "Lettre de la Rue Saint-Guillaume,"* July 2001. Likewise, the International Commission on Intervention and State Sovereignty recommends that the five permanent members of the Security Council "should consider and seek to reach agreement not to apply their veto power, in matters where their vital state interests are not involved, to obstruct the passage of resolutions authorizing military intervention for human protection purposes for which there is otherwise majority support." *Responsibility to Protect,* p. 75.

and, ultimately, to rebuild following an intervention.[86] The Commission's report contains a perceptive discussion of principles that should inform decisions to intervene with force for humanitarian purposes, including a high threshold and a number of precautionary principles.[87] The Commission is agnostic on the best sequence of steps to pursue and ultimately reflect consensus on these principles; it suggests the possibility of a General Assembly Resolution centered around the concept of "Responsibility to Protect" and a possible set of Security Council guidelines.[88] Whether pursuit of such initiatives could ultimately yield political agreement on core principles or guidelines for humanitarian intervention among UN bodies or governments remains to be seen – probably not any time soon. But by keeping the issue of protecting victims of humanitarian emergencies front and center and by offering relevant guiding principles, such efforts do contribute to a longer-term project of shaping political attitudes and encouraging more effective protection of human rights. Such efforts, moreover, cumulatively may contribute over time to a greater international consensus on when intervention for humanitarian purposes is warranted, including intervention with force in exceptional cases.

Most of the diplomatic efforts regarding political guidelines for intervention focus on making agreed Security Council action more likely in the future. This may not always be possible, however, which raises the question whether guidelines for Security Council action are relevant for interventions undertaken without Council authorization. The British and others have argued that guidelines for Security Council action may still be useful in exceptional cases, like Kosovo, if action without a Security Council mandate proves necessary. In such cases, proponents contend, agreed political guidelines would provide a basis for evaluating and justifying non-authorized action and for minimizing abuse. Others are even more explicit in calling for guidelines by which to assess the legitimacy of non-mandated humanitarian intervention.[89] Yet the very possibility of using potential

---

[86] *Responsibility to Protect*, chs. 2–5.

[87] As a threshold matter, the Commission argues that a "just cause" exists for intervening in circumstances that involve "large scale loss of life" or "large scale ethnic cleansing." In addition, the Commission articulates four precautionary principles that must be satisfied at the outset of an intervention: right intention, force as a last resort, proportional means, and reasonable prospects of success. Ibid., pp. 32–37.

[88] Ibid., pp. 74–75.

[89] The Dutch Study, for example, advocates an "assessment framework" for humanitarian interventions without Security Council authorization. Although the Study views such interventions

Security Council guidelines to justify non-authorized interventions makes other states (including some permanent Council members) uncomfortable about the guidelines initiative in the first place. So it remains an exceedingly difficult diplomatic endeavor. Nevertheless, the recent proliferation of efforts to articulate criteria for interventions even without Security Council authorization may put some useful public pressure on the Security Council to step up to the plate if and when situations like Kosovo arise in the future.

In short, the debate over intervention encouraged by Secretary-General Annan has had a valuable cumulative effect. It has altered the normative climate in which situations like Kosovo or Rwanda will be considered in the future. The question of intervention to protect the victims of atrocities is now a prominent – and legitimate – subject of diplomatic discourse. This may make some states uncomfortable, but every diplomat posted to the UN must engage the issue – and frequently. Furthermore, every tyrant who contemplates committing atrocities against his own people must think twice, knowing that the prospect of humanitarian intervention cannot be ruled out. In short, the debate over intervention – and over triggering criteria – has contributed to a larger process of shaping political attitudes, public expectations, and diplomatic possibilities over time. But, at the same time, as the Secretary-General recognizes better than anyone, the challenge of spurring *effective action* to protect human rights in the face of limited resources remains enormous.

Effectiveness: the missing factor

In the end, the normative debate over the circumstances warranting humanitarian intervention will be incomplete unless the question of the *effectiveness* of using military force for humanitarian purposes is fully addressed. For an intervention to be legitimate it should, at the very least,

as illegal under the Charter regime, it also believes such interventions will occur in the future because the Council sometimes will be unable or unwilling to authorize humanitarian interventions in compelling situations. The Study argues that, pending a clearer legal basis for non-authorized interventions, they should nevertheless be as legitimate as possible. An "assessment framework," argues the Study, could "provide the UN community of nations with a basis for assessing cases of humanitarian intervention that have already taken place and for tolerating them provided that sufficient account has been taken of 'legitimacy considerations.'" Ibid., p. 35. More ambitiously, the Study hopes that such a framework, if observed strictly, might ultimately contribute to international acceptance of a legal justification for non-authorized humanitarian intervention "in which humanitarian necessity prevails over the law banning the use of force." Ibid.

do more good than harm. It should, in short, have a humanitarian objective and a reasonable prospect of success in achieving that objective at acceptable costs. Otherwise, the risks to the intervenors and to the victims being assisted are very hard to justify. Reasonable prospect of success in achieving a legitimate objective was an important part of the "Just War" tradition.[90] But such analysis is absent from much recent writing on humanitarian intervention. Many lists of criteria for lawful intervention developed during the last few decades do not include the prospect of success as a critical factor.[91]

The issue of effectiveness has received a bit more attention recently. The International Commission on Intervention and State Sovereignty includes "reasonable chance of success in halting or averting the suffering which justified the intervention" as one of its precautionary principles.[92] The Independent International Commission on Kosovo includes as one of its threshold principles that "the method of intervention must be reasonably calculated to end the humanitarian catastrophe as rapidly as possible."[93] The British likewise have included in their proposed guidelines that a humanitarian intervention "must be likely to achieve its objectives."[94] Certainly, political guidelines that address broader issues of legitimacy should include effectiveness among the principles for humanitarian intervention and provide fuller analysis of what this entails.

At a minimum, a legitimate humanitarian intervention should have a reasonable prospect of success in stopping the atrocities that triggered the intervention in the first place. Otherwise, the intervenors will simply be exposing their soldiers and the target population to life-endangering situations without the hope of success that justifies the risks to be borne. I would include within "reasonable" prospects of success in stopping atrocities that the *means* used be reasonable and consistent with the law of armed conflict,

---

[90] Sydney D. Bailey, *Prohibitions and Restraints in War* (Oxford University Press for the Royal Institute of International Affairs, London, 1972), pp. 16, 30.

[91] See e.g. Burton, "Legalizing the Sublegal," pp. 449–53; Michael J. Bazyler, "Re-examining the Doctrine of Humanitarian Intervention in Light of the Atrocities in Kampuchea and Ethiopia," 23 *Stanford Journal of International Law* (1987), 547, 597–607.

[92] *Responsibility to Protect*, ch. 4, p. 37. Likewise, another recent initiative includes "reasonable chance of success at acceptable costs," as one of its guidelines for intervention, although it does not spell out how success should be judged. Noordwijk Seminar on Humanitarian Intervention, 16–19 April 2000, Conclusions of the Chairman, at 3 ("Factors for consideration before undertaking a military intervention").

[93] Independent International Commission on Kosovo, *Kosovo Report*, p. 293.

[94] Cook speech, "Guiding Humanitarian Intervention," at 4.

and that the *costs and risks* of the intervention be reasonable and acceptable in relation to the urgency of the situation. To be sure, one can never know for certain how situations will unfold, or control completely the consequences that flow from an intervention. But one can still make reasonable assessments of risk and develop a concept of operations for responding to circumstances that plausibly can be anticipated.

In order to have a reasonable prospect of success in stopping atrocities, a number of factors must be present. There must be a clear-eyed analysis of the underlying conflict and a plausible military concept of operations in support of the objective of stopping the atrocities. In some cases, interposing neutral forces between hostile factions can halt the atrocities, though at extremely high risk to the intervenors. In other cases, such as Sierra Leone, the nature of the conflict is such that perpetrators of atrocities will simply retreat into border areas or neighboring states and await future opportunities to resume hostilities. In such cases, stopping atrocities and preventing their immediate resumption will require both a longer-term presence and a sound political strategy for addressing the underlying conflict.

This raises the question whether interventions should have a reasonable prospect not only of halting atrocities in the near term but also of preventing their recurrence. Military force is more likely to be effective in stopping atrocities and restoring basic security than in addressing the underlying factors that lead to atrocities. That requires a longer-term political strategy and civilian presence. In the case of genocide, as in Rwanda, near-term success in halting atrocities alone would justify intervention because of the severity of the human rights abuses. Yet success in halting atrocities may not endure – and the atrocities may simply resume once the intervenors depart – unless there is a viable political strategy to address underlying causes (which may include lack of a stable legal system or police system; lack of willingness of combatants to negotiate and honor a peace settlement; unwillingness of other states in the region to support a peaceful resolution to conflict, etc.).

At a minimum, intervenors ought to have a plausible strategy both for halting the atrocities and for departing in circumstances that minimize the likelihood of their recurrence. An intervention can be deemed a success, at least basically, if the people of the target state are better off as a result of the intervention (in relation to their likely circumstances without it) at an acceptable cost for the intervenors. More challenging are the longer-term issues that accompany a fuller concept of success, which would include improvement of the political and economic conditions of life for the

population of the target state, development of basic and effective legal institutions, and establishment of a sustainable trend towards an enduring
peace.

The challenge of effectiveness is not only conceptual. It is also fundamentally a question of means, capacity, and political will. Success in achieving
even limited goals will depend profoundly on whether or not an international commitment exists to provide adequate resources to carry out the
mission. This may well be the most challenging aspect of all in humanitarian interventions. Often the impulse to assist suffering civilians is a
mile wide and an inch deep – it is not accompanied by a corresponding
willingness to commit forces or provide resources needed to respond effectively to the atrocities and their underlying causes. Yet if insufficiently
equipped and trained forces are deployed to carry out over-ambitious or
ill-defined missions, the likelihood of failure is considerable. This failure,
moreover, may have serious spillover effects on other potential interventions
of equal or greater need. For instance, the severe problems encountered in
the follow-on phases of the intervention in Somalia generated such severe
adverse reactions in the US Congress that a significant military operation in
Rwanda, which could have saved thousands or even hundreds of thousands
of lives, was viewed by US policy-makers as a non-starter. The credibility
and effectiveness of past and existing UN operations is a critical factor in
the willingness of states to commit resources and take risks in future operations; this argues for a cautious approach that avoids getting the UN and
intervening states in over their heads in situations where the conditions for
successful intervention simply do not exist and a commitment to stay the
course cannot be sustained.

Yet, even in compelling circumstances, the political challenge of convincing states to commit resources and take reasonable risks to assist victims
of atrocities remains daunting, particularly after 11 September has refo-
cused international attention on the imperatives of defeating terrorism. To
be sure, the primary responsibility to protect civilians from atrocities and
to safeguard basic human rights lies with the governments and communities in which they live; but better strategies and more effective means to
support constructive local actors are desperately needed. So much diplomatic, political, and academic energy has focused on the legitimacy and
legality of military intervention for humanitarian purposes. Yet such interventions generally occur, if at all, only at the back end of long-simmering
conflicts. Meanwhile, strategies for preventing and halting atrocities at

the front end of conflicts require more attention. The enormous international challenge of effectively marshalling resources and improving response capabilities must also receive greater political and diplomatic commitment, as the recent Brahimi panel report on reforming UN peace operations[95] emphasized in identifying critical areas for improvement and reform. These are challenges all of us must take up within our respective communities and political systems.[96] Addressing state failure and severe human rights violations more effectively can contribute to a wider effort to defuse situations that otherwise risk serving as potential breeding grounds for discontent, organized crime, and terrorism.

Conclusion

The diplomatic and public debates over intervention to protect victims of humanitarian emergencies have moved ahead considerably in the last decade or so. Old barriers to collective action have been eroded in many respects. In this dynamic context, it is better to continue the gradual process of normative evolution under the UN Charter framework rather than attempting to codify legal criteria for a right of humanitarian intervention. Over time, as the cases of the Kurds and Kosovo suggest, the elements of a normative consensus regarding intervention for humanitarian purposes may emerge. In this gradual process of normative evolution, any conflicts between the non-intervention norm and the human rights principles at the heart of the UN Charter are best addressed in concrete situations as countervailing values and pressures are confronted in all their complexity. As James Madison wrote in explaining the US Constitution's system of checks and balances: "ambition must be made to counteract ambition."[97] So too with the living UN Charter: when the non-intervention norm and the developing norm to protect victims of atrocities pull in different directions, as they sometimes will, the resulting tension is best resolved in practice rather than in a doctrinal formulation abstractly in advance.

---

95 Report of the Panel on United Nations Peace Operations, UN Doc. A/55/305-S/2000/809 (2000). Available at http://www.un.org/peace/reports/peace_operations (5 March 2002).
96 For one example, the Council on Foreign Relations has initiated a new Center for Preventive Action with the support of Secretary-General Annan. Available at http://www.cfr.org/public/resource.cgi?prog!97 (5 March 2002).
97 James Madison, "Federalist No. 51," in Jacob E. Cook ed., *The Federalist* (Wesleyan University Press, Middletown, Conn., 1961), p. 349.

In short, the most promising path for the future lies in the middle ground between rigid adherence to the text of the UN Charter and premature attempts to codify criteria for a right or doctrine of humanitarian intervention. This is not to argue against all discussion and analysis of criteria for humanitarian intervention. On the contrary, the public debate over guidelines for humanitarian intervention has had some useful effects: it has helped alter the diplomatic climate in which future cases will be addressed; it has put tyrants on notice; and it has highlighted the enormous challenges ahead in mounting effective and consistent responses to severe atrocities. Scholars can play a useful role, moreover, in identifying patterns and elements of a possible normative consensus in recent practice. But the temptation to codify criteria for humanitarian intervention – whether for legal or political purposes – should be resisted, lest the normative space for positive developments be frozen in time and future possibilities foreclosed.

PART IV

The politics of humanitarian intervention

8

Political authority after intervention: gradations in sovereignty

ROBERT O. KEOHANE

Military interventions for allegedly humanitarian purposes, not authorized by the United Nations Security Council, have created sharp disagreements among students of international law. At first, the principal focus of this debate was on the decision to intervene.[1] More recently, however, there has been increasing attention to policies to be followed *after* intervention. Both the *Kosovo Report*, issued in November 2000 by an independent commission co-chaired by Justice Richard Goldstone and Carl Tham, and *The Responsibility to Protect*, the Report of the International Commission on Intervention and State Sovereignty, co-chaired by Gareth Evans and Mohamed Sahnoun, issued in December 2001, have emphasized the importance of post-intervention action.[2] Economic and political reconstruction is widely seen as essential if the purposes of military intervention are to be achieved.

Attention to the prospects for successful institution-building is also crucial to a sensible evaluation of whether to intervene in the first place. That is, it is important to estimate the probability that intervention will lead

I am grateful for comments on earlier drafts of this chapter to Hein Goemans, Fen Osler Hampson, Jeff Holzgrefe, Michael Ignatieff, Nannerl O. Keohane, Stephen D. Krasner, Joseph S. Nye, and Anne-Marie Slaughter. I also benefited from comments by participants at a conference sponsored by the Carr Center for Human Rights Policy, Harvard University, in collaboration with the Kenan Institute for Ethics, Duke University, 27–29 September 2001; and by participants at a seminar at the United Nations University, Tokyo, 6 December 2001.

[1] For a thorough review of the debate, see J. L. Holzgrefe, "The Humanitarian Intervention Debate," ch. 1 in this volume. For a set of comments on the Kosovo intervention by eminent international legal scholars, see 93 *American Journal of International Law* (1999), 824–62. An excellent analytical discussion of these views can be found in Anne-Marie Slaughter, *International Law and International Relations* (Academy of International Law, The Hague, 2001).

[2] Independent International Commission on Kosovo, *Kosovo Report* (Oxford University Press, Oxford, 2000); International Commission on Intervention and State Sovereignty, *The Responsibility to Protect: Report of the International Commission on Intervention and State Sovereignty* (International Development Research Centre, Ottawa, 2001).

to a non-abusive, self-sustaining structure of political authority. Evaluations of the legitimacy, or prudence, of humanitarian intervention should be conditional on estimates of eventual political success. Decisions "before intervention" should depend, to some extent, on prospects for institution-building "after intervention."

For understandable reasons, the major commission reports referred to above have sought to reinterpret rather than to devalue the concept of sovereignty. *The Responsibility to Protect* explicitly states as one of its objectives to *strengthen* the sovereignty of states, although it also seeks to change the emphasis from "sovereignty as control to sovereignty as responsibility."[3] For political reasons in the short run, such attachment to the concept of sovereignty is probably sensible. Otherwise, no consensus among a diverse set of commissioners would be possible, and reports by independent commissions would be stillborn.

Academic commentators, however, do not labor under such political constraints. Our distinctive task in writing on policy issues is to question received assumptions and to put forward arguments that lie outside the contemporary political consensus. We need not be "politically correct." My argument about sovereignty is accordingly much more radical than that of the International Commission. In my view, classical notions of sovereignty provide a poor basis for policy with respect to post-intervention political decisions in troubled societies.

The argument of this chapter is that sovereignty needs to be "unbundled" in order to establish legitimate authority after intervention. Some aspects of sovereignty should be retained, but others are obstacles to eventual success and should be jettisoned. The "Westphalian" conception of sovereignty as implying exclusion from a territory of external authority needs to be distinguished from other types of sovereignty, based on domestic authority, legal status, and ability to control flows across borders.[4] For the troubled societies towards which humanitarian intervention is directed, domestic and legal sovereignty may be more appropriate than Westphalian sovereignty. Furthermore, the external sovereignty to which the Westphalian model refers should be seen as a matter of degree. Troubled societies may have more or less of it, but the classic ideal-type of Westphalian sovereignty should be abandoned even as an aspiration. Once sovereignty has been

---

[3] International Commission on Intervention and State Sovereignty, *Responsibility to Protect*, p. 13.

[4] Stephen D. Krasner, *Sovereignty: Organized Hypocrisy* (Princeton University Press, Princeton, 1999).

divided into its components, and these components have been evaluated separately, policy-makers can be more innovative about institutional arrangements. In particular, they can think about multilateral regional institutions that could make promises credible by limiting state power, and they can design *gradations of sovereignty* rather than treating it as an "all or nothing" proposition.

This is not to say that the state should be abandoned or that sovereignty should be discredited as a concept. On the contrary, the state remains the principal unit of protection and collective action in the contemporary world. Sovereignty, properly understood, reflects the loyalty that most people feel to their own states. It is also consistent with the principle that peoples should be allowed to govern themselves except when they inflict great and unjustifiable harm. Nationalism makes imposition of foreign rule unsustainable in the long run, and anarchy continues to be as horrible as Hobbes portrayed it 350 years ago. We somehow have to reconceptualize the state as a political unit that can maintain internal order while being able to engage in international cooperation, without claiming the exclusive rights, or having the "winner-take-all" quality, traditionally associated with sovereignty. We also have to accept that states are differentiated both in their capacities and in legal status: despite the legal fiction of sovereignty, states are not all equal. One person's double standard is another's recognition of reality.[5]

The same institutional arrangements may help both to reconstruct troubled countries that are in danger of becoming "failed states," and to constrain the autonomy of those states. However, the effectiveness of institutions depends critically on mutual interests, which means that institutions depend on the quality of the "neighborhoods" proximate to troubled regions. Hence, decisions about humanitarian intervention need to take into account the feasibility of institutional arrangements that "unbundle" sovereignty, and the quality of neighborhoods that may make such institutional innovations feasible or not.

This chapter is about the effectiveness of alternative institutional arrangements after intervention occurs, and therefore requires a brief discussion of what constitutes effectiveness, or post-intervention "success." In my view,

[5] For an excellent discussion of three different types of states – "modern," "weak post-colonial," and "postmodern" – and the "distinctive rules of sovereignty" pertaining to each, see Georg Sørenson, *Changes in Statehood: The Transformation of International Relations* (Palgrave, London, 2001).

standards of effectiveness must vary with the situation. In good neighbor-hoods, the bar might be relatively high: significant movement towards an internally sustainable liberal democracy. We can hope for such develop-ments in Bosnia and Kosovo, even though we may have to be satisfied with very slow progress. But such a standard of success seems impossible for failed states such as Somalia or Afghanistan. In such societies, reconstruc-tion of state institutions that can provide internal order, prevent starvation, and fulfill their external obligations would be a relatively satisfactory re-sult, even if these regimes do not even reach Rawls's standard for "decent hierarchical peoples," much less liberal ones.[6]

The first part of this essay discusses what I mean by "troubled societies" and indicates why holding onto a unitary conception of sovereignty is in-imical both to human rights and to political stability. The second part explores the concept of sovereignty in greater depth, describing how a con-cept that began life as part of absolutist theory has been altered under the democratizing and pluralizing conditions of modern times. The third part argues that the political consolidation of gains from humanitarian inter-vention will depend on institutions that limit and unbundle sovereignty, permitting troubled societies to exercise some, but not all, aspects of classic sovereignty. Political authority needs to be institutionalized in a new, more multilateral, way. The final part suggests that the creation of viable institu-tions that enable troubled societies to govern themselves will be much easier in "good neighborhoods," where most countries practice self-government and are peaceful towards their neighbors, than in bad ones. Appropriate policies towards troubled societies will have to be different in good and bad neighborhoods.

The problem: troubled societies after intervention

I begin with J. L. Holzgrefe's definition of humanitarian intervention: "the threat or use of force by a state (or group of states) aimed at pre-venting or ending widespread and grave violations of the fundamental human rights of individuals other than its own citizens, without the per-mission of the state within whose territory force is applied."[7] My concern in this chapter is with *efficacious* humanitarian intervention, defined as

---

[6] John Rawls, *The Law of Peoples* (Harvard University Press, Cambridge, Mass., 1999).
[7] J. L. Holzgrefe, ch. 1 in this volume, p. 18.

humanitarian intervention that creates political structures in which external actors exercise substantial authority. I am not concerned here with situations characterized only by empty threats, ignored or defied by power-wielders within the state.

I also assume that authentic humanitarian intervention occurs only in what I call "troubled societies." That is, intervention is actually stimulated by widespread and grave violations of human rights, rather than merely justified by allegations of such violations and carried out for other reasons. My concept of "troubled societies" is indebted to John Rawls's concept of "burdened" peoples – societies unable to create well-ordered regimes due to unfavorable historical, economic, or social circumstances.[8] "Troubled" societies for me are a subset of burdened peoples: societies unable, *due to political conflicts*, to create well-ordered regimes. If the areas in which such people were demarcated are spatially sufficiently distinct, they can simply dissolve their union, creating two or more countries in its place – as in the example of Czechoslovakia becoming the Czech and Slovak republics in the early 1990s. Frequently, however, such a spatial solution is impossible, either because rival ethnic groups are spatially interspersed, as in Bosnia, Kosovo, and Rwanda, or because the political conflicts are not ethnically based, as in Cambodia during the 1980s and Haiti. Troubled societies may exist in relatively benign regions (Haiti is an example), but they often exist in troubled regions: regions unable, due to interstate as well as intrastate and transnational political conflicts, to maintain peaceful regional relationships. The Balkans and Central Africa during the 1990s, and much of the Middle East since 1948, could be viewed as troubled regions.

When humanitarian intervention has constructed new authority structures in a troubled society, a new set of problems arises. Once the UN, NATO, or another international organization finds itself in a Bosnia, a Kosovo, or a Macedonia, on what basis can it construct a coherent political structure that enables it to renounce its proconsular role and exit, having established the basis for self-rule?

Groups that were formerly oppressed, which called for intervention, seek to manipulate the intervenors to support their agendas, which may well imply repression of their former oppressors. In the wake of human rights abuses of the magnitude necessary to generate military intervention, both mutual confidence and willingness to compromise are likely to be

---

[8] Rawls, *Law of Peoples*, p. 90.

close to zero. Handing over full authority to the newly favored group, even if it is a majority, becomes an unattractive strategy for anyone dedicated to humanitarian principles, since such authority is likely to be abused. And even if the wielders of such authority would for some reason not abuse it, their willingness to exercise democratic restraint is unlikely to be credible to the minority. The minority will not only fear their motives but also worry that people more ruthless in their exercise of power will replace relatively moderate leaders of the majority group.

Holding onto a classic unitary conception of sovereignty in a post-intervention situation seems likely to create unresolvable dilemmas. The most fundamental problem is that unconditional sovereign independence creates "winner-takes-all" situations. The faction that first takes control of the territory may gain the ability to perpetuate its rule by repressing opponents. In an ethnically divided space, unscrupulous leaders of the majority ethnic group may well find that their best chance of gaining and keeping power is to mobilize politics along ethnic lines. Madison's "politics of faction" is turned on its head: rather than faction limiting faction, a majority faction, based on supposed ethnic affinity, can be created by demagogic leaders who appeal to fear or hatred of the other group.

It may be useful for the UN and regional organizations to seek some domestic institutional formula that will assure responsible use of sovereignty by an ethnically divided state. David Wippman has creatively discussed how consociationalism, as defined by Arend Lijphart, could help ethnically divided societies. Institutions, as Donald Horowitz has argued, can be constructed to provide incentives to politicians to mobilize support across ethnic lines.[9] But as Wippman and Horowitz both admit, prospects for success of such domestic institutional solutions are mixed at best. Institutional arrangements for consociationalism or to encourage cross-ethnic political mobilization have often broken down. International organizations, with their troops, have not dared to withdraw from ethnically divided societies such as Bosnia, Cyprus, and Kosovo, fearing renewal of civil war.[10]

The problem of creating order in an anarchic society is of course a Hobbesian one. Like Hobbes, I believe that people who are in endemic

---

[9] See David Wippman, "Practical and Legal Constraints on Internal Power Sharing," in David Wippman ed., *International Law and Ethnic Conflict* (Cornell University Press, Ithaca, 1998); Arend Lijphart, *Democracy in Plural Societies* (Yale University Press, New Haven, 1977); and Donald Horowitz, *Ethnic Groups in Conflict* (University of California Press, Berkeley and Los Angeles, 1985).

[10] Many civil conflicts are not ethnic; some are based on ideology (as in Central America during the 1980s) or on political factions simply competing for political power. But ethnic conflicts are

conflict with one another, and mutually suspicious, are typically unable to solve the problem of order by themselves, although from a human rights perspective, effective rule by an international institution is preferable to Leviathan. The key point with respect to humanitarian intervention is that, in the absence of an external authority structure, people in troubled societies may lack the capacity to act collectively, even if they should want to do so. The necessary trust and credibility just do not exist.[11] Hannah Arendt once defined power as the human ability to act in concert.[12] In troubled societies, the debilitating problem is that people are unable to act in concert and are, therefore, in Arendt's terms *powerless*. Introducing an external authority structure can actually increase the power of people in a troubled society by making it possible for them to act in concert.[13]

It is important to see that the severity of the dilemma faced by the intervening powers is worsened by the persistence, in much thinking, of a unitary conception of sovereignty. In this view, "self-determination" is the goal of the intervention: that is, restoring full sovereignty to the troubled society. But full sovereignty, with its exclusion of external authority, is more part of the problem than part of the solution. As long as the alternatives are "no sovereignty" or "full sovereignty," there is unlikely to be any viable "exit option" for the humanitarian intervention. And anticipating that they will not have such an option, cautious policy-makers will be reluctant to intervene in the first place, even when threats to human rights are severe and, on moral grounds, intervention should be threatened or used.[14] The consequences of a rigidly unitary conception of sovereignty are therefore adverse for human rights. It is worthwhile, as a consequence, to consider

---

often among the most difficult to resolve, since the perceived differences among groups tend to perpetuate themselves from generation to generation. Hence ethnic conflicts are a special focus of attention in this chapter.

[11] See Thomas Hobbes, *Leviathan*, first published in 1651 (Library of Liberal Arts edn, Bobbs-Merrill, Indianapolis, 1958). On the absence of credibility in troubled societies, see Timothy D. Sisk, "Democratization and Peacebuilding: Perils and Promises," in Chester A. Crocker, Fen Osler Hampson, and Pamela Aall eds., *Turbulent Peace: The Challenges of Managing International Conflict* (US Institute of Peace, Washington, DC, 2001), especially pp. 794–95.

[12] Hannah Arendt, *Crises of the Republic* (Harcourt Brace Jovanovich, New York, 1972), p. 143.

[13] It is noteworthy that, despite its claim to support sovereignty, the International Commission suggests that Chapter XII of the United Nations Charter, on trusteeship arrangements, could be adapted and reactivated to enable the United Nations to exercise, in effect, trusteeships over failed states. No time limit is set for such trusteeships, although the Report indicates that they would have to extend over a long time. The implications for sovereignty are obvious. See International Commission on Intervention and State Sovereignty, *Responsibility to Protect*.

[14] See Fernando Tesón, "The Liberal Case for Humanitarian Intervention," ch. 3 in this volume, and Fernando Tesón, *A Philosophy of International Law* (Westview Press, Boulder, 1998).

how sovereignty might be reconceptualized in a way that would promote the institutionalization of legitimate authority "after intervention."

Understanding sovereignty

The classic unitary conception of sovereignty is the doctrine that sovereign states exercise both internal supremacy over all other authorities within a given territory, and external independence of outside authorities. As the World Court said in the *Wimbledon* case, sovereignty means that the state "is subject to no other state and has full and exclusive powers within its jurisdiction without prejudice to the limits set by applicable law."[15] Sovereignty in this sense is a legal term, not implying either full de facto autonomy or effectiveness. It confers the *right* to act independently and with full domestic authority, not necessarily the ability to do so. In terms of formal sovereignty, all members of the United Nations are equally sovereign; or, as Dr. Samuel Johnson observed over 200 years ago, "in sovereignty there are no gradations."[16]

The notion that sovereignty must be unitary has its origins in absolutist political thought. Jean Bodin in his *Six Books of the Commonwealth* (1576) developed a theory of political order, based in part on the concept of a "puissant" and indivisible sovereignty. Bodin's notion of sovereignty was consistent with earlier and later French political thought: "Even before Bodin asserted clearly that sovereignty, by definition, cannot be divided, sixteenth-century Frenchmen took for granted that authority must have some specific unitary locus in the state...The disinclination to think in terms of a division of authority marked French theorists until the late seventeenth century, and was not seriously challenged until the *Spirit of the Laws*."[17] The period in which the concept of sovereignty was developed was a period of civil war. For long periods of time, both in France and in England, the king failed to have an effective monopoly of violence. Acceptance of a unitary concept of sovereignty reinforced the power of the king. Later, when sovereignty was interpreted as implying non-intervention, the

---

[15] Permanent Court of International Justice, Series A, No. 1 (1923). See Stanley Hoffmann, *Janus and Minerva: Essays in the Theory and Practice of International Politics* (Westview Press, Boulder, 1987), pp. 172–73.

[16] Quoted in Bernard Bailyn, *The Ideological Origins of the American Revolution* (Belknap Press, Cambridge, Mass., 1967).

[17] Nannerl O. Keohane, *Philosophy and the State in Seventeenth Century France: The Renaissance to the Enlightenment* (Princeton University Press, Princeton, 1980), pp. 26–27. See also pp. 67–72.

unitary concept of sovereignty inhibited intervention in civil wars, insofar as it imposed costs on potential intervenors.[18] But, in so doing, it denied potential external resources to popular rebels against monarchical power; so, from a democratic standpoint, unitary sovereignty is a problematic concept.

The absolutist conception of sovereignty is *agency-based*. The sovereign body is endowed with supreme authority to make the rules. Formerly, this body was the monarch; in traditional international relations theory now, it is, more broadly, the state. That is, the various powers to be exercised are exercised together, or *aggregated*.

In democratic theory, by contrast to absolutist theory, sovereignty is *rule-based*. In the United States, as one commentator has stated, "strictly speaking, we cannot even identify the sovereign until we have the rules in question," and "sovereignty is progressively more and more absurd as the rules which must be presupposed to identify the sovereign become more complex."[19] In a modern constitutional system, rules define the locus of authority, so rules are prior to sovereignty. The same is, of course, true in the European Union, which has certain attributes of sovereignty but in which the authority of its various bodies is determined by the treaty-based rules, which have gradually been "constitutionalized" by the European Court of Justice.[20] In a rule-based system, legitimate rules must be agreed upon, and these rules designate the holders of sovereignty. As Friedrich von Hayek wrote more than half a century ago, such a rule of law "means that government in all its actions is bound by rules fixed and announced beforehand."[21] There is no reason, furthermore, why sovereignty under such a system must inhere in a single entity; instead, it can be dispersed among governmental entities, as in a federal system.

The priority of rules over a specific agent means that for modern states not members of constitutionalized supranational organizations, the reality of sovereignty is more complex than it may at first appear to people used to traditional language. The first point to recognize is that sovereignty is quite consistent with specific restraints. Indeed, a key attribute of sovereignty is

---

[18] Krasner, *Sovereignty*, pp. 23–24, dates the articulation of norms of non-intervention to Wolff and Vattel in the last half of the eighteenth century. He does not deny the impact of such norms, but emphasizes that obedience to them has depended on calculations by rulers, rather than being necessitated by their constitutive or "taken for granted" quality.

[19] Kenneth C. Cole, "The Theory of the State as a Sovereign Juristic Person," 42(1) *American Political Science Review* (1948), 25 and 30.

[20] J. H. H. Weiler, *The Constitution of Europe* (Cambridge University Press, Cambridge, 1999).

[21] Friedrich von Hayek, *The Road to Serfdom* (University of Chicago Press, Chicago, 1944), p. 72.

the ability to enter into international agreements that constrain a state's legal freedom of action. For a state to bind its tariffs, or not develop anti-ballistic missile defenses, or not produce chemicals that disrupt the stratospheric ozone layer, is quite consistent with classical conceptions of sovereignty. But the issue becomes more complex when the state agrees to *rules defining a process*, over which it does not have a veto, that can confer obligations not specifically envisaged in the original agreement. Such obligations erode external sovereignty, which Krasner discusses in terms of an ideal-type of "Westphalian" sovereignty. In Krasner's words, "Westphalian sovereignty is violated when external actors influence or determine domestic authority structures."[22]

The clearest contemporary example of states accepting obligations that restrict external sovereignty, thus violating the Westphalian ideal-type, is the European Union. The European Court of Justice has ruled that European Union law is supreme over national law, and can have direct effect. Advisory Opinions of the European Court of Justice are routinely enforced by national courts. Partial restrictions on external sovereignty, with more ambiguous implications for Westphalian sovereignty, are found in the World Trade Organization, whose dispute settlement provisions provide for binding settlement of disputes, without a state veto. Hence a panel, supported by the Appellate Body of the WTO, can legally interpret international law in a way that expands the obligations of members, without receiving their assent. However, unlike the rulings of the European Court of Justice, WTO rulings are not, in general, enforced by national courts. The WTO, therefore, cannot require a state to change its rules, but rather can only authorize states whose trading interests have been damaged by such a state's actions to retaliate.[23]

Europe's experience is one of what Krasner has called "unbundling" sovereignty.[24] Krasner distinguishes four distinct types of sovereignty:

---

[22] Krasner, *Sovereignty*, p. 20.

[23] On the European Union, see Weiler, *Constitution of Europe*. On the WTO, see John H. Jackson, *The World Trade Organization: Constitution and Jurisprudence* (Royal Institute of International Affairs, London, 1998).

[24] Krasner did not originate this conception. John Ruggie writes of the "unbundling" of territoriality, a formulation that he adapted from Friedrich Kratochwil. See Ruggie, "Territoriality and Beyond: Problematizing Modernity in International Relations," 47(1) *International Organization* (1993), 139, 165; and Kratochwil, "Of Systems, Boundaries and Territoriality: An Inquiry into the Formation of the State System," 39(1) *World Politics* (1986), 27, 48. Kratochwil, in turn, refers to Joseph S. Nye, *Peace in Parts: Integration and Conflict in Regional Organization* (Little, Brown, Boston, 1971). Nye (p. 51) refers to David Mitrany, who wrote in 1943 that, "by entrusting an authority with a certain task, carrying with it command over the requisite

1. *Domestic sovereignty*: the effective organization of authority within the territory of a given state.
2. *Interdependence sovereignty*: the ability of a state to regulate movements across its own borders.
3. *International legal sovereignty*: the fact of recognition of an entity as a state, by established states.
4. *Westphalian sovereignty*: the exclusion of external authority structures from the decision-making processes of a state.

The principal value of Krasner's distinctions for the present discussion is that they indicate that types of sovereignty do not necessarily go together. On the contrary, they can be unbundled. Indeed, Taiwan currently "has prospered in a kind of never-never land where it has many of the attributes of fully sovereign states – territory, population, and domestic and Westphalian sovereignty – but only very limited international legal sovereignty."[25] The arrangements made for governance of Hong Kong after 1997 are inconsistent with international legal sovereignty, since Hong Kong can enter into international agreements; and with Westphalian sovereignty, since Hong Kong's Court of Final Appeal may invite foreign judges from common law countries to sit on its panels. Member countries of the European Union have lost interdependence sovereignty and Westphalian sovereignty, but they retain domestic sovereignty and international legal sovereignty.

In practice, Krasner's ideal-types are a matter of degree. Not only can Westphalian, or external, sovereignty be distinguished from domestic, interdependence, and international legal sovereignty; under different conditions, external sovereignty can be restricted to a greater or lesser extent. We have seen above that the European Union (EU) and the World Trade Organization (WTO) both restrict external sovereignty; but the EU's restrictions on external sovereignty are more severe than the WTO's.[26]

---

powers and means, *a slice of sovereignty is transferred from the old authority to the new*" (my italics). See David Mitrany, "A Working Peace System," in David Mitrany ed., *The Functional Theory of Politics* (St. Martin's Press for the London School of Economics and Political Science, London, 1975), p. 128 (first published in 1943). Krasner, however, reports that he got the unbundling term from Michael Ross Fowler and Julie Marie Bunck, *Law, Power and the Sovereign State: The Evolution and Application of the Concept of Sovereignty* (Pennsylvania State University Press, University Park, Pa., 1995).

[25] Stephen D. Krasner ed., *Problematic Sovereignty: Contested Rules and Political Possibilities* (Columbia University Press, New York, c. 2001), p. 17.

[26] When referring to the ideal-type, I will use Krasner's phrase, "Westphalian sovereignty." But, when discussing the *degree* to which domestic authority structures are independent of external authority structures, I will refer to "external sovereignty."

The general point is that in contemporary external sovereignty, there *are* gradations. States not only accept specific, treaty-based limitations on their legal freedom of action; they accept procedures that can limit their future freedom of action in ways that are not fully specified *ex ante*. These arrangements vary in their degree of intrusiveness. "Sovereignty" is a variable, not a constant. Humanitarian intervention certainly limits external sovereignty, since it imposes external authority structures; but it may be a necessary condition for restoring domestic sovereignty.

Unbundling sovereignty after intervention

Several other chapters in this volume seek to specify moral or legal criteria to govern humanitarian intervention. My focus, instead, is on the organization of political authority after intervention in what I have called a "troubled" country. In such troubled countries, as argued above, sovereignty can protect a majority faction that has seized power from interference with its oppression of minorities. As Michael Ignatieff points out in his chapter in this volume, democracy is no guarantee against abuse of a minority by a majority. Pledges by outsiders to protect minorities are unlikely to be viewed by those groups as credible, when made by states that at least nominally accept the sovereignty of the new state and that lack military forces in the contested territory.

After secession has taken place, full sovereignty creates the potential for international war. Once sovereignty has been handed over, the majority faction will have little incentive to compromise with minorities to ensure rights and privileges that may fragment the state and weaken the central government. States whose ethnic majorities are compatriots of minorities within the new state are likely to become its enemies.

Hence granting sovereignty in such situations of ethnic conflict is likely to lead to situations that seem only to have unpleasant options: (1) acceptance of majority oppression; (2) intervention by a state supporting the minorities; or (3) international intervention by a coalition seeking to stop the fighting. An example of the dilemmas that result is provided by the Mediterranean island of Cyprus, with a majority Greek, and minority Turkish, population. In 1964 the Greek Cypriot regime of Archbishop Makarios sought to revoke the minority guarantees of the 1960 constitution, which Great Britain had imposed as a condition of Cypriot independence. An imminent invasion by Turkey was only prevented by American threats to withdraw its protection of Turkey against the Soviet Union. A UN peace-keeping force (UNFICYP) was sent to patrol the dividing line between the two communities. In 1974 Turkey did invade the island after an attempted coup against Makarios by the right-wing military junta then ruling Greece. Turkey established a rump state in northern Cyprus.[27] Since then, neither side has found much reason to compromise its objectives, and the great powers, particularly the United States, have not been disposed to exert great pressure on them to do so. At the beginning of 2002 Cyprus is still divided and UNFICYP remains.

It is foolhardy to grant unconditional, unitary sovereignty to new states with severe ethnic divisions. The experiences not only of Cyprus but also of Bosnia and Macedonia provide further evidence for this proposition. Recognition of the sovereignty of Croatia and Bosnia, in the absence of a security guarantee for these new states, provided the catalyst for the war that raged in the former Yugoslavia between 1992 and 1995. Macedonia's appearance as a sovereign state seemed to rule out more complex interna-tional institutional arrangements that would have embedded Macedonia within a broader structure that could provide guarantees and credibility that a Slav-dominated Macedonian government cannot easily furnish to the minority Albanian population.

Limitations on Westphalian sovereignty require institutions. They must be built into a structure of authority that all major players accept. There is precedent for such action with respect to a larger country than Bosnia or Macedonia: the Federal Republic of Germany in 1954. The Paris Agree-ments, signed by seven European states, the United States, and Canada on 23 October 1954, prevented Germany from developing nuclear, biological, or chemical weapons and assigned German forces to NATO's integrated command. German pledges were reinforced by a joint pledge by Britain, France, and the United States to act against any resort to force, in violation of the UN Charter, by a German government.[28] West Germany became a "semi-sovereign state."[29] Its sovereignty was not merely conditional but institutionally limited, and it remained so throughout the Cold War.

[27] Lawrence Stern, *The Wrong Horse* (Times Books, New York, 1977).
[28] Joseph Joffe, *The Limited Partnership: Europe, the United States and the Burdens of Alliance* (Ballinger Publishing, Cambridge, Mass., 1987); Richard Kugler, *Commitment to Purpose: How Alliance Partnership Won the Cold War* (RAND, Santa Monica, 1993).
[29] Peter J. Katzenstein, *Policy and Politics in West Germany: The Growth of a Semi-Sovereign State* (Temple University Press, Philadelphia, 1987).

Such an international institutional solution requires a matrix of norms, rules, practices, and organizations, within which the new entity's status is not anomalous. The new rulers are more likely to accept constraints on their sovereignty when their neighbors' sovereignty is limited as well. One part of this process is essentially normative: the notion of unitary sovereignty should be discarded and Westphalian sovereignty should be seen as more of a continuum. External authority structures, on this conception, play some role in the decision-making process of all states, even the United States (as the dispute settlement process of the WTO shows). Where strong supranational authority structures exist, states can afford to accept less external sovereignty, since they are protected by their participation in the regional structures, and by the constitutionalization of those structures. Accepting less external sovereignty is not, therefore, necessarily a mark of weakness. On the contrary, it can be a mark of strength, and is entirely consistent with continuing international legal sovereignty and domestic sovereignty – the maintenance of coherent, purposive ordering of internal authority relationships.

Abram and Antonia Chayes have written that "the only way most states can realize and express their sovereignty is through participation in the various regimes that regulate and order the international system"; and therefore "the need to be a member in good standing of the organized international community is a powerful motivator of state behavior."[30] Such a motivation may not be decisive either for great powers, who can act on their own, or for failed states run by gangs whose principal concern is to exploit their resources. Yet it is likely to be particularly strong for new states seeking the benefits of association with more stable and prosperous neighbors.

United States policy towards international trade over the last century illustrates the propositions that accepting external authority structures can be a sign of strength rather than weakness, and that the long-run effect can be transformative of interests and policy. When United States industry was fearful of international competition, in the years before the Great Depression, the United States maintained high trade barriers and strict autonomy over its tariff policies. It was fully sovereign in the Westphalian sense, and sought to maintain what Krasner calls interdependence sovereignty as well. The first step away from this policy, taken in 1934, was to open the door

---

[30] Abram Chayes and Antonia Handler Chayes, *The New Sovereignty: Compliance with International Regulatory Agreements* (Harvard University Press, Cambridge, Mass., 1995), pp. 27, 190.

for negotiation by the President of reciprocal tariff agreements with other countries, up to a prior limit, set by Congress, of tariff-cutting authority. The next step, taken after 1967, was to institute "fast track" procedures that made it difficult for Congress to alter the bargains made by the President. Next, the General Agreement on Tariffs and Trade (GATT) developed a dispute-settlement procedure, which began serious operation during the 1980s, through which panels of experts could issue opinions on the consistency of national policies – including US policy – with GATT rules. Formally, these panels did not limit Westphalian sovereignty since any state had the right to veto formation of a panel and, after its judgment, to veto implementation of its conclusions. Finally, between 1986 and 1994 the major trading nations (and many others) negotiated the World Trade Organization, whose dispute resolution system yields legally mandatory judgments about national policies.

These changes corresponded to the increasing export-orientation, and multinationality, of American producers. US-based firms sought to compete on a worldwide basis. To secure open access to foreign markets, they had to ensure that the United States offered such markets to its competitors. In other words, as US producers became stronger relative to global competitors, the United States became more willing to accept limitations on its external sovereignty. As it did so, and as barriers to trade fell, a dynamic process was set in motion. The US increasingly lost the ability to control the flow of products across its borders, as American firms became dependent on foreign suppliers as part of intricately interdependent systems of production. And the political economy of the United States became more open: firms and groups with interests in open trade were strengthened relative to protectionist industries, which ended up fleeing abroad or being weakened at home – or even disappearing – under the pressure of foreign competition. This process was reinforced by the openness of the US political system, which provided access and information to outsiders, hence making them more willing to enter into agreements that made them more dependent on American decisions.

Trade illustrates how limiting sovereignty can result from greater strength, and how such limitations can also lead to greater economic strength, generating a "virtuous spiral." Such a process, however, is not easily generalizable to other issues. Indeed, with respect to sovereignty over security issues, it is all too evident that there is no universal consensus in favor of such limitations of sovereignty. The United States, China, and

Russia are certainly disinclined to go along, and many developing countries also fear explicit restrictions on their domestic, interdependence, and external sovereignty – all of which are de facto quite tenuous in any case. Hence, creating what I call an "anti-sovereignty matrix" of rules, practices, and organizations will only be feasible on a regional basis, first in Europe, perhaps later in South America.

Fortunately for the Balkans, Europe now has a dense set of such rules, practices, and organizations, some of which have been created as "human rights entrepreneurs" or "normative intermediaries." These institutions include the Organization for Security and Cooperation in Europe (OSCE) and its High Commissioner on National Minorities; the Council of Europe Framework Convention for the Protection of National Minorities; the European Stability Pact; and, of course, the European Union itself.[31] These institutions provide standards for state behavior towards minorities, and support by powerful members provides incentives – positive as well as negative – for implementation of the standards.

A Balkan entity that had seceded from an oppressively governed country, or that was struggling to maintain its existence in the face of ethnic divisions, could imitate Belgium or Britain. That is, it could have international legal sovereignty, entailing membership in the United Nations and the European Union, but it would not have Westphalian sovereignty. Its external independence and internal supremacy would be limited by supranational institutions, but these constraints would not single it out for inferior status. Unbundling sovereignty would, in Europe, have become the norm rather than the exception.

Institutions rely on incentives, and institutions that unbundle sovereignty would be no exception. These incentives cannot typically be provided by partners within a troubled region itself. They have to come from outside – from states that are genuinely willing to make their own involvement, and their resources, conditional on the construction and maintenance of such institutions. The arrangements for West Germany, discussed above, would not have been feasible except for the larger, highly beneficial institutional structures into which Germany was inserted after 1954, in particular NATO and the European Union. The states that served

---

[31] See Steven Ratner, "Does International Law Matter in Preventing Ethnic Conflict?" 32 *New York University Journal of International Law and Politics* (2000), 591–724; and Arie Bloed and Pieter van Dijk eds., *Protection of Minority Rights Through Bilateral Treaties* (Kluwer Law International, The Hague, 1999).

as guarantors of Germany's good behavior were also its strong allies and supporters, with a continuing and intense commitment to the stability of Central Europe.

By the same token, it would be futile to try to set up international institutions limited to the Balkans, the Middle East, Central Africa, or other troubled regions, and to expect them to facilitate the unbundling of sovereignty. Such institutions require support from outside. But "outside" cannot mean "far away and disinterested," since disinterested powers do not have sufficient incentives of their own to remain involved. Far from "disinterest" being a necessary condition for justifiable intervention, it should be regarded as almost a disqualification. The United States was all too disinterested in Somalia in 1993 and was therefore able to leave suddenly after a relatively small number of its soldiers were killed there. Great Britain and France felt too disinterested in Eastern Europe after World War I, so they were unwilling to enforce the minority rights provisions of treaties, which they had themselves imposed. One of the stabilizing factors in the Balkans today is that the United States has strong interests in seeing NATO's operation lead to political stability – not least because the United States is interested in maintaining NATO as its institutionalized military link to Europe.[32]

To summarize, the political consolidation of gains from humanitarian intervention will depend on institutions that limit and unbundle sovereignty. These institutions require outside involvement; and such involvement depends on continuing self-interest by the outside powers. Of course, as the NATO example indicates, this self-interest can itself have been generated by prior institutions, valuable to their members. Interests are not exogenous or inherent; they are created by action, including institution-building action. The transformation of world politics, here as in other areas, occurs incrementally. The gradual growth of the European Union, with subsequent bargains fundamentally structured and prepared by earlier institutional developments, demonstrates this point. Institutions "piggyback" on strong existing institutions, on the basis both of organizational support and of the interests that have been created by the earlier institutions. Institutions are not just created; they grow.

---

[32] The sharply increased American interest since 11 September 2001 in failed states such as Afghanistan and Somalia suggests that long-term United States involvement in those states is more likely than it would have been when the US was more disinterested. Involvement, of course, is not always benign, as the example of United States involvement in the Vietnam War between 1961 and 1975 shows.

Since institutions and interests are so closely connected, there is no contradiction between an institutional approach to policies "after intervention," and either a classical realist or liberal one. International institutions can reinforce domestic sovereignty while requiring states explicitly to renounce claims of Westphalian sovereignty. Such an institutionalist strategy is consistent with classical realism because it offers leaders the prospect of long-term consolidation of security and influence gains from humanitarian intervention. It is consistent with the brand of liberalism that emphasizes domestic politics, by offering a vision of the future that should appeal to democratic publics.

Intervention in good and bad neighborhoods

Theory and experience suggest that institutions grow best in institutionalized soil – where they are supported by other institutions. Conversely, the examples of Cyprus and especially of Somalia show that, under bad conditions, military intervention can be ineffective in the long run. Either the will to maintain it may collapse under pressure, or even if military action stops a civil war, it may freeze the political situation, preventing any stable long-term political solution. The *context* within which humanitarian intervention takes place is critical to the long-term political efficacy of any strategy to restore normal life and civil relations between ethnic groups that have been adversaries. The international context of humanitarian intervention can be viewed in metaphorical terms, as what the late Myron Weiner referred to as bad or good "neighborhoods."[33]

In a bad neighborhood, it is easy to act badly, but difficult – if not suicidal – to act well. In bad neighborhoods, there is little hope that the neighborhood itself will ever improve. People dislike or even hate each other; even more serious, they distrust one another. What James Coleman and Robert Putnam have called "social capital" is low.[34] Unless there is an institutionalized involvement of forces from outside the region, Westphalian sovereignty seems to be an essential attribute of a state in a bad neighborhood, since external authority structures in bad neighborhoods can be

---

[33] Myron Weiner, "Bad Neighbors, Bad Neighborhoods: An Inquiry into the Causes of Refugee Flows," 21 *International Security* (1996), 5–42.

[34] James S. Coleman, *Foundations of Social Theory* (Belknap Press, Cambridge, Mass., 1960); Robert D. Putnam, *Bowling Alone: The Collapse and Revival of American Community* (Simon & Schuster, New York, 2000).

assumed to be hostile or exploitative. In good neighborhoods, by contrast, there is substantial social capital, and trust is much higher.

Intervention in good neighborhoods

Mutual interests are essential for the success of international institutions, since they depend on at least a considerable degree of voluntary consent or acceptance. Hence, institutions thrive in good neighborhoods and wither in bad ones. In good international neighborhoods, Westphalian sovereignty is not a precondition for domestic sovereignty, since external authority structures can have limited powers and be responsive to the states involved. Hence, in good international neighborhoods, it is possible for institutions to develop that constrain states by unbundling sovereignty.

The problem is that good neighborhoods cannot simply be created. They must emerge on the basis of common interests, as the European Union grew on the basis of common security, and especially economic, interests. Such growth takes time. For humanitarian intervention to be capable of fostering liberal domestic institutions, it should occur in or near a good neighborhood. But, in the short term, it would hardly be sage policy advice to suggest the creation of good neighborhoods in order to make urgently needed humanitarian intervention successful. The construction of good neighborhoods is a long-term issue.

More promising in the short run is a strategy of *redefining the boundaries* of a neighborhood. Defining the boundaries of a neighborhood is not entirely an objective task, but partly an exercise in social construction. The Balkans have been seen recently as a "bad neighborhood," but Europe is a good one. Yet the Balkans are part of Europe, and strife in the Balkans affects the rest of Europe in a variety of ways, including refugee flows. Hence, if humanitarian intervention occurs in bad neighborhoods that border on larger, good ones, a plausible strategy is to redefine the neighborhood. Incentives must be provided for governments in the bad neighborhood to reform their behavior. These governments cannot provide sufficient incentives for each other, since they neither trust one another nor have substantial resources to invest, hoping for an eventual return. Resources and credibility have to come from outside the bad local neighborhood. But for resources to flow – and the expectation of further resources, as well as enforcement of agreements, to be strong – the providers of resources need to see the troubled region as within their own neighborhood. That is, they have to define the troubled region as part of their neighborhood, and they have to teach people in that region comparably to redefine their neighborhood.

In order to persuade states in the troubled region to abandon attempts to secure Westphalian sovereignty, institutional entrepreneurs need to be able to make conditional offers to join attractive, resource-providing institutions, such as (in the contemporary European context) NATO and the EU. That is, economic incentives to change long-established patterns of behavior are likely to be necessary. New causal beliefs may have to be taught: for instance, beliefs in the efficacy of the rule of law for attracting investment. At the same time, the norms and practices of the good neighborhoods must be extended to the bad ones. States from the good neighborhoods practice, but also require, reciprocity, and they should teach liberal democratic norms, through their own behavior as well as through educational programs. But to get the process rolling – to create virtuous rather than vicious circles – material incentives are likely to be necessary.

This analysis of the conditions for political success after intervention has implications for humanitarian intervention itself. Criteria for deciding whether to engage in such intervention usually stress, as one condition, the likely efficacy of the action. The key point about neighborhoods and institutions for decisions whether to intervene is that efficacy will depend not merely on conditions within a society, but on its neighborhood. Whether intervention to stop severe human rights abuses is sensible may depend on whether the troubled society is located close to a good neighborhood. If so, the neighborhood can be redefined to include them, and regional institutions may be constructed to support progress towards the creation of a liberal society. Successful institutions are self-reinforcing, and can gradually extend outwards, creating what Joseph Nye once called "peace in parts."[35] If the troubled society is in a bad neighborhood, however, potential intervenors must have lower expectations for success. Compared to any pre-intervention situation, therefore, the gains from intervention will be less. Hence potential intervenors should be more cautious.

One implication of the distinction between good and bad neighborhoods is that special efforts should be made to reinforce democratic institutions in relatively large countries that could serve as the basis for the emergence of good neighborhoods where they do not currently exist. Such efforts at development should not merely be evaluated in economic terms. Indeed,

---

[35] Nye, *Peace in Parts*.

were these the sole criteria, countries such as South Africa and Nigeria might be seen as poor candidates for support. Yet from the standpoint of effective long-term measures to solidify humanitarian intervention – and eventually to remedy the conditions that produce humanitarian abuses – nothing could be more important for southern and western Africa than to ensure that South Africa and Nigeria both strengthen their domestic authority structures and remain, or become, democratic.

Intervention in bad neighborhoods

To say that potential intervenors should be more cautious in bad neighborhoods is not to imply that whole areas of the world should be relegated permanently to a "zone of turmoil,"[36] in which humanitarian intervention is inappropriate. If abuses are extremely severe, intervention may be justified to stop them, even if the resulting political institutions are not likely to be decent by Rawls's standards, much less liberal. Furthermore, it has now become clear that failed states, such as Afghanistan or Somalia, in bad neighborhoods, can provide safe havens for networks of terrorists. Hence, the empirical line between humanitarian intervention and self-defense has begun to blur. Formerly, humanitarian intervention was seen as feasible only in areas away from great power control, which could therefore not threaten rich societies governed by powerful states. Decisions about humanitarian intervention were seen as decisions about the morality, legality, and political feasibility of intervening *for the sake of others*, or to uphold values – what Arnold Wolfers once referred to as "milieu goals" as opposed to "possession goals."[37] Now, however, interventions in Afghanistan, Somalia, or Kosovo have implications, positive or negative, for self-defense. The globalization of violence by small bands of people, as illustrated by the attacks of 11 September 2001 on the Pentagon and World Trade Center, seems to make it harder to defend possession goals without seeking milieu goals as well.

Traditional humanitarian intervention can be seen as having two phases: destructive and constructive. In the destructive phase, military action ends control over a society by a regime that abuses human rights; in the

---

[36] Max Singer and Aaron Wildavsky, *The Real World Order: Zones of Peace, Zones of Turmoil* (Chatham Publishers, Chatham, NJ, 1993).

[37] Arnold Wolfers, *Discord and Collaboration: Essays on International Politics* (Johns Hopkins University Press, Baltimore, 1962), pp. 67–80.

constructive phase, economic aid is provided and efforts to build state institutions carried out, typically under the auspices of an international organization such as the United Nations. In the next era of world politics we may observe a new phenomenon: the constructive phase of humanitarian intervention *following* traditional military intervention in self-defense. If states that harbor terrorists are to be "ended," as Deputy Secretary of Defense Paul Wolfowitz was quoted as saying in the days after 11 September, something must be put in their place.

In either variant, intervention creates a situation in which external authorities control the politics of a formerly independent state. It therefore creates a quasi-imperial situation in which outsiders rule by virtue of force, legitimated by their supposed good intentions and the pronouncements of international organizations. The NATO or UN "proconsul" is actually in charge. Such a situation is uncomfortable for post-colonial sensitivities, especially when it is prolonged. One of the costs of intervening in "bad neighborhoods" is that periods of external rule are likely to be longer there, in the absence of regional structures into which the troubled society can be integrated.[38] The alternative – leaving resentful occupants of the troubled area to figure out ways to strike back at the rich societies from which the interventions came – is increasingly unattractive due to the globalization of informal violence – violence wielded by non-state actors. Hence, in bad neighborhoods the nominal alternative of recreating Westphalian sovereignty may be even less of an option than in good ones.

In view of these long-term prospects for external authority, we should be thinking more seriously about constructing different categories of qualified sovereignty. These categories could provide procedures to help regularize movement towards the sort of limited independence that this chapter has suggested. At first, sovereignty may not be unbundled, but actually denied, as in trusteeship arrangements, about which there is increasing discussion.[39] Then, *nominal sovereignty* could be reintroduced, in which the country regains international legal sovereignty – and its seat in the United Nations – but domestic authority is in the hands of the United Nations or some other outside authority. As the troubled society begins to recover, it will make sense to grant its new state institutions a little bit of sovereignty at a time.

---

[38] I wish to thank Joseph S. Nye for suggesting rethinking the concept of trusteeships in world politics.

[39] International Commission on Intervention and State Sovereignty, *Responsibility to Protect*, p. 43.

The next step would be *limited sovereignty*, in which domestic governance is for the most part controlled by local people, but the UN or other external authority can override its decisions when they are seen to be abusive of human rights or to contradict agreements that have been made. The final stage could be *integrated sovereignty*, in which domestic authority is controlled by nationals of the state, and there is no continually functioning external authority, but in which there are constitutional restrictions, adjudicated by a supranational court and potentially enforceable by the country's neighbors – as in the European Union. In this array of degrees of external sovereignty there is no opening for Westphalian sovereignty: it is simply bypassed in the movement from limited to integrated sovereignty. The policies of major powers, and international organizations, ought to encourage such gradations in sovereignty.

Operationally, nominal sovereignty requires an extensive international presence, including military and police forces and civil administration. Cambodia under the UN operation (UNTAC) of the early 1990s and Afghanistan in 2002 provide examples. Limited sovereignty would require a smaller UN-legitimated force and a continuing civil administration, not as extensive as under nominal sovereignty. Finally, integrated sovereignty only requires constitutional arrangements and the rule of law at a supranational level, along with some residual means of enforcement in case of crisis.

Conclusion

Some of the most serious political and institutional issues concerning humanitarian intervention arise *after* military intervention has succeeded in stopping large-scale violence. Adherence to unitary notions of sovereignty – often merely nominal, and sometimes hypocritical – is likely to hinder innovative and constructive institutional innovations that could consolidate the short-term accomplishments of the intervention, and create the conditions for self-sustaining peace and security. Effective solutions to the problems that arise after intervention require reconceptualizing sovereignty. It should be thought of as limited rather than unitary. It should be seen as a multidimensional concept, the various aspects of which do not necessarily go together. Domestic sovereignty can be strengthened through a strategy that incorporates external authority structures, thus renouncing Westphalian sovereignty. Finding solutions to the political dilemmas of troubled post-intervention countries requires the unbundling of sovereignty.

The more difficult step is to devise and implement institutional arrangements that incorporate appropriate limitations on external sovereignty. External authority structures are crucial to reconstructing troubled countries and troubled regions. These structures, like most other enduring structures in world politics, need to be based not merely on normative beliefs but also on interests. The guarantors of institutions of political settlement need to be interested parties, not disinterested altruists. Finding such guarantors, and creating or extending appropriate institutional structures, is likely to be easier in troubled regions that border good neighborhoods, than in those surrounded by bad or indifferent neighbors. As the good neighborhoods expand, along with institutions that reshape interests and provide the infrastructure to pursue collective goods, the areas in which humanitarian intervention is likely to be politically successful can also expand. Yet even in bad neighborhoods, humanitarian intervention may be necessary, either to prevent human rights abuses or to reconstruct state institutions in the wake of more conventional military action, justified on grounds of self-defense. Over the long run, incremental expansions of zones of peace could, it is hoped, remove both the threats to liberal democracies posed by failed states, and reduce the need for humanitarian interventions, with all the risks and costs that these enterprises entail.

The policies suggested in this chapter have their roots equally in realist and institutionalist thinking. They take interests and strategic choices seriously; but they also reflect the fact that interests and optimal strategies can be profoundly shaped by institutional structures. Both the history of the European Community and of American trade policy over the past seventy years indicate how fundamental but enduring political change depends on mutually reinforcing "virtuous spirals" involving both interests and institutions. Strong multilateral institutions are needed for the long-term success of humanitarian interventions. The concept of sovereignty will need to be unbundled, and the Westphalian fetish of total autonomy from external authority discarded, so that stable domestic authority, and peaceful relations among countries in formerly troubled regions, can be restored.

9

State failure and nation-building

MICHAEL IGNATIEFF

During the Cold War, the chief threat to human rights came in the form of state tyranny in the Soviet bloc and in authoritarian regimes receiving American support. After 1991, with the end of imperial support for client states and satellites, together with the national independence of groups held in imperial tutelage, there has been an explosion of state formation and state fragmentation. Since 1991 more than fifteen new states have emerged, and while some have made the transition to stability, many of them, Georgia and Armenia for example, are struggling, others like Chechnya are staging a secessionist war that is being brutally put down, while other ex-Communist survivors like Yugoslavia have broken apart. Where states cannot control their territory and are fighting insurgencies or ethnic separatism, massacre and ethnic cleansing become ways of life.[1] As a result, chaos has replaced tyranny as the new challenge to human rights in the twenty-first century.

Some states are struggling to be born, while others that had benefited from imperial assistance, like Somalia, have collapsed altogether. Still others, like the Democratic Republic of Congo, remain states in name only. Sierra Leone has been torn apart by a civil war fomented by its neighbor Liberia, and in Afghanistan, the state was first dismembered by a civil war and then taken over by a terrorist group. In other places, collapse has not essentially been driven by imperial departure or conflict.[2] In Colombia and Sri

---

[1] Two classic articles on state failure are Gerald B. Helman and Steven R. Ratner, "Saving Failed States," 89 *Foreign Policy* (1992–93), 3–20; and Susan L. Woodward, "Failed States: Warlordism and 'Tribal' Warfare," 52 *Naval War College Review* (1999), 55–68. See also an early collection on the problem, William Zartman ed., *Collapsed States: The Disintegration and Restoration of Legitimate Authority* (Lynne Rienner, Boulder, 1995). And see the useful introduction by Robert Rotberg, "State Failure in the Developing World" in his forthcoming edited volume, *Why States Fail and How to Resuscitate Them* (World Peace Foundation, Cambridge, Mass., 2002).

[2] On Colombia see Brian Michael Jenkins, "Colombia: Crossing a Dangerous Threshold," *The National Interest* (Winter 2000–01), 47–55; on Sierra Leone see Joseph Opala, "Sierra Leone: The

Lanka, the central governments continue to function but they do not control all their territory and are locked in a bloody stalemate with insurgent groups.

If we look a little closer, we can begin to explain why so many of the new states are either struggling or coming apart. In the case of former Communist states, the chief problem causing collapse is a Communist political culture and a socialist system of production, both of which inhibit the capacity of the new state to manage entry into a global economy and to consolidate stable electoral democracy. Many of the new states in Central Asia remain Communist-style kleptocracies; while in the Balkans, the new microstates, with the exception of Slovenia, are populist democracies still hobbled by a socialist economic infrastructure. In these former Communist countries, an additional component of their pathology was the forcible suppression of ethnic and linguistic self-expression during the period of Communist rule. Now that the era of the dictatorship of the proletariat and "brotherhood and unity" is over, and democracy returns, new states find it difficult to contain these ethnic differences once they find electoral expression. Indeed, newly emerging democracies do not easily permit cross-ethnic or cross-religious party allegiance in politics. Such was the case in much of the former Yugoslavia. When democracy arrived there in 1990, the only available way for politicians to secure political support was to appeal to national pride and ethnic grievances. Those who sought to craft a cross- or trans-ethnic appeal were outvoted. Hence the coming of democracy sometimes brings ethnic majority tyranny followed by ethnic minority separatism.

The first disturbing lesson of the post-Cold War period, therefore, is that while in the long run democracy may be a very good thing – democracies do not go to war with democratic neighbors, they prove more efficient economically, and they allow the peaceful expression of internal conflict – in the short term the coming of democracy to a closed society with suppressed ethnic tensions can have explosive consequences. Rapid democratization in Yugoslavia has to be seen as one of the precipitating causes of the Yugoslav collapse. Democratic politics permitted the emergence of ethnic

Politics of State Collapse," unpublished paper presented to the conference "Irregular Warfare in Sierra Leone and Liberia" (Science Applications International Corporation, Denver, 1998); John Hirsch, "War in Sierra Leone," 43 *Survival* (2001), 145–62. See also International Crisis Group, "Sierra Leone: Managing Uncertainty," ICG Africa Report No. 35 (Brussels/Freetown, 24 October 2001).

demagogues and mobilization of nationalist anger on ethnic lines, both of which drove the Balkans towards state fragmentation.[3]

The 1990s were a decade of unprecedented democratization – there are more functioning democracies in the world than at any time in history – but they also brought with them ethnic war and ethnic cleansing.[4] Besides the Balkans, Indonesia could be added to the list of societies that have been making the agonizing transition from centralized, authoritarian rule to greater democracy and decentralization and have known increasing inter-ethnic and inter-religious violence as a result. Self-determination in East Timor, while intrinsically desirable in itself, given Indonesia's brutal record of invasion and oppression, may spur similar self-determination claims elsewhere in the archipelago. The long-term viability of a single state in the Indonesian archipelago is now in doubt.

Outside the Soviet and socialist bloc, in the post-colonial states of Africa, the chief driver towards collapse has been the slow but inexorable weakening of state institutions in a band of central, western, and eastern African states, stretching from Sierra Leone in the west to Somalia in the east, that achieved independence in the 1950s and early 1960s. In some cases, this is because the colonial inheritance was dreadful, as in the Congo; in another case, Sierra Leone, the British left behind a viable infrastructure. But even when the departing colonial power left adequate infrastructure and a relatively decent bureaucratic and legal tradition, it did not always leave behind a viable state. In many cases, as Jeffrey Herbst has argued, it is an illusion

---

[3] This chapter builds on – and occasionally repeats a section from – an earlier effort of mine, "Intervention and State Failure," 49 *Dissent* (2002), 114–23, and on earlier unpublished versions presented at the authors' conference for this volume, held at the Carr Center for Human Rights Policy, Kennedy School of Government, Harvard University, September 2001. I am grateful for useful comments from fellow contributors, and especially for the comments of Robert Keohane. The paragraphs on the Balkans build on two earlier studies of mine, *The Warrior's Honor: Ethnic War and the Modern Conscience* (Vintage, London, 1998), especially ch. 3, "The Narcissism of Minor Difference"; and *Blood and Belonging: Journeys into the New Nationalism* (Vintage, London, 1994), especially the introduction and ch. 1. For a survey of global armed conflict and state fragmentation, see Ted Robert Gurr, Monty G. Marshall, and Deepa Khosla, *Peace and Conflict 2001: A Global Survey of Armed Conflicts, Self-Determination Movements and Democracy* (Center for International Development and Conflict Management, University of Maryland, College Park, Md., 2001).

[4] Michael Doyle, *Ways of War and Peace* (Norton, New York, 1997), pp. 477–99; Freedom House, *Freedom in the World: The Annual Survey of Political Rights and Civil Liberties, 2000–2001* (Freedom House, New York, 2001); Robert H. Dorff, "Democratization and Failed States: The Challenge of Ungovernability," 26 *Parameters: US Army War College Quarterly*, (1996), 17–31. See also Spencer R. Weart, *Never at War: Why Democracies Will Never Fight One Another* (Yale University Press, New Haven, Conn., 1998).

to suppose that there was a state with a monopoly of the means of violence over the whole of the territory at independence.[5] Hence independence presented new leaders with the daunting and sometimes impossible challenge of consolidating national institutions over tribes, regions, and ethnic groups who had never known central authority. They had two generations to meet challenges of nation-building that took many European societies centuries. Faced with these challenges, some leaders wasted decades and threw away a good inheritance – as in Zambia and Tanzania, for example – by attempting to practice socialist forms of development that were never credible or realistic. Others have used the state institutions as a personal patrimony and have sold them off to the highest bidder, or, conversely, set out to destroy state institutions like the army or the bureaucracy, lest they pose a challenge to their continued rule.

The vicious circle of state decline will vary from state to state, but it has recurrent and common features. Rulers at independence may inherit a poor country, a weak infrastructure, a multitude of ethnic groups, and basically weak coverage of state institutions across the country. Mismanagement, corruption, and bad economic planning or simple misfortune cause the tax revenue base to shrink. As it does, ruling elites lose their capacity to buy off or conciliate marginal regions or minorities. When these minorities pass into discontent, the regime concentrates its political base on its own ethnic group, heightening the discontent and causing minorities to pass into open rebellion. Rebels seize the production of key commodities – diamonds, oil, drugs – and the state does the same. Neither side has the capacity to prevail, and as order disintegrates a new kind of war economy takes root, in which violence becomes the chief means of extracting surplus from the population, and the warlord and his units become the chief units of production.[6] As the weakening government struggles to regain control, both it and the rebel groups use more and more egregious attempts to terrorize the population on the other side. This slow process of

---

[5] Jeffrey Herbst, "Responding to State Failure in Africa," 21 *International Security* (1996–97), 120–44; Jeffrey Herbst, "War and the State in Africa," 14 *International Security* (1990), 116–36. See also Jeffrey Herbst, "Let Them Fail: State Failure in Theory and Practice: Implications for Policy," paper presented at the World Peace Foundation conference on state failure, 2001. I am grateful to my colleague Robert Rotberg for making this paper available to me.

[6] William Reno, "Economic Motivations of Warfare in Collapsed States," *National Strategy Forum*, (Winter 2000). Available at http://www.nationalstrategy.com/nsr (5 March 2002). See also David Keen, *The Economic Functions of Violence in Civil Wars*, Adelphi Paper No. 320 (Oxford University Press for the International Institute for Strategic Studies, Oxford, 1998).

fission – observable in Sudan, Somalia, and Sierra Leone – may spread beyond the borders of the state itself, as refugee populations flee across the borders and as insurgent groups use frontier zones for their base camps. A collapsing state thus has the capacity to metastasize and spread its problems through the region. These "bad neighborhoods" are not confined to Africa.[7] They include:

Colombia, Ecuador, and Peru
South Balkans: Macedonia, Montenegro, and Kosovo
South Caucasus: Georgia, Ossetia, Azerbaijan, and Nagorno Karabakh
West Africa: Liberia and Sierra Leone
Central Africa: the Congo
Southern Africa: Angola
East Africa: Sudan and Somalia
Pakistan, Afghanistan, Uzbekistan, and Tajikistan

These areas present a cluster of human rights catastrophes: forced population displacement; ethnic or religious massacre; genocide; endemic banditry; enslavement of captured populations; rape as a weapon of war; and forced recruitment of child soldiers.

Some of these spirals seem never-ending. Angola and Sudan have been convulsed by civil war for over twenty-five years, in large measure because mineral and oil wealth give the combatants a seemingly bottomless supply of resources to sustain their combat.[8] In addition, once these "war economies" take root, the combat itself ceases to become a battle to the finish, a battle to take the capital, to secure state power. War becomes a business to maintain and reproduce the profits of the various combatants and their supporters. Civil war endures therefore for three basic reasons: because a resource base permits it; because the two sides are so evenly balanced that neither can prevail; and, finally, because it is in neither side's economic interest to bring the combat to an end.

It is commonly said that state failure is a direct result of poverty, colonialism, and steadily more adverse terms of trade in a globalized economy.

---

[7] Myron Weiner, "Bad Neighbors, Bad Neighborhoods: An Inquiry into the Causes of Refugee Flows," 21 *International Security* (1996), 5–42.

[8] See Blaine Harden, "Angolan Paradox: Oil Wealth Only Adds to Misery," *New York Times*, 9 April 2000. See also Jane Perlez, "Suddenly in Sudan, A Moment to Care," *New York Times*, 17 June 2001; Jon Lee Anderson, "Oil and Blood," *The New Yorker*, 14 August 2000, p. 46. See also Ingrid J. Tamm, *Diamonds in Peace and War: Severing the Conflict–Diamond Connection* (World Peace Foundation, Cambridge, Mass., 2002).

It is certainly true that the collapse of the post-independence states relates directly to the poverty of many of these states and their adverse geographical situation. An adverse situation is then made worse by corruption, bad planning choices, or ideological dogma. As the developed world has accelerated into the fourth industrial revolution of computers and information technology, sub-Saharan Africa, for example, remains stuck at the bottom of the international division of labor as primary producers. Yet it would be wrong to imply that the problem of state crisis and failure could be fixed if only more foreign aid, development assistance, and debt relief were forthcoming. All of these would help but the reality is more complex. In many cases – Chad, Angola, Sierra Leone, Sudan, the Congo, Colombia, and Afghanistan – states are in crisis not because they are poor exactly, but because they are cursed with a highly profitable commodity – heroin, cocaine, oil, diamonds, or all of these – which ought to provide the resources for state- and nation-building, but instead provides the resources for interminable civil war.

The central role of key commodities – like diamonds, oil, cocaine, and heroin – in the pathogenesis of failed states simultaneously suggests that they should be the focus of policies attempting to prevent state failure. In Chad, for example, the World Bank is seeking to impose conditions on the loan it gives the government of Chad to build the pipeline carrying its oil and gas resources to the tanker port in Cameroon. These conditions require the government of Chad to invest in infrastructure, education, and healthcare. Whether these conditions will be respected is another matter, but the fact that they are being attempted indicates that not only in Chad, but also in Sudan and Angola, the most important remedy for state failure is international pressure to force local states to invest in state infrastructure and social services for people, instead of siphoning off revenue to their private bank accounts or purchasing arms.[9] The other function of international commodity regulation – like the attempt to control the export and sale of diamonds from conflict zones – is to shut off the funds going to rights-abusing rebel groups, like the RUF in Sierra Leone. These intervention strategies target the international markets, international lenders, and large corporations that deal with states, as much as the states themselves.

---

[9] Luc Lampriere, "The World Bank and Human Rights: The Chad–Cameroon Pipeline," Carr Center for Human Rights Policy Working Paper (January 2002). See also Genoveva Hernandez Uriz, "To Lend or not to Lend: Oil, Human Rights, and the World Bank's Internal Contradictions," 14 *Harvard Human Rights Journal* (2001), 197–231.

All of them involve direct infringements of the economic sovereignty of states. The Chad Government resents World Bank supervision of its domestic economy, but since it has given no evidence that it can spend the money on its own people without such supervision, it is hard to generate much sympathy for the claim that its sovereignty is being infringed. Structural adjustment programs that force governments to cut payrolls, slash services, and privatize state enterprises have been unpopular and sometimes counterproductive. Development programs that force governments to spend money on their own people in the interest of creating stability and effective governance may be open to the same objections from local elites in failing states. They infringe the external sovereignty and constrain the power of a local elite, but they do so in order, at least in theory, to improve internal or domestic governance. Such interference may be the only way to prevent failing states from collapsing altogether.

Each of the states in crisis is in crisis in its own way, yet all share the single property relevant here: it no longer possesses a monopoly of the legitimate means of violence, thus no longer meeting the classic definition of the state that we associate with Max Weber.[10] In all of these societies, violence has spread out through the social tissue, whether at the hands of armies and their paramilitary allies, or at the hands of rebel groups, secessionist movements, or terrorist gangs. Uncontrolled violence within societies threatens the human rights and the very lives of civilians caught in between.

To be sure, chaos is not the only explanation for the darkening human rights climate. There are still many nasty state tyrannies around: China and Iraq come to mind. They are a threat to the human rights of their own citizens and to their neighbors precisely because they are strong states. Elsewhere, however, human beings are at risk because their states are weak, unable to control violence from within. One of the enduring problems for human rights activists is that their movements were created to challenge tyranny, not to protect people from chaos. Thinking about how to recreate stability, governance, and, above all, a monopoly over the means of violence, has become the key challenge in developing new strategies of human rights protection.

The problem of intervention also needs to be rethought in the context of chaos rather than tyranny. The interventions of the 1990s were all in weak

---

[10] See Max Weber, "Politics as a Vocation," in Max Weber, *From Max Weber: Essays in Sociology* (ed. H. H. Gerth and C. Wright Mills, Routledge & Kegan Paul, London, 1948), p. 78.

states spinning apart in the fission of civil war and secession. In Kosovo, Bosnia, East Timor, and now in Afghanistan, intervention was centrally motivated by a concern not just for the human rights of victims, but for the destabilizing consequences of continued disorder. Interventions in Kosovo and Bosnia occurred primarily because the United States concluded that it had to reassert American leadership over NATO and to prevent endemic conflict in Eastern Europe both from destabilizing Europe and from splitting the alliances that maintain its security.[11]

Now that these interventions have been successful, at least in a military sense, the challenge has become to create stable forms of governance that deliver services and security to the population while respecting the rule of law. This task is both a matter of conscience – since without governance human beings are unlikely to have any human rights protection worth the name – and a matter of state interest. Failed states, as Somalia, Sierra Leone, and Afghanistan have shown, export terror, regional instability, organized crime, uncontrolled immigration flows, and drugs. These new challenges essentially solve the issue of triage that has dogged interventions: why here, why not there, and so on. In a post-11 September environment, intervention is likely to be targeted at those places that present a security or terrorist challenge, and not at those places where the challenge is merely humanitarian.

Moreover, where chaos and state collapse is the challenge, the test of a successful intervention is no longer whether it defeats an enemy or stops a human rights abuse, but whether it sets in train the nation-building process that will prevent the area from becoming a security threat once again.

One way to put the central question of intervention is: how does an external state best use violence (or coercion) to enable the population of another state to re-establish a legitimate monopoly on the means of violence? A related question is: if states have failed, *should* they be put back together, with the same borders, the same populations, and the same basic prerogatives as states? It is a mistake to assume that the aim of rebuilding failed states is simply to restore complete Westphalian sovereignty in these places. If these states are failing in the central sovereign function – maintaining a secure monopoly over the means of violence – what type of sovereignty should we try to re-establish?

---

[11] Michael Ignatieff, *Virtual War: Kosovo and Beyond* (Chatto & Windus, London, 2000); see also Ivo Daalder and Michael O'Hanlon, *Winning Ugly* (Brookings Institution, Washington, DC, 2000).

Following Krasner – and Keohane – we can distinguish between domestic sovereignty, independence sovereignty, international legal sovereignty, and Westphalian sovereignty.[12] If chaos caused by internal violence is the chief problem, then the sovereignty that really matters is "domestic sovereignty," self-rule defined as the capacity to provide governance, services, and basic security to the entire population within a determinate set of borders. In most collapsed or crisis states, it is not their external sovereignty that is in question. They are collapsing from within, rather than being attacked from without.

This helps explain another striking feature of many of the collapsed or failing states: they continue to be accorded international legal sovereignty and to be treated as Westphalian entities, when they do not exercise effective domestic sovereignty. They are "quasi-states," shell-states that perform on the international stage at the UN, when everyone knows that their governments barely control their own capitals.[13]

So the question then becomes, what are the real preconditions for effective domestic sovereignty? Are all the other attributes of sovereignty necessary for the exercise of effective governance within a state? There are plenty of governments that fulfill all the criteria for effective domestic sovereignty but do not have full international legal personality. Taiwan has effective domestic sovereignty without international recognition. Singapore is a formidably successful state, without the capacity to protect itself against external attack. Canada and many of the Scandinavian nations enjoy full domestic sovereignty, together with full international legal personality, without actually possessing the armed forces necessary to safeguard Westphalian sovereignty, i.e. to repel other states. Indeed, one reason these societies are successful is that they do not have to divert resources to external defense. They have transferred or shared their costs of external defense to other states or to regional alliances.

It does not follow that full international legal personality does not matter, or that it does not matter unless it can be defended by force. States that lack both the capability to defend themselves and international recognition are also likely to be unstable. Macedonia cannot secure full international

---

[12] See Robert O. Keohane, "Political Authority after Intervention: Gradations in Sovereignty," ch. 8 in this volume; see also Stephen D. Krasner, *Sovereignty: Organized Hypocrisy* (Princeton University Press, Princeton, 1999), ch. 1.

[13] See Robert Jackson, *Quasi-States: Sovereignty, International Relations, and the Third World* (Cambridge University Press, Cambridge, 1990).

recognition because of the objections of its neighbors. Nor can it fully defend itself. It is also in a state of suppressed or barely controlled civil war. Each of these problems reinforces the others and holds the country back. It cannot attract investment or seek protective forms of regional integration with its neighbors.

A new and increasingly important category is the protectorate: an entity which has neither domestic sovereignty nor international independence. Protectorates are formerly war-torn societies which are placed under international supervision and are being guided to an as yet undefined status in international law that will grant them, presumably, domestic sovereignty without the full trappings of Westphalian international personality. One such example is the Kurdish safe haven in Iraq, mandated by the Security Council after 1991, and currently policed by American and British overflights. The nominal sovereignty of the region remains with Baghdad. A Kurdish parliament and the chief Kurdish political factions exercise effective domestic sovereignty on the ground. Another example of a protectorate is East Timor, administered from 1999 to 2002 by the UN which was, in effect, the transitional holder of its sovereignty until it was ready to elect its own government and became a fully fledged state. Afghanistan is another post-sovereign hybrid. It is not a UN protectorate. The UN administration is there only to assist a transitional government which remains the holder of Afghanistan's sovereignty. Yet because the Afghan Government has no resources, the country remains a ward of the international community, and while Afghanistan is a sovereign state in name, in practice substantial powers are ceded, for example, to the coalition partners who are waging their campaign against Al-Qaeda. A further example is Kosovo, a province of the Federal Republic of Yugoslavia under international law, administered by a UN administration and being prepared for "substantial autonomy and self-government" according to Resolution 1244. What kind of state should Kosovo become? A full Westphalian state, with a seat at the UN, say the Kosovar political parties. A protectorate for the medium to long term, say most of the big European states. There is a third possibility, proposed by the Independent International Commission on Kosovo, which would give Kosovo conditional independence. This would be a hybrid status that combines full domestic sovereignty with a conditional international status. Kosovo would progress to full independence only if it met certain conditions. These would include leaving Macedonia alone, not merging with Albania, and protecting its internal minorities, the Serbs and Roma.[14]

If our concern is to reduce chaos and to improve domestic governance and stability, we do not necessarily need to multiply the number of Westphalian states in the world. We might consider protectorates, regimes of conditional independence, and other forms of regime which provide what matters, namely, domestic self-rule, without necessarily proceeding to full international legal independence. But this option is credible only if other states, or regional pacts or multilateral organizations like the UN, can enforce the conditions imposed on the conditional or limited sovereign. In Kosovo, for example, enforcement of these conditions – protection of minorities and respect for external borders – is entirely dependent on the presence of an international security force. Since Kosovo depends for its survival on the continued presence of these troops, a future government elected by the Kosovars can be counted on to respect, at least formally, the conditions imposed on its independence. It is questionable whether it will do so once these troops are removed. Conditional independence and sub-sovereign solutions of all kinds are thus dependent on credible guarantees of the conditionality, and this requires, in effect, an ongoing imperial or external presence with the military or economic capacity to keep these new entities in line. East Timor, Kosovo, and the Kurdish enclave face uncertain futures, since the security guarantees they require are not yet in place.

An additional question is whether states that have collapsed into ethnic fragments should be put back together. The defaults of the international system are set against recognizing secessionist movements, or at least granting them recognition as sovereign entities. Beyond the obvious realist reasons for wishing to conserve the existing state order as it is, there are some normative reasons why it is a good thing to try to keep states together.[15] Almost all secessionist claims are demands for ethnic majority rule, and,

---

[14] Independent International Commission on Kosovo, *Kosovo Report: Conflict, International Response, Lessons Learned* (Oxford University Press, Oxford, 2000), pp. 259–83. The author served on this commission and drafted the sections of the report relating to conditional independence.

[15] Krasner, *Sovereignty*, pp. 73–104; Chaim Kaufman, "Possible and Impossible Solutions to Ethnic Civil Wars," 20 *International Security* (1996), 136–75; Hurst Hannum, *Autonomy, Sovereignty, and Self-Determination: The Accommodation of Conflicting Rights* (University of Pennsylvania Press, Philadelphia, 1996); and Hurst Hannum, "The Specter of Secession," 77 *Foreign Affairs* (1998), 13–18.

with few exceptions, involve the potential for tyranny over ethnic minorities. Thus, were a government elected by the francophone majority in Quebec to demand secession, the normative issue at stake would be whether secession would harm or endanger the minority populations within Quebec – the aboriginal peoples and the English-speaking communities.[16] The normative justification for continuing the Canadian federal state would be that it provides an institutional structure for the protection of such minorities while entrenching constitutional protections for the rights of the French-speaking population who, in Canada as a whole, are a minority. What is true of Canada might be true elsewhere. Where there exist adequate federal guarantees for minority rights in the institutional structure of a country, there is always a prima facie case to maintain the federation and resist claims to secession.

Where these guarantees are absent, however, they need to be created. In Sri Lanka, there is no prospect of ending the Tamil insurrection unless Tamils are guaranteed self-government in their own majority areas, and minority rights guarantees are adopted in the country as a whole. Were these federal rights guarantees entrenched in a peace settlement monitored by credible international authorities and upheld by all political groups, as a very condition of their lawful participation in political life, there would be no case for the dismemberment of a small island and the creation of a Tamil state.[17]

This preference for solving minority–majority ethnic conflict within existing states, by rights guarantees and federalist devolution, could apply to the Catalans, Basques, Catholics in Northern Ireland, Québécois, Tamils, and Russian minorities in the Baltic states and other post-Soviet successor states. In these cases, the viability of federalist and rights-based solutions would depend on the institutional strength of the state structures themselves. Where these are strong and credible, solutions to ethnic conflict that do not require the splitting of the state would seem both possible and desirable.

---

[16] I discuss the Quebec case at length in *The Rights Revolution* (Anansi, Toronto, 2000), especially pp. 55–85. See also Will Kymlicka, *Finding Our Way: Rethinking Ethnocultural Relations in Canada* (University of Toronto Press, Toronto, 1998); and his *Multicultural Citizenship: A Liberal Theory of Minority Rights* (Clarendon Press, Oxford, 1995).

[17] Robert I. Rotberg ed., *Creating Peace in Sri Lanka: Civil War and Reconciliation* (Brookings Institution, Washington, DC, 1999); Neelan Tiruchelvam, *Transcending the Bitter Legacy; Selected Parliamentary Speeches* (International Center for Ethnic Studies, Colombo, Sri Lanka, 2000).

But there are other places where state structures are already weak, where blood has already been spilled, and where minorities credibly feel that they cannot live beside another group except at the risk of their own lives. In such situations, it may be inevitable that secessionist movements will fight until they secure national independence. The Chechens see no prospect of a future inside the Russian federation, and the Russians cannot permit independence, not least because they see an independent Chechnya as a potential terrorist base. Here war, not compromise, will be the arbiter of the result.

Finally, there are places – Somalia comes to mind – where the central state has collapsed altogether, and where the question arises whether the policy of external states should be to encourage the reconstitution of a state or simply to allow it to remain as it is. The evidence in Somalia seems to suggest the latter solution. Somaliland runs itself and appears to be growing and prospering. Puntland appears to be surviving.[18] It is only in Mogadishu and southern Somalia that conflict goes on, in part because there is a capital for warlords to fight over and some dribbles of aid and other external sources of income. Reconstituting a central state would certainly require a long-term colonial occupation by some foreign power. It is not clear that this is either possible or desirable.

Most thinking about what to do about failed, failing, and conflicted states does not seek to learn lessons from states that have successfully met these challenges. It is worth asking what successful states, navigating in an inter-linked international arena, tell us about what should be the desirable goals for weak states, struggling in the same environment. In Europe, states have begun experimenting, not with the dismantling of their sovereignty, but with ways to improve internal governance and enhance external influence by pooling or sharing sovereign functions. In doing so, they have volun-tarily both allowed the OSCE to have some supervisory role in relation to group minority rights within their territories and accepted a human rights oversight of domestic national legislation through the European Conven-tion and the European Court of Human Rights. They have done so, Andrew Moravcsik argues, not to derogate from or diminish sovereignty, but to con-solidate continental conditions of stability that will, in the end, enhance the governance capacity and security of each state.

[18] Jason P. Sorens and Leonard Wantchekon, "Social Order Without the State: The Case of Somalia," Yale University, Political Science Department. Available at http://www.yale.edu/ycias/african/as2.pdf (5 March 2002).

In the North American Free Trade Area, Mexico, Canada, and the United States hope to enhance, not diminish, their capacity as states to improve economic performance by reducing tariffs, increasing cross-border trade flows, and eliminating needless forms of governmental regulation of economic activity. In both Europe and North America, states are responding to the competitive challenge of enhancing their populations' share of global economic activity by entering into agreements with other states to improve the efficiency of their cross-border cooperation. These states, with their strong traditions and nationalist populations, would have no incentive to weaken themselves in these multilateral pacts. They seek multilateral cooperation to *strengthen* their capacity to deliver what their populations want, namely improved economic performance across borders.[19] Of course, things do not always turn out as planned, and smaller states, like Canada and Mexico, have paid the price for greater economic integration. Despite NAFTA, for example, the US imposes retaliatory duties on Canadian products whenever it feels the need to protect domestic producers or whenever it feels that Canadian produce is benefiting from some form of subsidy that breaks NAFTA rules. As a result, Canadians often feel that they have the costs of free trade without its benefits, namely full and equal access to the whole North American market. But this discontent has not translated into a political movement favoring withdrawal because the Canadian population is uncertain whether they would be less or more self-governing, autonomous, and, in these senses, sovereign if they had stayed out of NAFTA. In or out, Canadians realize that globalization reduces the quotient of sovereignty associated with autonomous self-rule. The conclusion most Canadians draw is that multilateral integration may have somewhat diminished the elements of sovereignty associated with autonomous self-rule, while enhancing those elements of sovereignty associated with efficient internal governance. The nation may be less independent, but it is more efficient as a state and more productive as an economy.

What is interesting about the sovereignty of the strong states in Europe and North America, therefore, is that the states' strength depends not on maintaining the attributes of Westphalian sovereignty – non-interference, omnicompetence, and full international legal personality – but on pooling and sharing some of these features. In addition, only two of the European

---

[19] Andrew Moravcsik, *Why the European Community Strengthens the State: Domestic Politics and International Cooperation* (Center for European Studies, Harvard University, Cambridge, Mass., 1994).

powers – France and Britain – could be said to maintain the final element of full Westphalian sovereignty, namely the capacity to defend themselves against external attack. Even these two, while maintaining independent nuclear deterrents, would be incapable of fulfilling the Westphalian function of defense against external attack were it not for a fifty-year alliance with another state, the United States. Canada likewise depends on the United States to defend it, and, here again, what she loses in strict notions of sovereignty, she gains in governance and efficiency, enabling her to divert only 1 percent of her GDP to defense and allowing her to spend more on those features of national life, e.g. publicly funded healthcare, which provide a key basis of her national independence vis-à-vis the United States.

What does the experience of rich, successful states have to tell us about the experience of poor, weak ones? First, there is the paradox that, with the exception of the United States, there seems to be a correlation between multilateral devolution of sovereignty and success in governance. The more implicated a state is in trade and border agreements and security pacts with other states, which, in one sense, diminish the autonomy of the state, the stronger and more efficient as an instrument of governance it becomes.

This has immediate policy relevance for small and weak states. Their future lies not in national self-reliance, autarchy, and Westphalian autonomy, but in seeking as many binding security and economic alliances as they can. If they can trust a stronger neighbor they should devolve the costs of security to another rich state as Canada has done; if possible, they should seek customs and commercial union with richer neighbors. Thus, in the case of the Balkans, the future for all the micro-states created by the break-up of Yugoslavia – Macedonia, Montenegro, Serbia, Croatia, Bosnia-Herzegovina, Slovenia, and Kosovo – would seem to lie in eventual integration in both NATO and the EU. Their chief goals should be to reduce, if not eliminate, the costs of defense, to open up to a continental market and to give their populations the chance to live and work anywhere in Europe.

This discussion, designed to illustrate the paradox that the best-governed states are not those that are most independent in the classic Westphalian sense, has three immediate lessons for less successful states in regions like the Balkans or Central Africa. The first is that their prospects are bedeviled by an ideological heritage of nationalism inherited from their former masters. Created by nationalist movements of independence, they aspired to a Westphalian model of self-reliant autarchy that, if this analysis is correct, is precisely the wrong way to go in a globalized and interdependent world.

These states should not be seeking independence as such, but partnerships with neighbors and ex-colonial countries in order to strengthen, not their sovereign independence, but their capacity as systems of governance to deliver services and decent economic prospects for their people. To the degree that nationalism reflects a yearning for Westphalian sovereignty it is a snare and a delusion.

The second lesson is that the chief difficulties facing weak or failing states are not just internal. They also include the weakness of their external environment and the absence of regional economic and defense organizations capable of protecting them and delivering a stable economic context for growth. All of these external difficulties make it much more difficult to exercise internal domestic sovereignty. In Central Asia, with the Russian state in both military and economic difficulty, there is no pole of strength around which newly emerging states can coalesce. In Africa, where state collapse and failure is most acute, there are no regional economic and defense organizations capable of acting to strengthen weakening states. South Africa and Nigeria have the potential to stabilize their neighbors but they have not yet done so. In Europe, the situation is more hopeful. The Balkans are on the doorstep of the EU, and it is possible to envisage the eventual integration of the Balkan peninsula into a European structure giving them security, access to markets, and a supporting environment for their otherwise weak state structures.

If the second lesson of this discussion of sovereignty is that weak states need powerful neighbors, the third lesson is that there may be a conflict between the desire of weak states to join the club of the rich and the willingness of strong states to let them do so. Joining Europe may be the ultimate solution to the Balkan tragedy, but there is no evidence that Europe is in any hurry to move the Balkan statelets from the waiting room in which they are currently sitting – the Balkan Stability Pact – to full membership, granting their populations the right to migrate to wealthier countries.[20] We cannot assume, therefore, that strong states have a clear interest in being good neighbors to weaker ones. Strong and capable states have an interest in preventing chaos in weaker states close to their borders, but an equally strong interest in denying entry rights to populations from these weaker states. Indeed, weaker states are kept in the waiting room – denied full

---

[20] On the Balkan Stability Pact, see Independent International Commission on Kosovo, *Kosovo Report*, ch. 8.

membership rights – precisely to insulate stronger ones. Yet this solution rarely works in the long term. Where strong states are bordered by weak or fragmented ones, immigration flows, crime, drug traffic, the trafficking of women and minors flourish and become the illicit means by which populations in weak states seek to secure revenue transfers from rich ones that will not grant them rights of citizenship.

Over the long term, say fifteen to twenty years, the strong states hold out the prospect of full membership in their customs and defense union in the hope that, in the shorter term, conditions in the weak states will improve sufficiently so that most of the population will remain where it is, satisfied with slowly improving prospects, rather than migrate – usually illegally – in search of more rapid improvement. In an ideal world (and the world is rarely ideal) weak states will eventually leave the waiting room of the club of richer states at the point at which conditions in the weak state lag behind by a diminishing margin. The prospect of eventual membership in the rich man's club keeps the lid on the discontents of the poor state. If the poor state fails to develop adequately, these pressures may build to explosion point. One form this explosion may take is uncontrolled and uncontrollable cross-border migration. Another form it may take is a renewal of civil war, by parties seeking to satisfy their discontented majority populations by promising them that the path to wealth lies in securing monopoly control of the state and the eviction of a competitor minority.

Rebuilding poor states, therefore, is not just a matter of getting them to see that it is in their interest to partner with richer ones near by. It is also a matter of finding incentives for rich states to take the risk of building stability in their neighborhoods. The obvious incentive – and effective political argument – is that investing to stabilize populations where they are is preferable to the costs of large-scale migration of people from states in trouble. Coupled with this might be the argument that a system of temporary work permits, allowing inhabitants of troubled states to work temporarily in rich states, and thus creating the inward remittance flow that helps troubled states to grow, would be a strategy that helps the weak state while simultaneously meeting labor shortages in the rich state.

Creating incentives for rich states to stabilize their weaker neighbors, conditional protectorates for states in trouble, regulation of the international trade in commodities that fuel civil conflict – all of these are ways to keep failing states from tipping over into collapse. What are the right policy options when states are actively convulsed by a civil war?

One of the strategic impulses that impedes effective intervention in zones of conflict is the desire to stay neutral, to interpose between two competing sides. Most strategies of humanitarian rescue, UN peacekeeping, and conflict mediation are premised on staying neutral in zones of conflict. In reality, as Bosnia cruelly showed, neutrality can become discreditable as well as counterproductive. Once the decision is taken to introduce humanitarian aid into a war zone, backed up by peacekeepers to aid in its delivery, the aid itself becomes a focus of combat. Its provision, even to unarmed combatants, becomes a way, not to damp down the fighting, but to keep it going. Neutral humanitarian assistance can have the perverse effect of sustaining the fighting it seeks to stop.[21]

All victims have some claim to assistance from those bystanders who can provide it. But if that is all that bystanders do, they may help to keep civil wars going, by sustaining the capacity of a civilian population to absorb still more punishment. In Somalia the incontinent flow of humanitarian aid into Mogadishu in 1992 actually exacerbated the internal civil war between warlords for control of the capital and surrounding countryside. Suddenly, the warlords had valuable commodities to fight over. Instead of damping down the civil war, aid caused it to flare more violently.[22] Aid, therefore, is rarely neutral. Those who secure control of it on the ground secure power and resources to continue their struggles.

Moreover, when mediators impose a cease-fire in an ongoing civil war, they invariably draw the line in such a way as to reward the side that has waged the conflict with the most aggression and the most success. That is why, when peacekeepers are deployed to enforce the cease-fire, they are usually viewed by the party that has lost most in the conflict as colluders in aggression. Such cease-fires rarely hold.

Neutral humanitarianism, when viewed more cynically, is a kind of hedged bet, in which intervening parties salve their consciences while avoiding the difficult political commitments that might actually stop civil war. For the key dilemma in civil wars is which side to back.[23] Unless one side is helped to win, and win quickly, nothing serious can be done to reduce

[21] David Rieff, *Slaughterhouse: Bosnia and the Failure of the West* (Simon & Schuster, New York, 1995).

[22] David Shearer, "Aiding or Abetting: Humanitarian Aid and its Economic Role in Civil War," in Mats Berdal and David M. Malone eds., *Greed and Grievance: Economic Agendas in Civil Wars* (Lynne Rienner, Boulder, 2000), pp. 189–203.

[23] Edward N. Luttwak, "Give War a Chance," 78(4) *Foreign Affairs* (1999), 36–44.

the violence. The basic choice is whether external intervention should be aimed at preserving the existing state or at helping a self-determination claim succeed. In Bosnia, Western intervenors thought they were intervening to keep warring parties apart. They failed even to understand that a recognized member of the UN – Bosnia-Herzegovina – was being torn apart by a self-determination claim, aided and abetted by outside powers – chiefly Serbia, but also Croatia. The crisis was seen as an internal affair, when its chief determinant was illicit foreign subversion: the arming and training of insurgents, and the provision of safe bases of operation in both Serbia and Croatia. The war within Bosnia was only brought to an end when foreign intervention was directed, not at the internal combatants, but at the chief external instigator, Serbia. It was only when outside intervenors took sides – by bombing Serbian installations, forcing the Serb government to exert pressure on its internal proxies – that the civil war stopped. In other words, the international community finally intervened to sustain the unity of a state and to *defeat* a self-determination claim by the Bosnian Serbs.

The same point could be made in relation to the genocide in Rwanda. The international response to the increasing intercommunal violence in Rwanda before actual genocide occurred consisted in dispatching a neutral peace force, UNAMIR, to patrol and reinforce a cease-fire which neither the rebel RPF nor the Hutu government in Kigali had any intention of observing. When the Hutu government set about massacring Tutsis in 1994, the UN force had neither the capability nor the political authority to take sides. It had to stand by and try to protect the small number of civilians who reached the safety of its compound. In retrospect, at least, it seems clear that a more effective strategy would have been to take sides with the RPF as soon as the genocidal intentions of the Hutu government became clear. By withdrawing UN peacekeepers, arming the RPF, and supporting them with air strikes, international assistance might have been able to secure RPF victory sooner. In any event, it was the RPF victory in June that brought the genocide to a close.[24]

The case of Afghanistan, however, illustrates that taking sides is not always easy. Prior to 11 September, the dilemma was as follows: if Western powers recognized the Taliban, they would help consolidate Taliban rule over the entire territory and thus help bring an end to a devastating civil war. Order would prevail, but it would be the despotism of rural Islam at

---

[24] Samantha Power, "Bystanders to Genocide," 288 *Atlantic Monthly* (September 2001), 84–108.

its most obscurantist. In such a situation, Afghan women would pay the price of a Western preference for order over justice. If, on the other hand, Western support continued to reach the Taliban's opponents, the civil war would continue, and Afghanistan would continue to bleed to death.

Until 11 September, Western powers placed a two-way bet, supporting the Northern Alliance just enough to keep it in business, while refusing to normalize relations with the Taliban. At the same time, the United States allowed the Pakistani secret service to funnel support to the Taliban, while American officials continued to denounce the regime for their treatment of women and the destruction of religious monuments. This double game has now come apart, and, in the wake of 11 September, it is apparent that it was bound to. Having washed its hands of Afghanistan after the Soviet departure, the US spent the 1990s conceiving Afghanistan to be a humanitarian or human rights disaster zone, and failing to notice that it was rapidly becoming a national security nightmare, a training ground for terror. Nothing enfeebled American policy more in the 1990s than the refusal to notice that untended human rights and humanitarian crises have a way of becoming national security threats in time.[25] Afghanistan is the most dramatic example of this tendency. Now, finally, the United States and its allies will take sides, but having defeated the Taliban, the problem they sought to avoid – namely how to rebuild a nation-state there – will not go away.

As in Somalia, the aid and reconstruction funds currently pouring into Afghanistan might well have the perverse effect of strengthening the political power of warlords at the expense of the central government. Accordingly, governments are seeking to channel reconstruction and rehabilitation funds to the Karzai administration directly. But this attempt to strengthen state functions by centralizing aid may be undercut if private non-governmental organizations, which have large resources, begin to enter the scene. As Kosovo, Bosnia, and Somalia all show, NGOs are competing for visibility, funds, and impact, and in this competition they are not always too careful about whom they negotiate with in order to secure access to victims. If they make strategic partnerships with local powerbrokers, allied to warlords, their relief efforts may end up perversely weakening the central government and inhibiting its capacity to establish effective governance over the whole

---

[25] Barnett R. Rubin, "The Political Economy of War and Peace in Afghanistan," 28 *World Development* (2000), 1789–1803.

of the country. At the same time, working directly with local communities, and not solely with central government sources, is also crucial, since nations cannot be rebuilt unless local communities are engaged and empowered. Hence the need to coordinate the relief effort and subordinate it to a clear vision of political change, aimed at empowering civilian leadership in local communities and enhancing the resources, administrative capacity, and legitimacy of the central authority.[26]

Taking sides is not the only dilemma. There is also the problem of triage. Given the fact that resources of willpower, diplomatic skill, and economic aid are always finite, there have to be criteria to determine which conflicts to take on and which ones to ignore. Intervention occurs, in general, where states are too weak, too friendless, to resist. The Chinese occupation of Tibet goes unsanctioned. The Russians reduce Groznyy to rubble with impunity. Yet the Serbs are bombed for seventy-eight days. These inconsistencies are a fact of life, rather than an argument against intervention itself. The fact that we cannot intervene everywhere is not a justification for not intervening where we can. Moreover, the fact that certain failed states – Sudan, Somalia, North Korea, and Afghanistan – have become harbors or exporters of terror will make the triage easier.

Nor is the experience of intervention as nation-building entirely negative. The UN Mission in Cambodia managed to oversee peaceful elections and the creation of democratic rule in a country ravaged by genocide.[27] NATO, the UN, and the European Union have joined forces to put Bosnia into a transitional trusteeship. It is a state whose internal peace and security are guaranteed by foreign troops. Resettling of refugees and rebuilding are both funded from the outside. The process is costly, but violence has not returned, and peace in Bosnia has hastened democratic transitions in Croatia and Serbia next door. Further south in Kosovo, another trusteeship experiment is underway. A former province of a state is being prepared for substantial autonomy and self-government. The UN administration has written the constitutional rules for a gradual handover of power to elected local elites, and there is even a chance that eventually the Serb minority will take their

---

[26] Barnett R. Rubin, Ashraf Ghani, William Maley, Ahmed Rashid, and Olivier Roy, "Afghanistan: Reconstruction and Peace-building in a Regional Framework" (Center for Peacebuilding/KOFF, Berne, Switzerland, 2001), pp. 1–46.

[27] William Shawcross, *Cambodia's New Deal* (Carnegie Endowment, Washington, DC, 1994), pp. 4–36; Trevor Findlay, *Cambodia: The Lessons and Legacy of UNTAC* (Oxford University Press, Oxford, 1995).

place at the table. Finally, in East Timor, a transitional UN administration is handing a new country over to its elected leaders.[28] All of these experiences are fraught with difficulty, but all indicate that an inchoate practice of state building, under UN auspices, is emerging. Afghanistan, though not under direct UN administration, will test every lesson learned in the 1990s about how to rebuild nations from the ground up.

An intervention strategy that takes sides, that uses force, and that sticks around to rebuild is very different from one premised on neutrality, casualty-avoidance, and exit strategies. Normatively, it is also based on different premises. These premises have been outlined recently in *The Responsibility to Protect*, a report sponsored by the Canadian Government and delivered to the UN Secretary-General in December 2001. Building on ideas of good citizenship and human security, the commission which produced the report argued that all states have a responsibility to protect their citizens.[29] In certain limited cases, where states are unwilling or unable to do that, and where the resulting human rights situation is catastrophic, other states have a responsibility to step in and provide the protection instead. The international responsibility to protect is a residual obligation that comes into play only when a domestic state proves incapable or unwilling to act and where the resulting situation is genuinely catastrophic.

The idea of a responsibility to protect also implies a responsibility to prevent and a responsibility to follow through. Action, especially of a coercive kind, lacks legitimacy unless every effort has been made to avert the catastrophe; once action is taken, its legitimacy depends on staying the course until the situation is on the mend. Thus the responsibility to protect is intended to provide a rationale for constructive engagement by rich countries through an intervention continuum that begins with prevention and ends with sustained follow-up.

All of these exercises in nation-building represent attempts to invent, for a post-imperial, post-colonial era, a form of temporary rule that reproduces the best effects of empire (inward investment, pacification, and impartial administration) without reproducing the worst features (corruption, repression, and confiscation of local capacity). Unlike the empires of the

---

[28] James Traub, "Inventing East Timor," 79 *Foreign Affairs* (2000), 74–89; James Cotton, "Against the Grain: The East Timor Intervention," 43 *Survival* (2001), 127–42.

[29] International Commission on Intervention and State Sovereignty, *The Responsibility to Protect* (International Development Research Centre, Ottawa, 2001).

past, these UN administrations are designed to serve and enhance the ideal of self-determination, rather than suppress it.

Taking responsibility without confiscating it is the balance international administrators have to strike. The trick in nation-building is to force responsibility – for security, for co-existence – back onto local elites. This is not easy. The spectacle of disgruntled locals, sitting in cafés, watching earnest young internationals speeding around to important meetings in Toyota Land Cruisers has been repeated in every nation-building experiment of the 1990s. The most successful transitional administrations are ones that try to do themselves out of a job. This is not always possible. The legacy of bitterness in places like Kosovo and Bosnia is so intense that international administration has to remain in place, simply in order to protect minorities from vengeance by the victorious yet previously victimized majority. Controlling the culture of vengeance usually takes longer than the time frame dictated by most modern exit strategies. Once Western forces intervene they are usually committed to rebuild, or at least patrol, post-conflict societies for a long period. It takes time to create responsible political dialogue in shattered communities, still longer to create shared institutions of police and justice, and longest of all to create the molecular social trust between warring communities necessary for economic development and community co-existence. The initiative for these developments has to come from the local people. Internationals can hold the ring – provide impartial administration, some inward investment, some basic security protection – but the work has to be done by the political elites who inherit the intervention. Nation-building takes time, and it is not an exercise in social work. Its ultimate purpose is to create the state order that is the precondition for any defensible system of human rights and to create the stability that turns bad neighborhoods into good ones.

SELECT ENGLISH LANGUAGE BIBLIOGRAPHY

The publisher has used its best endeavors to ensure that the URLs for external websites referred to in this book are correct and active at the time of going to press. However, the publisher has no responsibility for the websites and can make no guarantee that a site will remain live or that the content is or will remain appropriate.

Adebajo, Adekeye, and Landsberg, Chris, "The Heirs of Nkrumah: Africa's New Interventionists," 2 *Pugwash Occasional Papers* (2001), 65–90

Adelman, Howard, "The Ethics of Humanitarian Intervention: The Case of the Kurdish Refugees," 6 *Public Affairs Quarterly* (1992), 62–87

"Humanitarian Intervention: The Case of the Kurds," 4 *International Journal of Refugee Law* (1992), 4–38

Akehurst, Michael, "Humanitarian Intervention," in Hedley Bull ed., *Intervention in World Politics* (Clarendon Press, Oxford, 1984), pp. 95–118

Annan, Kofi A., "Peacekeeping, Military Intervention and National Sovereignty in Internal Armed Conflict," in Jonathan Moore ed., *Hard Choices: Moral Dilemmas in Humanitarian Intervention* (Rowman & Littlefield, New York, 1998), pp. 55–69

"Two Concepts of Sovereignty," *The Economist*, 18 September 1999, pp. 49–50

Baranovsky, Vladimir, "Humanitarian Intervention: Russian Perspectives," 2 *Pugwash Occasional Papers* (2001), 12–38

Bazyler, Michael J., "Re-examining the Doctrine of Humanitarian Intervention in Light of the Atrocities in Kampuchea and Ethiopia," 23 *Stanford Journal of International Law* (1987), 547–619

Beitz, Charles R., "Justice and International Relations," in H. Gene Blocker and Elizabeth H. Smith eds., *John Rawls' Theory of Social Justice* (Ohio University Press, Athens, 1980), pp. 211–38

"Non-intervention and Communal Integrity," 9 *Philosophy and Public Affairs* (1980), 385–91

Political Theory and International Relations (Princeton University Press, Princeton, 1979)

"The Reagan Doctrine in Nicaragua," in Steven Luper-Foy ed., *Problems of International Justice* (Westview Press, Boulder, 1988), pp. 182–95

Benjamin, Barry M., "Unilateral Humanitarian Intervention: Legalizing the Use of Force to Prevent Human Rights Atrocities," 16 *Fordham International Law Journal* (1992–93), 121–58

Berger, Lee, "State Practice Evidence of the Humanitarian Intervention Doctrine: The ECOWAS Intervention in Sierra Leone," 11 *Indiana International and Comparative Law Review* (2001), 605–32

Beyerlin, Ulrich, "Humanitarian Intervention," in Rudolf Bernhardt ed., 3 *Encyclopedia of Public International Law* (North-Holland Publishing Co., Amsterdam, 1982), pp. 211–15

Bonser, Michael, "Humanitarian Intervention in the Post-Cold War World: A Cautionary Tale," 8 *Canadian Foreign Policy* (2001), 57–74

Brilmayer, Lea, *American Hegemony: Political Morality in a One-Superpower World* (Yale University Press, New Haven, 1994)

"What's the Matter with Selective Intervention?" 37 *Arizona Law Review* (1995), 955–70

Brown, Bartam S., "Humanitarian Intervention at a Crossroads," 41 *William and Mary Law Review* (2000), 1683–1741

"The Protection of Human Rights in Disintegrating States: A New Challenge," 68 *Chicago-Kent Law Review* (1992), 203–27

Brown, Chris, "John Rawls, 'The Law of Peoples,' and International Political Theory," 14 *Ethics and International Affairs* (2000), 125–32

"Review Essay: Theories of International Justice," 27 *British Journal of Political Science* (1997), 273–97

Brownlie, Ian, "Humanitarian Intervention," in John Norton Moore ed., *Law and Civil War in the Modern World* (Johns Hopkins University Press, Baltimore, 1974), pp. 217–28

International Law and the Use of Force by States (Clarendon Press, Oxford, 1991)

"Thoughts on Kind-hearted Gunmen," in Richard B. Lillich ed., *Humanitarian Intervention and the United Nations* (University Press of Virginia, Charlottesville, 1973), pp. 139–48

Buchanan, Allen, "The Internal Legitimacy of Humanitarian Intervention," 7 *Journal of Political Philosophy* (1999), 71–87

"Recognitional Legitimacy and the State System," 28 *Philosophy and Public Affairs* (1999), 46–78

Bull, Hedley, "Recapturing the Just War for Political Theory," 31 *World Politics* (1979), 588–99

Burmester, Byron F., "On Humanitarian Intervention: The New World Order and Wars to Preserve Human Rights," 1 *Utah Law Review* (1994), 269–323

Burton, Michael L., "Legalizing the Sublegal: A Proposal for Codifying a Doctrine of Unilateral Humanitarian Intervention," 85 *Georgetown Law Journal* (1996), 417–54

Byers, Michael, and Chesterman, Simon, " '*You the People*': Pro-democratic Intervention in International Law," in Gregory H. Fox and Brad R. Roth eds., *Democratic Governance and International Law* (Cambridge University Press, Cambridge, 2000), pp. 259–92

Caney, Simon, "Humanitarian Intervention and State Sovereignty," in Andrew Walls ed., *Ethics in International Affairs* (Rowman & Littlefield, Oxford, 2000), pp. 117–33

Caplan, Richard, "Humanitarian Intervention: Which Way Forward?" 14 *Ethics and International Affairs* (2000), 23–39

Cassese, Antonio, "*Ex iniuria ius oritur*: Are We Moving towards International Legitimation of Forcible Humanitarian Countermeasures in the World Community?" 10 *European Journal of International Law* (1999), 23–30

Cassidy, Robert, "Sovereignty versus the Chimera of Armed Humanitarian Intervention," 21 *Fletcher Forum of World Affairs* (1997), 47–63

Chadrahasan, N., "Use of Force to Ensure Humanitarian Relief – A South Asian Precedent Examined," 42 *International and Comparative Law Quarterly* (1993), 664–72

Chesterman, Simon, *Just War or Just Peace? Humanitarian Intervention and International Law* (Oxford University Press, Oxford, 2001)

Chopra, Jarat, and Weiss, Thomas G., "Sovereignty is No Longer Sacrosanct: Codifying Humanitarian Intervention," 6 *Ethics and International Affairs* (1992), 95–117

"Sovereignty under Siege: From Intervention to Humanitarian Space," in Gene M. Lyons and Michael Mastanduno eds., *Beyond Westphalia? State Sovereignty and International Intervention* (Johns Hopkins University Press, Baltimore, 1995), pp. 87–114

Cotton, James, "Against the Grain: The East Timor Intervention," 43 *Survival* (2001), 127–42

D'Amato, Anthony, "The Invasion of Panama was a Lawful Response to Tyranny," 84 *American Journal of International Law* (1990), 516–24

"Nicaragua and International Law: The 'Academic' and the 'Real'," 79 *American Journal of International Law* (1985), 657–64

Damrosch, Lori Fisler, "Changing Conceptions of Intervention in International Law," in Laura W. Reed and Carl Kaysen eds., *Emerging Norms of Justified Intervention* (Committee on International Security Studies, American Academy of Arts and Sciences, Cambridge, Mass., 1993), pp. 91–114

Danish Institute of International Affairs, *Humanitarian Intervention: Legal and Political Aspects* (Danish Institute of International Affairs, Copenhagen, 1999)

Delbrück, Jost, "A Fresh Look at Humanitarian Intervention under the Authority of the United Nations," 67 *Indiana Law Journal* (1992), 887–901

Donnelly, Jack, "Human Rights, Humanitarian Crisis, and Humanitarian Intervention," 48 *International Journal* (1993), 607–40

"Human Rights, Humanitarian Intervention, and American Foreign Policy: Law, Morality, and Politics," 37 *Journal of International Affairs* (1984), 311–28

International Human Rights (Westview Press, Boulder, 1993)

"State Sovereignty and International Intervention: The Case of Human Rights," in Gene M. Lyons and Michael Mastanduno eds., *Beyond Westphalia? State Sovereignty and International Intervention* (Johns Hopkins University Press, Baltimore, 1995), pp. 115–46

Doppelt, Gerald, "Statism Without Foundations," 9 *Philosophy and Public Affairs* (1980), 398–403

"Walzer's Theory of Morality in International Relations," 8 *Philosophy and Public Affairs* (1978), 3–26

Dorff, Robert H., "Democratization and Failed States: The Challenge of Ungovernability," 26 *Parameters: US Army War College Quarterly* (1996), 17–31

Duke, Simon, "The State and Human Rights: Sovereignty versus Humanitarian Intervention," 12 *International Relations* (*David Davies Memorial Institute of International Studies*) (1994), 25–48

Elbe, Joachim von, "The Evolution of the Concept of the Just War in International Law," 33 *American Journal of International Law* (1939), 665–88

Elfstrom, Gerald, "On Dilemmas of Intervention," 93 *Ethics* (1983), 709–25

Fairley, H. Scott, "State Actors, Humanitarian Intervention and International Law: Reopening Pandora's Box," 10 *Georgia Journal of International and Comparative Law* (1980), 29–63

Farer, Tom J., "Humanitarian Intervention: The View from Charlottesville," in Richard Lillich ed., *Humanitarian Intervention and the United Nations* (University Press of Virginia, Charlottesville, 1973), pp. 149–66

"An Inquiry into the Legitimacy of Humanitarian Intervention," in Lori Fisler Damrosch and David J. Scheffer eds., *Law and Force in the New International Order* (Westview Press, Boulder, 1991), pp. 185–201

"Intervention in Unnatural Humanitarian Emergencies: Lessons of the First Phase," 18 *Human Rights Quarterly* (1996), 1–22

"A Paradigm of Legitimate Intervention," in Lori Fisler Damrosch ed., *Enforcing Restraint: Collective Intervention in Internal Conflicts* (Council on Foreign Relations, New York, 1993), pp. 316–47

Finnemore, Martha, "Constructing Norms of Humanitarian Intervention," in Peter J. Katzenstein ed., *The Culture of National Security: Norms and Identity in World Politics* (Columbia University Press, New York, 1996), pp. 153–85

Fonteyne, Jean-Pierre L., "The Customary International Law Doctrine of Humanitarian Intervention: Its Current Validity under the UN Charter," 4 *California Western International Law Journal* (1974), 203–70

Franck, Thomas M., "Break It, Don't Fake It," 78 *Foreign Affairs* (1999), 116–22

"The Emerging Right to Democratic Governance," 86 *American Journal of International Law* (1992), 46–91

"Intervention Against Illegitimate Régimes," in Lori Fisler Damrosch and David J. Scheffer eds., *Law and Force in the New International Order* (Westview Press, Boulder, 1991), pp. 159–76

"Lessons of Kosovo," 93 *American Journal of International Law* (1999), 857–59

"Who Killed Article 2(4)? or: Changing Norms Governing the Use of Force by States," 64 *American Journal of International Law* (1970), 809–37

Franck, Thomas M., and Rodley, Nigel S., "After Bangladesh: The Law of Humanitarian Intervention by Military Force," 67 *American Journal of International Law* (1973), 275–305

Gallant, Judy A., "Humanitarian Intervention and Security Council Resolution 688: A Reappraisal in Light of a Changing World Order," 7 *American University Journal of International Law and Policy* (1992), 881–920

Glennon, Michael J., *Limits of Law, Prerogatives and Power: Interventionism after Kosovo* (Palgrave, New York, 2001)

Goldman, Alan H., "The Moral Significance of National Boundaries," 7 *Midwest Studies in Philosophy* (1982), 437–53

Gordon, Ruth E., "Saving Failed States: Sometimes a Neocolonialist Solution," 12 *American University Journal of International Law and Policy* (1997), 903–74

Greenwood, Christopher, *Humanitarian Intervention: Law and Policy* (Oxford University Press, Oxford, 2001)

"Is There a Right of Humanitarian Intervention?" 49 *World Today* (1993), 34–40

Griffin, Michèle, "Where Angels Fear to Tread: Trends in International Intervention," 31 *Security Dialogue* (2000), 421–35

Guicherd, Catherine, "International Law and Kosovo," 41 *Survival* (1999), 19–34

Haas, Ernst B., "Beware the Slippery Slope: Notes toward the Definition of Justifiable Intervention," in Laura W. Reed and Carl Kaysen eds., *Emerging Norms of Justified Intervention* (Committee on International Security Studies, American Academy of Arts and Sciences, Cambridge, Mass., 1993), pp. 63–87

Haass, Richard N., *Intervention: The Use of American Military Force in the Post-Cold War World* (rev. edn, Brookings Institution, Washington, DC, 1999)

Harriss, John, ed., *The Politics of Humanitarian Intervention* (Pinter, London, 1995)

Hashmi, Sohail H., "Is There an Islamic Ethic of Humanitarian Intervention?" 7 *Ethics and International Affairs* (1993), 55–73

Hassan, Farooq, "*Realpolitik* in International Law: After Tanzanian–Ugandan Conflict 'Humanitarian Intervention' Reexamined," 17 *Willamette Law Review* (1981), 859–912

Hassner, Pierre, "From War and Peace to Violence and Intervention: Permanent Moral Dilemmas under Changing Political and Technological Conditions," in Jonathan Moore ed., *Hard Choices: Moral Dilemmas in Humanitarian Intervention* (Rowman & Littlefield, New York, 1998), pp. 9–27

Hehir, J. Bryan, "The Ethics of Non-intervention: Two Traditions," in Peter G. Brown and Douglas Maclean eds., *Human Rights and US Foreign Policy: Principles and Applications* (Lexington Books, Lexington, 1979), pp. 121–39

"Expanding Military Intervention: Promise or Peril?" 62 *Social Research* (1995), 41–46

"Intervention: From Theories to Cases," 9 *Ethics and International Affairs* (1995), 1–13

"Military Intervention and National Sovereignty: Recasting the Relationship," in Jonathan Moore ed., *Hard Choices: Moral Dilemmas in Humanitarian Intervention* (Rowman & Littlefield, New York, 1998), pp. 29–54

Helman, Gerald B., and Ratner, Steven R., "Saving Failed States," 89 *Foreign Policy* (1992–93), 3–20

Henkin, Louis, "Kosovo and the Law of 'Humanitarian Intervention'," 93 *American Journal of International Law* (1999), 824–27

"Use of Force: Law and US Policy," in Louis Henkin, Stanley Hoffmann, Jeane J. Kirkpatrick, and Allan Gerson, William D. Rogers, and David J. Scheffer eds., *Right vs. Might: International Law and the Use of Force* (2nd edn, Council on Foreign Relations Press, New York, 1991), pp. 37–69

Herbst, Jeffrey, "Responding to State Failure in Africa," 21 *International Security* (1996–97), 120–44

"War and the State in Africa," 14 *International Security* (1990), 116–36

Hoffmann, Stanley, "The Crisis of Liberal Internationalism," 98 *Foreign Policy* (1995), 159–77

The Ethics and Politics of Humanitarian Intervention (University of Notre Dame Press, Notre Dame, 1997)

"The Politics and Ethics of Military Intervention," 37 *Survival* (1995–96), 29–51

Ignatieff, Michael, *Virtual War: Kosovo and Beyond* (Chatto & Windus, London, 2000)

The Warrior's Honor: Ethnic War and the Modern Conscience (Vintage, London, 1998)

Independent International Commission on Kosovo, *Kosovo Report: Conflict, International Response, Lessons Learned* (Oxford University Press, Oxford, 2000)

International Commission on Intervention and State Sovereignty, *The Responsibility to Protect: Report of the International Commission on Intervention and State Sovereignty* (International Development Research Centre, Ottawa, 2001)

Jackson, Robert H., "Armed Humanitarianism," 48 *International Journal* (1993), 579–606

"International Community Beyond the Cold War," in Gene M. Lyons and Michael Mastanduno eds., *Beyond Westphalia? State Sovereignty and International Intervention* (Johns Hopkins University Press, Baltimore, 1995), pp. 59–83

Jhabvala, Farrokh, "Unilateral Humanitarian Intervention and International Law," 21 *Indian Journal of International Law* (1981), 208–30

Jones, Bruce D., "Intervention Without Borders: Humanitarian Intervention in Rwanda 1990–1994," 24 *Millennium: Journal of International Studies* (1995), 225–49

Kamminga, Menno T., *Inter-state Accountability for Violations of Human Rights* (University of Pennsylvania Press, Philadelphia, 1992)

Kingsbury, Benedict, "Sovereignty and Inequality," 9 *European Journal of International Law* (1998), 599–625

Kirkpatrick, Jeane J., and Gerson, Allan, "The Reagan Doctrine, Human Rights, and International Law," in Louis Henkin, Stanley Hoffmann, Jeane J. Kirkpatrick, and Allan Gerson, William D. Rogers, and David J. Scheffer eds., *Right vs. Might: International Law and the Use of Force* (2nd edn, Council on Foreign Relations Press, New York, 1991), pp. 19–36

Klintworth, Gary, *Vietnam's Intervention in Cambodia in International Law* (Australian Government Publishing Service, Canberra, 1989)

Knudsen, Tonny Brems, "European Approaches to Humanitarian Intervention: From Just War to Assistance – and Back Again?" in Knud Erik Jørgensen ed., *European Approaches to Crisis Management* (Kluwer Law International, The Hague, 1997), pp. 171–99

Krasner, Stephen D., "Sovereignty and Intervention," in Gene M. Lyons and Michael Mastanduno eds., *Beyond Westphalia? State Sovereignty and International Intervention* (Johns Hopkins University Press, Baltimore, 1995), pp. 228–49

Sovereignty: Organized Hypocrisy (Princeton University Press, Princeton, 1999)

Kratochwil, Friedrich, "Sovereignty as *Dominium*: Is There a Right of Humanitarian Intervention?" in Gene M. Lyons and Michael Mastanduno eds., *Beyond Westphalia? State Sovereignty and International Intervention* (Johns Hopkins University Press, Baltimore, 1995), pp. 21–42

Kresock, David M., " 'Ethnic Cleansing' in the Balkans: The Legal Foundations of Foreign Intervention," 27 *Cornell International Law Journal* (1994), 203–39

Kritsiotis, Dino, "Reappraising Policy Objections to Humanitarian Intervention," 19 *Michigan Journal of International Law* (1998), 1005–50

Krylov, Nicholai, "Humanitarian Intervention: Pros and Cons," 17 *Loyola of Los Angeles International and Comparative Law Journal* (1995), 365–407

Kumar, Radha, "Sovereignty and Intervention: Opinions in South Asia," 2 *Pugwash Occasional Papers* (2001), 52–64

Kuperman, Alan J., *The Limits of Humanitarian Intervention: Genocide in Rwanda* (Brookings Institution, Washington, DC, 2001)

Laberge, Pierre, "Humanitarian Intervention: Three Ethical Positions," 9 *Ethics and International Affairs* (1995), 15–35

Lang, Anthony F., *Agency and Ethics: The Politics of Military Intervention* (State University of New York Press, Albany, 2001)

Levitt, Jeremy, "Humanitarian Intervention by Regional Actors in Internal Conflicts: The Cases of ECOWAS in Liberia and Sierra Leone," 12 *Temple International and Comparative Law Journal* (1998), 333–75

Lillich, Richard B., "Forcible Self-help by States to Protect Human Rights," 53 *Iowa Law Review* (1967–68), 325–51

"Humanitarian Intervention: A Reply to Ian Brownlie and a Plea for Constructive Alternatives," in John Norton Moore ed., *Law and Civil War in the Modern World* (Johns Hopkins University Press, Baltimore, 1974), pp. 229–51

"Humanitarian Intervention through the United Nations: Towards the Development of Criteria," 53 *Zeitschrift für ausländisches öffentliches Recht und Völkerrecht* (1993), 557–75

"Kant and the Current Debate over Humanitarian Intervention," 6 *Journal of Transnational Law and Policy* (1997), 397–404

"The Role of the UN Security Council in Protecting Human Rights in Crisis Situations: UN Humanitarian Intervention in the Post-Cold War World," 3 *Tulane Journal of International and Comparative Law* (1995), 2–17

Lobel, Jules, and Ratner, Michael, "Bypassing the Security Council: Ambiguous Authorizations to Use Force, Cease-fires and the Iraqi Inspection Regime," 93 *American Journal of International Law* (1999), 124–54

Lowe, Vaughan, "The Principle of Non-intervention: The Use of Force," in Vaughan Lowe and Colin Warbrick eds., *The United Nations and the Principles of International Law: Essays in Memory of Michael Akehurst* (Routledge, London, 1994), pp. 66–84

Luban, David, "Just War and Human Rights," 9 *Philosophy and Public Affairs* (1980), 160–81

Luttwak, Edward N., "Kofi's Rule: Humanitarian Intervention and Neocolonialism," 58 *The National Interest* (1999–2000), 57–62

Mahalingam, Ravi, "The Compatibility of the Principle of Non-intervention with the Right of Humanitarian Intervention," 1 *UCLA Journal of International and Foreign Affairs* (1996), 221–63

Malanczuk, Peter, *Humanitarian Intervention and the Legitimacy of the Use of Force* (Het Spinhuis, Amsterdam, 1993)

Mandelbaum, Michael, "Foreign Policy as Social Work," 74 *Foreign Affairs* (1996), 16–32

Mapel, David R., "Military Intervention and Rights," 20 *Millennium: Journal of International Studies* (1991), 41–55

Mason, Andrew, and Wheeler, Nick, "Realist Objections to Humanitarian Intervention," in Barry Holden ed., *The Ethical Dimensions of Global Change* (Macmillan Press, Basingstoke, 1996), pp. 94–110

Mazarr, Michael J., "The Military Dilemmas of Humanitarian Intervention," 24 *Security Dialogue* (1993), 151–62

McMahan, Jeff, "The Ethics of International Intervention," in Anthony Ellis ed., *Ethics and International Affairs* (Manchester University Press, Manchester, 1986), pp. 24–51

McWhinney, E., *The United Nations and a New World Order for a New Millennium: Self-Determination, State Succession, and Humanitarian Intervention* (Kluwer Law International, London, 2000)

Mertus, Julie, *Kosovo: How Myths and Truths Started a War* (University of California Press, Berkeley, 1999)

"The Legality of Humanitarian Intervention: Lessons from Kosovo," 41 *William and Mary Law Review* (2000), 1743–87

Miller, Richard B., "Humanitarian Intervention, Altruism, and the Limits of Casuistry," 28 *Journal of Religious Ethics* (2000), 3–35

Moore, David, *Humanitarian Agendas, State Reconstruction and Democratisation Processes in War-torn Societies* (United Nations High Commissioner for Refugees, Geneva, 2000)

Murphy, Sean D., "Democratic Legitimacy and the Recognition of States and Governments," in Gregory H. Fox and Brad R. Roth eds., *Democratic Governance and International Law* (Cambridge University Press, Cambridge, 2000), pp. 123–54

Humanitarian Intervention: The United Nations in an Evolving World Order (University of Pennsylvania Press, Philadelphia, 1996)

Nanda, Ved P., "Tragedies in Northern Iraq, Liberia, Yugoslavia, and Haiti – Revisiting the Validity of Humanitarian Intervention under International Law – Part I," 20 *Denver Journal of International Law and Policy* (1992), 305–34

Nanda, Ved P., Muther, Thomas F., Jr., and Eckert, Amy E., "Tragedies in Somalia, Yugoslavia, Haiti, Rwanda and Liberia – Revisiting the Validity of Humanitarian Intervention under International Law – Part II," 26 *Denver Journal of International Law and Policy* (1998), 827–61

Nardin, Terry, "The Moral Basis of Humanitarian Intervention," 16 *Ethics and International Affairs* (2002), 57–70

Nederveen Pieterse, Jan, "Sociology of Humanitarian Intervention: Bosnia, Rwanda and Somalia Compared," 18 *International Political Science Review* (1997), 71–93

Nederveen Pieterse, Jan, ed., *World Orders in the Making: Humanitarian Intervention and Beyond* (St. Martin's Press, New York, 1998)

Nowrot, Karsten, and Schabacker, Emily W., "The Use of Force to Restore Democracy: International Legal Implications of the ECOWAS Intervention in Sierra Leone," 14 *American University International Law Review* (1998), 321–412

Nye, Joseph S., Jr., "Ethics and Intervention," in Linda B. Miller and Michael J. Smith eds., *Ideas and Ideals: Essays in Honor of Stanley Hoffmann* (Westview Press, Boulder, 1993), pp. 127–43

"Redefining the National Interest," 78 *Foreign Affairs* (1999), 22–35

O'Connell, Mary Ellen, "The UN, NATO, and International Law After Kosovo," 22 *Human Rights Quarterly* (2000), 57–89

Onuf, Nicholas, "Intervention for the Common Good," in Gene M. Lyons and Michael Mastanduno eds., *Beyond Westphalia? State Sovereignty and International Intervention* (Johns Hopkins University Press, Baltimore, 1995), pp. 43–58

Paris, Roland, "Peacebuilding and the Limits of Liberal Internationalism," 22 *International Security* (1997), 54–89

Pease, Kelley K., and Forsythe, David P., "Human Rights, Humanitarian Intervention, and World Politics," 15 *Human Rights Quarterly* (1993), 290–314

Pellet, Alain, "State Sovereignty and the Protection of Fundamental Human Rights: An International Law Perspective," in 1 *Pugwash Occasional Papers* (2000), 37–44

Petersen, Fredrick J., "The Façade of Humanitarian Intervention for Human Rights in a Community of Sovereign Nations," 15 *Arizona Journal of International and Comparative Law* (1998), 871–904

Phillips, Robert L., and Cady, Duane L., *Humanitarian Intervention: Just War vs. Pacifism* (Rowman & Littlefield, Lanham, 1996)

Philpott, Daniel, "Usurping the Sovereignty of Sovereignty?" 53 *World Politics* (2001), 297–324

Rajan, Mannaraswamighala Sreeranga, "The New Interventionism?" 37 *International Studies* (2000), 31–40

Ramsbotham, Oliver, "Humanitarian Intervention 1990–1995: A Need to Recon-
ceptualize?" 23 *Review of International Studies* (1999), 445–68
  "Islam, Christianity, and Forcible Humanitarian Intervention," 13 *Ethics and
International Affairs* (1998), 81–102
Ramsbotham, Oliver, and Woodhouse, Tom, *Humanitarian Intervention in Con-
temporary Conflict: A Reconceptualization* (Polity Press, Cambridge, 1996)
Ratner, Steven, "Does International Law Matter in Preventing Ethnic Conflict?" 32
New York University Journal of International Law and Politics (2000), 591–724
Rawls, John, *The Law of Peoples* (Harvard University Press, Cambridge, Mass., 1999)
Reisman, W. Michael, "Coercion and Self-determination: Construing Charter
Article 2(4)," 78 *American Journal of International Law* (1984), 642–45
  "Criteria for the Lawful Use of Force in International Law," 10 *Yale Journal of
International Law* (1985), 279–85
  "Hollow Victory: Humanitarian Intervention and the Protection of Minorities,"
91 *Proceedings of the American Society of International Law* (1997), 431–35
  "Humanitarian Intervention and Fledgling Democracies," 18 *Fordham Interna-
tional Law Journal* (1995), 794–805
  "Sovereignty and Human Rights in Contemporary International Law," 84
American Journal of International Law (1990), 866–76
  "Unilateral Action and the Transformation of the World Constitutive Process:
The Special Problem of Humanitarian Intervention," 11 *European Journal of
International Law* (2000), 3–18
Reisman, W. Michael, with the collaboration of Myres S. McDougal, "Humanitarian
Intervention to Protect the Ibos," in Richard Lillich ed., *Humanitarian Inter-
vention and the United Nations* (University Press of Virginia, Charlottesville,
1973), pp. 167–96
Roberts, Adam, "Humanitarian War: Military Intervention and Human Rights,"
69 *International Affairs* (1993), 429–49
  "NATO's 'Humanitarian War' Over Kosovo," 41 *Survival* (1999), 102–23
  "The So-called 'Right' of Humanitarian Intervention," 3 *Yearbook of Interna-
tional Humanitarian Law* (2000), 3–51
Roth, Brad R., *Government Illegitimacy in International Law* (Clarendon Press,
Oxford, 1999)
Schachter, Oscar, "The Lawful Resort to Unilateral Force," 10 *Yale Journal of Inter-
national Law* (1985), 291–94
  "The Legality of Pro-democratic Invasion," 78 *American Journal of International
Law* (1984), 645–50
Scheffer, David J., "Towards a Modern Doctrine of Humanitarian Intervention,"
23 *University of Toledo Law Review* (1992), 253–93
  "Use of Force After the Cold War: Panama, Iraq, and the New World Order,"
in Louis Henkin, Stanley Hoffmann, Jeane J. Kirkpatrick, and Allan Gerson,

William D. Rogers, and David J. Scheffer eds., *Right vs. Might: International Law and the Use of Force* (2nd edn, Council on Foreign Relations Press, New York, 1991), pp. 109–72

Schrijver, Nico, "The Changing Nature of State Sovereignty," in James Crawford and Vaughan Lowe eds., *The British Yearbook of International Law 1999* (Clarendon Press, Oxford, 2000), pp. 65–98

Schweigman, David, "Humanitarian Intervention under International Law: The Strife for Humanity," 6 *Leiden Journal of International Law* (1993), 91–111

Shulong, Chu, "China, Asia and Issues of Intervention and Sovereignty," 2 *Pugwash Occasional Papers* (2001), 39–51

Simma, Bruno, "NATO, the UN and the Use of Force: Legal Aspects," 10 *European Journal of International Law* (1999), 1–22

Sisk, Timothy D., "Democratization and Peacebuilding: Perils and Promises," in Chester A. Crocker, Fen Osler Hampson, and Pamela Aall eds., *Turbulent Peace: The Challenges of Managing International Conflict* (US Institute of Peace, Washington, DC, 2001), pp. 785–800

Slater, Jerome, and Nardin, Terry, "Non-intervention and Human Rights," 48 *Journal of Politics* (1986), 86–96

Smith, Michael J., "Humanitarian Intervention: An Overview of Ethical Issues," 12 *Ethics and International Affairs* (1998), 63–79

Stedman, Stephen J., "The New Interventionists," 72 *Foreign Affairs* (1993), 1–16

Stowell, Ellery C., "Humanitarian Intervention," 33 *American Journal of International Law* (1939), 733–36

Tanca, Antonio, *Foreign Armed Intervention in Internal Conflict* (Martinus Nijhoff, Dordrecht, 1993)

Tesón, Fernando R., "Collective Humanitarian Intervention," 17 *University of Michigan Law School Journal* (1996), 323–71

   Humanitarian Intervention: An Inquiry into Law and Morality (2nd edn, Transnational Publishers, Irvington-on-Hudson, 1997)

   "International Obligation and the Theory of Hypothetical Consent," 15 *Yale Journal of International Law* (1990), 109–18

   "Kantian International Liberalism," in David R. Mapel and Terry Nardin eds., *International Society: Diverse Ethical Perspectives* (Princeton University Press, Princeton, 1998), pp. 103–13

   "The Kantian Theory of International Law," 92 *Columbia Law Review* (1992), 53–102

   A Philosophy of International Law (Westview Press, Boulder, 1998)

   "The Rawlsian Theory of International Law," 9 *Ethics and International Affairs* (1995), 80–99

Thomas, Caroline, "The Pragmatic Case against Intervention," in Ian Forbes and Mark Hoffman eds., *Political Theory, International Relations and the Ethics of Intervention* (St. Martin's Press, New York, 1993), pp. 91–103

Trachtenberg, Marc, "Intervention in Historical Perspective," in Laura W. Reed and Carl Kaysen eds., *Emerging Norms of Justified Intervention* (Committee on International Security Studies, American Academy of Arts and Sciences, Cambridge, Mass., 1993), pp. 15–36

Traub, James, "Inventing East Timor," 79 *Foreign Affairs* (2000), 74–89

Turner, James, "Humanitarian Intervention, Christian Ethical Reasoning, and the Just-War Idea," in Luis E. Lugo ed., *Sovereignty at the Crossroads? Morality and International Politics in the Post-Cold War Era* (Rowman & Littlefield, Lanham, 1996), pp. 127–43

Vales, Hernàn, "The Latin American View on the Doctrine of Humanitarian Intervention," *Journal of Humanitarian Assistance*. Available at http://www.jha.ac/articles/a064.htm (11 February 2001)

Verwey, Wil D., "Humanitarian Intervention," in Antonio Cassese ed., *The Current Legal Regulation of the Use of Force* (Martinus Nijhoff, Dordrecht, 1986), pp. 57–78

"Humanitarian Intervention in the 1990s and Beyond: An International Law Perspective," in Jan Nederveen Pieterse ed., *World Orders in the Making: Humanitarian Intervention and Beyond* (St. Martin's Press, New York, 1998), pp. 180–210

"Humanitarian Intervention under International Law," 32 *Netherlands International Law Review* (1985), 357–418

Vincent, R. J., "Grotius, Human Rights, and Intervention," in Hedley Bull, Benedict Kingsbury, and Adam Roberts eds., *Hugo Grotius and International Relations* (Clarendon Press, Oxford, 1990), pp. 241–56

Non-intervention and International Order (Princeton University Press, Princeton, 1974)

Walzer, Michael, *Just and Unjust Wars: A Moral Argument with Historical Illustrations* (3rd edn, Basic Books, New York, 2000)

"The Moral Standing of States: A Response to Four Critics," 9 *Philosophy and Public Affairs* (1980), 209–29

"The Politics of Rescue," 61 *Social Research* (1995), 53–66

Thick and Thin: Moral Argument at Home and Abroad (University of Notre Dame Press, Notre Dame, 1994)

Weart, Spencer R., *Never at War: Why Democracies Will Never Fight One Another* (Yale University Press, New Haven, 1998)

Wedgwood, Ruth, "NATO's Campaign in Yugoslavia," 93 *American Journal of International Law* (1999), 828–33

Weiner, Myron, "Bad Neighbors, Bad Neighborhoods: An Inquiry into the Causes of Refugee Flows," 21 *International Security* (1996), 5–42

Weiss, Thomas G., "Humanitarian Intervention in War Zones: Recent Experience and Future Research," in Jan Nederveen Pieterse ed., *World Orders in the Making: Humanitarian Intervention and Beyond* (St. Martin's Press, New York, 1998), pp. 24–79

Weiss, Thomas G., and Collins, Cindy, *Humanitarian Challenges and Intervention* (2nd edn, Westview Press, Boulder, 2000)

Wheeler, Nicholas J., "Agency, Humanitarianism and Intervention," 18 *International Political Science Review* (1997), 9–25

  "Guardian Angel or Global Gangster: A Review of the Ethical Claims of International Society," 44 *Political Studies* (1996), 123–35

  "Pluralist or Solidarist Conceptions of International Society: Bull and Vincent on Humanitarian Intervention," 21 *Millennium* (1992), 588–99

  Saving Strangers: Humanitarian Intervention in International Society (Oxford University Press, Oxford, 2000)

Wheeler, Nicholas J., and Morris, Justin, "Humanitarian Intervention and State Practice at the End of the Cold War," in Rick Fawn and Jeremy Larkins eds., *International Society after the Cold War: Anarchy and Order Reconsidered* (Macmillan, Basingstoke, 1996), pp. 135–71

Wicclair, Mark R., "Human Rights and Intervention," in Peter G. Brown and Douglas Maclean eds., *Human Rights and US Foreign Policy: Principles and Applications* (Lexington Books, Lexington, 1979), pp. 141–57

  "Rawls and the Principle of Non-intervention," in H. Gene Blocker and Elizabeth H. Smith eds., *John Rawls' Theory of Social Justice* (Ohio University Press, Athens, 1980), pp. 289–308

Wippman, David, "Practical and Legal Constraints on Internal Power Sharing," in David Wippman ed., *International Law and Ethnic Conflict* (Cornell University Press, Ithaca, 1998), pp. 211–41

Wolf, Daniel, "Humanitarian Intervention," 9 *Michigan Year Book of International Legal Studies* (1988), 333–68

Woodward, Susan L., "Failed States: Warlordism and 'Tribal' Warfare," 52 *Naval War College Review* (1999), 55–68

Zacher, Mark W., "The Territorial Integrity Norm: International Boundaries and the Use of Force," 55 *International Organization* (2001), 215–50

Zartman, William, ed., *Collapsed States: The Disintegration and Restoration of Legitimate Authority* (Lynne Rienner, Boulder, 1995)

INDEX

Lightning Source UK Ltd.
Milton Keynes UK
UKOW02f0620260415

250334UK00001B/66/P